When You Come Home

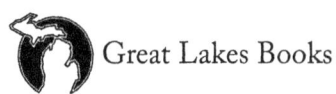 Great Lakes Books

A complete listing of the books in this series can be found online at
wsupress.wayne.edu

When You Come Home
A Wartime Courtship in Letters, 1941–45

Edited by

Robert E. Quirk

Wayne State University Press
Detroit

11 10 09 08 07   5 4 3 2 1

Library of Congress Cataloging-in-Publication Data

When you come home : a wartime courtship in letters, 1941–45 / edited by Robert E. Quirk.
    p. cm. — (Great lakes books)
    Excerpts of the letters between Robert E. Quirk and his wife.
    ISBN-13: 978-0-8143-3334-1 (pbk. : alk. paper)
    ISBN-10: 0-8143-3334-6 (pbk. : alk. paper)
1. Quirk, Robert E. 2. World War, 1939–1945—Personal narratives, American. 3. United States. Army—Biography. 4. Soldiers—United States—Biography. I. Quirk, Robert E.
    D811.A2W453 2007
    940.54'1273092—dc22
    [B]   2007013490

Grateful acknowledgment is made to the Department of History at Indiana University, Bloomington, for their generous support of the publication of this volume.

Publication of this book was made possible through the generosity of the Ford R. Bryan Publication Fund.

∞The paper used in this publication meets the minimum requirements of the American National Standard for Information Sciences—Permanence of Paper for Printed Library Materials, ANSI Z39.48-1984.

Designed and typeset by E.T. Lowe
Composed in ACaslon and Cochin Italic

Contents

Foreword:
World War II Detroit

The war began one Sunday when we weren't expecting it. By Monday the kids in the neighborhood and I had already begun to plan our role in the coming conflict.

In December 1941 I was eleven and living with my parents and two brothers in an upstairs flat on Lycaste, on Detroit's southeast side. When bombs were falling on the American warships in Pearl Harbor my brothers and I were where we were every Sunday afternoon—in the Plaza Theater on East Jefferson watching the double feature. That Sunday it was two forgettable films, *Two in a Taxi* and *Sign of the Wolf.*

We came home to a house sadly quiet. My parents sat on the couch listening to our old Zenith radio. The heavy-voiced announcer reported that the Japanese had bombed some place in Hawaii that we never heard of, and we spent the rest of the day sitting on the floor listening with our parents to news about the war that was sure to come.

The next day we gathered again in front of the big wooden radio and listened in silence while President Roosevelt asked Congress to declare war on Japan, calling the attack "dastardly." My brothers and I heard the word differently and decided that this war business must be something extremely serious for the president to use language like that.

Monday, December 8, was a holy day, the feast of the Immaculate Conception, and the kids who went to Catholic school had the day off.

After war was declared a handful of us from St. Rose School gathered on Richard Conover's porch to talk excitedly about all that had happened and what we needed to do. We stopped talking only to watch when fighter planes—called "pursuits" then—roared over our heads. The military airbase at Selfridge Field was not far away and it seemed that every one of its planes was in the air that day, scanning the horizon, we presumed, for signs of enemy activity.

In that working-class neighborhood, where life was, mostly, predictable and routine, this was heady stuff. For the kids in the neighborhood it was easily the most exciting thing that had ever happened.

The concept of modern war and its aftermath was alien to us. We saw it not as the cataclysm it was but as a kind of patriotic exercise in which we would be expected to do our part. Never for a moment did we consider the reality that this war would someday soon reach out and tragically touch the neighborhood.

As we sat on Richard's porch a kid passing on a bike shouted to us that there were soldiers with a machine gun guarding the gate at Waterworks Park. We ran the dozen blocks to the park to see for ourselves. When we got there we were disappointed to find not soldiers and a machine gun but a single policeman with a billy club and a civilian watchman in a long overcoat and gray fedora hat. Across the driveway at the park's entrance, next to the massive Hurlbut Memorial, a wooden sawhorse with WPA stenciled on it had been set up. A kerosene lantern hung from a nail on the barricade.

When we saw a copy of the *Detroit Times* later that day our disappointment deepened. The paper featured a photo of soldiers from Selfridge manning a heavy machine gun—a World War I vintage .30-caliber water-cooled weapon—at the entrance to the Detroit-Windsor Tunnel. Another photo showed an identical machine gun in place at the Ambassador Bridge, next to the tollbooth; two soldiers with .45-caliber pistols stuck in their web belts flanked the crouching gunner.

I later questioned the misguided priorities of a military that placed heavy weapons at border crossings with Canada while protecting the pumping stations that supplied drinking water to millions of Detroiters with one policeman and a watchman. Did anybody seriously think that we were in danger of enemy attack from Windsor when a more believable scenario involved the poisoning of the city's water supply? It was not, I decided, a very encouraging beginning.

How much of our unhappiness was inspired by our neighborhood being denied the opportunity to see real firepower close up is difficult to determine after all these years. I think it is safe to say that it was probably a factor.

Many of us tracked the war on newspaper maps taped to our bedroom walls, ever mindful of our responsibilities on "the home front." We believed it was naïve and probably careless to assume that Detroit was safe from "The Enemy." Posters in shops and businesses reminded us constantly that the enemy was everywhere, listening to our careless conversations, infiltrating our institutions, and living among us waiting for the opportunity to do us—and the country—harm.

The Detroit newspapers reported regularly about the apprehension of spies in our midst, reinforcing our belief that vigilance was our most effective defense.

A Hungarian countess, Grace Buchanan-Dineen, was arrested in her apartment, conveniently situated next to the Brodhead Naval Armory near the Belle Isle Bridge. Max Stephan, proprietor of a restaurant on East Jefferson and East Grand Boulevard was arrested and charged with treason for trying to help an escaped prisoner of war, a Luftwaffe pilot, make his way back to Germany. We took quiet pride in the knowledge that the restaurant had been on our "watch list" since the early weeks of the war—even before Mr. Stephan painted over the word "German" on the sign that had previously read "German Restaurant."

A German American Detroiter, Countess Mariana von Moltke, also was jailed as a spy. When she was released after the war she and her husband, a former professor of German at Wayne University, changed their name to Miller and bought the St. Rose Sweet Shop, the candy store across from our school. I was in high school by this time and I had difficulty reconciling the soft-spoken woman with the gray-blond braids behind the soda fountain with the person the FBI had decided three years earlier was a serious threat to the country.

The FBI's dark warnings in the early years of the war, however, kept us on the alert for people who fit the spy profile. One newspaper story pointed out that German spies, no matter how good their English, would still speak with the trace of an accent. We decided being on the alert for accents in our ethnic neighborhood was a losing proposition. Another story informed us that one way to tell the Japanese from our friends the Chinese was to look at their feet. The first and second toes of the Japanese were separated, the story said, because of the sandals they traditionally wore. The story also explained that while the Chinese have smooth faces, Japanese faces have a rougher texture. Since few people in that neighborhood walked around without their shoes we were denied the split-toes option, so we concentrated on complexions. We hung around in front of the Canton Hand Laundry and the Chinese Teapot Café on Jefferson Avenue studying the faces of every Asian who came out or went in, finally deciding that if there was really a way to tell the difference, we had not figured it out.

Our new priority became the tiny diner on the northeast corner of Kercheval and St. Jean, next to Gallagher field. It was, as were most of the small restaurants in the neighborhood, owned and run by Greeks. The man we decided was the boss because he was always there, day or night, had a small black square of a mustache that looked remarkably like Adolf Hitler's. A Nazi sympathizer? It did not occur to us that he might have had the mustache long before the war, or even long before Hitler. For a long time we watched the restaurant from the gas station across the street but never managed to see the man come to work (too early for us) or go home (too late for us). The patrons all seemed to be neighborhood folks, many of them from the nearby Department of Street Railways car barns, including my father, who was a streetcar conductor.

Interest in the man as a serious suspect soon waned, but the long-term effect of this episode is that from the early 1940s until the place was torn down a couple of decades later, the diner was known by all in the neighborhood—and still is by those who remember it—as "Hitler's."

Carrying copies of pamphlets showing the silhouettes of enemy aircraft, we lay on our backs in the playground scanning the skies for

Stukas or Messerschmitts or Zeros. All we ever saw were planes from Selfridge, the TWA airliners heading for City Airport, and an occasional Piper Cub. But I remain convinced that if the enemy had ever dared try to slip one of its airplanes into Detroit airspace, some kid in my neighborhood would most certainly have raised the alarm.

Although it was not nearly as exciting, we all worked together in something universally designated as, "The War Effort." We collected scrap rubber, old aluminum pots and pans, tin cans, newspapers, and fat drippings from our mothers' frying pans. If we had been honest with ourselves we would have determined that this was a much more tangible contribution to ultimate victory than keeping an eye on Hitler's clone in a Greek diner or searching the sky for enemy planes.

One night we stood near the swings in the Lingemann School playground while a Civil Defense worker demonstrated, with an actual bomb, the proper way to extinguish an incendiary device. The bombs were, the man explained, designed to pierce the roofs of buildings causing devastating fires that if not stopped quickly could wipe out entire neighborhoods. Demonstrating as he spoke, the man detonated the small bomb in a pyramid of wooden orange crates. He showed us how putting water on the bomb made it flare up. The only way to stop it, he said, was by smothering it with sand. It was important, he emphasized, that every home in the neighborhood have a pail of sand in the attic in case of an incendiary attack.

That night, when I told my mother we needed a pail of sand in the attic she informed me that since we had only one pail for use in all household chores that required a pail, she was not interested in tying up that pail by filling it with sand and sticking it in the attic. When I told her we could always buy another pail she told me she was not going to spend good money on a pail we didn't need on the off chance that the Luftwaffe was going to be able to get a bomber as far as Detroit with a pilot skilled enough to drop an incendiary bomb through the roof at 1532 Lycaste. She dismissed my arguments that she was putting the entire neighborhood in danger by telling me she was willing to risk it. The house was never bombed.

I remember at some point, as the oldest in my family, being unhappy at not having an older brother in the service. I was envious of kids who showed up at school with war souvenirs sent to them by their brothers, including the colorful unit patches they sewed to their shirts or jackets. I remember sitting in the locker room at the Hannan YMCA listening to a kid from Annunciation talking about his brother, a fighter pilot in the Pacific.

His brother had just sent the family a letter telling them he had shot down a Japanese Zero. His younger brother shared every exciting detail, using his flattened hands to demonstrate the dogfight maneuvers that finally ended when he sent one of his hands spinning crazily, complete with sound effects, toward the damp floor. Everybody cheered.

When the casualty lists started to include young men from the neighborhood and from St. Rose School, I realized my envy had been misplaced. I was suddenly thankful that I would never have to sit next to my mother in church, a folded flag on her lap, while she wept at the loss of a son.

By the end of 1944 it had become an unhappy ritual at St. Rose. Classes would be interrupted by a scratchy announcement on the public address system that someone from the school had been reported killed or missing. Before the announcement, one of the nuns would come to the classrooms and quietly take the siblings to the office where parents or relatives waited. After the announcement, we all would go next door to the church to pray for the dead or missing serviceman, for the safety all the young men of the parish, for a just and lasting peace. The pastor would close by reminding us how many boys from the parish had already died in the war and, naming each one, asking us to keep them in our prayers. By the war's end, eight young men from St. Rose had died, including the brothers of two kids in my class. When the short service ended we were sent home, the war suddenly a more serious and deadly business than it had seemed to us such a short time ago.

All the years the kids in the neighborhood and I were busy dealing with the war on our own terms, an east side kid from a different neighborhood from ours, Bob Quirk, drafted into the Army in the months before Pearl Harbor, was exchanging letters with his sweetheart back home in Dearborn, Marianne Gutzeit—letters about life in the army, about bad food and good books, about classical music and college courses, about their future careers, about their dreams of a life together, about abiding affection and the pain of separation.

What follows is a touching journal, an endearing compilation of correspondence that tells a story about two lives, one war, and the wonderful durability of love.

Neal Shine

Preface

"It could be a true test of our love." Marianne's voice was strangely muted, as though she were pondering the awesomeness of such a long separation. Twelve months apart seemed like an eternity. For both of us. We had been "going together," as they say, for only a few short weeks. And now this. I had been directed by the draft board to report the next day. Not that it was any surprise. I had known about it since early March. Still, the inevitable had been creeping up on me—and on Marianne—all too quickly. I just tried to put it out of my mind, as so many young people facing difficult problems would do.

We were sitting in the swing on her front porch. From time to time I gave a slight push with my toes to keep us moving. We had just come back from a walk in the park, and my coat lay twisted across my lap. I had been carrying it most of the way. The temperature was perhaps in the high eighties, and I had sweated quite a bit. She held out her hand. "Do you want me to hang it up for you?" Disorder annoyed her, even at important times such as this.

I shook my head. "I'll be leaving in a little while, anyway. I have to do some packing."

"Maybe you won't have to go." Marianne always tried to look on the bright side of things. "Have you ever thought of that? I'll hold on to you. Tight. Like this." Her cheeks were flushed, and she moved closer, linking her arm with mine. I could smell her perfume. Lavender, I think.

She did that often. Linked arms, that is. Especially when we strolled down Second Avenue after a class at Wayne. To drink a Coke most likely. A small Coke. In those days it was all I could afford to buy her. On Saturdays I worked downtown at the Kerns department store, selling ties. The pay was $3.50 for the eight hours, and I had to make it last all week. One Sunday in May we went to a Tigers game and got seats in the bleachers. Tickets were fifty cents each. Marianne paid her own way. And also for her bus fare to and from Briggs Stadium. During vacations I worked through the week and picked up enough money to pay for my tuition. In one way I lived in poverty. In another, I was the richest young fellow in the world. I had Marianne as my best friend. I put my hand on hers.

The year was 1941, the month June. It was still peacetime for the United States, though the American Congress had authorized "lending" and "leasing" naval equipment to the British. And United States forces had occupied the Danish island of Greenland to prevent the Nazis from moving in. Earlier that week the Germans had invaded the Soviet Union. Operation Barbarossa, Hitler called it. His people required more "living space," he said, as well as the Romanian oil fields and the rolling wheat lands of the Ukraine. The Super Race deserved only the best. If millions of lesser folk died in the process, so be it. Already Nazi tanks were deep into the border republics of Latvia and Lithuania, headed for Moscow and for Leningrad. Many Wayne students thought the European war was not their business. It was so far away. And America had its own problems. At a large college rally candies on a stick were passed out. Each had a paper attachment that proclaimed: "This sucker's not coming."

In the military draft I had drawn a low number, and my father was head of the district board. There was no way he was going to show favoritism and let me stay in school one more day. The board had given me until the end of the now-completed semester. My brother John, a naval midshipman, had finished his second year at Annapolis, and Dad believed his boys would "do their duty," as he put it. Both of us officers, probably. You might say that I had some isolationist views; or that I thought the French and British shared some of the blame for Europe's problems. But the thought of avoiding the draft never entered my mind. I was not a conscientious objector. If they took me on Monday, why, they took me. That's all. The decision was out of my hands.

Marianne and I had first met, in the sense that we talked with each other, in Harold Basilius's Intermediate German class. I sat behind her—by intent, I confess, and I often forgot my books, so I had to move up a row to share hers. Leaning over to read her notes, I let my hand touch hers. If she was suspicious of my motives, she said nothing. It was a tough course, probably the most challenging—and worthwhile—I ever took part in: At Wayne before and after the war, at Utah in the army, and later in graduate school at Harvard. All those other professors were cream puffs compared with Dr. Basilius. He was a great teacher, with high standards. And like all great teachers he made us work our butts off. A lot of students complained about that. Once he walked out of class when no one seemed prepared. We felt ashamed, as though we had let him down. During the semester we were required to read at least fifteen books. And in German yet. *Mina von Barnhelm, Iphigenia auf Taurus, Die Leiden des jungen Werthers, Die Brücke,* and a lot more. No translations. The professor was a bear on the real thing. And on Romanticism. It was his special research topic. The right atmosphere for two young persons exploring the many meanings and manifestations of love. In his class he and I recognized that perhaps I had the makings of a scholar. He encouraged me to write essays and to make translations of Goethe's poetry. I could become a teacher, he said.

I had discovered Marianne's existence a year earlier. We had both taken Carl Colditz's class, sitting on opposite sides of the room. But I never communicated with her. She was the mysterious, comely blond, silhouetted against the tall windows, who somehow knew all the answers. I looked her way a lot during discussions, thinking I really ought to say something to her. Or perhaps be "accidentally" close to her locker—near the chemistry lab—when classes were changing. I could say, "Oh, you're Marianne Gutzeit. I'm in your class." And see how she responded. But I kept postponing that moment. Maybe she already had a boyfriend. Much later she said, "I thought you would never ask me."

I'd heard she lived in Dearborn, light years from my neighborhood in East Detroit, near the Belle Isle bridge. I had no car. To get back and forth you had to transfer twice, take two streetcars and a bus. Or was it two busses and one streetcar? After all these years—more than sixty—I've forgotten. Usually it took me at least an hour, each way. I remember Sunday nights at midnight, or even later, standing in front of the Fisher Building, shivering in the cold February winds and waiting for some kind of transportation. And I still had an early-morning class to get ready for.

On our first real date I took her to Wayne's annual Thanksgiving football game. And brought her a large yellow chrysanthemum. A single flower. It cost a whole fifty cents. We were both sophomores. She was not quite nineteen. I was nearly three years older.

She and I had come to Wayne and to the German classes by widely divergent paths. My family moved to Detroit from northern Ohio in the summer of 1931, when Dad took a job with the United States Rubber Company. I was eleven. He was head of the tire-repair school, an executive who made $360 a month. To us it seemed like a million. We were well off, finally. We rented a large house on East Grand Boulevard and acquired lots of new furniture. In Ohio he had been a science teacher and a school principal, but during the middle 1920s the Ku Klux Klan had got him fired. No Catholics would teach in a country public school, they insisted. The only job he could find then was selling real estate at Silver Lake.

In Detroit things quickly got worse again. Within a year the Great Depression had devastated us. The repair school closed, and Dad was once more without regular employment. He bought an old Dodge truck, and during the summer he and I drove around trying to sell tire-repair kits at gasoline stations. That business failed because no one was interested. Few people patched their own tires.

Without an income, we moved into smaller quarters, sharing a house on nearby Helen Avenue with a Lebanese family. I can still recall the aromas of Middle Eastern cooking and the strange foods that were so willingly shared with us. My mother was always embarrassed and ashamed that foreigners were better off than we were. Most of our furniture had disappeared into the dark recesses of a storage company, including the valued Atwater Kent "superheterodyne console" radio that had introduced me—all too briefly—to the world of long-distance reception. KDKA, Pittsburgh. KYW, Philadelphia. WTMJ, Milwaukee. WTAM, Cleveland. And dozens more. A twelve-year-old DXer, twisting the dial and exploring the broadcast band.

We also lost the comforting overstuffed davenport and the dining table and wooden chairs, as well as all the beds. My folks had bought most of it on credit. Then, like so many unfortunates in Detroit, we went on welfare, and moved down the street to the third floor of a tenement house that had once been somebody's attic. I wore shoes that had belonged to older cousins in Akron. They were too big for me and had holes in the bottoms that couldn't be repaired, so every morning I stuffed them with newspapers to keep out the snow and water. The welfare office gave me ankle-height shoes that I hated, because no one else in my classes wore them. I did my best to hide my feet under the desk.

For a while Dad worked for the WPA—the federal government's Works Progress Administration. It was a step up, I suppose, from the shame of cashing our welfare checks at the Syrian grocery on Lafayette. Hoping no one you knew had recognized you. My father now inspected books that were taken in and out of our local library on Field Avenue. But we were still embarrassed when our friends said they had seen him there, standing at the door. That wasn't what our fathers were supposed to do. We knew that it was not a "respectable" occupation for a man.

When Dad finally did go back to the rubber company, it was to lift tires and throw them on trucks. He had become a manual laborer now. His pay was forty cents an hour, and he might put in ten hours a day, seven days a week. When he asked for Easter Sunday off, to go to Mass, the foreman took him to a window and pointed at the unemployed men milling about on Jefferson Avenue. "Goddamn it, Quirk," he said. "Would you like to be down there with those unlucky bastards?" But it was a job, a genuine job with regular wages. And we could get furniture. On credit, again. And our Christmas presents also. That was all-important. One year a Hallicrafter shortwave radio was there for me under the tree, a Sky Chief that cost my folks nearly sixty dollars. I had been getting by on crystal sets and single-tubers I built myself from used equipment and connected to the bedsprings for an antenna. I started then to listen to the BBC news each day. With earphones. And picked up Radio Australia and the Deutschewelle, as well as amateur operators around the world. It usually took Dad several months to pay off what Santa Claus had brought us in that one night. Later he was one of the founders of the union at the Detroit plant, negotiating working conditions and wages with the bosses. By then, because of New Deal legislation, workers had more clout.

For three years after high school I worked full time at Kerns, first operating an elevator—wearing a brown-and-gold uniform—and then taking charge of the employees' locker room. My pay was fifteen dollars for the six-day week. A third of that went for room and board. When I turned eighteen I had applied at the rubber company, but the personnel director wouldn't hire me. I should go to college and be a teacher, he said. Not spend my life in a factory. Wasting it, he implied. I had few truly marketable skills, except for an ability to put words together. And to build primitive radios and develop photographs. (For fifteen dollars I bought myself an Argus camera that did double duty as an enlarger lens.) I had applied at Wayne for a scholarship, but was told none were available.

During my third year at the department store I did take the first positive step toward a college degree when I signed up for a night class. I chose the basic course in German. That was because of my good friend, Irmagard Scholz. She was employed at Kerns too and majored in the language. Enrolling in that class was only one of the many happy fortuities in the twists and turns of my life. And subsequently Marianne's life as well. I was becoming competent in the language, while she was already fluent.

My one extravagance in those days was collecting books. I had been picking them up since I came to Kerns, mostly those that were on sale.

I acquired the complete works of Mark Twain. Of Shakespeare and of Charles Dickens. Also *The Bible as Literature, Theory of the Leisure Class,* and *Leaves of Grass.* And a lot of P. G. Wodehouse volumes. You could get books for much less than a dollar in those days. Paperbacks were a quarter, and even less during the many sales. I kept wishing I could go full time to school, like Irma, but there was no way my family could support me—and my brothers and sister—if I didn't have a sufficient income. The solution came about unexpectedly and in a strange way.

As far back as I can remember, Dad was a "politician"—in Ohio when Herbert Hoover was running for president against the Catholic Al Smith, and four years later in Michigan when Franklin Delano Roosevelt took on the Republican incumbent. The year I turned fourteen I passed out fliers at election rallies on Belle Isle, and helped pick up the trash when everybody went home. A born-and-bred Irish storyteller, my father salted his speeches with witticisms and anecdotes. "Vote early—and often," he would say. And he drew from the Bible to support the Democrats' cause. Jesus Christ had admonished us: "Suffer the little children to come unto me, and forbid them not." Whereas the Republican Hoover had turned things around: "Suffer little children, don't come unto me."

Through most of the 1930s he was the precinct captain and local delegate to the county convention. We were part of Michigan's First Congressional District, dominated then by a huge enclave of Poles in the city of Hamtramck. Our representative in Washington was George Sadowski, as honest as a Democratic politician could be in those days. Dad and he were friends, and the congressman and I once sang the Requiem Mass—as part of a quartet—for a Polish constituent in the St. Charles Borromeo parish church. (I received five dollars, a huge sum then.) In 1938 I took my father's place as precinct captain, working to get out the votes on election day and keeping silent at the county convention, so as not to antagonize the party leaders. Although I wasn't yet twenty-one, and couldn't vote, nobody seemed to care. I was most likely the youngest working politician in the district. And maybe the state.

But then political turmoil turned our private world upside down. Righting it, as it were. The Polish machine decided to dump Sadowski and replace him with Rudolph Tenerowicz, the current mayor of Hamtramck. A decade earlier Tenerowicz had held the same office, but he was charged with "conspiracy to protect vice" and sent to prison. Now he was back home, redeemed by a governor's pardon and with higher ambitions—the American Congress. He ran and won, easily. What Pole was going to vote for the Republicans? After some wrangling in the House of Representatives about corruption, he was seated. Sadowski, in his last months in office, felt betrayed. He had one more appointment at his disposal. The lame-duck congressman asked Dad if he knew a good Irish boy they could send to the naval academy. No Poles need apply, he said. Within months my brother John was in uniform, on the way to what he thought would be a career in the peacetime Navy. Then Dad was promoted to foreman at the rubber company with a sizeable raise—so he would stop making trouble as the union vice-president. Bought off, I suppose you would say. "You can go to Wayne, now," he told me. "And don't worry about room and board."

That fall, as a freshman, I signed up full time and included the Colditz classes in my program. Maybe I would become a journalist, I thought now, and write for the *Free Press*. Get to be the sports editor, and go to all the Lions and Tigers games. My future—to me—looked bright. And brighter still when I met my wife-to-be.

Marianne Elisabeth Gutzeit was born in Remscheid, in the Rhineland, and was brought to the United States in November 1924, a month before her third birthday. It was Germany's "Time of Troubles," when rampant inflation and food shortages plagued the country. A loaf of bread might cost a million marks, and savings accounts were wiped out, devastating the middle classes. Prices changed every day, and often more than once in the same day. On weekends her father would go out into the countryside to find something to eat for his family. He would trade an item from the household for food. The Germans blamed the French and British, who had insisted on huge reparations after World War I. And because the reparations were to be paid in gold, all backing for the mark had disappeared. The victors said the war had been the Germans' fault, and they owed money for the damage they had caused. In the 1920s and 30s Adolf Hitler capitalized on the widespread disaffection in his country.

Decades earlier Marianne's paternal grandfather, Friedrich Wilhelm, had moved to Remscheid from eastern Prussia, near the border with Lithuania—an area that was later part of the Soviet Union, and now Russia. In the 1860s and 70s Otto von Bismarck had defeated Austria and then France and brought the many German provinces together to form a powerful empire. But on the frontier remunerative work was hard to find for a young and ambitious peasant who had a sense of his own worth. (He refused to tip his hat to the wealthy landowners or to call them "sir." He was sixteen.) Without telling his family, the boy set out on his own to make a life in the West, ultimately settling in the industrialized Rhineland. He did well there, as did Ewald, his oldest son. Marianne's father became a skilled tool-and-die maker and in the early 1920s, like other Germans, was paid with junk money. Relatives suggested he might consider going to America. "Lots of us are doing that," they said.

Marianne's mother—Katharine—was from Caldern, a farming community near the Hessian city of Marburg. She too moved to Remscheid, and married Ewald during World War I. (He fought on the Russian front and was wounded several times.) In 1923 Katharine's uncle, who had earlier come to the Detroit area, signed papers backing Ewald's entry into the United States. The rest of the family followed him the next year.

In America, Ewald had no difficulty finding employment with the Ford Motor Company, which was expanding. And through the 1930s he was less touched than most workingmen by the economic depression. He was rarely out of work. If by chance the Ford plant were to close for a week or so, the family packed up and camped some place north of Dearborn, where they had bought a house. And her father fished. In Germany no workingman would be allowed to fish, he said. Only the upper classes. "America is a great country," he told me. The young Marianne had a good life in a good family. The Dearborn schools were excellent, supported by the Ford family. At Fordson High School, Marianne was an honors student.

But troubles mounted. After a long and painful illness, Katharine died of cancer. Marianne was fifteen, her sister Katie two years older, and for a time much of the responsibility for household affairs fell on the girls. Ewald subsequently married again—to Jane Fitzmaurice, a fine British American woman from the Upper Peninsula of Michigan. Jane supported Marianne's intention to go to college and to make a career for herself.

But that marriage quickly saddened. When I met Jane—the family had invited me to Thanksgiving dinner after the Wayne football game—she already showed evidences of Parkinsonism. Marianne was helping her more around the house. (Katie had married and moved away.) And Marianne worked weekends at Montgomery Ward's to pay for her tuition at Wayne and for her room and board. She was determined to be self-sufficient. When I met her she was already a pillar of common sense and resolve. If she gave me advice, I usually took it.

It was Monday afternoon. The army doctor poked at various crevices and orifices and listened to noises in his stethoscope. You have a cardiac arrhythmia, he told me. What's that? I asked. He explained: it was an irregular heartbeat. I had never noticed, I said. He seemed nonchalant about it. He put me on the scales. And you're underweight, he said. One hundred and thirty-nine pounds and almost six feet, two inches tall. I said nothing. I knew I was skinny. "How about sleep?" the doctor asked. "Do you get enough sleep?"

I laughed. In college? "Students never get enough sleep," I told him. That clinched it. "You'll have no trouble sleeping in the army," he said. "You'll get plenty of exercise. And good food. And they'll fix all those teeth. First thing." On June 27 I was sworn in as an American soldier, along with 382 other draftees. I wouldn't be seeing Marianne for a long time. A year maybe. The inductees left Detroit by train at 7:30 p.m.

A few days before I was inducted I had bought Marianne a birthstone ring, a zircon. I arranged to pay for it in installments, at five dollars a month. My father went to the jeweler's with me and guaranteed to back me up. He had a special place in his heart for the beautiful and talented Marianne Gutzeit and was determined that she should be part of our family. He saved his best items of humor for her. "I can tell Bob is smarter than you are," he said, as I introduced them. "He chose better than you did."

"What does the ring mean," Jane asked when Marianne showed it to her. "That you're planning on getting married?"

Marianne shook her head. "We never talked about it." And she would have to finish school first. "That's a long way off. Two years, at least."

I'd have been hard put to answer Jane's question. The gift wasn't intended as an engagement ring. Marianne and I had never talked about marriage. Our relationship was too new, our future too iffy. A stated, long-term commitment was not necessary as yet. Mostly, I think, I wanted her to have something tangible, to represent my feelings for her while I was away and to remind her of my existence.

Despite Marianne's and my fervent promises to write each day, that pledge was impossible to fulfill. Over the years there were occasional complaints and—on my part—too many pained "poor me" laments, followed by explanations and apologies. Mostly, however, we kept to the spirit of our compact. And because we were apart for so long, months at a time, we could think over important matters and avoid hasty judgments, while the many letters provided a vital sense of continuity.

Both of us began to talk of marriage within days of my arrival at Camp Roberts, California, on the fourth day of July, 1941. "Maybe we can take trips," Marianne wrote. "And some day we'll be together for always." On the phone I had suggested a train ride for our honeymoon. "For days I thought of you," she said, "on that train, going farther and farther away from me. It's funny how easy it's been to cry during the past week." Then the pragmatic nineteen-year-old spirit took over. "But really, dear, this could be a good chance for you." I'd have all sorts of experiences and adventures, she said. Meet interesting people, see

Private Quirk — in old-time blue denims — is ready for any cleanup job.

Marianne and Ellen.

things I'd never see otherwise. Read books and write stories, and maybe publish them. "Ellen stayed with me until Monday morning," she added.

Ellen Broderick was Marianne's closest friend from her Fordson High School days. For the duration of the war the two young women were often together, talking at night, writing letters, going to movies (usually double features), attending concerts, having lunch when both worked as secretaries for the same firm, and vacationing at resorts in the north of Michigan and in Canada. For me, Ellen was a godsend who could provide stability to a dear one who might otherwise have been constantly dismayed by the many pressures of a wartime existence. I owe to Ellen—and to Sarah Bailey, who was going to school in Kentucky, as well as to my sister Eileen—much that has subsequently been good and permanent in my life.

"It helps to dream," Marianne said.

Indeed it did. For more than four years of enforced separation. And because we were separated, we saved each letter, to be read and reread, mine in drawers at her home, and Marianne's in an army footlocker or, overseas, in my duffel bag. As my division moved through France and then across Germany the bag might fall behind. But it always caught up with me. When the war ended, first in Europe and then in the Far East, and I returned to civilian life, we stored them in my folk's house and in Marianne's. Somehow, we could never bring ourselves to throw them away. In Bloomington, Indiana, when I had gained tenure and we built our own house, they ended up in the attic, stowed away in a far corner. Decades later, after we both had retired, I found them again when I was looking for something else. As I leafed through them, I recognized at once that our many letters, combined with other memories and details, would make a wonderful story about two young people in love in a time of war. The rest, as the saying goes, is history.

When You Come Home

❦ 1 ❦

Basic Training

Guess what, honey. I've been assigned to the infantry! I had found some
ink at the post exchange and could begin sending Marianne real letters. To use a pencil would have been "banausic," I wrote. (That was
one of Harold Basilius's favorite words of deprecation.) I was sure she
would be as disappointed, as I was. I knew also that she would send an
ameliorating comment—assuring me that I might transfer to another
branch of the service in the future. After basic training. It was in my
mind as well. When or where we'd be located then was any man's
guess, and the subject was booby-trapped with rumors. On one day
consensus had it that we'd stay in California. In nearby San Luis
Obispo, maybe, where you slept in tents instead of wooden barracks.
The next day we were guaranteed that we'd go east. To Illinois. Or,
best of all, to Fort Custer in Michigan. I could almost commute from
there. And so it went.

I had been hoping for the Signal Corps where I could use my skills
as a photographer or a radio technician. I should have known better:
the evidence was all around me. There were a few artillerymen, but
Camp Roberts was constructed and equipped to turn out foot soldiers,
hundreds of them every thirteen weeks. The basic element of the
armed forces. That's what the army needed most of all, if war came.
And the news from Washington had worsened during the summer.

1

United States planes and naval vessels were now patrolling the Atlantic to warn the British about maneuvers by German submarines.

A dangerous precedent, I thought. As did a lot of other fellows who came with me from Camp Grant in Illinois where we had taken various tests and were given our summer uniforms. We talked about it on the troop train headed for California. And I had had such faith in Roosevelt when I worked for his reelection in 1940. I believed then that he would keep us out of "foreign entanglements." What if a U-boat were to sink an American ship? Would it mean war? That was one of the reasons the United States had entered World War I in 1917 and put millions of young Americans in the trenches.

There was more unwelcome news for Marianne. *It's pretty clear now,* I wrote. *We won't get out in a year.* Or even come home on a furlough, probably. And about writing letters, I told her: *Our address here is Company B of the 76th Infantry Battalion.*

Two days later they moved us into our permanent quarters, and units began to be formed. The heat was almost suffocating. A hundred and fifteen in the shade, the first sergeant said, and we had to walk at least a mile in the sun, carrying bags and weapons that must have weighed at least a hundred pounds. Toward the end I had to drag one of my bags. And trucks went up and down the line, collecting stragglers who were overcome from heat exhaustion. Four men passed out, that I knew of, and seeing them collapse and lie there on the ground, like dead men, made you think of yourself, and how dizzy you were. But I did make it OK, which was something, I thought. My first major accomplishment as a soldier. Marianne, as always when she wrote, had sound advice: *Be sure to wear your hat when you're in the sun.*

Most days they rousted us out of bed before five o'clock, and we trained until half-past three. That way we could be in the barracks, or some place else inside, during the hottest part of the afternoon. The lights were turned off at eight-thirty p.m. If you wanted to read then, or to write letters, you went into the latrine and sat on one of the toilets. Or walked over to the rec house.

The first sergeant explained the temperature anomaly to us. At night, he said, winds were coming off the ocean, which was just over the hills to the west. And you had to sleep with blankets. He made a pronouncement: "If you don't like the weather in California, wait a minute." He was always ready with an aphorism. On another occasion, when a trainee offered a lame excuse, he replied: "Yes, and if the dog hadn't stopped to shit, he'd of caught the rabbit." By and large, he was a reasonable fellow. Like most of the noncoms, he came to Roberts from a regular-army unit and had been in the service for several years. As for the rest of the NCOs, I gave them short shrift from the start. Unfortunately, I had brought with me to California a lot of Akron and Detroit prejudices. *It seems all you have to do to be a corporal or a sergeant,* I wrote, *is to be a hillbilly.* None were college graduates, nor indeed had attended a university. Only later did I come to appreciate their competence in what they did—teach us to be soldiers.

A lot of what we were required to do seemed at the time to serve no useful purpose. Early on I wrote: *Today we worked clearing off stones on the parade ground. I raked for hours till I got blisters on my hands, and the area is still stony. You can hardly tell the difference.* The most unfair part, I thought, was when someone made you work on a weekend. *On time that is supposed to be your own.* And I didn't mean KP [kitchen police], which rotated. Alphabetically and with fairness. None of the privates were exempted from working in the kitchen. But most of the fellows would be in town on Saturdays and Sundays. And I had stayed in the barracks, minding my own business, writing a letter or reading a book or a magazine. So along came someone in authority to give me a job. *Such as picking up cigarette butts around the officer quarters.* Why couldn't they shred the paper and scatter the pieces? *As any considerate human being would do?* Instead they treated us *like peons.* So we would learn, I supposed, to obey their every order and command, *no matter how ridiculous.*

I was writing this at the barracks, sitting up in my bed. The other men were back, most of them from nearby Paso Robles, but a few from San Francisco. And they were full of stories about this or that beer garden. One talked about the San Francisco night club that featured a "Topless Mother of Twelve." Awesome, most of the fellows thought. A corporal had had drinks at the Top of the Mark. I asked him about

3

the theater and the symphony orchestra in the big city, but he had no information. The train cost him almost five dollars for the round trip, he said, and I had to think that over. It would be a good part of my monthly pay. And where would I stay overnight? A hotel might be costly. One fellow said he had slept on a pool table. Another had gone to the YMCA. But you had to watch out for the homosexuals in the toilets, he said. He had been accosted twice.

Day by day, week by week, our training with weapons became more intense and increasingly taxing. On July 17 I wrote that we had gone out on *maneuvers,* which meant that we learned to fall down while running and carrying a rifle. *You turn in your left foot to trip yourself. Then you're falling forward on the outside of your left knee, catching yourself by letting the butt of the weapon hit the ground just before you do, rolling on your left elbow. Then you creep and crawl forward without lifting yourselves from the ground. Every once in a while I got sand in my mouth.* I didn't see any snakes or tarantulas, I wrote, though some other fellows did. *Those spiders grow up to ten inches across.*

The next day—it was Friday—I was out of sorts. More than usual, that is. We had walked four miles. *During the march I sweated so much the color of my fatigue uniform ran, and my undershirt turned a bright blue.* And when we got back to the barracks, and I had taken a good shower, they sent us out again, the whole squad, to clean up a field of matches and cigarette butts around the officers' quarters. *Those bastards!* So I was as dirty and sweaty as ever. And then we learned a general would inspect us the next day. *They said I had to wash my uniform. But I'm not going to do it. I washed it already. And besides if the general wants us to have clean uniforms, he should see to it that we have more than one. I'll probably have to do extra KP duty or haul rocks around the camp as a punishment. But what the hell.*

None of this happened. *Surprise, honey. The general never noticed. He just walked right by without saying a word about our uniforms. Which was smart of him. A half-ass second lieutenant would have awarded a slew of demerits, and then everyone would be unhappy. And the officer would feel he had done a great thing for humanity that justified his existence.*

Training was tough. But in July and August of 1941 the worst problem for me began in Washington. Congress was preparing legislation that would extend the draft another year. Or even more. In my letter of July 19 I sounded off: *We soldiers who must give up so much have nothing to say about the matter. Those who decide things are the ones who sacrifice nothing.* But worse, I continued, *We are slowly but surely being forced into the war by the machinations of international diplomacy.* But what could I do about it? A mere private. *The eternal low man on the totem pole.*

Marianne agreed. She had taken a summer job with a real estate firm in downtown Detroit and was writing during her lunch hour. *I know how you feel about our being swept into the war. Those are my sentiments too. I don't think we should have to pay with our time, our minds, our lives, for a cause we don't have any feeling for. The propaganda that's being thrown in our faces only makes me feel more antagonistic. I think I'm pretty capable of coming to my own conclusions. But you're right, dear. There's no point in airing our opinions, because it doesn't do any good. Look at it this way: the draft can't last forever. Maybe there won't be a war.* And there were compensations. *Things like this have come and passed before, and the experience of living through it, of being in it, is valuable. Especially for people like you who want to be a writer. And if we never have to make sacrifices, or had to adjust ourselves, we'd be pretty shallow people. Wouldn't we?*

Nevertheless, life went on in the military camp, with new skills acquired and new problems to cope with, almost every day. *I'm writing this letter, honey, from the guardhouse. No, don't worry. I've done nothing wrong.* I was a member of the guard, I wrote, for that one day, guarding some trucks. Walking around and around them. *Probably the reason they gave me this duty is the ROTC* [Reserve Officers' Training Corps] *I had before I came in the army. And the tests I took at Camp Grant. The first sergeant thought I ought to know something about being a sentinel.* It was in my record, he said. I didn't tell him the ROTC was while I was still in high school. And I had been trying to avoid some phys. ed. courses I disliked. *Whether I did any good, I don't know. No one checked on us, and without a war we have no enemy to watch out for.* Besides, who was going to steal a two-ton truck in the middle of Camp Roberts?

Another letter went out the next day: *It's tomorrow now, honey, and I'm still doing guard duty. I'm the only one this time, and it's just for a few hours.* Why? *Because I was posted to the officers' quarters, outside the door of a second lieutenant charged with going AWOL* [Absent Without Leave]. I was sitting in the hall, I told her, on an armless chair, across from his room, again with a pistol in my belt. *They told me it was loaded, but I didn't check. Besides, I had never fired one before. Or knew how to load it.* And I had to see that he didn't leave his room until the MPs [Military Police] came to pick him up in the afternoon and carted him off somewhere. *I didn't think officers did things like that,* I wrote. *They have so much more to lose than we do.* In the end, the company commander came without the MPs, and the two officers just strolled away, chatting, as though nothing was amiss. *So perhaps nothing more will come of it. An enlisted man would have been in the hoosegow,* I wrote.

You referred to my writing about things in your letter. In fact, I have an idea for a series of stories, and I embroidered on them in my mind while I was guarding all those trucks. I don't remember if I told you about the fellow in our barracks who was sleeping late on a Sunday morning. I came back from Mass at 9:30, and someone had taken him, his mattress, and his bed-clothing and put them in the middle of the floor. He didn't wake up for another hour or so, and then he lay there, batting his eyes and wondering how he'd got himself in that fix. Pranks can be fun and funny—if they're played on somebody else. But another morning a fellow was lying on the floor, in his own vomit. I thought to myself: Never would I drink that much liquor. Even an animal wouldn't do that.

After another training session: *Today was a red-letter day. We were issued more clothes. Finally. And to top it all off there was a letter from you. I put it in my shirt pocket, next to my heart. Coming back from the bayonet course I was tired, naturally. But I just thought about other things. Mostly about you and the first time I said I loved you. And you told me your cousin Gertrude said there was no such thing as love. Do you remember?*

Marianne's reply: *Yes. I remember very well. When you gave me the bracelet. But it wasn't my cousin. Anyway, that has nothing to do with us. It was just after you went to the track meet at Notre Dame, and I'd become sort of used to the fact that you were pretty important in my life. But I hadn't thought of it in words. In fact, I guess I was a little afraid of being in love with anyone. And I wanted to be sure that the way I felt about you was really love. I still don't know. I just know that I couldn't ever feel about anyone else the way I feel about you. When you took the psych. course did they ever talk about imagery? How a person can really see and hear another person thinking, no matter how far apart they may be? It's midnight here, nine in the evening where you are. And you're in bed. Can you hear me say it? I love you very much. There I said it.*

I was between maneuvers now: *No. We never talked about "imagery." But then I had a different prof. He was more interested in true-and-false tests than in subjects like romanticism. Which leads me to an important question. Have you made any decisions yet about your classes in the fall? And the School of Education? Did you fill out the applications yet? And another thing. Do you remember what Dr. Basilius said once about too many women teaching for a few years and then quitting to get married? If they don't intend to make careers in education they shouldn't start in the first place. What are your thoughts about that?*

I thought seriously of going to San Francisco next weekend. It turns out that it doesn't cost as much as people said. If you don't take the train or the bus. Hitchhiking is against the law in this state and also forbidden by army regulations. But if you just stand there in your uniform, beside the road, some civilian will pick you up. I decided, though, to postpone it for another month to have more money. There's a play in that town I'd like to see, about two old ladies who are poisoning people. It doesn't sound like much, but it's supposed to be funny. And it has Boris Karloff in it, I think. Incidentally, the Frisco paper said the temperature at Camp Roberts yesterday was 125 degrees! In the shade.

On August 4 Marianne wrote: *You asked me what the score is, what the relationship is between my wanting to be a teacher and to be your wife, really. I think that is what you meant. What Harold Basilius was talking about. I don't know what to tell you, when I don't quite know myself. I used to think I'd like to finish college, to teach for several years, perhaps the first two or three after we were married. And then to give it up when we'd had a start, especially if there were children.*

7

But now I see that there are loopholes. In the first place, as you say (and Dr. Basilius agrees), that it isn't fair to the school system to give up my job and career when I'd just begun to become proficient. And personally, I wouldn't have any enthusiasm for undertaking something, which all the time I knew was only temporary. In the second place, it would be very difficult to give up the additional income once I was teaching—and was married. And to give up a profession I liked and was good at. So where does that leave me? Gee, I don't know yet, honey. It's all so confusing.

And I haven't finished the application for the School of Education yet. I keep putting it off. Education courses are all so darned practical. If I entered, there'd be no more background courses, things I like, such as economics and sociology. And especially the German literature, which will always be special to me. And I'd be taking nothing but penmanship and spelling, children's literature and games, things I know all about anyway. Things I've read and done all my life. I've been asking myself lately what I wanted from college, and I don't think that so far I have enough background to begin to be a teacher. Or anything else, I suppose. I don't think I'm ready to enter the College of Ed. In fact, I don't think anyone else is better prepared. But that doesn't help the situation. If it were up to me, I'd go on taking things I like and wait with entering the College of Education for a year. But I don't know what to tell my folks. That I want to take five years, instead of four. I don't know if they'll understand.

But then I'm paying my own way through school. And I should be able to take what I'll enjoy most and do me the most good. In the long run. So maybe they won't mind so very much. Also you and I can be in classes at the same time, if I do that. What do you think about it?

It was Saturday, and I was reading her letter and trying to get ready for our weekly inspection. But I found time to write. *I washed my ammunition belt and mess kit, shined my shoes (I have three pairs now), and cleaned my rifle. Its funny how we work so long for an inspection that is over in a few minutes. And they don't even look closely. But woe be it if you haven't cleaned something. You'll catch it for sure. Unless it's the general who's doing the inspecting, as we've seen. But maybe he's nearsighted!*

As it turned out, the inspection wasn't so bad. *But I can't say the same for the rest of the day. A sergeant came around the barracks and got me into fatigues before I could disappear. I had to haul gravel, he said. It was hot and dirty and plenty hard work. He came again in the afternoon, I heard, but I was at the barbershop. Luckily. Getting that brush cut I told you about on the phone. You won't recognize me probably. And I decided to stay the rest of the afternoon at the library, just in case. I read* Studs Lonigan *by J. T. Farrell. The first part, that is. It's the same stuff as* USA *and* The Grapes of Wrath. *Have you read them? How can anybody read them and still vote for the Republicans?*

After another week of hell: *Every day they find a hundred new muscles to exercise and to make sore. Then they march us that two miles back to the barracks. I'm hot and dusty, and my feet drag. And my mouth tastes like dry leaves. The temperature on Monday was 115, the cook said. And Tuesday was even worse—120 degrees. The lieutenant told us just to drink more liquids.*

About the liquids, we carry with us a canteen of water on our belts. It holds about a pint or so. We fill them in the evening because it cools the water to stand outside all night. So the water is reasonably cold in the morning. But we usually don't need water before lunch, which is at 11:30. And by then the sun has got at the water and it's tepid. Each company has large containers of cool water, but they don't last much past lunch. We fill up our canteens with ice-cold water at noon, but within an hour it's hot. With the temperature at 140 degrees in the sun you feel a need for liquids. But if you drink the hot water, you'll feel worse than ever. Still nobody has keeled over because of the heat. So I guess we're all getting tougher. And one good thing, I guess, we don't have to worry about snakes any more. No self-respecting serpent would be seen out on days like these.

I've been thinking about things more than I used to: This morning we marched out into a fog that settled over everything. You couldn't see more than fifty feet ahead or behind you. Other soldiers were marching and disappearing into the fog, and it occurred to me that the fog resembled life. You go forward blindly, not knowing what's in store for you, and with no way of finding out. You just put one foot in front of the other, and hope for the best. You have to trust the Captain—in the fog and in your life.

I see by the papers that Congress is about to lengthen the term of us draftees to 2 1/2 years. That's really a slap in the face, isn't it? You said this

9

year would be a test of our love. Now this added separation will make the test a million times more difficult. And make it that much harder for me to finish school. But I know I am going to do it, go back to Wayne, that is. And if necessary I can finish everything in a year and a half. Or even less, if I go to summer school and take extra classes. If we love each other enough, and I know we do—am sure we do—it will eventually turn out all right.

About the firing exercises: *Tomorrow we go out on the range to actually fire the rifle for the first time. It will probably be a strenuous day before it's finished, with the heat and all. And with our elbows and shoulders giving us a lot of pain in the practice sessions. The officers told us to fix up some pads. From old rags, maybe. The fellows in Company A were way ahead of us, though. They must have talked with somebody. At any rate, they went into Paso Robles and bought themselves boxes of Kotex. Also rolls of adhesive tape. It provides a lot of protection for elbows, they say. Better than rags. And it's ready-made. I don't know if I could do that. I'd be too embarrassed to ask the drugstore clerk. Especially if it was a woman, which is mostly the case in Paso Robles. So maybe I'll just suffer the pain. I could ask Bud Rollins to get some for me. Or I can share a box with him. Did you know him at Wayne? He lives in the barracks next to ours. What a coincidence! And he has more guts than I do, for things like that.*

(Later: The idea spread, and soon there were no supplies of sanitary napkins in the town, which was small. The women were complaining, including, we were told, the wife of the general. Within days notices appeared on each bulletin board in camp warning that army personnel were forbidden to purchase sanitary napkins in Paso Robles. But it's difficult to outwit a bunch of soldiers when they put their minds to a problem. Even for a general. And I think they continued to buy pads in other towns and cities. There were a lot of them in our barracks.)

As it turned out, though, the firing wasn't as difficult as I expected. Without the pads, I mean. We had heard about the jolt into the shoulder when we fired the Aught-Three.[1] But that didn't hurt me. I just grunted when my elbows gave me trouble. Maybe I can stand pain better than some people. I fired ten shots from the prone position and made one bulls-eye

---

1. Springfield rifle.

and nine fours for a score of 41 out of 50. Later we fired from the sitting, kneeling, and standing positions. I made 172 out of 250 possible points and qualified as a marksman.

Not much to brag about, I suppose, but when I turned in my scores, the first sergeant said: "Very good shooting, Quirk." Things like that make you feel good about yourself. Recently I noticed that for some reason the sergeant has been watching me. More, maybe, than the other fellows. I wonder what's up.

Payday! Many a soldier will get royally drunk on his pittance and have to borrow all the rest of the month to get along. Which reminds me of something funny. No, let me change that. It wasn't funny at all. Quentin Rollins has soured on life. Or if he hasn't, he should have. He's a "soft touch," as we say. A few weeks ago he loaned a Pontiac fellow $11 until the guy got a check from home. A couple of days later the fellow went "over the hill." There's a rumor that he surrendered himself in Detroit, but we don't know whether it's true or not. Then last night, after we were paid, one of the sergeants borrowed $5 from Bud and a private borrowed $10. This morning, at roll call, those two were missing. The sergeant had taken his suitcase, so it doesn't look as if he, at least, is coming back. Or the private either, I think. So Bud is out another $15, of the less than twenty-one he was paid. Maybe his folks send him money. I hope so, anyway.

As for me, I got $23.80, because of the four days extra in June. And then they took out a dollar for laundry and another three for canteen checks. And now I know what I can count on. I plan to put aside five or ten dollars each month to save for the time when I am out of the army. I know that whenever my term is up, whatever it is, readjustment will be difficult. Demobilizing our vast army—and navy—is going to be catastrophic. All of a sudden 2,500,000 or more men will be dumped on the labor market. From your economics class you will know that isn't good. It could be difficult to find employment. When the boys were drafted and left their jobs, they were promised that when they returned, those positions would be open to them. At the same time, I know that after two and a half years it will be difficult to take a civilian out of his job to make way for a soldier. Promises will long since be forgotten. So I don't want to be caught short. I'll need to have enough money to go back to school. Then, with a B.A., I can find a place more easily."

Chapter 1

The day after my first payday: *You asked in one letter if I'd changed. You can say what you like about the army, but when it claims to build men, it does just that. Already, my muscles are harder, and I feel better than I did in civilian life. Much better. I can do a lot harder work than I ever could before, and not tire so much. And while the food isn't always the best I have eaten—my mother is a great cook—it is scientifically proportioned, as to proteins, vitamins, etc., and it is wholesome. We have meat practically every meal, and that is a muscle-builder. I have been stowing away plenty of it since I came here, and I intend to stow away a lot more before I leave. The bread is especially good. With lots of butter. I have heard that everyone who comes in the army gets heavier. I've gained almost ten pounds in the short time I've been at Roberts. And my teeth have been fixed. Twenty-two of them at one sitting!*

So I guess the answer is yes, I have changed. But only physically. Mentally and spiritually I will always be the same fellow who loved you so much in those good old days at Wayne University, and at the Cass-Warren drugstore, and during the walks down Second Boulevard. When we should have been studying, I suppose. Remember? Come what may, I will always love you. That can never be changed by mere events or time.

And the next day: *I feel kind of tired this evening, as if I could go to bed and never get up anymore. I don't know what we did especially today to make us so tired, but everyone was completely done in. When we came in from the firing range this afternoon a good many of us thought we couldn't possibly get over that last hill. True, it was hot, but not as hot as it has been. Perhaps it was the release of tension after our record firing was over. I'm glad it's finished, though I did enjoy some of it, and I have some mementos—a skinned hand and a bruised shoulder from the Browning submachine gun. And more praise from the first sergeant. Especially when I fired the Browning. I was the top man in the platoon in that department. And before that, fourth highest with the pistol. Sharpshooter in both. That rating is just below expert and higher than marksman. Lucky, maybe. But anyway we are all tired. And it's a good thing we don't have to get up early tomorrow. We can sleep until 5:15, I think. Though with my luck, I'll probably wake up at 4:15. As usual.*

Most likely I'm let down by the latest news from Washington. The long wait is over, and it's certain that I'll be spending at least 2 1/2 years in the army. It's funny how the destiny of millions of people can be determined by the vote of one man in the House of Representatives. Whoever he is. If he had voted differently, the extension would probably have been for only six months, or at the most a year. Am I angry about it? No, because that wouldn't do any good or change anything. And I had been expecting it, so I wasn't surprised. Still, it makes my near future look rather bleak. Sometimes I think it's too much to ask of you, that you must wait so long for me to come home. But before you bite my head off, let me say that I believe you implicitly, that no time is too long to wait for me. No, I don't mean it that way. It sounds too egotistical.

I guess I'm all mixed up. Or tired. Or both. What I mean is that we love each other, and in view of the years of happiness ahead of us, we can wait a couple of years for the consummation of that happiness. And who knows? We may come out of the crucible a lot more finely tempered. It may even be good for us in the long run, for all we know. So let's make the best of it, you in school and at home, and I as a soldier. Meanwhile, we can have our frequent letters and our once-in-a-while long-distance phone call. And once in a long, long time I'll have a furlough, a reunion for a few days, at least. And before we know it, I will be home again, for all time, my own dear one.

Marianne had quit her daytime job at the office: *I'm writing from a little cottage on the lake about twenty miles north of Port Huron. I brought a couple of books from the Dearborn library. One was* Democracy and Education *by John Dewey. Dr. Basilius said no one was fit to teach until he had read what Dewey had to say about the subject. So I thought I'd better find out. I'll have a lot of time on my hands here. When I'm not swimming or lying in the sun. Two whole weeks. Or even longer, I think. It depends on the others. Ellen and Sarah Bailey are coming, and my sister Katie is here already, with her family.*

About the two and a half years. The only thing we can do is resign ourselves to the fact and do our best in the meantime. In two and a half years we'll both be a lot wiser. And older, of course. I'll be all of 22. I can see us—in 1947, say—looking back to these days when we were separated. And we'll laugh, because it will be just a memory, nothing more.

You asked me on the phone where I would like to live. And you talked about "country folk." They were always the romantic ideal, weren't they? At least, in German literature. Small towns are very nice, but I don't think we would be happy for a very long period. There would be a lack of culture, no symphony orchestra or theater. I like your idea of living near enough to a city that transportation is no problem. You would have the benefits of a big city and all the freedom of the countryside. And the land around the house is very important. I'd rather have a home in the right place. Long after, the children will remember the setting about the house, as well as the house itself, which altogether form the picture they'll think of as home.

But we don't want a large house, do we? For me only eight rooms is enough. And maybe a Cape Cod. But the rooms would have to be large, with wide casement windows. And of course a big fireplace in the living room. I can see the smoke curling up from our chimney at night, while we talk about so many things. And most of all, it must be very colorful and cheerful. Our future together is a wonderful dream, isn't it? No length of time is too long for me to wait for you. Funny, isn't it, how two people could get to know each other so well, in such a comparatively short time. And now at such a distance. P.S. The little radio on my desk is playing "It's So Peaceful in the Country." What a coincidence!

The next day, from Camp Roberts: *I think your idea of choosing a five-year course is a good one. That is, for me, from a selfish point of view. Then you wouldn't have to wait so long after you are graduated for me to finish. But aside from that you would be taking the classes you liked. The College of Education courses might be more practical for what you are going to do, but do you remember what Dr. Basilius said about the Ed College? That they cover all the mechanics of teaching, and then forget to give the prospective teachers anything to teach. For instance, a person could, by fulfilling the college requirements, teach German in high school with only a minor. I could do it now with my few credits. But I know I am not capable of teaching it, no matter what the education college says. I can read it pretty well, and speak it, but I'm far from fluent in the language.*

So, with you, you might acquire all the mechanics of teaching, but would you have the background necessary for an educated woman? Would you know economics, sociology, philosophy, literature, and the other subjects that make for a rounded education? Isn't that a rhetorical question that you have already answered for yourself? And quoting from the sociologists, how about this: *A marriage between two university graduates has the best chance of succeeding. The couple are more tolerant and more capable of working out difficulties amicably. Such as our different religions. I've been thinking about that problem for a long time. And we need to talk about it.*

First of all, we have to recognize that the problem exists. I am a Catholic, though not a good one, and my background has been Catholic for more than twenty years. Yours, on the other hand, has been Lutheran. There are many matters on which our religions differ hugely, and these are what we want to watch for. And to guard ourselves against becoming antagonistic. In case you didn't know it, you are starting with a huge disadvantage. That is, if we were married by a Catholic priest, as my religion demands, you would have to swear that all our children would be raised as Catholics. I know that is a difficult decision for a non-Catholic to make. But the Church wants to keep its members from marrying outside the "One and True Church." Unless I am married by a priest, I am not morally married. We would be living together out of wedlock. In sin. I would be denied the rites and sacraments of the Church. That is the crux of the matter.

I can well imagine that it would be difficult for a devout Lutheran to raise his or her children as Catholics. Centuries of religious strife are against it. For us I can see only two possibilities. The first is that you promise our children would be raised in my Church. Then we would be both legally and "morally" married. But if you could not agree to that, the other possibility is that we not be married by a Catholic priest and raise our children as we see fit. Neither would be easy. Both are loaded with dynamite. It would be a hardship for each of us. It is for that very reason that both Catholic and Protestant authorities try to discourage mixed marriages.

But I would be willing to give up a lot for you, darling. I love you so much that even my religion could not stand between us. You are the greatest thing in my life, and you always will be. I don't mean to say I would change my religion, because I know I could never do that. I have a lot of grievances against the Catholic Church. They go a long way back to when the priests asked us to pray for that "great Catholic leader," General Franco. It started me thinking about a lot of things. And when, for example, the pastor at St. Charles denied that the Church and the popes had ever been corrupt. Especially during Luther's time, for example. We studied that last year in Frank Kemmer's class. And used the Bossenbrook and Johannesen textbook. Remember? Anyway, I showed it to the priest. It was trash, he said. Which was not true. It was well researched. I can tell that. And Kemmer was convincing on the subject. I do mean that I would be Catholic in thought, if not in deed. And I'd still want to sing in the choir, if they'd let me. So that even if it were very, very difficult, we could still work out our profound differences, if we look at them squarely. So let's not concern ourselves too much about the future. It will come, and all will be well.

Marianne's reply was prompt and forthright: *You suggested two alternatives: The first is to be married by a Catholic priest, and I would swear to keep a Catholic home and give our children a Catholic education. I love you very much, but I don't think I could do that. I believe certain things that—for me—are true. My love doesn't change that. To say I would raise my children as Catholics—something I don't believe in—would be hypocritical. I'm sorry. I hope you won't be too disappointed in me. But I could never make such a promise. You said your church does not recognize a marriage performed by any authority but a priest. And they regard two people married by anyone else as living together out of wedlock. In sin—as you said. That's very drastic. And important for the both of us. If, for instance, we were married by a minister or a justice of the peace, would you feel that you weren't morally married to me at all? If you did, I don't think you would be happy. And I don't think I could marry you if I knew it was causing you to do something that was contrary to your own convictions. So I guess it all depends on what your feelings are about it.*

Since I read your letter, I have been trying to think what a marriage is and when it is *one. Truly one. Of course, the ceremony must be performed by a properly authorized person. For legal purposes. But most of all—and this is important—two persons must feel that they want to belong to each other, forever and ever. And they must believe—sincerely—in the vows they make to each other. I'm sure then that God will recognize them as married forever. On the other hand, no matter who spoke the text of the ceremony, if they didn't sincerely believe in what they were promising, I wouldn't regard that as a marriage.*

But then, as you say, it's not something we have to settle here and now, is it? Luckily. We're both young, and two and a half years may make a difference. Somehow, the problem could be solved for us.

And she changed the subject. I had asked her earlier about a Sunday-night program I heard on the radio: *Yes,* she said, *beautiful music makes me feel the same way, and I think of you, dear one. You said you were listening to Mendelssohn's "On Wings of Song" by the Fred Waring Choir. I haven't heard it yet. But there is a recording just now that I like very much—an arrangement by Freddy Martin's orchestra of the "Piano Concerto in B-flat." It's by Tchaikovsky, I think. Every time I hear it, I get an exultant feeling, of being on top of the world. I want to hear it the day I am with you again. Right now—incidentally—the radio is playing "Estrellita." Pretty, isn't it?*

It was a Sunday morning, after Mass, and I had been at Camp Roberts for fifty-one days. I put the theological arguments behind me and went directly to the practical matters that were easier to deal with in my letter to Marianne: *Not right now getting married, I should say, but when I am out of the army and back home again. I mean should we wait until we have enough money to get a good start, or should we plunge into it, on a shoestring, as it were? Sometimes I think I like the idea of the latter. Of the two of us starting out together, fighting against the world, taking the tough breaks with the good. But then it would be a lot easier if we both were working and had good incomes. So we'll see. But I do want us to have a home of our own. A really nice home, costing maybe $10,000.*

It seems to me the FHA [Federal Housing Administration] *plan is the best. You put ten percent down and the rest on monthly payments for twenty years. It usually comes to less than you would be paying in rent—and you would have your own home. You said in your letter "only eight rooms." That's a large house, my love, by my standards. It would be nice, certainly, but could we afford it?*

And there's something I meant to bring out. I think one of the reasons why my folks lost all of their possessions in the Depression was that they bought so much on credit. In recent years they've had plenty, but I've always distrusted buying on credit. You'll say I've done it a lot myself, and you're partly right. For instance, the only way I could have bought you your ring was on credit. Either that or to wait a long time till I had saved the money. By that time I'd be far away in the army. I wanted to give it to you while I was home. But I hope that when we are married we can use credit as little as possible. It will mean more budgeting, but I think it will be worth it. Don't you, darling?

I'm closing now. I have to get up at 4:15, and Bud Rollins just came in with a pint of ice cream for each of us. He had gone to the movies to see "Manhunt," with Walter Pidgeon and Joan Bennett. He said it was very, very exciting. So maybe I'll go tomorrow evening, and then write you a letter about it. In the meantime, I'll be thinking of you, as always. As you know, you are the center of my world. And always will be.

The next Monday: *We had to clean rifles after supper, so I didn't have time for the movie. And now only for a short letter. I told you before about firing the B.A.R.[2] Well, I still have a bump and a sore place on my forehead from that. It's funny, when I shoot the Browning in the kneeling position, the gun jumps up and smacks me. It doesn't do that in any other position. It got so that every time I fired it, the tears would run down my cheeks from the sudden pain. Automatically. It didn't help my shooting to know that each time I pulled the trigger it would hurt me. I guess I must have flinched with each shot, because my score for that position was only 17 out of 25. Who knows? I might have been rated "expert" otherwise. Like Ralph Matthews. He's the best in everything. Incidentally, Ralph is planning to volunteer for the paratroopers when he finishes basic training here. He says he's afraid of high places—I think the Abnormal Psych. prof called it acrophobia. Anyway, jumping out of airplanes would cure him, Ralph says. I don't believe it, but who knows?*

I meant to tell you also that they issued us gas masks a week ago. They let us smell various gasses used during past wars, so we would be able to identify them. They all smelled pretty bad, but there wasn't enough to hurt us. It reminded me, though, of the chemistry class at Eastern High, and how Mr. Beddow told us that in the 1917–18 war the soldiers, if they didn't have masks, would urinate on their handkerchiefs and breathe through those. Anyway, they marched us into a chamber filled with tear gas, and then we

---

2. Browning automatic rifle.

put on our masks. It really hits you in the eyes and makes the tears run. With the masks on it doesn't bother you at all. I told the other fellows about Mr. Beddow's story, and they dared me to try the handkerchief method. I just laughed, but I'm still wondering about it. If we have any more tests I might experiment. If I can get someone else to do it too. But then where would I urinate? A real problem.

Another day they wanted to show us the consequences of mustard gas, as a warning. They didn't spray us, but they dipped something, a stick maybe, in the gas—it was liquid. Then they touched us on the inside of our bare arms. The doctor wiped off the gas from the right arm with a substance he called British anti-lewisite. You'll see the difference in a few days, he said. And he was right. The right arm was OK. But the spot on the other arm raised a blister the size of a two-bit piece. Very painful, it was. And still is. It will leave a scar, he said, "for the rest of your natural life." Some warning! I don't want to do that again. But I know what mustard gas can do to a person.

August 30, 1941: Another army payday, the second since I came to Camp Roberts. I got only $11.79 this time, since we were paid early, and a lot was deducted for laundry, canteen checks, theater books, etc. But I went into Paso Robles, because I wanted needles and some thread for mending, and I did something rash. I was passing a restaurant—at supper time—and I decided to treat myself to a steak dinner. With french fries. Smells were coming out the door. It cost me all of $1.95. I can't afford to do that too often, if I want to save for our future. It seems I've developed such a large appetite in the army. I'm always hungry. If I keep that up, you will be marrying a fat man.

I wanted to tell you, though, about last night and the hike. This time we wore our denims with wool shirts and the canvas leggings. Also our new field jackets. And we needed them all, what with the cold winds from the coast. Several squads were sent out with compasses to find a particular point where a truck was parked. The difficulty was that they had to go around hills, instead of over them, and that tended to throw them off the course. I was a runner for the lieutenant—a new man, from Maine, I think. He has a funny way of talking. Down East, he says, and he elides his r's. I followed him around all evening, and carried messages and got information for him.

19

He's only five feet, four or five inches tall, but he surely set us a fast pace. He's a "good Joe," somebody said. So far, he seems impressive. Not like most of the officers in this outfit. Sometimes I wonder where the army got them. My job was to make sure the squads got in OK. And were not lost. I was really tired, as you can imagine. I just flopped into bed and slept through the night without dreaming. Not even of you, dear heart. And they let us sleep late this morning. Until 6:30. Imagine that!

What have you decided about the College of Ed? To enter this semester or wait till next year? I won't try to influence you one way or the other, but you do know which way my sentiments lean. I really did enjoy going to Wayne. Because of you, first of all. But I liked the classes and the instructors. Kemmer and Kelly in the History Department, most of all. Kelly never used notes the whole semester, and he was well organized. And Raymond Miller too was fine. He could tell funny stories about his Scottish grandfather. And Bossenbrook was good, but crazy. He would bend over and look students in the eye, especially in the first row, and he'd say: "See what I mean?" Then he'd shake his head and say: "I thought not." And he kept telling us more about Soren Kierkegaard than we wanted to know. Some days I think I should be a history teacher. It's the most interesting subject I've taken, by far.

I felt I was getting to be someone at the university when I left. People who counted for something asked to meet me. And people whom I didn't know would know me—and call me by name. And my writings for the Collegian *were appreciated. I was probably conceited, as you have pointed out more than once. But I was proud of my work there. When I come back, it could be different, I suppose. I'll have to start all over again. My classmates will be new and strange. And lots younger. But with you at my side, I know I'll do well again. And things are looking better in Europe. If the tide turns against the Germans by next summer, I'm sure to be out in a year. And back at Wayne again.*

That is, if the Russians are winning. If not, we're in trouble, I'm afraid. I don't have much confidence in the British and French. They can't beat the Germans. And unless Germany goes down, I will have to fight. I know that. In the infantry. And we both know what that means. Lots and lots of casualties. We'll just have to hope and pray, won't we? And depend on the Russians.

I hate to talk to you about Germany's being defeated. You must think of your relatives over there. But it must be done. Not that I hate Germans. But our country has clearly put itself on the side of England and the Allies, and I am part of the American army. It's a matter of my future happiness—and yours too—that Germany be defeated as quickly as possible. I know you will understand. If we never have to fight, it will be perfect. But only time will tell.

I have been hearing some beautiful music lately on the radio too, the Bell Telephone Hour and the Voice of Firestone. And as I listen I imagine that we are together again, this time in our own home. Let's have a good record player and make a collection of the best music available. Handel's "Largo." "The Intermezzo" from "Cavalleria rusticana." "Berceuse" by Paul Joslin. I heard the "Largo" on the Fred Waring program, sung by Stuart Churchill. It actually made chills run up and down my spine. It's beautiful beyond all description. And it makes me think of you. And of the symphony concerts we went to. And will, when I am home. The romantics saw music as the ultimate expression of love and beauty. Didn't Dr. Basilius say something like that in one of his classes?

By the way, I've been acting-corporal in our platoon for almost a week. One good thing is that I don't have to walk guard. Or come to think of it, do KP either. Bud Rollins had to take my place in the kitchen, which teed him off somewhat. They go alphabetically, and his name comes right after mine on the company roster. He had been planning a trip to SF. I think he has some relations up there.

Today is my last day as squad leader. Did I tell you about it on the telephone Sunday? I've forgotten. I always feel so rushed and flustered when we're really talking together. In a way I enjoyed the responsibility. And I know I didn't do a bad job. Pretty good, in fact.

From Dearborn, September 2, 1941: *I got back from the lake yesterday evening, and it feels good to be home again. I found four letters from you. I'll try to answer those this weekend. It's been a pretty good test this far, hasn't it? Though sometimes I cry myself to sleep, when I haven't heard from you*

*for a while. For four or five days, sometimes. I wonder if something has hap-
pened to you. And then I get several letters at the same time, and all is well.
I like what you say about our "Shangri La" life together. A place where we
can be completely happy. For all time.*

*I'm still working at Ward's on weekends, until I find out for sure about
the NYA* [National Youth Administration] *job at Wayne. The woman in
charge there has asked me to help out. Ward's has raised my wages a lot, and
I'm not going to quit there until I decide which would be most profitable for
the time I have to spend. I wonder, though, if I could handle the two jobs, as
well as a full program of classes, without killing myself. That way I can put
more money in our joint account. I'll have to think about that.*

Two days later, September 4, 1941, in the army, from Camp
Roberts: *I'm still wearing corporal stripes on my left arm. But for how long
I don't know. I talked the other day to one of our fellows who works in the
company office, and he heard the first sergeant say he was not going to change
the squad-leaders, as I expected. He was keeping his "good men," he said. Was
that why he kept watching me? And I was worried about it. I have to admit
that it makes me proud of what I have done so far. If I make permanent corporal I would get $54 a month, instead of only $30. And we could save a lot
more. The catch, though, is that I would have to stay at Roberts, while
maybe the other fellows go east. If I had my druthers, I'd prefer to be a private in the Middle West. If I got out in a year, that is. It's confusing, isn't it?*

A week later: *It's official. For good or for bad, I'm staying right here.
And I'll be an instructor for the next batch of trainees. The good point is the
money and the corporal rating. And I could fly home, if I got a furlough. It's
not a rough job, and I'll have more time to myself. I have to admit that it is
an honor to have been chosen. That I am one of only six in the company of
250 men. And I might even go higher. I could be a sergeant, and then I'd
really be rich.*

*On the other hand, it's hard to leave friends like Bud Rollins, or for a
corporal even to have friends. Noncoms live apart from the privates and eat
at separate tables. And there's always that chance that the fellows will go
east. In the end, though, it's not up to me. I have no choice in the matter. As
the Bible says: "They say stay, and I stay. They say go, and I go." This is the
army, and everyone just takes orders from somebody. Even the generals.*

And that reminds me of something else. One of the trainees in our platoon—he was from Arkansas—was a real knucklehead. It turned out he had been in ROTC at the university, and during the tenth week here he suddenly became a captain! Silver bars and all. As though someone had waved a magic wand, and the toad had become a handsome prince. They didn't know what to do with him until they could send him someplace else, so the major put him to work training us. He lasted less than a day. For one thing, he couldn't think of the simple marching orders, outside of "forward march." The result was that he got us going toward the barracks—the whole platoon—and then he just kept hollering "Stop! Stop!" as we all crashed into the side of the building. The fifty of us trying not to laugh. He couldn't even think of "column right" or "column left." Or of the simple word "halt." And no one was going to help him. Human beings can be cruel sometimes. He looked as though he wanted to cry.

Our lieutenant was watching the whole thing, and he chewed us out royally. "Stop fucking around!" he said. But I could see he was smiling, just a bit. And I wondered what would happen if that ROTC captain ever had to lead a company of more than 200 men into battle. He could be the enemy's best weapon. The next day he was nowhere to be seen. The company clerk said he'd gone someplace no one had ever heard of. I think it's in Alaska, but I'm not sure. It sounded like an Eskimo name, with lots of Ks.

❦ 2 ❧

Pearl Harbor

The United States will do "everything in our power to crush Hitler and his Nazi forces." This was Franklin Delano Roosevelt speaking as he addressed the American people on Labor Day, 1941. The same week Herbert Hoover, also in a radio broadcast, countered that the German dictator would be destroyed by the "vicious forces" within his own regime, and that the Democratic administration should stop the "provocative steps that could take our sons into war." In the North Atlantic a German submarine attacked a United States destroyer. A government spokesman in Berlin complained that the Americans had dropped depth bombs first, and that the Germans were only protecting themselves. Which they had every right to do, he said. In London General Charles de Gaulle announced the formation of the Free French National Council, a government-in-exile. And in Washington, Martin Dies, chairman of the House Un-American Activities Committee, told the press that he was "looking into the possibilities" that Japanese on the West Coast could "spread yellow fever" in the event of a war between Japan and the United States. And in faraway Tokyo, an army official threatened that if his country could not reach a peaceful settlement of all outstanding problems with the Americans, there would most likely be a war. It appeared that there would be no compromise in Japan's drive to dominate the countries of Southeast Asia and the islands of the Pacific.

In Louisiana large-scale war games involving a half-million soldiers came to an uncertain and disappointing end. The troops complained of fighting one another through the area's swamps, of the viscous mud, the chiggers and snakes, and the intolerable heat. While the generals, wrote one sergeant, sat in their comfortable offices and "played with us as though we were pawns on a chessboard." Lesley J. McNair, the army's chief-of-staff, spoke with reporters about the woeful lack of equipment and of training. The officers were as unprepared as the enlisted men, he said. "It was a matter of the blind leading the blind." As a consequence, six high-ranking officers, including a major general, were relieved of their duties and assigned elsewhere.

In the Camp Roberts barracks, I read the daily newspapers and the American president's current articles in *Collier's* about New Deal policies, but I tended to push unpleasant information to the back-crannies of my mind. I concerned myself, rather, with the duties—and problems—of an acting corporal who was no better prepared for military action than the soldiers in Louisiana. And at home in Dearborn, Marianne wrote me about the first week of the fall semester at Wayne University. She said nothing concerning the prospects for American involvement in a war, either in Europe on in the Pacific.

Ellen is reading the booklet you sent about Camp Roberts and distracting me with her questions. But I'll do my best to get down to business and ignore her. I decided I wouldn't enter the College of Ed this fall. At first I was inclined to take the five-year course, but that way I'd be in the college for three years, and my schedule would be pretty much regimented the whole time. So now I'm just enrolling in classes that sound interesting—some of which are requirements, anyway. Like the Economics course "Contemporary Problems" from Dr. Levin. He's the department head, and is supposed to know his stuff. So far he seems to me to be rather dull. But maybe it's the subject. I'll wait awhile before I make a judgment. I'm also taking Biology 101 from De Forest, who is very good, I think. And a geography course from Stilgenbauer; German 286 on the period of Realism from Dr. Colditz, to help complete a minor; and Art 128, a course in elementary sculpture that I like very well. Fifteen hours in all. And I decided I could handle the two jobs. I hope so anyway.

Bob Swarthout is editor of the Collegian *this year. Neither he nor Verne Gibson was drafted. Verne was deferred on account of his eyes, and Bob because he has a misplaced vertebra, or something like that. Paul Juntunen, who sat behind us in Dr. Basilius's class, has your job as sports editor, and his page is doing pretty well, considering the handicap he is suffering under—that he's not you, I mean. I think I'll send a copy of the paper with this letter, so you can see for yourself.*

I responded from Camp Roberts: *I'm sitting here on my bunk this lazy Saturday afternoon, with your sweet picture before me for inspiration. And I'm sending you some photos that were taken last week. It seems to me that I look disgustingly healthy—in contrast, at least, to the pictures taken before I went away. And please note the corporal stripes on my left arm. They're only temporary until I get the real things later on—four months after I was inducted. And they won't give me the pay increase until then. I could sure use the money right now. But everybody calls me Corporal Quirk anyway. I sort of like the sound of it, don't you?*

I'm glad you're not trying to do too much work this year, honey. I am sure you won't regret your decision. And you'll be enjoying school that much more. I would like nothing better than to be with you, having classes together, maybe hitting you on the head with my ruler again. You never did say if you minded it. Those were happy times weren't they? We didn't realize then how lucky we were to meet each other every day. And I'd like to be in Detroit now to see the fall coming in. A real autumn, with the red and yellow leaves and all the chrysanthemums. We don't have the traditional seasons out here. Everything is the same, except that it rains for a while in February and March. And it's a bit cooler then, before we start the long summer all over again.

Sunday, September 21, from Marianne in Dearborn: *It's the middle of the night, and I can't get to sleep. I went to bed early because I have a morning class, but I've been crying and crying, so I thought I'd get up and write you this letter. I feel as though the bottom has dropped out of everything.*

All week I'd been counting off the days until Sunday, and then counting the hours until nine o'clock, sitting in the living room and twisting my handkerchief. Then the phone rang, and I thought I'd never get to it. My

Robert E. Quirk as corporal of the guard, with World War I helmet.

knees were so wobbly, and my heart was pounding. Golly, the next four minutes flew by, didn't they? It was so good to hear your voice after the years—it seemed—since I talked to you last. And there were so many things I wanted to say to you, but somehow nothing would come out. Then you were suddenly gone, and I had such an empty feeling. It's strange, and at the same time, terrible. I can't feel near to you, no matter how I try. And I don't know for sure that you love me. Please love me. Please. As much as I love you. If only I could talk to you again, this very minute, and hear you say it, I know everything would be fine. It's so easy to doubt when a person is that much in love.

Tell me, how much would it cost to call me at night, station to station. And if it's not too much, maybe I can have you phone me again, very soon, and reverse the charges. I'd like to do that. I guess I'd better go back to bed, dearest, and get some rest. After I have read again the poems you wrote for me. Especially "Black Velvet Night." And you know, I think I feel a lot better now. Happy Birthday, dear. Did you get the book I sent you? And the Worry Bird? I guess not, or you would have mentioned them when we were talking. I couldn't think of anything else you would especially like or could use.

The same day, more than 2,800 miles away: *I'm in the barracks now, sitting on my bunk, and I just got back from talking to you, my darling. And—well—I don't know exactly how I feel. I'm elated that after so long I have heard your sweet voice again. At the same time, though, I feel sad and very, very lonesome. Hearing you again makes me realize how empty my existence is without you. It's funny how I couldn't think of all the things I wanted to tell you. How much I loved you and missed you. I was so excited, and my heart was going like a trip-hammer. The time we talked certainly went by fast, didn't it? I think the telephone company must have gypped us, though, because it didn't seem like four minutes to me. It's funny how time goes so fast when we are together, or when we are talking with each other, and how slowly when we are apart. Some day, soon I hope, we will not be separated, and we'll never need to concern ourselves with time.*

I've been thinking about "when we are together again." It's nice, isn't it, to have that we feeling both of us read about in Sociology? We, and us, and our. "Our problems." "Our future together." Not as separate persons.

29

Dad wrote to ask if I was considering the Officer Training Program, and that has some advantages. When I finished training—at Fort Benning I suppose, in Georgia—I could specify where I wanted to go. In the East, for example. But I'd have to join the regular army and enlist for three years, which I don't want to do. This way, staying at Roberts, the chances of getting out sooner, and finishing my education more quickly, are a lot better. Those are the percentages I am working on. And if I can come back home in a year or so, as the army is saying now, why it won't be so bad, will it? I must say, I've learned a lot about life in the months I've been here. Talking with so many of the fellows, from different parts of the country.

I've been wondering about something, dear. You say that you haven't as yet entered the School of Education. Was it mostly because you wanted to wait for me? Or you wanted to take those background courses before you entered? Or maybe you haven't filled out all those application forms as yet? Come on now, honey, was it the third? Confess it. And by the way, I've written to the University of Wisconsin to get information about their correspondence courses for soldiers. If it's possible, I'd like to take a basic economics course. That way, if I could get credit for it at Wayne, I could take the more advanced courses later when I return. I'll let you know what happens, if anything.

A quick retort came from Marianne in Dearborn: *No, you worm! I didn't stay in the College of Liberal Arts because I hadn't completed my Education forms. I could still turn them in, even now. And I've taken all of the tests. But the main reason is that I have seen the education courses my friends have to take—and they're just a lot of stuff to do that didn't teach them anything. I was reluctant to spend the next two years practicing penmanship and spelling and making booklets and carrying out projects. All that would be, for me, a great waste of my time. I already know enough about them. So I was thinking that some kind of Special Education would be much more interesting to me, and useful. Such as speech-and-hearing therapy. The curriculum isn't trivial, and it presents problems and challenges that make it more interesting.*

I thought first I'd take courses this fall that I like. The sculpture class, for instance. And a lot of physiology, anatomy, and psychology that are an integral part of the Special Ed. Curriculum. Then in January I'll enter the

School of Education. I know that some of the courses will still be a waste of my time, but I do want to get a teacher's certificate and be prepared to earn a living. And I really would like to go to school with you again, if I can. If I want, though, I can still finish in four years. So there, Mr. Smartypants!

You asked a while ago if I'd like to be married as soon as we could, instead of waiting until we were financially established. The answer is yes, because I love you so much. With you beside me it would be fun to "take the bad breaks with the good," as you say; there is nothing in the world I'd be afraid of. But there could be one thing that makes me hesitate, that it might not be fair to you if we married before you were definitely set on what you wanted to do in life. You wouldn't be able to take the chances you could if you were still single. But then, in the end, we might prefer to make the sacrifices of living together, both working and planning for our "little home in the country," with the fireplace and the wild flowers, because—most important—we would have each other. So we'll see. I know we are both rational people who have to consider the consequences of our actions. And maybe we'll be the better by having patience for a year or two.

Two days later, in Camp Roberts, I responded: *Thank you very much, dear, for the swell birthday presents. The Worry Bird came yesterday, and from now on—for the rest of my life—I will have nothing, absolutely nothing, to worry about. And then the book came today, and I've already read some of it. As you know, Wodehouse is one of my favorite authors. Now that I know I am staying here, I can start collecting more books for my—for our—library. There was a birthday cake from my mother, the traditional chocolate with white icing, and some money from my sister, Eileen, which was generous of her. I don't think she earns very much. I shared the cake with the fellows who will be leaving in a few days. They pronounced it first-rate.*

You said in your letter that you cried because you couldn't be sure what I told you was true. Don't ever doubt my love for you. I mean every word I've said. And if you ever have even the vaguest feeling that I am not close to you, will you do something for me? Just read the poems I sent you, and you will know that you are always in my thoughts and my heart. And will be forever.

A week later, in the barracks: *I am quite exhausted this evening, having just finished playing a rugged game of basketball out in the company area. So I feel in the mood for writing a long letter and just lying in my bed and resting at the same time. But there's a group of fellows all around me, including Bud Rollins, who are telling various and sundry stories, mostly dirty ones. About women naturally. And they are distracting me, I must confess. Maybe I'll repeat them for your edification some day when I know you better. And I'll do my best now to write a coherent letter.*

About calling you on the telephone and reversing the charges, honey, the cost is $2.95 for the first three minutes and 90 cents for each additional minute. If you think you can afford that, let me know, and I'll arrange the time. I wouldn't think of it, except that I've found $21 doesn't go as far as I thought. I have paid for your ring, though, so I'm not as strapped as I was before. Won't it be wonderful when we aren't all this distance apart, darling, and we have no worries except for the prosaic ones, like how are we going to pay the grocery bill. And whether Robert Jr. has the croup or not.

And that leads to a different question. How do you feel about naming our firstborn after me—and my father. Presuming, of course, that it's a boy. I kind of like my name and would be glad see it passed on to another generation. You've never said whether you liked children or not, but from the gleam in your eye when you held Katie's baby, I suspect you might have that "maternal instinct" people talk about. And what size family do you think appropriate? Of course, a lot depends on the financial situation, but I don't intend that our family be in the lower-income brackets. For me, having just one child is not wise, but on the other hand, too many can be equally bad, like so many Catholic families. What are your thoughts on the subject, dear?

On October 1, 1941, Marianne wrote about her latest news: *I'm sorry that it will have been quite a few days since you got a letter. We've had company from Marquette all week, Jane's relatives. And I haven't had much privacy to write. Congratulations on your being promoted. Did I say that before? I was wishing you could come east, but it's probably for the best this way. At least if you are not continually moved from place to place, I'll always know where you are. I knew they couldn't keep as good a man as you, down.*

I find I have quite a little homework to do tonight. I'm getting back to the good old routine, and I want to keep up in everything and not fall behind. All my classes seem interesting, after all. I had been sort of disappointed with the economics course, but things are looking up. It's not so bad.

Dr. Levin is a very peculiar person, though. At first I could hardly understand him, and he has just about the homeliest face I ever saw. He scares me every time he smiles. But he is supposed to be a very brilliant man. The sculpture class is the most interesting and a lot of fun. Right now our project is Abstract Design—in Surrealist Art.

I have to make some maps for geography, though, so I'd better close, honey. Is Sunday the best day for you to call me up? Let me know, and we can arrange the time. And you can reverse the charges. Whenever you like.

Three days later, October 4, Marianne in Dearborn wrote of not feeling well: *It's cold and misty out tonight, and it's been raining for the last few days. I just got home from work a short while ago, and after looking anxiously for mail from you, and taking off my damp clothing and making myself a cup of hot tea, I decided to write to my one and only. My throat feels rather sore. I guess it's a combination of the weather and my talking all day at work. One thing, honey, you certainly have to learn to have patience if you work in an office. I felt like swearing a blue streak several times today. You said in your letter that college graduates' marriages have a very good chance of success. But then I've been told that office girls make the best wives, because they have to deal with all sorts of situations, and they must develop both efficiency and systematicness. So you see, dear, what a bargain you are getting! Had you thought of that?*

You asked me what I felt about children—our children. I don't know how many would be ideal, but I think your family is a nice size. Do you think four is too many? I've always thought Michael would be a good name for a firstborn. Like your grandfather. But if you have your mind set on Robert, you ought to have something to say about the matter. As long as he wasn't just "Junior." Have you ever been called that? Wouldn't you just hate it? I think you're wrong, though, about my having any maternal instincts. The last time I played with Barbara Jean, my sister's baby, she cried, and I thought she must be thirsty. So I just filled her bottle with hot water from the spigot. When I gave it to her she looked happy. But Katie worried when she found out the water hadn't been boiled. So I guess there's a lot to learn about babies that I know nothing about.

It's getting pretty chilly in my bedroom—there's never much heat up here on the second floor. I wish you were here to keep me warm. But since you're not, I'll just gargle my throat and pile up a lot of blankets. Good night, dear one. P.S. Jane brought me a clipping about some soldier at Camp Roberts who ran over a mountain lion with his car. Good heavens! Not only do you have rattlesnakes and huge spiders out there, but dangerous animals too. Please take care of yourself. And I'll pray for you every day that you survive.

Three days later, on October 7: *It's about 9:30 in the evening, and I've just got up to write you this letter. It will be shorter than usual though. I felt kind of dizzy during the Geography class, and I thought it was never going to end. So I cut my other classes and came home and went to bed. I've been sleeping ever since. I'm feeling better now, though. My father brought me some hot wine, and that did the trick.*

A week later, on October 14, Marianne started another letter: *I got your swell long letter yesterday, and I would like to answer it today. But the sorority meets tonight, and I don't think I'll have time when I get home, so I'll write again tomorrow, if I can. I've started a letter almost every day this week, but then something happens, and I don't finish it. And I find it's hard to complete a letter I've started the day before. So I just start over again. I'm sorry, honey. Please forgive me for not writing to you for over a week.*

My school work is getting stiffer now. We're having pre-semifinal exams in almost all my classes. I got a bluebook back in Economics today. It was a B−, which is not so bad, since Levin is supposed to be a hard marker. There'll be an exam in Biology next Monday, and one in Geography on Wednesday. Oh yes, dear, we criticized our abstract sculpture things, and mine was judged fourth best in the class. It's really a sort of a mess. I know you would laugh if you saw it. Maybe I'll send it to you to put up on your mantel. Do you have mantels in your barracks?

From Camp Roberts in October: *I took charge of the platoon this evening for retreat (or flag-lowering). I was kind of nervous at first, but as far as I could tell everything turned out all right. And I'm going to be charge-of-quarters for the company tomorrow. That means I'll be the boss of the orderly room, arouse the KPs, turn the lights out at night in all the barracks, take bed-check, and have various and sundry other duties. It was nice to see my name on the bulletin board: "Acting-Corporal Quirk." I should have some time to myself tomorrow to write you a longer letter.*

We'll be going out on the last maneuvers of our basic training tomorrow at 3 p.m. They will last until eight the following morning, and then we will be finished. Finished, in more ways than one. The men are scheduled to leave here on Friday. I'll really be sorry to see Bud and Ralph and all the other fellows leave. Bud wants to transfer to the military police, now, but I think they'll all go to the infantry. Except for Ralph Matthews, that is, who's going to the paratroopers. I wonder if I'll ever see them again.

In the maneuvers I was very, very lucky. My squad rode out in trucks, while the other fellows walked. We acted as flank guards for the Blue forces, which were Companies B and C. To protect them from the enemy. We were fighting against A and D. For us it was a lot of fun at first, riding up and down the steep hills. These army trucks, with four-wheel drive, can really get around. It was a lot like a roller coaster at the amusement park, but without the girls squealing. I had five men in my truck, including Ralph and Bud. We would drive a while, and then I'd give orders to stop and scout around for the enemy. We didn't find any.

We got to our bivouac area about six, and it was already dark. (The days out here are really short now.) From there we spread out and set up outposts. I was the leader of one of them. And both Rollins and Matthews were with me. I had given my own rifle to a man who had hurt his arm, and I was carrying his Browning automatic in the truck. Our mission was to guard a road junction, and to keep enemy troops from passing that point. But no one told us how. Or even how we were to fight our "enemy."

About that time a car without any lights came through the intersection. We hollered and tried to stop it, but it kept on going. It turned around, though, and came back with a white flag, which meant it was an umpire's car. We waved it through. We learned later that it was an enemy trick. Neither side was supposed to use cars or trucks in the maneuvers. We also learned later that their captain got a dressing down by the battalion commander. For not fighting fair, I suppose you would say. If you could ever "fight fair" in a real war. We went back to the outpost to get some sleep.

I had scarcely tucked my blankets around me when a truck came along, this time with its lights on. I got out from under the covers and took my squad down to the road. I was carrying the B.A.R., and I stepped into the middle of the road and signaled it to stop. There was an officer in the front seat, but because it was so dark, I couldn't tell his rank. He looked angry. "What the hell are you doing in this area?" he said. "You're way out of the problem." I explained that there was no left boundary to the problem, and that we were where we should be. Bud and another fellow had their rifles sticking into the back of the truck, and I was covering the officer with the B.A.R.

Suddenly, while we were talking, another truck pulled up, and twelve men with rifles jumped out. "You're captured," said the officer. I could see now he was a lieutenant. A not-dry-behind-the-ears second lieutenant. Someone grabbed Kleppe, and he hit the fellow with the butt of his rifle. "Like hell we are!" he said, and ran. I stepped back and held the automatic rifle in front of me, wondering how I could defend myself. Were we supposed to use physical force? Like Kleppe? That didn't make sense. The officer said: "Get that man." He was pointing at me. I decided that the better part of valor, as Shakespeare said, was to get the hell out of there too. I turned and took off into the hills to get help from someone. I thought sure I would be caught, because I was carrying the sixteen-pound B.A.R., and it felt like it weighed a ton. I got away, though. The enemy must have decided a corporal was not worth running after.

I did find the captain and told him all my men had been captured. And how. (Actually it was only three of them, including Bud Rollins. The rest got away.) But he refused to use our truck to find the others. It was against the rules, he said. And when I got back to our outpost I found that all our equipment had been taken by the enemy—blankets, packs, water carrier, and mess equipment. Except for one measly tent pin that I stuck in my pocket. For the rest of the night I was up the creek. I couldn't sleep, because I had no blanket, and it was too darned cold to sleep without it. I had no water, and when we ate breakfast—at two a.m., I had to borrow a plate and cup from the cook. For the rest of the night I just didn't care much what happened.

At 3:30 our side launched an attack on the enemy. We were supposed to support Company D in their attack, but as it turned out, we did most of the assaulting. The officers were pretty dumb, it seemed to me. The enemy were situated on a steep hill, and we were led across a field at the foot of it, while a full moon made it as bright as day. The enemy had their simulated machine guns going the whole time. If it had been a real war, we would never have got through them. The little we learned about small-unit tactics in basic training should have taught us that. And then we made a bayonet charge up the hill, whooping and hollering like all get-out, and seemingly captured the enemy positions. I myself wrested a machine-gun from an enemy emplacement. And then I realized I would have to carry the darn thing all the way back to the barracks. Eight miles of agony.

As I struggled past the Company D headquarters, an officer stopped me. "Where did you get that machine-gun, corporal?" he said. I told him I had captured it. "Give it to me," he said. Which I did gladly. Let some poor fellow in his company do the hard work.

I asked our lieutenant from Maine—the good Joe—what I should do about my equipment, and he led me over to one of the enemy trucks. It was all in the back, together with the other fellows' stuff. Should I sort out mine here? I asked him. Everybody's leaving, he said. Get in the truck and sort it out when you're back in camp. I didn't need any urging to ride those eight miles. While the rest of the fellows walked. All in all, it was about 17 miles, coming and going. And I rode both ways. I had showered and shaved and was in my warm bed two hours before the rest got to the barracks. They called me a "gold-brick," but for once I didn't care. I think, honey, that I might write something for the Wayne Collegian *about the maneuvers and Bud's being captured. It ought to make a good story.*

October 13, 1941, in Camp Roberts: *I have finally moved into my new quarters, and while they are not as private as I might hope for, they are better than the old barracks room. It will be a little crowded, because four of us will be sharing the new room. One thing that is good about the new quarters is that I will have a table to put your picture on. Instead of hiding it away in my foot locker. Now I can see your beautiful face the last thing at night and the first thing in the morning. Wouldn't it be swell if it were really your face and not a reasonably accurate facsimile?*

I have been moved to the second platoon of Company B, but my address will be the same. I wish I could have stayed in the first platoon, but this is better than the fourth or third. They distributed the men according to height, from the first, down to the fourth. That's why I was in the first platoon before. I'd look out of place, wouldn't I, as a corporal with a lot of shorties? We call them "feather merchants," from the Barney Google comic strip, and say that they walk around in holes in the ground! So the new men in my pla-toon will all be reasonably tall, I presume.

I've been thinking about something lately. The army life wouldn't be too bad for a fellow who had no aim in his life. It's secure, and he has few wor-ries, because everything is set and prescribed. He is told when to get up, when to eat, and what work to do, and there is always someone higher up to do the worrying for him. The life is tough, but it's healthy, and it builds up a man remarkably. All that is good. The army has done a lot for me, and for that I am grateful. But in spite of all that, I am not in favor of the army per se. And I'll tell you why.

You asked me once if I ever thought of making the army my career. When I told you about what my father had said. For me there is one big deterrent. The army is equivalent to war and destruction, and that is bad from what-ever angle you look at it. Some have said there was never a good war or a bad peace, and I believe that wholeheartedly.

The army wouldn't be so bad, if it were for the sole purpose of building up the health of the young men of our country. I would favor a year's train-ing for every boy when he finishes high school, and before he goes to college or to a job. But behind our army lies the implicit threat that some day it will be used to kill people of other nationalities. Our men will kill and be killed. I can see no sane reason for that. And I will never make the military my aim in life. You can rest assured about that.

Have you seen Irma Scholz around lately? For some reason I was think-ing about her when I read in the Free Press *about Professor von Moltke. She's one of the top students in the department, and I think he gave her an A-plus. I don't know if I told you she was my girlfriend when I was work-ing at Kerns, and the reason I took those basic German courses. Lucky for me, I would say. I was nineteen at the time, and her parents didn't like my being a Catholic. Ask her if von Moltke still praises the Nazis, after all that's hap-pened. When I was in his class he kept pointing out that the overseas Ger-mans were returning to the Fatherland in droves. "Denken Sie mal," he said. "Freiwillig kommen sie zurück."[3] She was a big help to me when I ran into grammar problems.*

---

3. "Just think. They're coming back (to the homeland) of their own free will."

From Marianne in Dearborn: *It's sort of funny, Bob, your asking me about Irmagard Scholz. And no, I didn't realize that you two had been that serious. Last Thursday I invited her to the first Pi Kappa Sigma rush party. I thought she was very nice. We danced together, and she told me she went out with you three years ago. I don't know why you didn't keep going out with her instead of me—she is such a swell person. But I guess there is no accounting for people's tastes. I hope that Irma joins our sorority, but I doubt if she will, because she is already a senior, I think.*

Bob, you've talked about the Fates in your letters. So many things have happened to change the course of our lives, because our paths might never have crossed. It's scary. What if my father and mother hadn't decided America would be a nice place to come to. Or if your folks had preferred to stay in Akron. If you had kept your job at Kerns, instead of coming to Wayne the same year I did. If we had not taken the same class with Dr. Basilius, and you hadn't been fresh and hit me on the head with your ruler. But in the end that's all irrelevant, because the Fates have decreed what is happening and what will happen. Like your twelve months in the army. A year or so apart can't matter, because in the end we will be together—and forever.

Troubles in California: *This letter can't be very long, dear, because it's almost nine o'clock, and I'll soon be making my rounds to put out the lights. This weekend I had an unpleasant problem to take care of. It all started last Sunday when I was charge-of-quarters. Remember I told you when I called? Well, there was a little drinking party going on in a sergeant's room. I didn't know what to do about it, because I'm so new. And I didn't want to get in bad with the other cadremen. So I neglected to tell the officer-of-the-day when I reported to him. And although I didn't learn about it until the next day, there was also a fight. People were drunk, I think. Everybody in the company got wind of it, including the officers.*

Anyway, this evening while I was eating my supper, I was told to come to the captain's office. And when I got there, two of the sergeants were being interrogated about it. They both swore up and down they knew nothing about it. I knew they were both lying. Then the captain asked me what I knew about it, and I had a hot time trying to keep from implicating them, and at the same time keeping my own neck out of trouble. I had to resort to quite a few white lies, when what I wanted to do was tell everything I knew. I have no use for the men who were in on it. In keeping my mouth shut, I only succeeded in making myself look like the biggest ass in God's creation. And the captain knew exactly what was happening. They don't call him "Hardrock," for nothing.

Then, to top it off, the staff sergeant called all us cadremen into his room and wanted to know who had told the officers about the affair. I know who they think it was, but no one would admit it. Needless to say, it wasn't I. But the next time, if it happens again, I'm not sure I wouldn't turn them in. You can bet your bottom dollar that I won't be put on the spot again. I felt like telling them all off this evening, but then maybe it's just as well I didn't. I have to live with them for thirteen weeks more, at least.

Armistice Day, 1941, in Camp Roberts: *Well, honey, I finally did it— went up to Frisco, I mean. Saturday noon, when we had finished everything, I started out and didn't get back here until Monday morning at four o'clock. I really had a swell time. And it's a swell city. I could tell that from the small part I saw—the downtown, Fisherman's Wharf, and especially Chinatown. And I slept on a chair at the YMCA. I had $10 when I left camp, and only $2 when I got back, which will have to last for the rest of the month. But it was sure worth it to get away for a while.*

I picked up a statue of the Laughing Buddha for you. It's made of cinnemal, a substance somewhat like jade. I think you will like it. At first, I was sure I couldn't afford it. The shopkeeper said it was only a hundred dollars. "Only," he said. But when I told him how much money I had, and showed him your picture, he said he would let me have it for five dollars. Mostly, he said, because it was his first sale of the day. It's a Chinese superstition, I think. I'll send it as soon as I can find something to wrap it in. A strong box, probably. And there was a romantic story attached to it.

He told me it had once belonged to a Chinese princess, Tai Li (Laughing Flower). And that it was captured by some pirates on the Yangtze River, while she was on her way to a faraway city to get married. (I had told him you and I were planning to be married some day.) The beautiful princess and all the wedding party were said to have been foully murdered. The pirates sold it to a rich merchant from Shanghai. And it was discovered a hundred years later in the walk of his house when the building was destroyed by a Japanese bomb. A Chinese smuggler slipped it through the Japanese block-

ade and took it to Manila. This shopkeeper happened to be there a few weeks ago, looking for curios, and he recognized that it was a genuine Laughing Buddha. From there he took it to San Francisco, and on a dingy street in Chinatown I bought it for a mere pittance. Take good care of it, honey. Some day it will be a family heirloom.

On Roosevelt's early Thanksgiving in Dearborn:[4] *I wanted so much to write you Thursday, on our first anniversary, but I was so busy helping Jane get the Thanksgiving dinner. And about noon a messenger from the florist arrived with the most beautiful big and yellow mums I've ever seen. Thank you so much for remembering me from so far away. I'll always treasure the memories of this day. And your fat little Chinaman arrived on Friday. He got chipped a little bit in the mail, but I fixed it with some glue, and it looks as good as ever. Even better, maybe. I'm not taking that sculpture class for nothing, honey. You should be proud of me. I wonder, though, if it isn't cinnabar, which is fairly soft. I was reading about it the other day. After surviving in all those bombings in China, though, a few more bumps won't bother him too much. Right now he is beaming away on my dresser, where I can see him and talk to him every morning. And I'll keep him safe until we can have our own mantel and fireplace, as you say.*

I got most of my mid-semester exams back today, and I had a C-minus in Economics, which isn't very good. I thought I did better than that. I wonder where I went wrong. In German it was a B-plus and in Biology an A. Is that record all right with you, sir? There's an exam in Geography this Friday, so I'll have to read four chapters before that. Aren't you glad, honey, now that you don't have to worry about tests you haven't studied for? Until the night before, as I remember.

After my first army holiday meal: *Today, being Thanksgiving, we had an enormous chow in Camp Roberts. I feel as though I were ten pounds heavier. We had turkey and ham, cranberry sauce, two kinds of potatoes, gravy, peas, salad, fruit, dressing, three kinds of cake, two kinds of pie, ice cream, candy, and probably some more stuff I can't think of just now. One of the new trainees just came in my room and gave me a bunch of assorted shelled nuts, which was very nice of him. I wonder if I can eat nuts and*

---

4. The president pushed back the holiday to give merchants an extra week of business.

write this letter at the same time. We didn't have supper—understandably—but one of the cooks dropped by a while ago when I was writing to Dr. Basilius, and he told me I could come over to the kitchen and take whatever I wanted. Leftovers, that is. I couldn't face the prospect of another meal, but I did take a couple of apples, a piece of apple pie, and some fruit cake, for a snack later tonight. I'm warning you, honey, this man's army is turning me into a regular glutton.

I mentioned I was writing to Dr. Basilius. I hope I get an answer from him, since I have an especial affection for him. All in all, I think we learned a lot from him, not only about the German language and literature, but about life itself. Taking that course was one of the most important decisions of my life. And I owe a lot of it to my dad, as well. I had planned to enroll in French that semester, but he said it was better to perfect my German first. How right he was!

Have you noticed, at the head of this letter, that it says Corporal Quirk? After all the waiting, I finally got the rating and the stripes that go with it. I took all my shirts and my jackets into Paso Robles, so a professional tailor could sew them on. And now I'm strutting around the campgrounds like a peacock. Maybe one of these days I'll get around to having my picture taken, so you can see for yourself. I hadn't heard from you for a while, and I was wondering if you were OK, when I received a card from the Roosevelt post office in Detroit informing me that they were holding a letter that had no stamps. If I would mail them 6¢, they would send me the letter. Which I did, by airmail. And lo and behold, it was from you, dear. You had forgotten to put stamps on it. I must tell you that if I have to keep paying 6¢ for my letters, and 12¢ for yours, I will soon go broke. Even though I am now being paid the munificent sum of $54 a month. So kindly take heed for the future—eh.

The last week of November 1941: Secretary of State Cordell Hull has given the Japanese America's terms for settling differences between the two countries: Japan must withdraw from the Axis, renounce further aggression, remove its armed forces from the Chinese mainland,

and agree to equal trade opportunities in the Orient. Franklin Delano Roosevelt returned from a brief vacation in Warm Springs, Georgia, to resume talks with Japanese officials. At a news conference the president told reporters he had questioned the Japanese about troops that were "pouring" into Indochina. He hoped to get a satisfactory reply "very shortly." And a Japanese spokesman said there was no reason why all issues could not be settled peacefully. "War will not settle anything," he said. On December 5 the Japanese government told Roosevelt their troops in Indochina were there primarily to protect the area against a possible invasion by the Chinese. And the next day the president sent an urgent personal message to Emperor Hirohito, appealing for peace.

News from Dearborn: *It's December, and in only a few more weeks we'll have Christmas. It doesn't seem like Christmas at all, I suppose because we've had such mild weather for the past few weeks. And I could feel a lot more like Christmas, if I thought you would be here. I'd sort of resigned myself to your not coming home. And now you say there's a chance again that you might. I'm so glad! It would really be wonderful, dear, if I could see you again. I've been wishing on my ring, and rubbing our fat little Chinaman's tummy, and now it's all up to the Fates. And the Army, of course. Be sure to call me as soon as you know something, any time of the day or night. And reverse the charges, as usual. It's much easier that way.*

I finished a very good book this evening. It's The Keys of the Kingdom *by A. J. Cronin. It tells the story of a man who became a priest and served in China. Although he was a Catholic, the basis of his philosophy was tolerance and the brotherhood of man. I know you'd like it too. If my prayers are any good, I'll see you for Christmas. Good night, Corporal Quirk. Congratulations. P.S. I'm sending you a clipping from the* Free Press. *It does say some nice things about you and your promotion. I think your father must have sent them the information.*

A Date Which Will Live in Infamy, December 7, 1941: *Just a line, darling, to let you know I hadn't forgotten you. It's Sunday morning, and I am up in Frisco shopping for a Christmas present for my loved one. I hope you will forgive me if I haven't written you for a whole week, and if this letter is brief. I'll be going out this afternoon to take pictures of the town.*

I really had a strenuous week since last Sunday. We were out on the firing range every day with the trainees, and the days were long too. And then I walked so much around this town yesterday that I was dead tired. I came back to my hotel room at about 6:30 last night, and stretched out on the bed, thinking I would get up in a little while and go out again. But when I woke up it was a quarter to eleven, so I just undressed and went to bed. I didn't get up this morning until nine, and right now I feel right chipper. A lot better than I have in a long time. In addition to my regular duties, I have been going to choir practice on Mondays and Wednesdays, and now they have made me manager of the company basketball team. I don't play, but I do run the show. I wonder sometimes how I can do it all, but I must say I enjoy that part of my life, with the music and sports.

I'm going to close now, with this single page, so I can get out of the hotel on time. The checkout is listed as ten a.m., and I don't want to pay extra. I'll send your presents when I get back to the camp. I hope you'll like them. I look forward to seeing you in them. It's still not clear whether we'll have our furloughs or not. I'll let you know whenever the powers that be make their decision. So we can still pray. I'll drop the letter into the mail chute on my way to the lobby. I hope I can get some good pictures at the waterfront.

"What's up?" I asked. I was handing the room clerk my key, and great numbers of people were milling about in the lobby.

"The Japs have attacked Pearl Harbor," he said. "They bombed the naval base today."

"Where's that?" My knowledge of the Pacific area was not what it should have been for a fellow who was halfway toward his BA.

"Somewhere in the Pacific," he said. "I think in Hawaii. I suppose there will be a war. That's what they say on the radio." Numbed by the news, I decided to go a movie. My bus back to camp wasn't leaving for a few hours yet. Within minutes, a message appeared on the screen. All army personnel were required to return to their bases.

December 7, 1941, in Dearborn: *We've been listening to the news all day, dear, about the bombing of Honolulu and Pearl Harbor. It certainly looks as though we will be in it very soon, and it makes me worried to think you are so close to all the trouble. Take care of yourself, dear. I'm going to pray very hard that you will always be safe. It certainly looks as though any hopes we had of seeing each other at Christmas time are squelched—as well as those of a lot of other people in this country. I guess we were asking too much. Think of me, dear, and write to me often. Your letters mean so much to me, especially in times such as these.*

I've just finished knitting Jane a pair of bed-socks for Christmas, and I think they are cute. Would you like some too? I think they would go fine with your long underwear. If the army has no objections. And I'm going to the dentist tomorrow. He says my wisdom teeth will never come through the gums. So I suppose that means I'll be a dummy for the rest of my life. P.S. I love you very much.

Two days later, from the camp: *I hardly know how to start this letter, my darling. It seems as though it must be a dream, and that I will finally wake up and find it so. I think the men are glad it has happened this way. As it was, we were all just marking time, waiting for something to happen, and with only vague thoughts about our futures. There was no telling how long we would have to wait. Now we know what we have to do, unpleasant though it may be, and we all want to get it over with in a hurry.*

You must know that any faint hope we have had for a leave has vanished. All furloughs and three-day passes have been cancelled. So now I have no idea when I will be home. Maybe, if I am still in the United States, later on you could come out to see me. If I can save enough money, that is. Would you do that for me, honey. Our "little test" is turning out to be quite a formidable obstacle, isn't it?

And I must say something to you I hate to say. Dread to say. It just isn't fair, dearest, to hold you to a promise that was made with the expectations that I would be in the army for only a year. Now, only God knows how long it will be. Therefore, in all fairness to you, if you should feel that it is too long to wait, well—you know what I am trying to say. But if, on the other hand, you decide I am worth waiting for, and I pray to God that you do, I shall be

45

eternally grateful. So, I ask you, darling—will you wait for me no matter how long it is? You have my word that there can never be anyone for me in the world but you. If you will wait, I shall spend the rest of my life making it up to you. And when this war is over, we'll have our time for happiness. Time does pass, and it won't be too long, I hope.

It's hard to believe that it has been only two days since I wrote you last from San Francisco. And so much has happened in that short time. To me and to the world. I had left Camp Roberts—I was wearing my civilian clothing—on Friday night with a feeling of semi-security. War was the farthest thing from my mind. And I was thinking and wondering what I would get you for Christmas. Then everything broke apart with a fury. In those two days the European war was transformed into a world war, with more belligerents, even, than the last great conflict. Sunday morning, in my hotel room, I would have thought it impossible that we would be fighting against Japan. Germany yes, but not Japan. In fact, in the bus coming up from Roberts, I told a civilian that the Japs would never dare to attack the United States. I had studied history, I said, and I knew what I was talking about.

If you have been wondering what I am going to do, well, so do I. There hasn't been any talk here of an A.E.F.[5] as yet. The trainees are being issued tropical clothing, which indicates they might be going to the Philippines. I can say what I'd like to do, and that is to stay right here in Camp Roberts and train the men for the duration of the war. I don't know if the cadremen will be sent out with the privates, but there is one good omen. They haven't given us any tropical clothing. So we'll see. One rumor has it that we will go to the Boulder Dam, to guard it from some attack. But, as I said, it is just a rumor. You can rest assured, darling, that as soon as I learn anything, I will let you know.

They are taking this thing pretty seriously out here on the West Coast. There has always been a lot of anti-Japanese sentiment. There have been blackouts in Frisco, and also in L.A. and in Sacramento, where the State House is. But so far there have been no sightings of enemy planes. We haven't had a blackout yet in the camp, but we may tonight, as a sort of practice. But things have certainly changed a lot since Friday. Then there were only a few

---

5. American Expeditionary Forces in World War I.

guards in the whole camp. Like the time I guarded the trucks. Now it's an armed fortress, with guards everywhere, even inside the barracks, watching over the rifle racks. Did they expect that the enemy would be sneaking into our barracks and stealing our weapons? And on the way back to camp, MPs stopped our bus and removed all of the Japanese soldiers—National Guardsmen, maybe, or draftees. There were five or six, I think. And a civilian too. I still wonder what they did with them.

Then yesterday they told some of us we would have to form a camp guard—to keep an eye on the water supply, sewage system, warehouse, etc. So I'm the corporal of the guard. One of them, I should say. There are several. We went on at 3:30 yesterday afternoon and will be on until the same time today. At first I stayed in the guardhouse, but about eight last night I was taken in a truck to watch over part of the sewage system, a large device known affectionately around here as the "turd-whirler." So far as I know, it has never had a guard before, though there might have been a night watchman, a civilian, but just to make sure the device was working. I have three privates to walk post, which gives me time to write this letter. In fits and starts, I should say. There's a large tent, which was all rolled up, and it just seemed too much trouble to put it up. We slept last night out in the open on our cots.

About midnight I woke up to find it was raining, but I stayed under the covers, and hoped the rain would stop. Incidentally, I slept with my clothes on, and haven't removed them or washed myself since yesterday morning. Nor have the other fellows. So there is a dank feeling and atmosphere about this place. We unpacked the tent and tried to put it up, without any success. Several hours later the officer-of-the-guard came around and asked me why we weren't using the tent. I told him we didn't know how to put it up, and besides we had no flashlights. They probably thought lights might attract an enemy attack or something like that. So the lieutenant sent for one of the sergeants to show us how. At which time I realized that we had been trying to put the darn thing together upside-down!

They haven't started censoring our mail as yet, but they may before long. So if you get a letter with words or lines inked out, you will know I have written something I shouldn't have. I sure as heck hate to have some officer reading the things I say to you. That are made to be private. But if censorship comes, and it is a matter of national policy, there is nothing you or I can do about it. But a lot of people's letters would certainly be much more drab and uninteresting.

Right now they have banned all social long-distance calls and telegrams. I suppose it has something to do with national security. I hope the ban is lifted pretty soon, because I had been planning to call you on Christmas—or the next day, on your birthday. Will you be home then? On either day, or both, maybe? And if so, which is better for you? We might make it the early seconds of the 26th, which is the anniversary of the first time I kissed you. You were sitting on the piano bench, remember? And I had my coat on, ready to go home. It was a pretty important moment in our lives, after all.

I've been wondering about a statement you made in your last letter, honey. Writing about The Keys of the Kingdom, *you said: "Although he was a Catholic, the basis of his philosophy was tolerance and the brotherhood of man." Don't you think that is also the basis of Catholic philosophy? It certainly is mine. What about that? I hope my future letters will hold nothing but good news for the both of us, darling. Please write me often.*

A week later, from home: *Bob, darling, I guess I will have a serious talk with you about something you brought up in your last letter. You asked me, if now that our future has become a little more uncertain, I would like to be released from all the promises I made. You may release me if you like, dear, but that wouldn't change the fact that I love you with my whole heart, not for a year or for two years, but so long as I shall live. And I could never change that. No length of time, nor wars, nor fifteen-year drafts can keep me from loving you. Or keep us apart for very long. No matter what happens. Is that clear, Mr. Picklepuss?*

I never thought the time would come when I wished you would remain at Camp Roberts, but now I am praying every night that you will be instructing the trainees until the end of the war, however long that will be. Please let me know what happens when you find out.

I heard an announcement on the radio about blackouts along the West Coast, and we had one in Dearborn last week. No one took it very seriously, though. I don't think anyone is getting awfully upset about the war. Maybe that's because we don't realize yet what it means. But I will say that after the first surprise wore off, most everyone felt a desire to do something. This talk you hear about a suddenly united national feeling is very true, I think. The sponsor of our sorority is in charge of a Red Cross unit, and last week she asked Jean Larson and me to help out. So now, every Wednesday from 4:30 till 7:00, both of us have a steady job. There have been almost a hundred blood donors each day, and Jean and I give them food and see that they are all right before we let them go home.

I'm sorry, honey, for the misleading statement I made about The Keys of the Kingdom. *And I'm glad you pointed it out to me. Funny, isn't it, how you can think one thing, and then write something else. What I meant to say was that every religious group in the world regards its faith as the sole true one, and its church as the only way to heaven. That's why it was unusual for the old priest to preach tolerance of all other beliefs. He believed that the adherents to all faiths were in the right, if they were sincere. And he refused to believe that God would allow entrance into His Kingdom to be determined by accident of birth. For that, the priest was regarded as a heretic by his own church, and would have been called a heretic by every other church, I suppose.*

But I believe those things too, and I can never think they are inconsistent with the Holy Bible and with Christianity. I didn't mean for this to be a sermon, and I'm afraid I've confused you completely. So, you'll just have to read the book, yourself, I guess, and make up your own mind.

Marking time in Camp Roberts: *It doesn't seem possible, dear, that there are only nine days until Christmas. The sun is shining brightly, and it is so warm. Even the Yuletide decorations don't make me feel like Christmas. What we need is snow, good old S-N-O-W. And that will never happen out here, of course. I'd give anything in the world to be able to hold you in my arms again. They seem so empty these days, and my heart is empty too. But then I think they can't keep us apart forever. Time does pass, and as surely as there is a God in heaven I will come back to you. If not this year, or the next, then the year after that. It's a promise, dear. And in the meantime, there will be furloughs. Or you could come out here to see me. Have you thought of that? I would love it if you could.*

I was thinking the other day about our joint bank account—I'm earning $54 a month now, and that is more than I could spend in the army. If I did get a chance to come home, or if you came out here, we would need money.

And we would need some financing when we were married. For a honey-moon, maybe. Or to buy some furniture. I could easily put $25 a month in our joint account, and for a year that would amount to $300. The longer I am in the army, the more we'd have to get started. It's all well and good to talk about marriage in a romantic way. But at some point we have to start thinking of the practical too. A nice little nest egg would provide a good start to our life together. Incidentally, they lifted the restrictions that have con-fined us to camp, but I didn't go into town, because I was flat broke from my jaunt to Frisco last week. It's a good thing we'll be paid on the 19th—because of Christmas. I can do the rest of my shopping then.

On the winter solstice in Dearborn: *I spent a quiet day at home get-ting my Christmas cards off and all of my packages wrapped, and then in the evening I went to church to the children's service. Except for one little boy in my class who was frightened and couldn't remember a thing, all the pupils recited very well. When I've written you this short letter, I'm going to bed, because I have to be at work early tomorrow morning.*

About your last letter, I've often thought of the possibility of going out to see you, all the more if it's impossible for you to come here. But I don't know whether it's a good idea, for a couple of reasons. I wonder if it would be all right to come alone. It's a pretty long and expensive trip, so I can't just ask one of my friends to drop everything and go out there with me. Another thing, are visitors still allowed in camp in spite of the war? And a big "if." Do you think it would be okay to come unchaperoned? If you do, then I would love to come. You decide.

No longer a teenager, December 26, 1941: *Right now the little radio in my room is playing "Liebestraum." I love that song so much, don't you. As I write, my room looks very pretty with the red roses you sent me for my birthday. Thank you so much. There were so many, and I shared them with Jane, and probably half of them are downstairs in the living room. And thanks for the beautiful pajamas. They fit just right. How did you know what size to buy? And what a pretty blue. They're my favorite color. I got an awful lot of things for Christmas from my dad—a dress, a hat, and a purse. Also a nice overnight bag that I'll need when I come to see you.*

Also thanks to you for the telegram. I was waiting for your telephone call on Sunday, and then it was long after twelve, so I called the operator. She told me there was a six-hour wait for calls from California. So I gave up and just went to bed. I'll make it a point to be home the next two Sundays—at nine p.m. your time, if you want to try again.

Well, honey, I'm twenty years old today and suddenly a grown-up, though I don't feel any different than yesterday. And so much has happened since last year on this day when you kissed me for the first time, and I suggested you stay a while longer. Let's hope that before next Christmas and my birthday we'll be together. And for the rest of our lives.

The mix-up at Camp Roberts: *You don't know, honey, how sorry I am that I couldn't call you on Sunday. When I found how long the wait was, I decided to send you a telegram instead. But thanks so much for the sweater. It fits me perfectly. I know how hard it is to buy something for a soldier, but you hit on the best thing you could have sent. All the fellows were admiring it and wishing they had one just like it. And I hoped you liked the pajamas. I don't know whether they're an appropriate gift from a young gentleman to a young lady of twenty. But I liked them in the shop, and so I just bought them, right off. It was in Chinatown the day war was declared. Blue always was my favorite color, and I knew you'd look scrumptious in them. And if you wonder how I knew the size, I just held them up against myself. Was that a good method or a bad one, dear?*

But the big news here was a lot of commotion on Christmas Eve that might interest you. During the evening an order came, cancelling all passes for the holidays and ordering us to fall out at once with full field packs, blankets, toilet articles, leggings, and rifles. And to be ready to leave the camp at once. What a scare! Some of the fellows were actually sick to their stomachs. Not even the officers knew where we would be going. We had visions of being sent any place in the world, from North Africa to the Philippine Islands. At the last minute, though, I was taken off the list, because I was slated to be on guard duty the next day.

I watched while an entire company was formed from the cadremen of our regiment and a few trainees who were over 28 and were scheduled to be discharged. Each man was issued 88 rounds of ammunition and a Garand semi-automatic rifle. All 150 of them were taken to a warehouse for the night where they slept on the floor with no mattresses or blankets. By then, I was more than glad that I was out of it, at least for that one night. Then on

51

Christmas morning they came back to the barracks for blankets, socks, and heavy underwear. And people started talking about Alaska. A long line of trucks was formed—we call it a convoy—along the parade ground. The men were then inspected by the general and a bunch of other officers. You can imagine that all of them were sure they were not coming back.

But then they were marched to my barracks, which were empty, and were quartered here. They were told to be ready to move out at a moment's notice. But this afternoon, they were all sent back to their respective companies, with a warning that this might happen again, at any time. So a Christmas holiday was ruined for all of us. We heard on the radio today that all this hoop-di-doo was ordered by General DeWitt, commander of the Ninth Corps Area. So it was not solely a Camp Roberts directive. You can imagine we were pretty damned sore about it. I couldn't go to church. Even midnight services, the first time I had missed the Christmas mass for as far back as I can remember.

Anyway, now that it's over, I'm glad none of us had to leave the camp in that fashion. The rationale was that General DeWitt had wanted the army personnel to be doubly alert during the Christmas season. And to see that they were ready for any contingency. What contingency, I don't know. Nobody ever said. Maybe they were seeing boogie men. I hope that in the New Year the generals will order more sense-making operations. And give us more forewarning when they do.

❧ 3 ❧

Jack-of-All-Trades

On January 6, 1942, Franklin Delano Roosevelt spoke to the U.S. Congress. "The militarists of Berlin and Tokyo started this war," he said. "But the massed, angered forces of common humanity will finish it. . . . Let no man say it cannot be done. It must be done, and we have undertaken to do it." During the month that followed, the Japanese drove American troops from Manila, and, according to Cordell Hull, the secretary of state, threatened to shoot white civilians in the streets. He accused the enemy of "descending to the lowest possible level of animal savagery." In the Malay Peninsula the Japanese now controlled eight of the nine states and were closing in on Singapore, while preparing to invade the Dutch East Indies. Radio Tokyo reported that the country of Thailand had declared war on the United States. And army headquarters in Washington announced the organization of the 93rd Infantry Division as an all-Negro unit.

On the home front, the federal government banned the production of civilian automobiles and trucks for the "duration of the war." Congress approved a price-control bill and sent it to the president for his signature. The Interstate Commerce Commission authorized a 10 percent increase in rail passenger fares. The director of the Price Administration announced the rationing of sugar—fifty pounds per capita in the year 1942. At the end of January, Attorney General Francis Biddle ordered the removal of all Japanese aliens from the San Francisco area. Republican Senator Robert A. Taft of Ohio said that in his opinion the war would last "for at least five years." And colleges and universities across the country were making plans to reduce the length of the undergraduate curriculum from four years to three.

After my first wartime telephone call home from Camp Roberts: *It was swell to hear your sweet voice again after so long. Isn't it funny how we couldn't think what to say at times, when there was so much that needed to be said, and so little time to say it. But the main thing was to hear you saying again that you loved me. It cost me $6 exactly, but it was worth every penny. I hope to heaven that I will be here at Easter time, and that you will be able to come out to see me. If you can get the time off, I'm sure we'll be able to swing it. We'll really have a swell time. There is a guest house where you can stay, and we can go into Paso Robles. Or there are lots of things on the post we can do. And maybe by that time we'll be able to travel farther away from camp. We could go to Frisco or Los Angeles. It would be great to see Chinatown together, and to walk around the city holding hands, the way we used to at Wayne. If there is any way possible, please come, because I want to see you so much. It seems strange that with thousands of soldiers all around me, I should feel lonesome. We can use our bank account to pay your way, if necessary.*

You seemed surprised when we talked this evening that we had no trainees in our battalion. I thought I'd written you about it, but maybe I forgot. We haven't had any for nearly four weeks. And there's been almost nothing for me to do, except go to cadre school and loaf. I'm getting very lazy, and worrying too that they might be sending us somewhere.

From Dearborn: *Thank you, Bob, for calling me tonight. They say love is fed by kind deeds and words, and that must be the reason I love you so terribly much. If only we could be together now instead of just united from time to time by long-distance wires, and that for only a few minutes. If you don't get a leave before spring, I promise I will come out to see you, by hook or by crook. And I might not be coming alone! Sarah says she would like to come with me, and so did Ellen. Just tonight your sister Eileen told me she would like to go along. Wouldn't you be surprised when you find that instead of the one girl you expected, a whole carload is dumped on your lap?*

It's pretty darned cold here tonight. The wind is blowing, and the house refuses to get warm. You used to say you knew that it was really, really cold when the moisture in your nose freezes. Well, it's even colder than that here. Five below zero, the radio says. And the frost on my windows is at least a half-inch thick. I know you'll be very glad to be out there in sunny California. Do you think, dear, that if you were home, you'd love me enough to come over on a night like this and hike the six long blocks from Warren? Freezing your ears? If you did though, I'd make you very glad you came. I'd feed you hot chocolate and waffles and sausages. It's much too cold to leave again and to stand in front of the Fisher Building. So you'd just have to stay until morning. How does that sound?

You asked how conditions are in Detroit. My dad has been working ten hours a day, seven days a week, and so have a lot of other men in defense industries. Non-defense production is being shut down altogether, so many men are out of work right now. Especially in Pontiac and Flint, where a lot of the auto companies are. I guess it will take a few months for the transition to be made to all-defense production, and the unemployed men are absorbed again.

From Camp Roberts, two days later: *It looks as though my days of enforced leisure are over. And none too soon. We received word that men would be coming in tomorrow, beginning with forty of them at 7:30 a.m. In a way, I'm both glad and sorry at the same time. Glad because our weeks of being in a quandary are over. And sorry that we are not moving east. Most of all, it's good that we are not being sent to combat divisions. Staying here certainly has its advantages, as you tell me. But I have to caution you that our every move is subject to change at a moment's notice. So don't be surprised if one day you hear that I have gone somewhere else. We'll just have to keep our fingers crossed, won't we?*

Now, concerning the subject you asked me about on the phone, it's true the army has had a reputation for being promiscuous, as Bill Rollo said. But from what I have seen, it isn't any more so than the average of people from which it is drawn. You might be surprised to know that according to polls, a large percentage of college men and women have had some sexual experience.

55

And the fraternity fellows talk about it all the time. Boast about it even. I would say that if the men who come to the army have consort with prostitutes, it is because they had sexual intercourse when they were civilians. Very few men lose their virginity in or because of the army. It's certainly true that there are prostitutes around Camp Roberts, both amateur and professional. But I would be safe in saying that no more than one or two out of ten soldiers that I have known here have had anything to do with them. The army is not a den of iniquity. Sure, we swear a lot. And we tell vile jokes. But that's superficial. And not the same as being "corrupt," as he says. So you don't have to worry about it one bit.

It's too bad you've had such cold weather in Michigan. For a while here it rained often. But lately the sun has been shining with regularity. Not that it's warm in January, because we had a frost this morning, meaning that the temperature approached 32 degrees. Which is, of course, nothing like your five below. But I can say, here and now, that I would walk those six blocks from Warren if it were twenty below, and the snow was knee-deep.

News about the spring semester: *You'll be interested to know, dear, that I am now officially in the College of Education, after all. It seemed wisest to get my teacher's certificate as soon as possible. That way, I can start earning money and saving up for when you will be coming back. These are abnormal times, and I should have an important part in building our future home. With our combined efforts, our new life will get off to a happy start. And it could be worse. I'm sure glad I don't have to take classes on how to make beanbags or play skip tag. I don't think I could have stood it. I'll be specializing in corrective speech, which I like. And these are the courses I'll be taking next semester: Survey of Education, Child Psychology, Survey of Special Education, Pathology of the Organs of Speech, Anatomy and Physiology, and the Philosophy of Education. My advisor is Dr. Hahn, head of the department. The other day he asked if I'd like to work in his clinic, and I told him I already had two jobs. He said it would be to my advantage, because it's the sort of work I'm interested in. And he offered to meet my present wages. So I think I should stop working at Ward's and accept his offer.*

Last semester's grades averaged out as B. I thought they'd be better, especially in Biology and in Economics—in the Econ final I wrote an awful lot, but I have to admit that most of it was blarney. The real problem, I think, was that I didn't do enough studying all semester.

I'm sorry about our "little controversy." About the soldiers and all. Perhaps disagreements are best settled when we are together, and we can talk all we like. And not just for a few minutes on the telephone, when you might say something you don't mean. On a more happy subject, I loved the poem you sent me. It sort of made me hurt inside. And especially the verse about the northern lights like tiers of gothic organ pipes. Last autumn they were more beautiful than I've ever seen them. I remember waking up one night, and happening to look out of the window. There they were, just as you say, and I wondered if you were looking at them too. Something about seeing the northern lights always restores my faith in God, like watching waves roll up on a beach, or a beautiful sunset.

Two weeks later: *This afternoon I went to the Red Cross center, as I do every Wednesday. And I thought when I got home I'd have lots of time to write you a long letter. I'm usually through by 7:30. But Jean and I were sent out as nurses' aides on a mobile unit. They were having a blood-donor night at the Hannah Y, and we didn't get through until after ten. Right now it's past 11:30—time for no more than a note, I'm sorry to say. It was interesting, though, working on a mobile unit. We had to work so much faster. A makeshift canteen and some beds were rigged up in the lounge, and we even had a German band that came in to play for us. Except for one big, fat lady who fainted on me, and a boy who almost did, everything went all right. So I'll write you again tomorrow.*

The next day: *I don't know how our plans for me to visit you at Easter time will work out, honey. I think all spring vacations are going to be cancelled. The registration board at Wayne is considering a plan for three semesters in a year, with no summer vacation. That way people will be able to finish their college in three years. The U of M has adopted the trimester plan already, and it looks as though Wayne will too. If so, I might come out to see you anyhow. I could just take the two weeks off, and try to make up the work when I got back. It's been so long since we've seen each other. I'm sorry, dear, that I ever said anything about a test. I know now that no amount of time could cause a breach between us or estrange us. No matter what happens in the war.*

January 24, 1942, at Camp Roberts: *It's raining pretty hard, and it looks as though it's never going to stop. I don't mind it so much today, because I'm charge-of-quarters, and I don't have to go outside. I guess maybe the rainy season is here at last. We've been having some pretty hard downpours lately. Here in California they don't do anything halfway. When it's hot, it's very hot, and when it rains, it pours, as the saying goes. I suppose it's still pretty chilly there, with all the snow you've been having. And have you noticed that the papers don't give much information about the weather these days. Too many Japanese spies, I would guess.*

You said once you were rereading my letters—because I hadn't written you lately, and it reminded me of the picture "I Want a Divorce." Joan Blondell is reading Dick Powell some of the letters he had sent her before they were married. And he has an agonized look on his face, as much as to say: "Did I write that stuff?" Do you think we'll ever feel that way when we are two old married people? In our eighties, maybe? I don't think we will. And I know that I'll never grow tired of saying: "I love you very much." Never.

I'm back in the old routine of training draftees. Almost all of them are from Arkansas, which means they aren't too educated. Most never even went to high school. But one thing in their favor is that they work hard. Really hard. We don't have much trouble with them. When it comes to keeping the barracks clean, they pitch right in. And they seem to know a lot about weapons. Maybe they'll all be second Sergeant Yorks. I saw that picture the other day, and I liked it very much. There was a lot of propaganda, but it was a good film.

They've started to issue 24-hour passes on the weekends. We can't go very far on that. But maybe when you come it will be longer. I'll talk to the first sergeant about the possibility. We could take the bus to Frisco, and stay a few days. The city ought to be very beautiful at that time of the year. We could take walks and ride the cable cars. What do you think of that?

January 26, 1942, in Dearborn: *I haven't heard from you for an awfully long time, dear, and of course it worries me. I have visions of you on a transport, far out at sea. Please let me know that you are all right. Reading your letters again made me feel so blue and very lonesome for you. Oh, Bob, I wish we could be together tomorrow, someplace where there is no war—in our own private Shangri-La. We can take lovely walks in the countryside and breathe fresh air, and love each other with all our hearts. Some day in the future, dear one, that will be a reality, instead of just a dream, won't it?*

I forgot to tell you that I had seen Dr. Basilius in the hall the other day, for the first time in a long while. He said: "Hello, I had a very nice letter from Bob. And he said some nice things about you." I can't imagine what you told him about me, but thank you. He still calls me Miss Gutzeit, though. I have some studying to do now, and it's late—a couple of the Deutche Novellen *I need to read before the exam on Wednesday. I'm afraid I don't know very much about that subject.*

Confinement to barracks, January 31, 1942: *I won't be doing very much for about three weeks, so you will probably be hearing from me more often—for a while, at least. It sounds funny, but our whole platoon is being quarantined for—of all things—the mumps. We can't leave the barracks except to drill, and we are completely separated from the rest of the company. We have to eat in the barracks from our mess kits. The KPs bring the food and leave it outside the door for us to carry in. It isn't so bad now, but I expect it will pall before the three weeks are up. I haven't ever had the mumps, so far as I know, and I am hoping for the best. Can't you see me, honey, with my jaws all swollen up, eating nothing but ice cream? I'll let you know if I detect any signs of a swelling under my jaws. In the meantime, keep your fingers crossed.*

Today was payday, so I'm a rich man. For a while, at least. I drew down $52.20, but I had to pay a company bill, so I now have some $48 and $2 worth of canteen checks. I'm not supposed to go to the PX, so I'll have a corporal in another platoon get me a money order to send to you. That ought to make our account a little larger. By spring we should have enough money for you to come visit me. Because of the quarantine, I won't be able to spend much money this month, anyway, so I should be able to contribute a little more later. Also I've heard that corporals are due for a twelve-dollar raise in a couple of months, and that will make it even better. I think maybe you'd better take a quick course in business management, if you are going to control the purse strings of our huge investments!

I was thinking the other day about what I wanted to be when I get out of the army and finish my schooling—if that is possible. I've changed my mind so many times since I left high school, and each of the positions was different. Now lately, with the war and all, I've been thinking I should do something about conditions in our country and in the world. I could go into politics or the diplomatic service. Can you see me as a consul to Australia or maybe to South Africa? I might write to the State Department for information. Would you ever like to live in a foreign country? Say in Germany after the war? Or how about being a congressman's wife? After all, I've had that political experience as delegate to the county convention and precinct captain. What do you think of all this? Incidentally, did you ever have the mumps? And if so, what are they like?

The first week of February, 1942: *We had a second fellow go to the hospital, which is very bad news. I'm told the whole platoon will stay in quarantine 21 days after the last man gets the mumps. Theoretically, we could stay here for the duration of the war. And today the second platoon heard the bad news, so that leaves only the fourth platoon uncontaminated—the feather merchants. Maybe they're tougher than we are. There'll be a show for us "germs" tonight in the 78th rec hall. But I decided to stay here and write letters. It probably wouldn't have been very good, anyway. Is that sour grapes?*

I had a discussion with our lieutenant today about a problem in target shooting, and I tried to show him what I thought was a simple solution. Everyone else I explained it to understood, even the platoon sergeant, who is not very bright about scientific matters. But do you think the officer would agree with me? You can bet your life he didn't. These second lieutenants with the shiny brass bars seem to think they know everything there is to know. And a lowly corporal is a second-class citizen. I prefer to be what I am, though. I can't see myself mixing with the lieutenants. Of course, there are some exceptions, like the man from Maine. But they are the exceptions that prove the rule, as they say.

A response from Dearborn: *I'm sorry, dear, that you are quarantined. I never had the mumps, so I can't tell you what they're like. In fact, I don't think I was ever sick, except for the whooping cough when I was little. And having my tonsils removed in the doctor's office. I'll have to tell you about it some day. It was very traumatic, to say the least. Katie running out the door with blood all over her mouth. And then it was my turn. Dreadful! I hear that in grown people mumps can have serious consequences. So for me, kindly be careful and stay away from your infected friends. I'll try to cheer you up by writing you frequent sunshiny letters.*

As for your future, I know that sometime, after the war, you will get your degree. Or degrees, I should say. I believe that things you really want always work out in the end. I know you will finish school, and probably get even more out of the courses because of your war experiences. By that time I should be teaching, and I can help out financially. And maybe I'll take some graduate work and go to a night class or two with you. Your real forte is writing, so you could be a journalist. Or a professor. Or a diplomat. They all sound very impressive, and you'd be very good at any of them. And you would have made a very good doctor or singer. But then perhaps we never would have met.

I don't think I told you that I almost decided to enroll at Mt. Pleasant College, because I thought Ellen would be going there. I applied for a scholarship, but they turned me down. And I couldn't afford both the tuition and the housing. Also, before my mother died, my folks were talking about sending Katie and me to a German school some day. So the fates have worked very hard to bring the two of us together, and I know they are not going to stop. So the most useful thing I can say is to just wait and see what happens.

Remembering in Camp Roberts: *I was thinking of calling you next Sunday, but now I know I had better not. I could get six months in the guardhouse for breaking quarantine, and I don't think you would want that, would you, dear? So I'll call you just as soon as the quarantine is over. I promise. So far, I have not acquired the mumps, so Lady Luck is still with me. And our confinement will be up in a couple of weeks, if there are no new cases in the platoon. Knock on wood for me, if you please.*

Earlier I was listening to the Ford Sunday Evening Hour, *and it made me think of the concerts we went to in Detroit. Do you remember "Messiah" the first part of December? We had been going together for only a week or so. Afterward, we were riding home on the bus, and I took off my glove to measure hands with you. We were sitting just in front of the rear door. And we laced our fingers together and held hands all the way home. I was in love with you even then, though I couldn't tell you at the time. It's funny how I can remember so clearly the seats we sat in, or the shows we saw, or what you gave me to eat when we got to your house. Or even what dress or shoes you were wearing.*

Lincoln's Birthday, 1942: *We've been working long hours since the training period has been shortened and speeded up. At the end of every day, I just collapse into bed. Right now it's the weapons period. I got to fire a few shots today while the trainees were just practicing. I did a lot better than when I was a trainee. I made a bulls-eye almost every time I shot. I even made a bulls-eye shooting left-handed, and the men are thinking I'm some kind of super shot. It's probably because I'm not afraid of a gun, now that I can shoot so much better.*

Speaking of marksmanship, there's a fellow in Company A who is only 14 years old. Boy, that is really getting them young, isn't it, honey? He lied about his age—said he was 17 when he volunteered. And he had his mother's consent. I think he is from the mountains of Tennessee, or some place like that. He's really good with the rifle. Still, I don't see how he got in. He's so young looking, and his voice hasn't changed yet. If your back is turned you would swear there's a girl in the barracks. I guess they tried to get him out, when they found out how old he really was, but he wouldn't go. I hear now that he couldn't get out, even if he wanted to, after refusing to leave when he had a chance. The noncoms in the company really take good care of him, like a bunch of mother hens.

Valentine's Day in Dearborn: *Thank you very much, honey, for the red roses and carnations. They make a wonderful bouquet. A little while ago I turned on the radio, and they were playing all the music of "Fantasia." And right now Marian Anderson is singing Schubert's "Ave Maria." It's so beautiful, and it reminds me, dear, of last spring when you and I went to see the movie. I'm still planning on coming out to see you, and counting on two whole weeks—seven days traveling and the other seven with you. Would that give us enough time to see San Francisco? I hope so. Right now, though, my father is a problem. He doesn't like the idea of my going alone. I'm too young, he says. And he won't let me miss all those days of classes (because the spring vacations have been cancelled). But I think I can get him to change his mind. I usually do.*

A week later in California: *I had a pretty bad cold Sunday night, but it's almost broken up by now. I went on sick call Monday morning, and had a fever of 100 degrees. That's not too bad, but the doctor gave me some medicine—probably aspirin, and I went out on the firing range anyway. Because it was damp from the rain, I wore the sweater you sent me under my jacket, so I was quite warm. As the day passed, it got warmer, and by evening I felt a lot better. It made me think of when I was a kid and had something wrong with me, my mother would give me some hot lemonade and put me under several blankets. I would "sweat out" whatever was making me sick. And it always worked. I don't know what the medical doctors would think of that. I haven't had very many colds out here, and this was the first time I've been on sick call since I came to Camp Roberts.*

You asked what I thought of the classes you're taking this semester. The Pathology of Speech Organs sounds interesting. Maybe you can find out why women talk so much. Ouch! I felt that smack way out here. Anatomy and Physiology is a good course, I'm told, but very stiff if taken from Wann. He makes you memorize every bone, muscle, blood vessel, etc. in the human body. I have heard all kinds of stories about girls who have led sheltered lives being traumatized by the frankness of his course. I'm afraid that by the time you finish that class, you will know more about me and my functions than I do myself.

You never did say if you told your parents how things stand between us. Your mother must know something, since I asked her permission to give you the ring. And more important, does your father know we intend to get married some day? I've told my family, and the whole world in general, including Dr. Basilius, how I feel about you. And that I hoped to marry you in the not-too-distant future. It's important to me that they both know what sort of guy will be their son-in-law.

Two days later and still confined: *It will be four weeks this Friday we have been in quarantine. And today there was another case of the mumps, so that makes two more weeks, at least. I guess you can get used to anything eventually. And we're supposed to get yellow-fever shots any day now. They must be thinking of sending us someplace in the tropics. If I have to go, I think I'd prefer Europe, where I'd have an opportunity to use my German.*

Chapter 3

The end of February in Dearborn: *About my coming out to see you, dear, I'm afraid it's going to be more expensive than we thought. All transportation rates have gone up ten percent lately. I called the ticket offices, and the round trip by rail is $123 and $73 by bus. That's a lot of money, isn't it? Jane thinks the bus would be more interesting and enjoyable, because it goes through all the main cities. They make rest stops frequently, and I'd probably have to stop overnight someplace. I wouldn't like to stay alone in a strange city at night, so maybe I can still induce someone to come with me. Also there would be the cost of meals on the way and my expenses while I'm in California. So maybe we should wait until June when we'll be better off financially. As it is, our bank account will be exhausted. Would you mind very much? And in any event, you might still be in quarantine all through the spring. And in June I could possibly stay longer.*

As for staying with me when you come home on furlough, that's just fine. My father would probably greet you in the morning with a shotgun, though. He has funny, old-fashioned ideas. I've never announced to my folks that you and I intend to be married. But I'm sure Katie and all my friends know it. And we didn't decide it all of a sudden, so there was no occasion to make an announcement. We sort of realized it gradually, didn't we? My father does know that you are the first man I have ever taken very seriously, and he likes you, I think. He won't approve of my marrying a Roman Catholic, but he doesn't say anything about it. He just grunts.

From California, March 1, 1942: *I meant to ask you, dear, about your idea of bringing someone along with you, and I wonder if you have considered what that might entail? In the first place, what would she do out here? Not having seen you for such a long time, I should naturally want to monopolize your time. I wouldn't want to share you with another person, even with my sister. And there would be expenses for her. As of now, I think we have enough money set aside for the bus trip and perhaps for your staying here a full week or more. Admittedly, the bus takes somewhat longer and is tedious. And it does make stops, for eating purposes and for you-know-what. But then these new busses, like the ones that go up to San Francisco, are pretty comfortable, with reclining seats and all. Do you think you could stand riding the entire way out and back on a bus? I sup-, pose I seem selfish in this matter, but I hope you can understand and ap-*

preciate my reasons. I'm enclosing a money order for $40 to add to our account. That leaves me with about $15, but we'll be in quarantine another two weeks anyway.

I have been collecting coins to be ready to call you the instant I am a free man. Day or night, so be prepared. It's difficult in a camp this large to get the nickels, dimes, and quarters for pay phones. Soldiers don't have many occasions to pick up change, because most of our needs are taken care of by the army. So all the fellows tend to hoard what coins they have. And the stores don't like to give you more change than they need to.

Four days later, on March 5, 1942: *Marianne, I've been busy the last few days, and will be for a while yet. I have charge of the men in our company who have not fired the rifle—ten in all. And I have to give them their weapon training. Since we are still in quarantine, the lieutenants can't help in any of the instructing. We can't risk an officer's having the mumps going down on him, can we? So I do the lecturing, demonstrating, and everything else. It's going to be tough tomorrow—on the range all day, and then a night problem that will last until 11:30 p.m. I'll be pretty tired by the time Saturday rolls around.*

Friday the 13th: *By all rights it should have been an unlucky day in Camp Roberts, and it almost was. For a while it looked as though we were stewed, screwed, and tattooed, all at the same time. This morning the first sergeant told us that from now on we'd be working seven days a week. No more Sundays off, he said. I can safely say that morale, already sagging in the company because of the quarantine, hit a new low. You can imagine how everyone felt. There was even talk of "going over the hill."*

But, as it turned out, it was just a rumor initiated by our first sergeant to get even with the mess sergeant for starting so many rumors. It was really a dirty trick, and thoughtless to boot. And it possibly endangered what has been good relations between the sergeant and the men. The incident shows how easy it is for a rumor to spread. The sergeant told the charge-of-quarters, and he passed it on to me. I told a few of the other noncoms. And before long, every one of the trainees had heard about it, and even the officers. When nerves are on edge, it's very easy to get people excited. I suppose you have rumors back there too, don't you, honey? We're constantly being warned, by the army and by the newspapers, not to spread rumors. And when anyone asks us where we get our information, we say it's a latrine rumor, right off the third hole from the left.

And three days later, March 16, 1942: *I have never—and I mean never—felt more nasty in my entire life. If I have heretofore thought of the big shots and brass hats as dirty bastards, I hereby take it back. They are a hundred times worse than that. I wish I could think of words colossal enough in scope to express my feelings on this fateful evening. In the language of the army, I feel as though I have been royally screwed, and without any Vaseline.*

Don't be alarmed, dear, at the vehemence of my words. It's just that I am in great need of an emotional catharsis, and I'm taking my feelings out on you. Have you ever felt that if you could put something on paper you could get it out of your system? Is that something I got from the Abnormal Psych class? And what am I so overwrought about? Well, we were supposed to get out of quarantine today. After all this time. But we just heard this evening that one of our men has the measles. It wouldn't be so bad if he had caught them here. We could understand that. We'd be pissed off, but we could understand it. But he has been in the hospital since March 5, and he caught them up there, not down here in the company. So they should just keep him there and leave us alone. I've about given up all hope of being a free man again.

I feel a lot better, now. Sorry to use you as a punching bag, dear, sweet Marianne. And I promise you I will never use language like that in front of our children. Good night. I love you very much.

The same day in Dearborn: *I'm sorry you haven't heard from me for a while. I do have so many things to do these days. I'm afraid my anatomy class is getting me down. You were right when you said it was a tough course. I never realized there could be so many parts to the human body. And every Thursday we have a two-hour quiz. Also I have to write a paper about my conception of the ideal education and read a book and give a talk next week on John Fletcher's opinion of the stuttering problem for the pathology course. And I haven't even started. Then I have to make a detailed "child study," though I have until the end of the semester for that. I'll try to find out just as soon as I can what time the bus arrives in San Francisco, dear. It depends largely on when my last final exam is, and how long I'd take to get there. The schedules have been changing, but I'll keep checking with the people at* *the bus station. Right now the fare is $73.55, and I can get stopover passes. Up to six-month's worth, if I should want.*

An end to the quarantine in Camp Roberts, March 19, 1942: *After all my sounding off, it looks as though we're going to be out of quarantine to-morrow morning. That is, with the grace of God and our GI doctor, and our having no more cases of either the measles or the mumps. What a relief! To be able to go to the PX and to shows. And to make telephone calls. I hope you weren't overly offended by my last letter. I doubt if you will ever get another like it. And it's better, probably, that you learn now instead of later that I am, by nature, an old reprobate.*

At this point I took on a responsibility that I was unable to write about in letters, or indeed to mention to anyone at Camp Roberts or at home. A secret mission, in a way. I was directed to come to the adjutant general's office where I was interviewed by a colonel. They wanted me to keep my eyes and ears open, he said, for evidences of disloyal talk or behavior. I was to send a personal letter each week to a Paso Robles post-office box belonging to Alice Green. If I had anything to report, on the one hand, I should say something positive. That I was able to buy a certain book; or go to San Francisco; or take in a movie, etc. Then someone from the colonel's office would call me in for a detailed report. On the other hand, if I had nothing to report, I would send a negative message: "Sorry, I can't go to the movies with you," for example. By the time I left Camp Roberts I had written more than fifty letters, all of them negative. And I had quickly realized that "Alice Green" was not a live human being, but a pseudonym for adjutant general. My activities as an army counterintelligence agent were exceedingly unproductive and boring. And my biggest problem was trying each week to think up new activities to be sorry for. But there were never any spies or traitors in Camp Roberts that I knew of.

April Fools' Day, 1942, in California: *I had an experience today that was quite interesting. The charge-of-quarters came around and said a sergeant, two other corporals, and I were detailed to give some officers a demonstration on how to roll packs and pitch tents. So after lunch we took our paraphernalia and went over to the classroom. Leonard Bristol—he's a corporal—first showed them how to make the bed roll for a full-field pack. I think I told you before all it contains—blanket, shelter-half, raincoat, tent-pegs, and so forth.*

After the officers had watched us do our tricks, they tried their hands at it. So why were officers taking lessons from us? Well, they had just been called into active service, and they had never before had to do lowly things like that. They probably had some college ROTC, and got their commissions in the reserves. They are taking a course now that is the equivalent of a recruit's 13 weeks, only faster. You should have seen the bed-rolls those second lieutenants put together. They were worse than any of the recruits we have had since we came. Worse than the inept captain from Arkansas. Some of the rolls were skinny and overly long, like a Navin Field hot dog, without the bun. Others were too short and bulgy.

Then we went out and set about pitching tents. We acted as squad leaders for the officers who posed as privates. We nearly died laughing at the jeeps (lieutenants) when they marched around the parade ground with their packs hanging low on their backsides and bouncing each time they took a step. They looked ridiculous. And for a time I felt superior to those officers, which made me feel good, of course. But then I thought they're what they are because they lack training. And if the United States is to win this war, those officers have to lead the men under them into dangerous and difficult situations. And it does no good to poke fun at them. Instead we should help them as much as we can. Perhaps there could be an organized program here for the poorly trained ROTC men and the reserves. I would know how to do it, based on my experience with the trainees. But then nobody has asked my opinion, so there's no point in even discussing the possibilities.

I had a chance recently to be something more than a noncom, but I turned it down. Somehow I couldn't see myself in the role of an officer. Some people might say I'm unpatriotic, but I think I'm more patriotic than— say—a lot of the flag-wavers. I just want to show my patriotism in a different way. I want to do something constructive for mankind. So I guess that makes me a pacifist. On the other hand, if they sent me to the front I could fight just as hard as the next guy. I've found that I have most of the skills required by a soldier. What do you think about it, dear?

A reply from Marianne: *At first, I was sorry you didn't go to the officer training program. I know how much your father wanted you to. And I always thought it was the officers who took the least risks in battle. Personally, I don't give a darn about prestige or about your wearing bars on your shoulders. If you can remain a corporal and stay at Camp Roberts for the duration, I hope you do. Nothing would suit me better. I agree that it's very important to society, as well as to me, that you come out of the war all right. There is so much you can give to the world.*

It's been sort of cloudy and cool all week, and Jane's daughter-in-law from Hawaii and her two grandsons are nearly freezing to death. Today I took Mark and Donald to school for the first time. I hope they get along all right in a strange environment. They are both very bright, but they have peculiar mannerisms, and every now and then they forget themselves and ramble on in their native language. They have the idea that the whole world is made up of islands. Yesterday Donald was looking at a little globe, and he said: "Show me the island where all the cowboys come from, Marianne." And he told the little girl next door that her puppy was the "dumbest dog on the island." Their father Bill is my half-brother, and he has been in the navy for some time. Everyone is worried about his being out in the Pacific on a ship.

What the boys mind most is having to wear such a lot of clothes, and especially shoes. At home kids go barefoot, evidently, even to school. Both have thick calluses on the bottoms of their feet. They've started at the same primary school I went to—so many years ago, it seems. And something interesting. The principal told me that whenever I was ready to teach, he had a place for me. Isn't that nice?

Freedom, April 10, 1942: *I am writing this letter from San Francisco. I was lucky enough to get a three-day pass, the first one in the company since Pearl Harbor. I left camp yesterday morning at nine. I got one ride of only twelve miles and then another to Salinas. After that, a truck driver picked me up and brought me all the way to Oakland. I had meant to stop in San José at the state college and visit a few classes, if they would let me. I sure miss Wayne and all it meant—and means—for both of us. But it had started to rain there, so I decided to go on through. I'll have to close now, as I want to go out and look over the city while it isn't raining here in Frisco. I'll write you again on Sunday. P.S. We can mail our letters free now, but I'm going to continue to send yours by air. Each will cost a whole six cents, but that way, they'll get there faster.*

Two days later, back at camp: *I've been having trouble with my eyes lately, and I may need to see about ordering glasses, if they get any worse. I'm thinking of getting them with tortoise-shell rims, which are all the vogue at Wayne. Very professorial, I would say. Would you mind very much if I changed my appearance? I meant to get started on this letter earlier in the evening, but I took the story I'm working on over to let one of the corporals read it, and I noticed that his roommate had a book on sex. Since I'm always trying to improve my mind with a little knowledge here and there, I scanned through it. So now I am an expert on the subject. If you have any questions, just ask old Dr. Quirk.*

And speaking about sex, I saw a movie while I was in Frisco called "The Unashamed: Life and Love in a Nudist Colony." There wasn't much to it, except a lot of "Bodies Beautiful," both male and female, cavorting across the screen, playing volleyball, tennis, golf, swimming, etc. Very bouncy for the women, I must say.

I bought another cinnabar statue and will send it to you when I can find a suitable box. This one is a woman, and it's about the same size as the Buddha. I found it in a Japanese shop that was being closed out, so it was a bargain. All of the Japanese on the coast, alien or not, are being moved into the interior. It seems a shame, because most of them are good American citizens. But we are in a war, and I suppose the army thinks we shouldn't take any chances. I've been wondering what the government intends to do about the farms they are leaving. It's a matter of record that some forty percent of all the celery, lettuce, tomatoes, etc. in this country has been raised by Japanese here on the coast. There's bound to be a shortage in vegetables unless somebody can take them over. And even so, no white person would ever work the soil like a Jap. He takes every available square inch of land he has, and works it over by hand until the whole thing is covered by plants. No white American would be so meticulous. On the way up here on Friday, I passed farm after farm that had belonged to the Japanese and are now overrun with weeds.

Oh well, it's none of my business, some people might say. It's the war. And soldiers are not supposed to express their opinions about national affairs. But you know me, honey! Remember how I used to sound off on the second page of the Collegian? *I made a lot of people mad, including the dean of Liberal Arts when I reported his jokes instead of the substance of his serious lecture. One of these days, sooner than we think, I can do it again. Sound off, I mean. And not just in private letters to you that nobody else will ever read.*

I also bought some books in a secondhand shop. Two were choice selections from Greek and Roman literature—Plato, Aristotle, Livy, etc. The third was Preface to Morals *by Walter Lippman. It was recommended to me by Mr. Ryan, who taught us Journalism and supervised the* Collegian. *He said that it was a "must book," for an understanding of modern morality. The fourth is one you no doubt are familiar with—*Mina von Barnhelm *by Lessing. I thought it would give me a chance to brush up on my German.*

Military affairs, April 15, 1942: *I'm leaving tomorrow on a short trip by troop train. I can't say where we're going or for how long, because it's a military secret. And the reason I know we will not be going very far is that we're taking pack lunches with us—no mess kits or dining cars. That means it's some place in California, so I'm not worried this time. And we'll be taking 1,000 men with us. You can guess that that is approximately the number of trainees who have finished their training here and are being shipped somewhere else, but I have not told you so.*

Four days later: *I'm back, safe and sound, which is all I'm allowed to say. Everything else is still a "top secret." These days the enemy is supposed to be listening to every word we utter. So we can't allow any American Japanese to remain in this great state.*

Another week passes in the army: *Just a short letter this evening to let you know I'm back from a "camping trip." And all tired out. A week ago we—most of the cadremen in our outfit—went out about ten or twelve miles from here. Luckily we rode in trucks, so we saved on the wear and tear on our feet. We drilled each morning from 8:30 to 10:30, and then we were free for the rest of the day. It was really a vacation of sorts. Or an extended picnic, after we'd been working so hard and for so long. We could play baseball or any other sport we wanted—go hunting, swimming, or hiking. Or just plain loaf, which is what I did mostly. In the evenings there was free beer for everyone.*

On Tuesday, there were some girls from San Luis Obispo who came out to the camp area to visit. The officers grabbed them off immediately, according to seniority. Since there were only ten girls they didn't go very far. Come to think of it, though, maybe they did go pretty far. Off into the woods. Needless to say, everybody had a good time.

The final week of April 1942, in Dearborn: *I meant to write you last night, but I was so tired. I had an anatomy mid-semester, and I don't think I did very well. I got the circulatory system all mixed up and had the blood in different veins running in the wrong direction. It makes me mad to know the right answers and just don't put them down in that way. I guess you might say I hadn't "overlearned" the materials. Or maybe it was lack of sleep. I have so much to do these days.*

Anatomy is an interesting course, though, and I like it very much. And it's funny the way that every time we study a new disease, everyone in the class develops all the symptoms. It's the same way with psychology—after reading about all the abnormalities of human behavior, you begin to feel sort of abnormal yourself.

When I come out in June will I be able to see the ocean and the great waves rolling up on the beach? Sometimes I think it would be very satisfying to live near the sea. Or on a lake, perhaps. I told you on the phone that I could be out there by the tenth. But now I think we should make it the fifteenth to be on the safe side. To allow for any late exams, etc. It would be too bad if I got to San Francisco and found that it was the last day of your leave. Is that all right with you, dear?

Later in the week: *Believe it or not, honey, for the past two days I've been a teacher. Shirley and I have been substituting at the Thayer School in Dearborn. Some of the regular teachers are helping register people for the draft, and Shirley's father, who teaches here, arranged for us to fill in. So I am teaching reading, writing, and arithmetic to a bunch of third graders. It certainly gets exciting. Yesterday a couple of the boys brought two snakes to class, and I put the jars on the window sill. And a little later, while I was on the other side of the room, one of the fellows took out a snake, and was playing with it on the floor. Today I'm not letting them get away with anything, and so far I've not had any trouble. Just now they've all gone to the gym, and it's nice and quiet in here. But I had better close soon. They'll be back in a few minutes, and it wouldn't do for the little hellions to see their teacher writing a love letter, would it?*

A reply from California: *I think it's swell that you have this chance to do some practice teaching. Though I can think of many things I would rather be doing than teaching a bunch of third graders. It's bad enough working with grown men, without having to worry about what kids are doing behind my back. Tell me more about your days as a school marm. I think I'm jealous though of those little boys in your class. They get to look at you all day, and when they do something good you probably pat them on the head and give them a hug.*

In a way, dear, I'll be a teacher of sorts out here in California. I've been chosen to give daily lectures to the company on current events. I need to be prepared at any moment to talk for from five minutes up to a half hour. That means I have to read the newspapers and the magazines a lot more, and listen to the radio. I think I will find it interesting. At this point I don't know what kind of lecturer I will be, but if I'm going to be a politician or a professor when I come back, I should be getting some experience in public speaking. I'd like, for example, to talk about Nazi Germany. Several officers, usually the chaplains, have been conducting orientation lectures. Mostly, they have been focusing on Japan, rather than Germany and Russia. The trouble has been that our chaplain knows very little about the subject. And if he were not a man of God, I would have to say that he doesn't know his you-know-what from a hole in the ground.

May Day, 1942: *Bob, your little Chinese statue from San Francisco arrived today, safe and sound. Thank you very much. She and the fat old Buddha are grinning down from the top of my dresser. I would say that they look like a contented husband and wife, except that it might be blasphemous in the Chinese culture. I hope you will take me to Chinatown when we are in San Francisco.*

From the school marm, May 6, 1942: *I taught again yesterday, to the same class. Teachers are rationing sugar this week, so they asked me to come back. It turned out though to be quite an expensive and embarrassing adventure. On the way home after school I found that someone had taken all the money from my purse. I know it's my fault for leaving the desk drawers unlocked, but I was truly disappointed that one of the little kids would do such a thing.*

Maybe I wasn't cut out to be a teacher, or maybe I was just too nice to them, but they didn't take me very seriously. In the middle of a penmanship lesson a little boy popped up and said: "Teacher, do you know the difference between an aeroplane and a baby?" And before I could stop him, he said: "The aeroplane goes from city to city, and the baby goes from titty to titty." Which broke up the class, as you can imagine. I'm beginning to think that all this modern education theory about letting children follow their own interests, is a bunch of baloney. I asked them to take out their arithmetic books, and a little boy in the corner said: "Aw, I want to draw dive bombers."

I guess the worst thing that happened—though it sounds funny when I tell you about it—was in the afternoon. I think their teacher is a nature enthusiast, because on the window sill she had a collection of snakes and all sorts of stuff, including a speckled egg. A little girl, Patsy, kept running over to show me the egg, and I warned everyone to leave it alone. If it broke, I said, it would make an awful smell. A few minutes later Patsy Busybody came up and said: "Teacher, you know the egg that was on the window? Well, I hardly even touched it, and now it's cracked a little bit." It was on the floor, smashed and smelling to high heaven, and the kids were walking around, holding their noses and saying: "pee-yoo! pee-yoo!"

In the middle of it all, the principal walked in, with his nose in the air, sniffing. He asked if the smell could be coming though the ventilator. I explained that it was only a small egg that had been broken. Which seemed to satisfy him, because he didn't ask the details. It's a good thing the school day didn't last longer or I might have torn every hair out of my head.

A reply from California: *I told the fellows in my barracks your story about the baby and the airplane, and they thought it was pretty good. Did I tell you I went to a school here for movie projection? Anyway, I got 97 percent on the final exam, the highest in the class. Once more I proved my skills in cramming for a test. At Wayne no one was my equal at crowding an entire semester's work into the final week or so. It wasn't wise, I know, but I never could exert myself until the final minute.*

They also gave me the job of setting up the company's public-address system. It isn't hard work, but it's been fun putting all the wires together. I gave my first orientation lecture yesterday. It was about the German invasion of Russia last year. I was going like a house afire, when the company commander cut me off. My limit was fifteen minutes, he said, and I had gone beyond it. It taught me to watch the clock better, but in my own defense I can say it's darned difficult to put all those campaigns into a quarter of an hour. Every two minutes there was a big battle. The good thing about my lecturing is that I have been keeping abreast of the national and international news. The sea battles in the Pacific, for example. It looks as though the tide has turned in favor of the Americans. Maybe the war won't last as long as we thought.

May 21, 1942: *I learned today that my lecturing days are over. The captain said that all talks to groups as large as a company must be given by one of the company officers. Which leaves me out. I think his orders must have come from higher authorities, probably the general's office, because the captain had been complimenting me on my work. I really liked the lecturing, and I'd be more than glad to keep it up, if they'd let me. I was just getting so I could make a pretty good presentation. Maybe one of these days I'll have the chance to do it again. So I'll still try to keep up-to-date on the news.*

Travel plans, May 27, 1942: *Hey there, what goes on? Here it is nigh onto two and a half weeks, and I haven't heard a word from you. The mail system between here and Dearborn must have collapsed, or maybe the postman fell down and broke a leg. And with June approaching and the time for you to come out and see me. You are coming, aren't you, dear? If possible it would be best if you could arrange to arrive in Frisco on a Saturday. That way I can meet you, and we could have several days there before we came down to Camp Roberts. Write me about what you have decided. Or if you are in a hurry, you can send a telegram.*

The first day of June, 1942, in Dearborn: *You said, Bob, that I should try to be there on the 13th or the 20th, so I will make it the former. My finals will be out of the way by then. Also bus service has been getting worse, and it's too risky to put off taking a trip much longer. The people at the depot said it would take me about five days. Can you tell me more about the furlough situation? I have been offered a summer job as counselor at a children's camp near Port Huron, and I wouldn't want to be out of town, naturally, if you were coming home in June. Let me know about that as soon as you can, dear. I'm going to buy the ticket on Wednesday, and then I'll mail you the rest of our bankroll. You have been very generous with your contributions lately. Thank you very much, especially for that last fifty dollars. Shall we meet at the bus station? And do you think you will recognize me, after all this time? I'll be the girl wearing a white rose.*

Three days later: *By the time you get this letter, I'll be on my way to see you, dear. Last night I was a little discouraged. I came home at about 11:30 after an individual oral exam in the pathology of speech, which lasted until 10:15. It was nerve-wracking, to say the least, and I was very tired. Then I heard the news broadcast about the Japanese raid on Dutch Harbor in the Aleutians, and golly I was afraid that would upset our plans. Maybe your pass would be cancelled. But nothing has been said in the papers about it, so I'll start packing tomorrow.*

From Omaha, Nebraska, June 9, 1942, en route to San Francisco: *I'm almost halfway to California, and in about 96 hours I'll have a date with you in San Francisco. I left Detroit Monday morning at 7:15. My father brought me to the station. He has been very good about it, although I know he isn't keen on my making this trip all alone. I would have wired you the time of my arrival, but I couldn't be sure. There are so many changes being made, and without notice. But I believe now that I will be arriving in Frisco sometime in the early hours of Saturday. I'm going to stop again overnight in Cheyenne. That way, I'll feel fresher when I get there. I'm staying here at the Hill Hotel, and I've just had a shower and a very delicious dinner. So I feel fine now, except for being so sleepy. Last night on the bus I was able to sleep for only a couple of hours. I'd certainly love to be taking this trip with you. Is there a chance you could get a leave or a furlough and ride back with me?*

I'm not afraid of traveling alone any more. At first I was a little scared, and Monday night in Chicago I felt like just turning around and going home. I had a four-hour stop there, so I took a shower and had dinner at the YWCA. And then I met a girl there I once knew, and we talked. So I felt a lot better about the whole thing. I really like Omaha, what little I have seen of it. Tonight I'm going to write my folks too. My father will be worried until he knows I am safely in San Francisco. See you then, dear.

Memories: *That was a nice day, wasn't it, Bob, when we met again after a year. I was never so glad to see anyone in my life. It was funny the way I wore myself out, all those days on the bus and then at the hotel in San Francisco, waiting and worrying about whether you'd get there, and whether things between us would still be the same. I finally fell asleep in the afternoon and never woke up until 7:15, when the phone rang, and I got your telegram saying your bus would arrive at 7:00. I was so excited I could hardly get my clothes on, and I ran down the stairs, still half-asleep, expecting to find you waiting for me in the lobby. Then I waited another nervous 25 minutes in the bus depot, until suddenly I looked up, and there you were, standing beside me! Your bus had been late, you said. After that, I was in your arms, and all the doubts were gone from my mind. And everything has been perfectly right ever since. We had such a beautiful time together in California, didn't we, those heavenly days in Paso Robles and in San Francisco? Seeing Chinatown and Fisherman's Wharf. And eating ripe figs at the YMCA Hotel. I'll never forget any of it. We grew closer together in a few days than we ever had in a year. I love you, darling, with all my heart, then, now, and forever.*

About going home, June 28, 1942: *I have bad news about my furlough, dear. We have a new regimental commander, and he has just cut leaves from fifteen to ten days. It will be difficult to get to Detroit and back in that time and still spend many days at home. But if that is all I have, I will try it anyhow. At least I could buy you our engagement ring, and let me see my folks. Most important, you and I could spend a little time together. Also it's possible I can get a three-day pass attached to the furlough. And the first sergeant might let me leave a day early. So we'll see.*

Well, darling, you have been my fiancée since Tuesday, June 23 at five p.m. That means that we have been engaged for five days, three hours, and forty-two and a half minutes. I have to smile to myself when I recall the way it happened. You always hear about the fellow's getting down on one knee and holding his hand over his heart while he's asking for her hand in marriage. And then speaking to her father about it. Or is it the other way around? All I said was: "When I get back to Detroit, if I buy a diamond, would you wear it?"

It doesn't sound like the proposal every girl dreams of, does it, honey? If I had been thinking of it, and planning, I would have prepared a pretty speech, but it just popped out as though it were the most natural thing in the world. Which it was, of course. I guess you and I didn't need words to tell about our feelings. And since we had long ago spoken of being married some day, it was only natural that we should become engaged.

July 5, 1942, in Camp Roberts: *I'm sitting on my bunk in nothing but my G.I. shorts and a T-shirt, because it's so doggoned hot. It's a good thing in some ways that you didn't stay any longer. I heard from someone that today it was 122 degrees in the shade. And it's supposed to be warmer tomorrow. How is it in the Detroit area? Most important, I do have good news for you. My furlough has been approved for the full fifteen days. And the first sergeant says I can tack on the three-days weekend pass at the end. Also, I'll just leave on Friday. The charge-of-quarters on that day will cover for me. All in all, it should be a great trip. See you on Saturday, honey.*

❦ 4 ❦

The Old CCC Camp

July 6, 1942, Marianne wrote about her summer job: *You remember that I had turned down an offer from a camp in Cheboygan, because I knew you would be coming home on your furlough? Well, when I got back from California I had a call from the director of the camp, asking if I'd consider a summer job nearer the city. It's the Methodist Children's Village, and it's on Six Mile Road about three miles west of Redford. They needed a recreation leader, she said, and she brought me out here to see the place. It really is wonderful. There's a park with a swimming pool nearby, and lots of trees and a creek in the village. There are five homes for the forty children, as well as a school and an administration building in front—that's where I live. The children are all "problem cases," sent here by the courts or some social agency. A lot of them seem to be victims of broken homes. My job is to keep them occupied throughout the day.*

I thought at first this would be sort of a nice vacation, because I'll be outside most of the day, and I'll have lots of exercise. But from what the social workers have told me I'll certainly have my hands full. Today went just fine though. We played games and went on a hike, and I had no trouble at all. Maybe they were on their good behavior. I took the job with the understanding that I will have four days off when you come home on your furlough.

John and Betty were home, and then I thought they were on their way to Norfolk, where he was to be stationed on the Wasp. *It's a new aircraft carrier,* he said. *But now your mother tells me they are going to San Diego, so maybe you can see them out there. I hope I have that story straight. P.S. You wanted to know if I'd have married you if you had asked me when we were in San Francisco. I'm not sure, dear, but I don't believe so. Being married is too important to do on the spur of the moment. I don't think we would like the kind of life where we'd be living together only a couple of days each week, never knowing how long that would last. You could be shipped out at any time. And even if I could get a job there, which is not a certainty, I don't think we'd have enough money to live on. We'd be much better off, I think, if I continued to live here, and to work here, saving our money for our happy life later. So I don't know what I would have said. Maybe I would have weakened. It was wonderful being with you for those few days in San Francisco. And I thank you for asking.*

After my first furlough, July 26, 1942: *I'm back again in California, and now as far away from you as ever. About the trip, there is not much I can say. You took the same trip, so you know what it is like. I made the train in Chicago with plenty of time to spare. When I got on, though, the train-man tried to steer me into an old rattletrap of a car, but I ignored him and looked around till I found a new stainless steel job with comfortable seats. Every once in a while, though, the air conditioning would go on the blink, and it would be hotter than hell. And I did get to see Cheyenne, when we stopped there for about an hour. I agree with you that it is a very interesting town. It was Frontier Day, and everyone was dressed in old-fashioned clothes. Quite a novelty.*

One strange thing happened that might make a good story, if I can find the time to write it. In the Chicago station a GI was saying a weepy farewell to his wife who was getting on the train. There was a lot of hugging and kissing. (I know they were married, because later on I saw the ring on her finger.) She was in the same car I was, and she was sitting next to a sergeant. That same night they too were hugging and kissing. And when the lights were turned off, there was a lot of interesting activity—and noise—going on in their seat! It looked as though various articles of clothing were being removed or pushed aside. When we arrived in Oakland, the two of them got off the train together and disappeared, walking hand in hand. Toward a hotel, I would imagine. So much for marital fidelity in this war-torn world.

I rode the train as far as San José, and then hitchhiked the rest of the way to the camp. I got here about seven hours before the time I was due, so the charge-of-quarters didn't need to fix anything up for me. As you can imagine, I really did hate to be back. We are in the middle of a heat wave, and it sure smacked me in the face. At that, I was lucky maybe, because the day before it was 127 in the shade—so they tell me.

My glasses aren't ready yet, so I'll just have to go without them for a week or so. And there are so many things I want to be reading, like the Minna von Barnhelm. *And today I found another book in the orderly room that was in German. It was a soldier's manual with a lot of vocabulary that might be helpful by and by, if they send me to Europe. I'll try to "borrow" it on a permanent basis. I doubt if any of the officers can read German or would miss it.*

The next day in Dearborn: *You are back in camp by now—3,000 miles away. It was wonderful to have you home for a while, darling. I enjoyed every minute we were together, especially bike riding in the park. It was so peaceful, and we could quite forget the war for a while. When I got back to the village, I found that my little friend Gerald had been misbehaving all weekend, and finally he and two friends left the village and started out hitchhiking to California. To find you, maybe. They were picked up at about midnight by the police. So he has spent this past week at the juvenile Detention Home. And I've had trouble with a lot of the others all week too. One kid hit another little fellow on the head, and he had to have three stitches taken. I'm sorry not to have written you sooner, but each night I'm too tired to do anything but fall into bed. There are twice as many children here now—and it keeps us twice as busy.*

Major changes at Camp Roberts, August 2, 1942: *I spent the last hour, dear, at the supply room looking through a huge pile of clothes for a pair of pants that would fit me, and also a good shirt and a cap. When I first came here—more than a year ago—they gave me 30/33 pants, when I needed 32/35. And I had been trying all that time to get them exchanged, without any success. I had just the one pair I could decently wear off the post. The others were too tight and too short. You remember that was why I bought the pair of trousers when we were in Frisco?*

And the reason I was able to exchange them today was that the troops moved out this afternoon and had to turn in all their summer clothes. You

81

might have some idea about where they are going when I tell you they were issued a mackinaw coat, and they took two wool blankets apiece with them. We don't know for sure, but one thing is certain—it's not North Africa! I hate to see them go, because all in all they were a pretty good lot.

And now about my new job. I start tomorrow, and it is supposed to be permanent—so, if I want to, I can be staying at Camp Roberts for the foreseeable future. Which will make you happy, I am sure. Earlier this week I got a call to go down to a certain building to see a Colonel Lawrence. He and a captain interviewed me, and asked a lot of questions about my present job—how I liked it, etc., and why I hadn't gone to the Officers' Candidate School at Fort Benning. I stayed only about five minutes, and they said would let me know what they had decided later.

I didn't know until yesterday what it was all about. Then a notice came down from the camp headquarters saying that I was attached to the I.O.P.S. I went back to see the colonel and was told what I will be doing. They have taken the NCOs' school, the Officer Candidates' school, and the refresher course for ROTC officers, and combined them into a single school under Colonel Lawrence. Someone told me that before the war he had been head of the ROTC unit at Michigan State. In our brief talks he didn't impress me as a military man, more like an arranger of things. I will be one of the instructors, the only one chosen, incidentally, from our battalion. There is a possibility that I will make sergeant, and anytime I decide to, he said, I can go to Fort Benning. The work will be harder, because we will be dealing with a much larger group, and with a lot of commissioned officers. So if you want to feel proud of your old man, I give you my permission to do so. I was also struck by the fact that this new organization is remarkably like the plan I had dreamed up only recently. And which I told you was probably an impossibility.

As soon as all the arrangements are made I'll move out to an old CCC [Civilian Conservation Corps] camp, about three miles north of here on the Nacimiento river. You might remember that you and I walked out there when you were staying at the Guest House. The big disadvantage is that it is so far away from the shows, the PX, and the bus depot. I imagine they will have trucks going in and out in the evenings. But until we move, the training will be in the 84th area, and I'll still be quartered here in B-76, with my friends. I sure hate to leave them, but then this was too good an opportunity to turn down.

And now some tough, tough news, darling. Because we are now engaged, I talked yesterday with the Catholic chaplain. He went on and on about the dangers involved in mixed marriages, and he kept asking questions about you. What kind of girl were you? How long had I known you? What sort of "crowd" did you "run around with?" As though you might be some dangerous loose woman. And he cited examples of Protestant girls who had had pre-marital sex with decent Catholic fellows. "Six months before they were married," he said. He stressed the things you and I have already talked about: I would be excommunicated if we were married by anyone but a Catholic priest; you must take lessons and promise to raise our children as Catholics; and no form of birth control could be used, even condoms. He pointed out that the states of Connecticut and Massachusetts had banned the sale of those devilish devices. There would be no compromises, he said. He wants you to talk with a priest in your area, and he will send you the name of one.

So there we are. We know the circumstances and the consequences, and we shall talk about them. In the end, I will marry you, come what may. I love you too much to give you up. It wouldn't hurt, though, if you did talk with the priest in Detroit.

Two days later: *I started work on my new job yesterday, and I think I am going to like it. I am an assistant to the instructor in tactics, which is both a difficult and an interesting subject. I needed to improve my knowledge in that phase most of all, so I volunteered for his class. It would give me a good background if I ever did decide to go to Benning. I plan to do a lot of reading about small-unit tactics as we go along.*

The next day in the Methodist Village: *I know I have been treating you badly, honey, not writing you the way I should. I'm kept so busy at work, typing plans until the middle of the night, that I don't have time even to think. I'm sorry if I worried you, which I'm sure I did. From now on I will try to stop everything at 9:30, so I can write you—and also get some sleep for a change.*

Your new job sounds wonderful. Congratulations! When you were at home and talked with your father, I had resigned myself to the fact that you would be going to officers' school and then leaving the country in a few months. But now it seems you might be staying on indefinitely. Your superior officers aren't so stupid after all.

I want to write you about your talk with the chaplain another time. It certainly isn't going to be easy to choose between mutually exclusive alternatives. It worries me that we have to make such an issue about what concerns just the two of us. Why do churches—the Catholics and the Lutherans—build up such intolerant walls that keep people apart? And require us to make promises we might not be able to keep? I'm going to talk to our pastor soon. He is very understanding and easy to talk to. But I think I know already what he will say. And I'd like to see the priest you mentioned, if you will send me his name. I haven't heard from your chaplain yet.

I'd better cut this short and say good night. It's almost 1:30, and I have to get up early. There's just too much to do around here. I think I have most of the children figured out and under control, and I get along pretty well with them. Except when it rains, which it did yesterday, cats and dogs. But I'll talk about that problem another time. Again, good night, dear. I love you very much.

More memories from Camp Roberts: *I kept thinking today about the time I met you at the bus depot in San Francisco, and you had been waiting so long, looking this way and that. Worried, you seemed. You were wearing your pink coat and the blue jumper you had made. And those crepe-soled shoes that I liked. You had just had your hair curled, the way I liked it. There was an aura about you, and I thought you were the most beautiful creature I had ever seen in my life. And then you were in my arms, and I didn't wanted to let you go.*

In Michigan, August 12, 1942: *A little while ago Miss Hatch and I drove in to the Redford police station to pick up a truant from the village. On the way back the air-raid siren sounded for the blackout throughout the Middle West. It was interesting the way brilliantly lighted Grand River was in total darkness and quiet in just about a minute. We had to pull over and park for half an hour until it was over.*

Everybody in the village has seen my engagement ring and admired it, even the janitor and both cleaning ladies. Little Billy Ewing asked if the soldier who had come out here to visit had given it to me. I said yes. "Gee, he sure must be awful rich," he said. *"Where does he get all that dough?"* By the way, dear, what is—or are—tactics?

A week later: *It's late and I'm awfully tired, sweetheart, so I'm just writing you another short letter before I go to bed. Let me explain. The kids were to have a play this evening, and it was quite cute and went off pretty well until about the middle of it, when there was a commotion in the audience. It seems that one little fellow had brought four frogs, and he set them down on the floor—to "get some exercise," he said. While they were jumping about they drew more attention than the play. All the actors on the stage screamed and stamped their feet because no one was watching them. It was all very confusing, and I finally had to send the boy and his frogs outside.*

And then after the play was over, no one wanted to go home. They all howled for more and whistled and tore around behind the stage and got grease paint on their faces, until I was ready to line them up against a wall and shoot them, one by one. I have just ten more days at this job, and I must say I will be happy to be back in peaceful Dearborn again. And back at Wayne. Besides, they are paying me only five dollars a week for all I'm doing. I guess they figure the "experience" will further my educational career.

From Camp Roberts, August 16, 1942: *Something funny happened the other day, though it was obviously not funny ha-ha to the person involved. Quite the contrary. It was shortly before I started my new job, and I was still with the trainees. When we fell out that morning all of us were told to roll up our sleeves, and the officers made an inspection of our arms and hands. We thought, naturally, that they were looking for some kind of skin disease, that might be contagious. We found out later that a young lady in the area had been raped by a soldier, and she had bitten and scratched her attacker on the arms. I never did hear whether they caught him or not. But it would have been awkward, to say the least, if some innocent fellow was found to have scratches that he could not account for. If the crime was committed on a government reservation, which Camp Roberts is, the penalty for rape could be death.*

You wrote me about the blackout there being "interesting." I think people in Detroit are too complacent about this war. A blackout is a game to them, and everybody has a lot of fun. They have no idea what a real emergency is like—people waiting for planes to come over and bombs to drop on them, the way we did in December right after Pearl Harbor. We were never bombed, but we expected to be. It's not a nice feeling to have. Detroiters should realize that their city is as close to Alaska as Los Angeles is. If the Japs ever took Alaska, I think Detroit would be bombed before Los Angeles. After all, our city is the center of the defense industries. The people there who are squabbling and not putting out enough weaponry and equipment should realize that the blue stars in their windows could easily turn into gold stars. I think the war in the Pacific is in our favor now—after the fighting at Midway. But the enemy has been in Alaska, and could come back. And a lot of boys will die before the Japs—and the Germans—are defeated. War is more than playtime blackouts.

More on the last day of August: *I had a letter from Dr. Basilius today. I had asked his advice about how to understand philosophers such as Plato, Kant, etc. Of course, he was pleased to be asked, and he said that Will Durant's* The Story of Philosophy, *while not a substitute for college courses, would give me a good start. I'm going to check out the library and see if they have a copy. If not, I think they might order it for me. Or I could buy it, of course. Wouldn't it be funny if your fiancé turned out to be a philosopher like Emmanuel Kant and the other thinkers we studied in German 105? And generations of the future might be talking about Quirk's Categorical Imperative!*

Leamington, Ontario, September 5, 1942: *For a week now I have been relaxing at the beach—swimming and lying in the sand. I must say I am not sorry to be finished with that job. It was vexing work, right up to the end. I know the kids had a lot of problems that were not their fault. But I was mighty tired of their cussing and quarreling all the time, and hearing about their sordid, mixed-up lives. I went out to the village with some idea of helping underprivileged children, but I ended up being bothered by everything. I guess I was never cut out to be a social worker.*

The next day in California: *You asked me about tactics. In the first place, like politics, it is considered a singular word. It is a subject that can be taught. Also it is always thought of in connection with strategy. Put simply, strategy is for generals and admirals, while tactics are what the underlings do to carry out the aims of the people at the top. At Midway, both the Americans and the Japanese aimed to destroy the enemy and to occupy territory.*

That was the grand strategy. And each side sent planes to bomb ships, particularly the aircraft carriers. Those sorties were the tactics. And I can give you a good example at the local level.

Two days ago, for our class, we set up a problem. The enemy was in control of a hill, and we formed squads of the trainees to try to capture it. It turned out that my squad was the fastest. I maneuvered the men and sent them up in short dashes, two at a time. Then we charged up with fixed bayonets. Obviously, we didn't really "capture" it. And no one was hurt. But what we were doing, at some time and another place, might pay off. And I can say that it was the most strenuous morning I've put in since I started my training a year ago. Running up hills is hard work, which is why the people on the top usually win. And why a lot of artillery ammunition is expended before the infantry does its business.

The new school year, September 8, 1942: *I had a swell time with my sorority sisters at the lake, but all the same it is nice to be home again. You really appreciate running water and bathtubs and toilets that are sanitary after being without them for a while. I think summer cottages were invented to make people thankful for the comforts of home. I have to start directed-teaching tomorrow morning, but classes at Wayne don't begin for about two weeks.*

You asked again about when we might be getting married, and I guess I feel the same way about it as before. I do wish it could be soon, but practically there are so many arguments against it. For instance, I've seen a lot of young women lately who have just had babies, or are about to have them, whose husbands are in the service. I think it is too bad for everyone involved, especially the babies. For me, being married is pretty important—important enough to wait a little while longer to insure our being together and being happy.

I've already read most of Durant's Story of Philosophy, *honey. Shirley had a copy, so I borrowed it from her. It was interesting, though I didn't understand or agree with some of the theories. I got a good laugh out of Schopenhauer's views of the woman's place in the world. He had a very sour opinion about the future of mankind. He said that the only hope for the male's development lay in the complete sublimation of his desires to the intellect. But this could never happen, because of the evil influences of women.*

To him all life was painful and futile, and if men could only exercise com-
plete control over their minds, there would be an end to senseless reproduc-
tion, and the human race would be extinguished. Amen! No wonder most
philosophers never get married. When you read the book, I suggest that you
just skip over Schopenhauer. He would give any thinking person the willies.
With that bit of advice, dear, I close this letter. I love you very much.

In camp, September 9, 1942: *I have read a couple of Shakespeare's*
plays lately, As You Like It *and* Twelfth Night. *I had never read either of*
them before, and they were very good. Hamlet *was the only one I was well*
acquainted with, though I had read The Tempest, *also in high school. Mrs.*
Cook at Eastern had me write a paper on a quotation from Hamlet: *"I am*
but mad north-north-west. When the wind is southerly, I know a hawk
from a handsaw." It was whether the prince was really mad or just pretend-
ing. And I still think he was pretending. That way I have more respect for
the Danish prince.

I have a book now of Shakespeare's comedies and one of the tragedies.
They're both paperbacks, so I can carry them with me if I'm transferred. His
plays are as true for us today, as they were in the 16th century. Some day I
hope we can have a library of all the great books, from Homer and Plato to
George Bernard Shaw and Upton Sinclair. But then we'd have to be mil-
lionaires, wouldn't we, dear?

A new semester, September 23, 1942: *I'm sorry I didn't write you yes-*
terday, on your birthday, but for some reason I wasn't feeling well. I was
woozy and couldn't eat anything. It seems that there has been a lot of that
sort of thing going around lately. I didn't register until Monday, the day
classes started, so I missed a couple days of teaching last week. I'm better now,
but already things seem to be piling up. I have a full schedule of classes this
year, but then I'm not going to be working at Wards or at the university, so
maybe it won't be too bad. These are my classes: Anatomy and Physiology
(cont.), Phonetics, Methods in Teaching, Student Teaching, Pathology of the
Speech and Hearing Organs (cont.), Methods in Teaching Speech Correc-
tion, and the Modern Novel. Total hours—19. I find that I have to take that
many hours to complete my major in education, if I hope to graduate in June.
Because I entered education late, remember. And I'll be carrying nineteen
hours next semester also. By the way, I've started on Lord Jim *for my Mod-*

ern Novel course. It's by Joseph Conrad. Have you ever read it? We will be reading a book each week this semester.

Word from California, September 28, 1942: *You certainly do have a tough schedule this year, honey. I hope that you can handle it all. Nineteen hours of classes is bad enough. But then you have your practice teaching in addition, a hard chore all by itself. I know you can do it, but try to get enough sleep and don't work too hard. It's not worth it if you injure your health. I have one request about your anatomy course—try to find out if women have one less rib than men, as Genesis seems to indicate. I have always wondered about that, and I meant to check it when you were out here, but I forgot.*

And about scientific discoveries, dear, the other day I figured out a way to follow a compass course at night, with no lights, and to go around hills while still keeping on the course. It turned out to be very simple, but none of the officers here had ever heard of it, including Lt. Fedderson, with whom I'm working now. They are going to incorporate it into the tactics course and try it out the next time we have a night maneuver.

More from California, October 4, 1942: *I'm sitting here on my roommate's bunk in a state of extreme dishabille—in fact wearing only my underwear and my socks. And why? you might ask. Well, Corporal Smiley took off yesterday on a five-day pass, so he won't know about it. Besides, the light is better on his side of the room. And best of all, I can listen to anything I like on his radio. I'm rather handicapped in that department when he is here. He doesn't like classical music, or care anything about the Michigan football games, which is a backward way of looking at the world, to say the least. Pretty soon, though, I'll be getting the Hallicrafter from home, and it has earphones. I can listen to anything I please, without bothering anyone. Mostly, though, I need to listen to the short-wave stations, so I can keep up with what foreign stations are saying about the war.*

That novel course must be quite a grind. Reading a book every week, with all the other courses, is a bit much. I can see how you could do it—physically—but how could you appreciate it? I can see a student reading it at the last minute, skipping large sections. Do you have any choice in your readings, or does the professor just assign them to you? If it's possible, you might read The Big Money *by John Dos Passos. I think it's one of the best of all modern novels. Every thinking American should read it.*

89

I was dreaming daydreams and building air castles the other day. What if we finally do get settled down at the CCC camp? I might be staying here indefinitely. Especially if I made staff or technical sergeant. Then I could live off the post and draw ration and rent money. So—what is to prevent us from getting married? After you are graduated, of course. And provided you could get a job in the Paso Robles school system. I'd be drawing about $150 a month, and you'd have a salary. And the government is putting up houses. Also you have a car for transportation. I know it is all so iffy—and a long way off. But why not talk about it, and make plans, even if they are tentative? The main thing is that we would be together, which is what we both want, more than anything in this world. Tell me, dear, what you think of my ideas?

There's no word yet about when we are moving to the CCC camp, but when we do, I'm going to send for my photographic equipment. They are going to build me a darkroom out there, and I will be taking pictures and enlarging them for the school. Lt. Fedderson says there are many possibilities for us to do good work with photographs as teaching aids. We could make something very important of it, he said. And also it would be fun for me to be doing it.

A reply from Dearborn, October 10, 1942: *Your plans about being married next summer sound very nice, darling. Wouldn't it be wonderful if things could come out the way we have hoped. I think when two people are as much in love as we are, they should be married as soon as they can. But there are a lot of things to be considered first, even in times such as these— especially in times such as these. I know, with conditions as they are, you can't expect that anyone could settle down normally. But unless the two people can be together, what's the point in being married? Is two or three days together being truly married, if they are followed by long separations that cause more sorrow and unhappiness than ever? It's all right for people to say they are grabbing their happiness while they can. It sounds romantic. But too many, I think, are being shortsighted, as though the war were the end of all things. The most important part of their marriage will be after the war. They need to plan more, not less. Some of the finest feelings can turn bad, if there are too many bumps in the road ahead.*

When I first went out to see you last summer, I met a lot of the wives and talked with them. And I began to wonder, because most of them were unhappy. They complained about the climate, the prices of things, the conditions they lived under. They might better have been at home, because they weren't making their husbands happier or helping their marriage. When you love someone so very much, you want that person to be contented. And not thinking about the consequences of what you are doing is both selfish and harmful.

So thank you again, dear, for asking me. And I really do look forward to being married as soon as possible. But first I want to finish school, to graduate, and then to have a real job that will give us an income and some stability. I won't have any trouble being placed in Detroit or Dearborn. I'm sure of that. But I doubt if I can say the same about Paso Robles. I can come out and stay with you for the summer, and you will be coming home on your furloughs. And the war will not last forever. Things are looking better month by month on the battle-fronts. I'm glad you feel you will be staying at the I.O.P.S. for a good long time now. That gives us a kind of stability. And by the way, dear, what do those letters stand for?

I'm glad you understand about my course load this semester. It's a good deal heavier than I thought it would be. There just don't seem to be enough hours in the day anymore. Practice teaching is what is taking so much of my time. Plus the novels class. It takes me so long to get home after my night classes, and by the time I've finished my plans for the next day, it's after midnight. So I just collapse into bed. I find that too much of my work is doing crazy things, like cutting out soldiers to illustrate arithmetic problems. Now my class is giving a play, so last week I was making monkey faces and tails. And I wondered why mothers don't take on those jobs to help the teachers.

Don't worry about me, though. If I think I'm carrying too many hours, I'll just drop a course or two. But then I wouldn't finish in June, would I? And I'd have to make it up by taking courses in the summer. And that makes more difficulties. If Wayne should adopt the trimester system, would there be any summer classes? So I guess I'll just have to work harder and more efficiently, if that is possible. And if I don't write you for a week or two, you will understand my dilemma. Good night dear. I love you very much.

A week later: *Last Friday Ellen and I went out to see Father Keating, and he was one of the swellest men I have ever met. He's a jolly Irishman, with curly black hair and snapping dark eyes, and he spoke to me in German—he's much better in the language than I'll ever be. He said he had only a few minutes, but then he talked to us for more than two hours. He didn't tell me anything altogether new, though he was very understanding and sympathetic and made things very plain. He showed me some forms I would have to sign if we were to be married by a priest. And he said there were two promises I would have to make: 1. That I would never attempt to influence your beliefs. And 2. That our children would be brought up in the Catholic faith.*

I asked him if that wasn't pretty difficult, even for a mother with the best of intentions. The children couldn't help being influenced by my background, which is German and Lutheran. He agreed, but he said it was up to us to choose godparents who are good Catholics, and it would be their duty to see that we kept our promises. On the matter of birth control, dear, he said that was entirely your responsibility—which both Ellen and I interpreted as leaving a way out for us, without his actually having said that. A matter of the confessional, Ellen said. Only a venial sin. Saying ten "Hail Marys" would take care of it each time, she thought. Whatever that means. He did say, though, that birth control had brought about the ruin of nations where it was practiced.

About our plans for marriage, he thought we were wise to wait at least until I graduated. He had been discouraging war marriages, he said, because he had seen so much heartbreak and disappointment. And in general, he told us, he opposed mixed marriages, but he was quite sure you and I would work things out. I'm glad I talked to him, but it's clear that we are no closer to a solution to our problem.

From California, October 27, 1942: *I finally learned why John is back in the States. He was on the* Wasp, *the aircraft carrier that was sunk by the Japs in the Solomon Islands. That brings the war pretty close to home, doesn't it? Everybody will be grateful that he survived. About 90 percent of the crew were saved, which was remarkable. I called him last Saturday, but we didn't get to talk much. Of course, he didn't say why he was in San Diego, because at the time the Navy hadn't released the news. He did say he would* call me later, but so far I haven't heard from him. I'm going to see if I can get a weekend pass to go down to his base. I would like to get the lowdown on his experiences, while they are still fresh in his mind.

I.O.P.S. You asked, dear, what those letters stand for. I should have told you before this. It's the Infantry Officers' Pool School, an awkward way of saying we do a lot of different things with different groups. But mostly we deal now with officers who need some kind of additional training. I'm still in the main camp, but the word is that we'll be moving between the first and the fifteenth of November. But knowing how the army operates, I don't guarantee that.

An order came down this week that all officers who have been here a year will be replaced as soon as possible. Lt. Fedderson has been trying to leave for some time, and now he thinks he is going soon. I hope not, because he and I work well together, and he is really a swell guy. And we've had such great plans for our classes, once he and I get settled. I don't know where they will find an officer who can fill his shoes. Not around here, certainly.

He wants to take a ten-day leave before he is transferred, so he told Col. Lawrence that I would be able to handle his classes, if necessary. I don't know whether I could or not, but I have heard his lecture so many times, I could do a passable job, I think. Anyway, it is flattering that he thinks I could teach tactics to officers, because it is such an important subject. It's what wins wars. I'm going to ask him if I could give one of his lectures in a couple of days. It's on the Principles of War, and I have been collecting materials on the subject for some time—going back to Hannibal and the Battle of Cannae in 216 B.C. I'll let you know if I get a chance to do it. Sometimes I think I ought to be a historian. History is the basis of everything we know.

For the past week or so I have been working on sand-table problems. Lt. Fedderson gave me a lot of diagrams of different types of terrain, and I set them up on the table. I made powder from various colors of chalk and sprinkled it on the sand to give the appearance of ground. Green chalk for grass, etc. And I cut up pieces of sponge and stuck them into the sand with pins to represent trees. I also dyed some acorns green to be pine trees, and pieces of Spanish moss to be oaks. After I was finished the whole thing was so realistic, hills, woods, rivers, towns, and all. Even railroad tracks. Then we carried the table outside and I took photos of it from all angles. We are going to *use them in a slide projector to teach tactics—that is, when it is raining, and we have to have our classes indoors. I like this sort of work. It is interesting and useful, but also a lot of fun for me.*

In Dearborn, October 31, 1942: *Yes, honey, I heard your brother was on the* Wasp *when it sank. I'm certainly glad that he got off safely, and I know your folks are relieved too. It was an ill-fated ship, wasn't it? After being reported sunk once before, and scaring everyone to death. When I saw the headlines Monday night, it gave me an eerie feeling. It must have been the same for you, dear. But the important thing, of course, is that he is back safely.*

Jane has been worrying about her son Bill for some time. He has really been in the thick of things since the war began. On December 7 he was at Pearl Harbor. And then he was in the Battle of Midway and has been in the Solomons for several months. He is on the repair ship, I think, that saved the Wasp *crew, Jane said, which is a wonderful coincidence. Belle has moved to California with her two boys to be closer to Bill. I think they will like the climate better out there. I'll try to get her address so you can look her up, if you have the opportunity.*

Miracle of miracles, today I got my license to drive! I drove a big, fat policeman around, and I didn't have any trouble at all. (With getting the license, that is.) I was really surprised. I could hardly park the car before, even when I had the entire block free. But he had me pull in—backing up—between two cars that were parked close together. And lo and behold I did it! Actually, I won't have much use for the car now, with gas rationing starting in a month. Mostly I'll be taking the bus, as before. But the car will come in handy if Jane and I are home alone, and we need to go somewhere. Besides, my father won't have to do the shopping in the morning before he goes to work. He has so little time to himself these days. He works such long hours at the Ford plant.

I hope you get the chance to take your lieutenant's place for a while. I have no doubts whatever that you can handle it. Your work does sound pretty soft, though, if all you do is sit and cut up rubber sponges to make trees. I guess being in the army isn't as tough as it's supposed to be, dear. It sounds like the sort of things I do for my classes. Today I made a cardboard movie machine for my reading class.

On becoming the gambler, November 2, 1942: *I started a letter last night, but some of the corporals were playing a game of poker in my room, and they inveigled me into joining them. At first I begged off. I told them I didn't know how to play. But they kept pushing me, insisting that they would show me how. It's easy, they said. Well, I thought maybe I could join them for a few hands, anyway, and then write the letter later. If they were willing to take my money, thinking I was a greenhorn, I would try my luck. Well, to make a long story short, I took them to the cleaners, as we say, to the tune of $4.65. Which is not a bad night's work for a corporal, considering that I was in the hole several times. And I did teach them a lesson in poker. All those Saturday-night sessions with the fellows on Helen Avenue, and figuring percentages, were paying off.*

There is another game going on right now, and they are trying to get me in, to see if they can win back at least some of their money. But this time I'm resisting. I wonder sometimes if the others don't have girlfriends or a family they need to keep in touch with. If they're not playing cards or shooting craps, they are off the base somewhere. Of course, yesterday was payday, and later in the month they may not have the wherewithal. There wasn't as much card playing when I was working in the 76th. We'll see.

From home, November 5, 1942: *I had an anatomy class this evening, but I cut it and came home to write you a letter. I seem to be writing you so seldom lately. I can see you shaking your head and hear you clucking your tongue, but it's really the first time I've missed a class this year. A university class, that is. I just didn't think I could stand to listen to a dull lecture about the platysma and the auricular supinus tonight. Why can't scientists speak plain English? We have a new fellow this semester—a doctor from one of the hospitals. And he has the rare knack of making a boring subject seem even more boring. He sits and talks into his mustache all evening and never knows—or cares, I think—who's there anyway. Really, Bob, I have never worked so hard as I have this semester. I don't think I knew what work was before. It's something that is grinding me down. I have dark circles under my eyes so deep I could get a good job—I think—haunting a house.*

I had a very nice dinner at your folks' house last Sunday, dear. They are all looking just fine. They don't know anything about John yet, except that he is well and in San Diego. Evidently he can't say much about his experiences. You will be glad to hear that I drove my car all the way to the East side through all kinds of traffic, without running down any old ladies. So there is hope yet that I will turn out to be a competent driver. Your dad constantly amazes me, Bob. He seems to have a general knowledge of everything, no matter what you are talking about. I've been studying speech defects for more than a year, but I think he knows more about the subject than I do. It's no wonder he has such a smart son.

News from California, November 8, 1942: *Well, honey, I finally got to see John and Betty. I didn't go to LA after all, because they stopped here on their way to Seattle where he is going to join the USS* Idaho. *It's one of the older battleships and is scheduled to be re-gunned for use in the Aleutians, he says, so he could be there a while. It's kind of a secret, though, so don't let any of this go farther than yourself. Not even to your family or mine. He and Betty were here for two days and stayed in Paso Robles at the Taylor Hotel. Does that name bring back fond memories, honey?*

One surprising thing I found out was that he was never on the Wasp. *He was on another ship on his way to catch up with the carrier, when she was sunk. In a way I'm disappointed, because I had been wanting to hear firsthand information about what must have been an exciting adventure. But of course, we can all be thankful that he is safe and sound. And he did have a lot of stuff to tell me, none of which I can put on paper. I can say, though, that when he left the Academy, he worked at a very confidential job at Pearl Harbor. He sure knows the ins and outs about what goes on in the Navy's high places.*

I stopped writing a minute so I could hear Frank Nunn sing the "Lullaby" from "Jocelyn," which is one of the most beautiful songs I have ever heard in my life. It made chills run up and down my spine. I had a feeling that you and I were suddenly brought closer together. And it gave me an idea—that we should keep a list of great music as it occurs to each of us, so we won't forget. You can be the caretaker, if you will. For a start I suggest the "Lullaby," as well as Handel's "Largo" and Bizet's "Agnes Dei." Nothing but the best. And then, when the war is over, we can put the records on the automatic changer and listen to them to our heart's content—while we are sitting before a warm fire. Wonderful eh?

From the news we got last night and today about the Allied invasion of North Africa, it may not be so very long before you and I are home together.

With the start of a "Second Front," the Allies for the first time are on the offensive. It will be a hard fight, in Europe and in the Pacific, but we can say—definitely—that we are on the road to victory.

You remember the poker game I told you about last week, honey? Well, the great thing is that all the money is in change. So now I can call you. Is early Sunday morning OK with you? Six o'clock out here. If I wait too long, the lines are usually busy. And if you don't hear from me on time, or don't hear at all, don't worry. I won't be sent anyplace for a while yet. But it's been increasingly difficult to get private calls through, that's all. I'll keep trying.

Follow-up news the next day in Dearborn: *Maybe you read out there that Wayne had won it's first football game of the season, defeating Akron 25–6. They didn't do any worse than usual this year, considering there are no grown men left on the squad. Verne Gibson was inducted a couple of weeks ago, and he was sent to a camp in Missouri. I can get his address, if you want it. Bob Swarthout is still here somewhere. The last I heard, he was driving a D.S.R. bus. In order to get some "sociological background," he said. That's according to Ruth Coulter, my sorority sister, who went with him for a while. It certainly sounds like Bob, doesn't it?*

On moving, November 19, 1942: *We are getting ready to move to the CCC camp this weekend, and everything is at sixes and sevens. It will certainly be a relief to have all of the school facilities right at hand, and I won't have to walk so far to and from work each day. One thing I want to do right away is to put up a long aerial for the short-wave radio. I'll have to buy some wire in Paso Robles. I also have an old two-tuber that I put together a long time ago. It runs on batteries. I'm going to work on it, if I have spare time, that is. In case we had any blackouts, for example.*

Here's some news about the faculty: A new lieutenant and a captain have been taking Lt. Fedderson's classes the last couple of days, and they sure don't know their you-know-whats from the proverbial holes in the ground. You can see puzzled looks on the faces of the students. I could do better, as I've been telling you, and the colonel knows it. But his hands are tied, so I just wince and try to look the other way. Sometimes the students ask me about something an instructor has said, but I can't just come right out and tell them it's a bunch of bullshit. I sure hope Lt. Fedderson doesn't ship out very soon. This school would be in bad trouble for a tactics instructor. And one last thought: If a corporal can do the work well, the government could save a heck of a lot of money by shipping out the officers.

Dearborn, November 22, 1942: *Our church had a Sunday School convention this afternoon, and my class was asked to give a demonstration lesson. Afterwards I got two offers by pastors for jobs in the Lutheran parochial schools. I thanked them, but said "no," because I'm eager to finish school and get my degree. You can see how bad the teacher situation has got to be, with so many men away in the services. Besides, the Lutheran Schools don't pay very much, and their standards are a lot lower, according to kids who have been transferred. I hope you have a nice Thanksgiving, and I wish I could be with you to celebrate a very important second anniversary.*

A new home, November 23, 1942: *Well here we are, finally, in the CCC camp, honey. It's really not a bad place at all, though it is run down. And there are many inconveniences, such as cold water for shaving and for showers. It gives you quite a thrill on a cool morning. On the credit side is the food. So far, the chow has been the best I've eaten since I've been here in California. I've stowed so much away in the past couple of days, that if I keep it up I'll actually get fat. Well, pretty fat, anyway. The water too is much better—from a well and not chlorinated. All in all, the culinary problems seem to be solved.*

The buildings are all old deserted barracks, and not in too good repair. They are heated (?) by wood or coal stoves. The beds and mattresses are CCC leftovers—too short for a grown man, unless he is a feather-merchant size. I find I have to sleep catty-cornered and not turn over too suddenly in the night. Otherwise, they are comfortable enough. As of now, I sleep in a barracks with the trainees, instead of a small room, like I had in the main camp. So it is all pretty rude. But I guess I can get used to it. And the pleasures of eating in the mess hall will more than make up for any amount of discomforts.

On the phone you asked me what CCC meant, and I forget to tell you. It's Civilian Conservation Corps, and was started up by the New Deal to provide work opportunities for young fellows during the Depression. I think, when the war is over, it should be made permanent. It was really a fine idea.

Thanksgiving on the home front: *I wanted to write you on Thursday, dear, our anniversary, but I was so busy all that day and the next. I* went to church in the morning and then came home to help Jane get the dinner. It wasn't so much like a holiday at our house, because there were only the three of us this year. We did have a roast turkey, though. My father had won a live bird in a raffle at the Catholic church. I arranged to be someplace else when he cut its head off, because there's so much flopping around. And then, while we were eating, your mums arrived to make it more like Thanksgiving. Such a big box, and so lovely. Thank you, thank you, thank you. Did you win another poker game, dear? P.S. Tell me more, honey, about what you do now at the I.O.P.S. Anything besides giving talks and showing movies? Are you helping teach men who are going to be commissioned officers? I'm not quite clear about that.

A week later: *Did I tell you that I had got an A in teaching at the Marr school? My critic was supposed to be an old picklepuss, who never gave high marks, so I must say that it's more of an accomplishment than usual. And while I'm bragging, dear, I can tell you that I got the highest grade on both my Pathology and my Phonetics mid-semesters. So maybe all the studying I've been doing lately is not in vain. I have to confess, though, that I'm not doing so well in the novels course. I haven't read* The Big Money *yet, and I keep falling behind. The last thing I read was* For Whom the Bell Tolls. *Have you read that one, dear?*

By the way, I will be handing in my forms for Detroit or suburban placement this month or the next. That way, I may have a job by June or July. I'm going downtown tomorrow afternoon to have my picture taken for the placement records. So I'll be washing my hair in a little while before I go to bed. Or maybe I should stop at the beauty parlor in the morning, so I'll look more like a grown-up teacher!

An explanation about the I.O.P.S., December 11, 1942: *You asked me what I do at the I.O.P.S. In a way it is difficult to say specifically. There are so many things, and often at the spur of the moment the colonel has me do something for him. Officially, I am Lt. Fedderson's assistant. He has all the tactics and terrain-appreciation courses. I've mentioned them before, I think. So when he needs charts for a particular class, I have to see that they get to the room on time, and that they are hung up in front of the trainees as he needs them. In one way, I suppose, that makes me a stooge or a lackey. But there's more to it than that. If we have a demonstration, I have to organize and take care of the demonstrating group, and see that everything goes off smoothly.*

For instance, tomorrow we have a class in the advance guard. I'll take a group out early and give them blank ammunition and place them in a position where they can fire on another group coming down the road. And that group has to "seek cover," as we say, and then report back. Also, when we need blanks, I take regular shells and replace each bullet with a wax plug. It's an invention of my own, the way I make them, and they are pretty good blanks, if I do say so myself. Then, after that class is over, I'll have to give the second-week group its weekly exam. The lieutenant trusts me to prepare the questions and to grade the officers. It's somewhat like graduate assistants at the university, I would think. And the testing involves quite a bit more, because I must be able to answer their questions about tactics. And so far no one has stumped me. I do have to keep busy, though, reading books and manuals on the subject.

Yesterday, I had to lay out a compass course for the men to follow last night. Often we are busy until almost midnight. And there is more. I have to take charge of each new group as it comes into barracks four and then leaves in a couple of weeks or so. And I keep the records for the 19th increment of trainees, the current group. For that I am working in Colonel Lawrence's office. All this keeps me busy, as you can imagine. But I love my work, and I think it is an important part of the war effort.

No, I never did read For Whom the Bell Tolls *in its entirety, honey. And right now I am too busy. But I hope to some day, especially the parts about the sleeping bag and "the earth shook."*

This and that in Dearborn, December 13, 1942: *I'd like to write you a long letter tonight, but as always these days, I have so much to do. Sometimes I wonder if I will ever catch up. There are several papers that are due before the holidays, and an inspector is coming this week from the national office to check over our sorority's records. As secretary/treasurer, I need to bring those up to date. Maybe I'll have a chance to write you during the next few days. I hope so, anyway.*

The same day in California: *I have been listening, dear, to "Album of Familiar Music," and just now Phil Spitalny's all-girl orchestra is finishing the piano concerto of Edvard Grieg. I think it is wonderful. Do you want to add it to our list? It must be getting pretty long by now.*

I worked all yesterday afternoon putting up an aerial for my radio—it's about 200 feet long, and it surely makes a big difference in my reception. This evening I have been listening to Japan, Germany, England, and Russia—to their English-language broadcasts. And on long wave, stations roll in loud and clear, from Chicago to New Orleans and from Mexico to Calgary. There is hardly any static or interference out here at the CCC camp. It's so far away from major electrical devices. Listening to the foreign broadcasts will serve me in good stead if they ever do ask me to talk again about current events.

Christmastide in Dearborn: *I spent a busy day washing and polishing my furniture and moving it around, and then wrapping the last of my Christmas presents. I'm afraid the long letter I was going to write you will not be so long after all. I'm awfully tired, and I'd probably fall asleep with the pen in my hand. I'll write for a while, and then finish up in the morning. Your presents arrived earlier this week, and when we have a tree, I'll put them under it. My dad usually waits until Christmas eve to buy one, because it is cheaper that way. But if he is working late, as he might be, it could be after midnight before he puts it up. I've shaken the package you sent, and smelled it, but I have no idea what it might be. Your mother says she already knows, though she didn't drop any hints, so I'll just have to wait until Christmas.*

More at the end of the year: *Thank you so much, dearest, for the lovely pearls. I was certainly surprised. I have always admired pearls, especially with a simple dress. And these are perfect. I will cherish them all my life. I had a very happy birthday too, thanks to you. The red roses were so beautiful. They came just before dinner, and they gave our house such a festive look. And Jane says thank you, also. I've been nursing them along with aspirin and cold water, so they should last for a long while. I wish, dear, that we could be together in these days, but I know that is impossible. So I will send you all my love vicariously, and pray for peace on this earth. Again, thank you for everything. I love you so much. P.S. I think I'll begin the new year by looking seriously for a job. Now that I am 21, I can't let my father continue paying the bills I run up. Because I have been carrying an overload of classes, and all of the other things I am required to do to get my degree, I have been unable to earn any money. He has been very generous, and for Christmas and my birthday he bought me a black chesterfield to go with the red suit you have never seen. Also he has given me money to buy things for school as I need them. It's about time, I've decided, to start standing on my own feet. Again, thank you, dear, for the pearls. I love them. And you too.*

A day later: *Yesterday evening I was on my way to see your folks when something awful happened. My dad had been telling me not to drive at night, but I had been doing pretty well. So I just started out and was within a few blocks of your house. East Grand Boulevard is wide, but it's not well lighted. I was nearing your neighborhood, watching the side streets for Agnes or St. Paul. And I was going very slowly, reading the street signs, when a man pulled out in front of me, and I smacked him in the rear. On my car I smashed the grill and one of the headlights. The man apologized, but I felt that it was my fault, because I hit him from behind. After that, I just wanted to go home, so I turned around and drove back to Dearborn. I haven't driven since, and the way I feel, I may never drive again. And my father has to pay the bill. He didn't complain, but I could see he was unhappy with me.*

At Camp Roberts: *I've had a pretty nice Christmas, dear Marianne, but as Iphigenie reminds us, it's a lonesome place out here. Thank you for the wallet and the scarf. But most of all for your photograph. It's the best picture of you I have ever seen, so beautiful and life-like. I suppose I don't say it enough, or maybe I take it for granted, but you are the nicest, the most wonderful person I have ever known. Thank you again. How long did it take you to knit the scarf, honey? It's a masterpiece! I never knew you had so many skills.*

A present from John and Betty arrived today. It was Ulysses *by the Irishman James Joyce. I looked through it, but I didn't get much that was coherent out of it. I suppose you've heard about the book, maybe in your modern-novels course. The critics say it's a classic, and it is supposed to portray the jumbled and mixed-up life of the twentieth century. So he does that in a jumbled way. Boy, is it ever mixed up! But since I took that literature course at Eastern High with Mrs. Cook I have always believed that the author owes it to the reader to put his message into understandable English. And then to portray the mess we are in, if he wants to. He doesn't need to use those four-letter words in every other sentence to show that people talk that way. They don't, even in the army, with that profusion. And I doubt if the Irish do either. I'm not a prude, as you know. But shocking people just for an effect, to me is not literature. If I'm ever shipped out, I'll send it home to you. It's a pretty heavy load to carry around in my duffle bag. And after the war I might find time to read the whole book to see if I have changed my mind.[6]*

It won't be long, dear, until 1942 is just a memory. And though for all but a few weeks of it we have been apart, in a way it has been the best year of our lives. I think that I have grown, in ability and in outlook, and that I am a better person, for myself and for the world. And I think I am doing a good job here at the camp. I hope that this next year will bring an end to the war and a beginning for our life together.

We are going to have a practice alert late this evening. The men won't be told about it beforehand, so it will come as a surprise for them. Everyone will be going to a special predesignated area. The colonel asked me to check it out this afternoon, and I cut down all the barbed wire in the way, so no one would fall over it in the dark. I don't think we will ever have a real alert here. The Japs will never get this close. Once they might have—in the weeks just after Pearl Harbor. But not now. At least I hope so.

Goodnight and Happy New Year, dear, dear Marianne. I love you very much. A year from now perhaps we shall be married.

---

6. And after sixty years I still haven't found the time—or the wish—to read it.

ℬ 5 ℬ

A Corporal's Duties

From the CCC camp, January 1, 1943: *Here it is, the start of a new year—the second that you and I have been apart. And even though we are apart again, the prospects of being together look better all the time. Twelve months ago both of us made resolutions, mostly to write more often. And though we had our difficulties there, as I go through the stack of your letters to reminisce I have to say that we have not done badly. It's always a pleasure to reread them and to remember and relive the wonderful times. In this year I'd like to write at least two or three times a week. If I set up a schedule of writing on Sundays, Tuesdays, and Fridays, it ought to work out just fine.*

Night before last, Sam Hopkins took me outside and had me look through his binoculars at the planet Jupiter. I could see four of its moons, all in a row on the left side. It was an impressive sight, because they are not visible to the naked eye, and I had never seen them before or known they could be seen. I looked for them again last night, and two had moved to the other side. Hopkins has a book on astronomy he brought with him, and he is going to tell me about the various stars. Because our camp is so far from lights, he says, it's a fine place to observe the night sky.

"Black Velvet Sky." I showed Sam the poem I wrote for you, and he thought it was pretty good. "First-rate," was how he put it. "You must really love her," he said. And he let me read some poetry by T. S. Eliot. Sam says he is going to memorize "The Love Song of J. Alfred Prufrock." I asked

105

him why, and he said because it was a challenge. It's why people climb mountains, he said. And do other difficult things. We talked all evening about it, and I could see what he meant. Anyone could commit a sonnet with fourteen lines to memory. But the Eliot work was long and craggy and hard at times to comprehend. I wondered, though, if it was a "good" poem. The first lines, for example, bothered me. For some reason they reminded me of the Joyce novel.

Something was wrong with the meter, I said. "Let us go then, you and I, when the evening is spread out against the sky." The words "the evening is spread out" seem awkward. In fact the whole poem is rickety. It seems he is just finding some rhymes and throwing a lot of words together. But Sam said I shouldn't be looking for iambic pentameters and other ancient line schemes in our time. How about beauty? I asked him. Where is it in this poem? Or love? There is no evidence that Prufrock loved anyone. That's what Eliot was rebelling against, Sam said. Romanticism. And that's what I'm for, I said. Otherwise poetry has no heart. We talked until after midnight and agreed the first chance we had we would take a long hike together. I feel so fortunate to have someone like Corporal Hopkins to talk to.

The same day in Dearborn: *It's been a very sleepy sort of day. My father worked—as did almost everyone we know, and he and Jane are asleep in the living room, both of them fagged out by all the late-night doin's. Thank you again for the lovely pearls and the little poem you sent about the "black velvet sky." It makes me look at the night in a totally different way. And I am very glad you liked the muffler and the billfold. I really did knit the muffler, as you probably noticed from the mistakes I made. When I started I thought it would take me maybe a week, but that week turned into four, and at the end I was very rushed. Part of the time I took it to my night classes to work on during lectures, so even my professors have an interest in keeping you warm.*

I'll never forget the evening I took it to Kay and Bill's, and before I knew it his mother, who is Scottish and knits all the time, was pulling it all out. When I asked her what she was doing, she said she had seen a dropped stitch way back. I didn't tell her it had taken more than a week to do that much. But she knitted it up again that very night. It took her maybe an hour. So you can thank her too for a big part of your Christmas present.

I spent a quiet New Year's Eve at home, finishing The Big Money, *while Sarah typed some of her homework. We celebrated with a couple of highballs, but I found I didn't much care for them. I prefer a Vernor's or a Coke—without the whiskey. And I do like peach brandy and most wines. I have to say that I never would have finished the book, if I hadn't had to read it for my class. I found it hard going, and I certainly didn't enjoy it. I know you are going to tell me I'm an ostrich and like to stick my head in the sand, the way you did one day at the Cass-Warren when we were talking about* The Grapes of Wrath. *But I just don't think this sort of people are worth writing a novel about. I'll admit, though, that it is a very effective book. And the author certainly didn't leave very much to the imagination, did he?*

Camp Roberts business, January 6, 1943: *I'm not doing too well about writing you so far, am I, dear? I've been cleaning rifles a good part of the day, and yesterday I was at the firing range with my friends in B Company. I ended up by shooting 49 out of a possible 50 in rapid-fire sitting—the best I have ever done, in fact. If I had been firing for record I'd have made expert. I was trying some new ideas about marksmanship Col. Lawrence had told me about, and I'm sure it helped a lot. He and I have been talking together a lot these days. He seems more like a professor than an army officer.*

It's too bad, darling, that you dented up your car, and I am greatly disappointed that you quit driving. If I had been there I would have made you turn right around and drive back to my folks' house, whether you wanted to or not. It's no good being a quitter just because you had one accident. And from what you say, it was probably his fault anyway. You know, in any profession, when people make a mistake, they are forced to do it over again. If a pilot wrecks a plane, he goes right back up. That's the only way to cure it. I hope by now that you have started again. You said you had been helping Jane with the shopping. And you will be needing the car, I am sure, when you are practice-teaching, won't you?

It's hard to realize, dear, that you are now twenty-one years old. It seems to me as though you must still be the same age you were when I first met you. But now I look at the picture you sent me and compare it with the ones from before I came in the army, and I realize that you are a mature woman and not a girl anymore. I guess both of us have grown up quite a bit in the past two years. And I like us better this way—don't you? And now you can vote.

107

That's something to really be proud of. Be sure you are registered, dear, before the next elections.

Remembrances in Dearborn, January 10, 1943: *I was looking through some of your letters today, and before I knew it I had spent almost two hours reading them again. I wouldn't give them up for anything. They are the link between us during the year and a half we've been apart. It is interesting to see how they have changed. At first we wrote about the year you'd be away, and then about my trip to see you. And now both of us seem more confident, more grown-up maybe. And our future looks brighter, as the Allies seem to be doing so much better. Perhaps the war will be over sooner than we thought.*

A week later: *I haven't done any driving since Christmas night, honey. The driving had never bothered me before. But after I hit the man's fender, driving back across town on the way home I was conscious of every car on the road, and I worried so about what everyone was going to do. By the time I got home I was almost a physical wreck. I haven't had any inclination to get behind the steering wheel since then. Damaging a car isn't so bad. Dents can be fixed. But I think if I ever hurt someone badly I'd never get over it. It would haunt me for the rest of my life. I realize that isn't a sensible way to feel—especially when you see some of the dumb bunnies that are out loose on the roads driving every day.*

The night I got back, my dad and Jane's brother, Uncle Bob, tried to make me take the car out again. They said the same things you told me in your letter. But I was too glad to be home—safely—I just couldn't. One of these days, though, I will drive again, when it is spring time and the ice and snow are gone. And maybe you will be sitting beside me in the front seat, giving me confidence.

More from Dearborn, January 17, 1943: *It's Sunday evening, and I think I will turn in early for a change. I've been reading all day to catch up with my modern novel class. I just finished* Fame Is the Spur *by Howard Spring. I thought it was quite a good book, and I got a lot out of it. I think you would like it too, honey. Now I have two more to read before final exams—*Darkness at Noon *by Arthur Koestler and* Only One Storm *by Granville Hicks. They are both about the communists, I think. If you were to read them too, we could have an interesting discussion by mail. What about that? Besides the books, I have a paper to write, so maybe I spoke too* *soon when I patted myself on the back about keeping up in my classes. I'm not doing as well now as I was at the beginning of the semester.*

Some time ago you asked me about coming out to California to marry you next summer, and I'm sorry I didn't answer you sooner, dear. I couldn't say "yes," because there were so many "ifs." And I didn't want to pour cold water on our dreams. Anyway, if we talk about it now, maybe you will know the answers—you usually do. In the first place, I've found that California requires teachers to go to school in their state for a year before teaching there. And I doubt whether they would hire speech clinicians in children's hospitals either, without their having studied in California. Anyway, would there be such a hospital near to Camp Roberts? I would have to come out there and take a chance on what I could find. Would I end up being a waitress in a restaurant—or something like that? It would be much easier convincing my father that going out there to get married was a good idea, if I already was certain I had a good job there.

And then there is the money problem. Rent and food seemed pretty high when I was visiting you last summer. Would we be living in Paso Robles, or is there housing close by your camp? And finally, I'll be practically penniless by the time I finish here and get my degree. So maybe we should wait awhile, till late summer. Or in the fall. And should we think about getting married here, so our families can be with us? They are an important part of our lives. There are so many things to think about, aren't there, dear, before we can make a decision?

The long weekend in Los Angeles, January 18, 1943: *I just got back from a three-day pass in Los Angeles. At first I hesitated to go to the big city because of the many stories of loose women there. You know what happened to good old Errol Flynn and the teenaged girls. But then I decided to brave it and just go to safe places like the U.S.O.* [United Service Organizations] *and the Hollywood Canteen. At the U.S.O. one of the hostesses attached herself to me, and I played several games of Chinese checkers with her and lost every one. For some reason I never could comprehend the strategy of that game. I could probably lead an army unit into battle—even a company, but Chinese Checkers is beyond me. One of these days you will have to explain it to me. The girl said she was studying to be a nurse, and she told me about her family in LA. We played two games of Ping-Pong, and ungallantly I*

109

beat her both times. She gave me her telephone number, but I told her I was engaged to be married. She said keep it anyway, just in case. Things might change. But when I left I tore it up and dropped the pieces of paper in a wastepaper basket. Back at camp, Bill Stanton said I was crazy. But you know about his views by now.

The U.S.O. was a nice place with an atmosphere that was family-like. The Hollywood Canteen was ritzy, with genuine movie stars all over the place. The only one I knew by name, though, was Fred McMurray. He had an apron on, and was picking up dishes from the tables and carrying them back to the kitchen. He was busy, so I didn't have a chance to talk with him. I did talk at some length with a woman who had a big role in Street of Chance, *which was about amnesia and starred Burgess Meredith and Claire Trevor. I told her I had seen it last year, and thought she was very good. She said she was Frieda Inescort, and then I remembered seeing her name at the beginning of the film. She told us she was in the movies because of her "classic profile," which she showed to us. And she didn't play ingenues because she had a crack between her front teeth. She displayed that also. Now, she said, she played nothing but "bitches," though I thought she looked nice and homelike, more like a favorite aunt. All in all, I had a quiet but successful weekend.*

Complaints about the army, January 20, 1943: *Well, honey, it looks as though I might remain a corporal for the rest of my life. If I had stayed in Company B, I would be a sergeant by now. I know that for darn sure. The other day there was an opening here for a corporal to make sergeant, and it went to someone else. In a way, I was not surprised, because he deserved the promotion. But now another corporal is making sergeant, and I know I am better than he is, by a long shot. The only thing I can figure is that they told the colonel they would go to OCS, and I said I wouldn't. It doesn't seem fair, but that is how the army is. I'll just stay here as long as he can stand me, and do the best I can, which is pretty good, I think. Incidentally, this is for your eyes and ears alone. Please don't say anything to my folks or anyone else about it. Especially my father. He'd likely take up the matter with the commander-in-chief of the armed forces. Or more likely write a letter to the* Free Press.

I got some books through the mail today that I had bought when I was in LA. One is Durant's The Story of Philosophy, *and another is on ciphers* and codes. *Those ought to keep me busy for a while. I spent a good deal of time roaming through used bookstores. It was a delight just to touch the books, to look through them and wish that all of them were mine. From time to time I'll send the ones I buy home to you, dear.*

Most of the men are gone from the school now, and we won't have any more until February. My barracks is completely empty, and I am working mostly in Col. Lawrence's office. He hasn't mentioned the promotions, but I think he is disappointed in me about OCS. From now on, all of the men will stay for four weeks before they are shipped out to Benning, he says. I've heard that the quotas for OCS have been cut in half this year. They must think they have enough officers now, or else they are reaching the bottom of the pool of eligible officers.

About marriage, January 24, 1943: *From your letter, dear, you don't seem very enthusiastic about our being married in June. As you say, there are so many "ifs" involved. And I suppose I might be rushing you too much. I still think we could do it, even if I remain a corporal. One of the corporals here is married and goes into Paso Robles every evening. He assures me that he never regrets for one minute his decision to get married or to bring his wife out here. Or that they are going to have a baby in June. That's just swell, he says. About the rent, they pay $22.50 a month, which doesn't seem very much, does it? And they buy all their food at the post commissary. A loaf of bread, for instance, costs only four cents.*

As to our income, as a corporal I would be making $60 a month, after my war bonds and laundry are taken out. We could get a $28 a month allotment from the army, and you could easily make $100 a month working at an office. We wouldn't be living on easy street, of course, but we could handle it. All my clothes are furnished by the army, and because of the climate here, you wouldn't need to bring too many things.

A new group at camp, January 28, 1943: *This is one of those rare Thursday evenings, because I have no night classes to teach. In fact, no classes at all. And I haven't a letter of yours to answer, but I will write to let you know I am thinking about you and loving you very much. For some reason or other it seems very hard to push the pen around. Maybe it's the cold weather that's making my hand stiff. But in any event, if my penmanship is worse than usual, you will have to excuse the California climate.*

111

I just interrupted the letter to run down to the other end of the barracks—which is almost empty—and turn up the volume on my radio. It was tuned to my favorite Mexican radio station—XERB—that broadcasts classical music every evening at this hour, and I recognized "La Danza" by Rossini. It's one of my most favorite favorites. I read somewhere that it's a tarantella—an Italian dance like somebody's been bitten by a spider. Have you ever heard it, darling? If not, I know you would like it as much as I do. And I think we ought to put it at the very top of our list. I told Corporal Keller, the assistant barracks leader, that it sounded like Jan Peerce—and sure enough, it was. He is supposed to sing "Faust" on Saturday with the Metropolitan. Maybe you will be listening too. Something else he sings a lot is "The Bluebird of Happiness." I like that too, but it is a bit gooey.

The ranks of our school have been virtually decimated, but we expect 256 new men in a couple of days—the largest group to ever come here at one time. We'll be kept busy, but I like that. I'd rather be overworked than just loaf around doing nothing. The funny thing about it, though, is that more than a hundred of them are second lieutenants who have just finished their training at Fort Benning. I wonder what we are supposed to do with them. One thing might be to teach them more about tactics. I've noticed that it is a weakness of a lot of officers who come here. And maybe at Fort Benning, who knows? The reason they're coming out to us, so I am told, is that Camp Roberts is overflowing with them. The classes leaving OCS have been so large, and then there is nothing to do with them until more divisions are formed and fronts are opened up in the Pacific and in Europe.

With so many officers here we are going to have to change a lot of things, such as the mess rooms. They will be eating separately, the cook told me. And also the latrines. Already, the toilets, showers, and washrooms have been divided into two sections, so they can use one, and we peons use the other. It seems ridiculous, but I suppose the second lieutenants don't want us to see their penises. If they were small, that might reduce our respect for them. Something like that.

End of semester business, February 1, 1943: *When I sat down to write you, dear, I owed you three letters. And now it is four. Another just arrived in the mail. Thank you so much for your patience at this difficult time for me. I'm sorry I have neglected you for so long, but during the past week or so things have piled up for me. Now, though, all my finals are over—except for one tomorrow in Speech Pathology. And all morning I have been typing furiously on a Phonetics Notebook that is, unfortunately, long overdue.*

I was going to write you a couple of days ago, but Sarah called to ask if I would like to hear Paul Robson sing at the Masonic Temple that evening. I just couldn't pass it up, could I? How many times can we take part in such a great occasion? I only wish you were here to go with me. He sang "Creations Hymn," "Steal Away," "Ol' Man River," "Bye and Bye," and some other Negro spirituals. I have to confess that he brought tears to my eyes.

Winter in Michigan, February 6, 1943: *It's the worst kind of weather imaginable. The wind is howling outside my windows, and it's been storming all day. For two months we've had the most wintry kind of weather I've ever seen. Almost every day the snow trucks are out, clearing the streets and roads. For about a week my dad has left his car in the garage for fear of being stuck in the snow. He takes the bus to his work. It's a good night though to be inside where it is warm and friendly. I'm glad it's Saturday, so I don't have to be going anywhere.*

I have my schedule for next semester pretty well planned, but I'm going to have to carry quite a load to finish in June. Thank heaven I will be graduating. I have several Psych courses—Mental Testing, Abnormal Psych, and Study of Mental Deficiency. Also a course on testing the deaf and hard-of-hearing, and an English course that I haven't decided on yet. I have a speech-correction contact at the Roosevelt School and five cases at the Wayne speech clinic. I'm taking three night classes again, but I won't mind that so much in the spring. I saw Dr. Hahn the other day who is home on leave from the navy. He told me he would be very glad to recommend me to teach in California. He got his degrees in speech correction out there and knows the state director of speech correction. So things are looking better day by day, aren't they, dear?

The German connection, February 7, 1943: *I started to write you about an hour ago so I could make this a very long letter, but one of the officer-students came over and asked me if I ever heard the Deutschewelle on my radio. I said all the time, and we got into a discussion about the German situation. He told me he had been born in that country, so I said my fiancée was from Remscheid. He said he had been there many times, that he came from Duisburg, which is near that town. He is Jewish and has been in America for six years. He has a slight accent, but otherwise his English is impeccable. He graduated from Columbia, he said. He sure hates Hitler, as you can well imagine. And he told me stories of concentration camps that I had never heard of. It doesn't seem to get into the papers. And he said that the fault was not the Führer's alone, that the German people as a whole must be held responsible. We talked for a long time, and he said he was a Social Democrat and had fought against the Nazis since the twenties. I finally said I had to write you a letter this evening, so we broke off our discussion. I spoke a little German with him, and he complimented me on my use of his language, which was nice of him, because I feel I am getting rusty after all these months away from Wayne.*

Actually, I have written to the University of Wisconsin to enroll in a class they offer in Military German. I thought it might come in handy some day, and I would like to start collecting credits I can transfer, when I am back after the war. I was thinking too of economics or history, etc. That way, I might finish up in a year, and I wouldn't be too far back of you. By the way, dear, the army will pay half the fees, which for this particular course amount to $17.60. So it is a real bargain. I played a little blackjack with the boys today and came off very much to the good. So I took my "earnings" and bought you something nice for St. Valentine's day. Let me know if you get it, because the package was insured. And I still have enough to cover the cost of the course.

Every chance I get now, I take a walk out into the hills, because the exercise does me so much good. Last Sunday Sam Hopkins, Bill Stanton, and I started out right after breakfast and walked all day—covering about twenty miles in all. We took three of Hopkins's .22 pistols, but none of us hit anything. We saw lots of quail and thousands—it seemed—of wild pigeons, and several deer. I was thinking that the pistols represented part of Sam's character—doing things the hard way. Anyone could kill a pigeon if he used a shotgun. But only an expert could do it with a pistol. A week ago he killed a coyote, and he's talking about trying to bring back a deer.

I sure felt the wear and tear of going up and down steep hills, and I was very stiff before I got back. The other guys said I walked so bent over my hands almost touched the ground. Because it was warm, I had taken off my jacket and tied it around my waist—with the arms hanging down. Someone said I looked like a spider. So ever since, they have been calling me by that name, even the trainees, who have added my rank to the nickname. They seem to consider it a term of respect or affection, so I probably should accept it. Another corporal is called "Red Dog." What do you think, dear? Corporal Spider?

Quarantine again! February 18, 1943: *Surprise! Surprise! I'm writing this letter from the camp hospital where I am confined with a horrible disease—the German measles. After all this time those germs have finally caught up with me, way out here in the CCC camp. But don't be alarmed, dear. I don't feel at all ill. And it might have been the mumps. I could jump out of this bed and go right back to work. Except then I might infect other fellows, if indeed I have not already done so. They'll probably keep me here the full seven days.*

It's funny, because I'd been telling people I would like to get the measles, so I could come here for a vacation—just lying around while pretty nurses held my hand. Except the only time my hand is held is when they take my pulse. Then I started getting the symptoms, though at the time I didn't know that. I had sore muscles in my right arm. Also sore eyes and a cold. Anyway, I was supposed to go on CQ yesterday noon, and before lunch I went to take a shower. Lo and behold, my chest and abdomen were a mass of red. I took myself to the dispensary and was packed off to the hospital forthwith.

And it really is a vacation up here. Not a bad deal at all. I get to lie in bed as often and as long as I want. The food is good. They pass out apples every so often and bring us fruit juices and eggnogs between meals. I thought to bring my copy of Will Durant's book, and I might be able to finish it before I leave.

For some reason I was thinking of the B-Company sergeant some months ago who decided to be circumcised so he could take a vacation in the hospital. (Furloughs had been cancelled, remember?) Anyway, when the medication wore off, he got an erection, because of some stimulus, I guess. So the ladies came and put an ice pack on it, which did the trick. But then the ice melted, and the problem came up again, followed by the same remedy. And each time there was much merriment as the nurses gathered to observe the consequences of their ministrations. The sergeant of course was very embarrassed. I was told that the doctors were never informed about the incident until later. They might have suggested another remedy—like a meat chopper, maybe—and thus spoiled the fun for the nurses.

I thought maybe I could finish the Durant book while I am here, but there have been too many distractions. Not only the nurses, but just people coming and going. It's the kind of book you have to keep paying attention to, or you will lose the train of thought. As a result, I'm about one-third through it. I haven't reached Schopenhauer yet, but when I do I'll keep in mind what you said about unmarried philosophers.

A reply from Dearborn, February 26, 1943: *I hope that by now you've got over the effects of the measles bug, though you don't seem to have been so very sick. Thank you very much for the good chocolates you sent me, honey, for St. Valentine's Day. Chocolate candies are practically nonexistent these days. My family and I appreciated them very much. Are they what you bought with your blackjack winnings? If so, you can thank your friends as well. But if you are always taking their money from them, will they still be your friends?*

I have two new cases at the clinic now. One is a 26-year-old man who has spastic paralysis. It's a tough case that I didn't want to take, because the improvement, if any, is so slow. But Mr. Bilto thought I needed the valuable experience. Everything can't be easy, he said. And I guess he is right. The second one is a stuttering case, a very pretty little girl of sixteen. I've had to change one of my classes. Waldvogel's Abnormal Psych was closed, so I'm taking Interpretative Reading instead. It's a good course, but I had wanted to have the same Psych professor you had when you were still here. When you learned about triskaidekaphobia, and other interesting and useful things, remember?

Back on the job in Camp Roberts, March 3, 1943: *I took a hike this afternoon—or rather the men hiked, and I rode most of the way in a truck at the end of the column. The driver wanted to get some exercise, so I steered the truck, and he walked alongside. I let the motor idle, so I did nothing but hold the steering wheel and keep us on the road. I've been practicing with Sam Hopkins's car, and before long I should be able to drive fairly well. I'm glad you liked the chocolates I sent you, honey. It's hard to realize here in the army, where we have just about everything we want, that people back home can't get very much. So I'll send you an anniversary present—which anniversary I don't know. But we have so many, there must be one this month. Incidentally, I finally got my photo equipment, and Col. Lawrence is arranging a darkroom for me. At present we don't have a sink, but I'll figure some way to process the pictures.*

While I was at the train station, picking up the equipment, the lady in charge asked me to take some boxes addressed to the camp that had never been picked up. Among them were two crates of apples from the state of Washington. They'll just spoil, she told me. And if the recipients were not at our school, she said, I should keep them. Well, they are not here, and I have a lot of large Delicious apples on my hands. I have been eating some, but mostly I am giving them away. I gave several dozen to the corporal whose wife is expecting a baby. She was here at the camp last Sunday, and she looked so young and pretty—and plump, that I just filled a couple of sacks for them. I surely do envy them, having their baby, and they seem so happy.

Four days later: *There was an article in the* Saturday Evening Post *recently by Malcolm Bingay—the* Free Press *editor—in which he referred to the Grosse Pointe people as the "better set." I wrote him a scathing letter this afternoon, asking him what he meant by "better set." Not the Helen Avenue people, I would assume. I suppose he will relegate it to the waste-paper basket, but there's a chance he could mention it in his column. You might check on that for a couple of weeks or so. By and large, I like his ideas, so I was surprised he would say something like that.*

Thinking about the near future, March 10, 1943: *The other night when I was charge-of-quarters, Col. Lawrence asked me again why I didn't put in for OCS. We had been talking for some time about how the records were kept, and I had suggested various changes. I told him I just didn't care anything about being an officer, that I liked what I was doing right now and thought I was useful to the army. He said that was no reason, that if I was qualified, I should go. The army needed people like me, he said, who were well prepared to lead troops. But I shook my head and said I didn't want to go, and there is no way they can make me if I don't fill out an application. I want to stay here at Camp Roberts as long as I can. I've never discussed these matters with Sam Hopkins, but from things he has said, I think he feels the same way.*

I had to go to a talk this evening about tactics by a colonel who had been on Guadalcanal when the Americans captured the island. It was quite boring and all stuff I had heard before. He could have made it lively, telling us how the Japanese attacked in a jungle setting, and how the Americans reacted, but he didn't. That would have been very helpful. He sounded as though he was reading to us from a military manual. I have to admit, that fighting in a jungle must be different from the tactics in an area of hills and plains. So I'll have to start thinking about that, in case I get a chance to teach classes again. A lot of the people we work with will be going to Pacific islands. I have a class tomorrow in which I have to put on a demonstration of night sounds and lights. I'm going to try to organize an especially good one this time, to make it more true to life. Lately the lieutenant in charge hasn't allowed me enough time to prepare the demonstration group, so everything has been slap-dash. When I told him about it, he didn't seem much interested, but he did say I could have more time. So we'll see. I sure miss Lt. Fedderson these days. I wonder if he is in the Pacific.

Doings in Dearborn, March 14, 1943: *I'm writing this letter in bed, darling, and I think I'm getting spots of cold cream all over the paper. You can see what horrors you will have to put up with after we are married. I planned to write you last night, but I went shopping with my folks, and we ended up going to the movies. We saw* The Black Swan *and* Street of Chance, *both of which you have seen, I think. Your friend Frieda Inescort was especially good, I thought. I made a point of looking for her profile, but she was always too quick for me. Ditto the crack between her teeth. But you are right, she is a good actress.*

It seems I'm always making apologies for not having written you, honey, but right now I'm breaking my neck to keep abreast of the work that piles up. I'll breathe a little easier when I have made up my incomplete in Methods of Speech Correction from last semester. I have twenty hours of observation that I just couldn't fit in then, and also there is a paper to write. I'm afraid my grades are suffering, but the main thing is to get everything done by June. Last semester I had two C's, which is not at all indicative of what I can do. One of them was in the "Modern Novel," which I neglected shamefully, I'm afraid, just zipping through some of the books. But as I said, I simply have to graduate in June.

Religious questions from Marianne, March 19, 1943: *At last, dear Bob, I have an evening free to do what I please, and to write you the important letter I have been owing you for so long. It bothers me terribly when I don't write, but this week, for instance, I haven't been home any day between 7 a.m. and 10 p.m. My father keeps worrying about me until he sees me coming through the front door. And I have classes and a clinic all day. I have nightmares lately about the work I have left undone, and it is beginning to get me down. Weekends are the only time I have to catch up on my homework and to write letters.*

I want to talk about our marriage plans and the religion question tonight and to tell you what Rev. Boecler had to say about it, darling, because I know we should settle it soon. I told him I had considered being married by a priest and about the talk I had with Father Keating, and that I'd read some literature about your church. He asked if I could be willing to consent in writing to something in which I did not believe. I told him that whatever we decided to do would not change what I believe, but that I would probably have to give in rather than you, because your church is so much more severe than mine, and you would be excommunicated. I said that you were quite a devout Catholic, and so it meant a good deal more to you than it otherwise might. He said he could understand what conflicts it would cause for two young people faced with this situation; that no earthly church had the right to take advantage of the tenderest human emotions to enforce its beliefs; that this should be done only through persuasion, not dictation. He said that no matter how dearly I loved you, I ought to consider carefully before promising something that would affect both of our lives—all of our lives. He asked me about you and what you had been studying and said you must be a very fine person—which I assured him you are. He said that whatever we decided, he would do all he could to be of help to us.

Since then I have been thinking about—and anguishing about—what he said and what Father Keating told me. My family came to this country believing that it is the land of the free. That's what this war is all about. The one thing that America promises its people is the right to live their lives without restraint, and to determine their own destinies. And I feel that no individual or group, no church or state, has the right to infringe on our liberties. No group can make me swear to live or to raise my children in a certain way—whether it is a good way or not. That must be my decision, based on my beliefs. A person's beliefs are a matter between him and God, and he owes ultimate allegiance only to God.

April 1, 1943: *My darling Marianne: I have some news for you that will probably alter our life plans considerably. I don't know whether you will consider it good news or bad. Things are still somewhat iffy. I have an opportunity that seems simply too good to pass up. But before you burst with curiosity or worry, I'd better tell you that I am going to go to a college to study Military Government. And all expenses will be paid for by the army. It seems to me the chance of a lifetime. All of my credits could be transferred to Wayne, I would think.*

Perhaps you have read in the papers that the army is taking over some of the universities and colleges for the technical training of its men. The plan is very new, and it's just been a week or so since the first candidates from this camp were sent to Oregon State to study engineering. I made inquiries about it, and was asked to come in to camp headquarters and take some tests. I had been told that the exams were very hard, and that they were chiefly on math. I was prepared to fail them, because, as you know, the sciences have never been my forte. My science grades in high school and in college are a monotonous string of B's.

But I decided to give it my all, and the night before the exams I borrowed a book from a lieutenant and soaked up as much information as I could. The way I used to do at Wayne. I stayed up most of the night. The result was that I not only completed the exams, which was more than most of the fellows did, but my score turned out to be the third highest of the bunch. And I had to guess at the last few questions! Thank God for all those multiple-choice examinations at Wayne!

Then today I went before the camp board for an interview. A lot of men had indicated Military Government as their first choice, but I was the only one who got it. Most of those who had passed the exams were lumped together into something called "Engineering." I had listed Foreign Languages as my second choice. I didn't want science or math, but I suppose I would have taken them if they had been offered to me. Anything to get a lot of college credits.

When I met with the board (there were five officers), they asked me a lot of personal questions. They said I had to know German quite well to get into

Military Government. I told them I was a bit rusty, but that I was start-ing a correspondence course in Military German, and I was getting practice with books like Iphigenie *and* Die Meistersinger. *They also asked if I had taken classes in government at Wayne. I said no, but that I had always been interested in politics and had been the precinct captain and delegate to the county convention in Detroit. That led to a lot of questions about politics, and a captain asked me if I thought Roosevelt would run again in 1944. I told them I was sure he would, if the war were not over. And he'd be elected again, naturally. It was a long and detailed interview.*

Then I was dismissed and waited outside the room for no more than a couple of minutes. I was called in and informed that I had been accepted for advanced training in Military Government. I was very much surprised— and elated, as you can well imagine. I don't know what college I'll be going to, but one of the officers did tell me it might be Virginia. It would be swell to be so much closer to home, wouldn't it, dear? It isn't certain, as yet, because I still have to be okayed by the Ninth Service Command in Utah. But the officers did seem to think my chances were pretty good. When the war is over in Europe, I would be part of the army of occupation in Germany, helping in the transition to civilian government. It sounds pretty exciting, doesn't it, honey? And it behooves me to work very hard on my German while I am still here.

April 6, 1943, in camp: *It's been almost a week now, and I'm still here, dear. I asked Col. Lawrence about the program. No one else from our school had applied, he said, and those from the main camp who were going would probably be in the Engineering section. They were all privates who were finishing their basic training. I asked Sam Hopkins if he were interested in Military Government. He has traveled to a lot of countries. But he doesn't speak any foreign languages well, he said. And anyway he has a good deal here, being close to his home and his girlfriend. And he always has plenty of gasoline for his car. His family seems to know a lot of the so-called "right" people. He knows the Hearsts and has been to their castle in San Simeon. I will miss him when I go. He's a good friend, and I like to talk about things with him.*

I don't think I told you, honey, that I could be reduced to a private. I would miss the extra money, but the education and the opportunity to serve in a military government, make it worthwhile. Besides, a reduction isn't certain. Hopkins says army regulations forbid a reduction in rank, unless I have done something bad. "With prejudice." So we'll see.

A reply from Marianne in Dearborn, April 11, 1943: *I want to tell you first of all that I think the news about going back to college is pretty swell. It's a wonderful opportunity for you, darling, and needless to say I am very proud of you. You will be working in a field that is very important. As for postponing our marriage, I'll be sorry, as will you. But it does give us more time to deal with problems such as my job and career, as well as our religions. And we can discuss those in a more leisurely fashion.*

I'm sorry I didn't write you last Sunday, but you'll understand when I tell you that I spent all of three days—and most of the nights—finishing work for my incomplete. The deadline was Monday afternoon at five, and I made it with a few minutes to spare. I wrote eight reports, made a card file, and wrote an 8,000-word paper. I always swear I won't let things pile up like that, and then they do! I had two mid-terms also last week, and I'm afraid I didn't do too well. Would you do something for me? Pray that I graduate in June. A few "Hail Marys" might help, whatever they are. At the rate things are going, I'll need a lot of praying. Your father said your train-ing in military government would probably last for the duration of the war, and I certainly hope so. And Mr. Bilto says there are courses in it at the Uni-versity of Michigan and at Harvard. Going to Harvard would certainly be prestigious for you, but being in Ann Arbor could be fine too—and closer to home. But maybe that's too much happiness to wish for.

More from Marianne at home, April 18, 1943: *Thank you, dear, for the two letters in German. You are doing very well in that language. And how is your correspondence course going? I was reading in the paper last night about an army program at the U of M for courses such as you will be taking, and it sounds as though you will be in for a grueling time. Accord-ing to the article, you will be studying more than twelve hours a day. But then, I suppose it won't be much harder work than you are doing now, and at least it would be more interesting.*

A week later: *Happy Easter, honey! I hope you've had a good time, though you are "fern von Eltern und Geschwistern" to quote Iphigenia. I wish the dumb old army would hurry up and decide where you will be* sent. I suppose your heart isn't in your work at the OCPS. I'm still praying that you will be sent east, but so far my prayers aren't helping you very much.

By the way, honey, the woman who is in charge of graduate records at Wayne tells me I am a couple of Education hours short. So, If I don't find them somehow, I'll probably have to go to summer school, after all. For so long I had set my mind on graduating in June, and I'll be very much disappointed. And my father too. I got your new letter in German, and I think you are doing just fine. Some of your words I wasn't sure of, though, and I had to look them up in the dictionary. Your vocabulary in technical matters is far beyond mine. Some day you will be speaking and reading the language like a native. And in Germany.

No news from California, April 29, 1943: *Thank you, dear, for your good words about my linguistic abilities. They buck me up when I'm having trouble with military terminology. So many of the words are made up, like* Gestapo *and* Stuka, *that didn't exist a few years ago. I'm going fairly slowly through my lessons, but at least I am doing them thoroughly. Last Sunday I went on a hike by myself and took my* Iphigenie *with me. Up in the hills, a million miles from anybody, I read the first act aloud to all the little creatures in the vicinity. Maybe declaimed would be a better word, for I was altering my voice with each change of character. And then I thought why not memorize the lines. If Sam Hopkins could memorize T. S. Eliot, Goethe's immortal prose would be a cinch. And then I thought I should get back to camp, because somebody might be trying to call me to say I was going to Princeton or to Yale. And I realized that I was just going crazy. No one will ever call me, and I'll rot away with the files in Col. Lawrence's office. Which is where I am working right now.*

More from Camp Roberts, May 4, 1943: *An officer from Classification came out here today, and I asked him about my status regarding the ASTP* [Army Specialized Training Program]. *He said if my orders have already gone in, I won't have to go before the board again or take any more tests. If they haven't, I will. There have been so many applicants around the country, I think, they are having to cut back. I can't get a furlough before I go, so there is no point in our hoping for that. They are starting to send men now to the Military Government, he said. And that course is being given at*

Princeton. It does clear up some questions, but not the main one, which is why are they keeping me waiting—for more than a month now.

The same day in Dearborn: *I was mighty glad to hear from you, dear, but at the same time a little disappointed. I had pictured you on your way to some university, not too far from me, and we could see each other from time to time. I was thinking, though, probably the reason you haven't been transferred sooner is that the program is so new, and the schools for military government are still in the process of being set up. So classes just haven't started yet. And I'm sure they will be very soon, and you will be on your way. Can the credits you receive in your program be transferred to Wayne? If so, you could have your degree sooner than you expected. And you could even start thinking about a graduate school!*

Concerning furloughs, if you did come home now, I wouldn't see much of you, unfortunately. Today, for instance, I have classes from eight in the morning until ten in the evening. It would be worse than ever for you, if you came all this way, and we couldn't be together. And I couldn't cut any classes, if I expect to graduate. Or have any incompletes. You wouldn't know me these days, honey. I haven't cut a class in weeks. I had an interesting offer today for a summer job in the Upper Peninsula, north of Marquette. Mr. Bilto is very anxious that I take it, because it's for speech-handicapped children, and I would be working with a Dr. Heidema, who is State Director of Special Education. Mr. Bilto said that after working with him, I could get a job almost anywhere. But it is such a long way from home, from any place really. And what if you were being sent somewhere. Is there any chance you'd have a furlough then? There are so many ifs in our lives, aren't there dear?

A reply from Camp Roberts, May 12, 1943: *I'm still here, as you can see from the envelope, and there is no indication as to when or where I might go. I've decided to be a stoic about the whole thing. If I go, I go; and if I stay, I stay. That's logical, isn't it? Though hardly comforting. Stoics must lead a shitty life. But then maybe they just don't give a damn. What news I do have is hardly worth writing about.*

The school right now is in the middle of a minor crisis. A main broke, and our camp is without water. It's been difficult, because we have to use the river water for washing up, all 300 of us. And doing the dishes even. It can't be very sanitary. And worse, the natural functions of humans keep on producing waste materials that need to be dealt with! Oh, to be at Princeton University right now!

From Dearborn, May 15, 1943: *The news about the war has been very good lately, hasn't it? On Wednesday we heard that the last German troops in Africa had surrendered. And now the British and Americans are getting ready to invade Italy. From the sound of it, you may be going to help govern an occupied Europe sooner than you expected, dear. I have quite a bit of homework to do, and I have to finish some drapes I'm making for the Speech Clinic. So I doubt if I will be writing you tomorrow. Goodnight, I love you very much. P.S. First you talked about Military Government, and now about the ASTP. Are they the same?*

Graduation daze, May 26, 1943: *Last weekend I had to go to the personnel board to take routine intelligence and culture tests for people graduating in education, and they lasted all day. Part of the testing is a psychological interview by one of the psychiatrists at the clinic. You have to be interviewed when you enter the College of Ed, and again when you graduate. A couple of interviewers are well known for being very insulting and asking intimate questions. I had one of them for my first interviews, but nothing unusual happened to me. One of my friends, though, got this Miss Nosy Parker, who asked her if she was a virgin. And my friend said: "No, are you?" Which I thought was very funny, because Miss N. P. is a stiff-necked old maid. And when she started asking Shirley Johnston personal questions, Shirley just got up and walked out. I think young women these days are standing up for their rights more than they used to.*

This time, I was glad to get a young man, who treated me courteously. He asked if you and I would be married, and when I said I hoped so, he said "good." He had seen enough trouble-making single women at the clinic to be convinced nobody should be one. I guess he meant "old maids." I spent all day Sunday writing and typing some reports that were due Monday.

I'm writing this part of the letter in a night class, the last of the semester. Dr. Williams is reading us the diary of a feeble-minded child, so if it gets incoherent, you will know why. (One of the women in the class handed me a page of jokes, so I'll copy it and send it to you later. But here is one short one. A silly definition: Pajamas—an item of clothing newlyweds place beside their beds in case of fire.) I can see you frowning at my doing this sort of thing in class, but Dr. Williams is the hardest person to listen to, and she always says the same thing anyway, so you're not missing anything. You just have to be careful to read the textbook, so you can pass the examinations. Just now two men in the back of the room are playing tic-tac-toe. And the woman on my right brings a crossword puzzle to class each week. And always finishes them. It's not surprising, is it, that this course (Mental Deficiency) has been a complete waste of my time?

More about graduation, May 31, 1943: *I will be graduated this June 17th, if I don't break a leg and can't go to my exams, or if I don't go batty with all the work I still have to do—in two short weeks. I haven't decided whether I will scream with relief when they hand me my diploma or just pass out quietly and have to be carried off the stage. I will really need you there, honey, to hold my hand and to prop me up. For a while I was afraid I might have to carry extra hours in summer school. It's a long story that I will explain later, but when they added up all my credits, I was short exactly one hour! But good old Mr. Bilto came to my rescue by offering me a reading course. I didn't have to do anything, but he signed his name to the arrangement. He said it might not be strictly legal, but that human relations were more important than mere technicalities.*

An ASTP explanation, June 3, 1943: *I finally found out why I haven't heard about my school. Captain Farleman, who is my good friend, went to Classification the other day, and they told him someone had forgotten to send my application in. That's army efficiency for you. I have been waiting for two months, on needles and pins, without any furlough, and someone, somewhere, has been remiss, they say. Captain Farlemen thinks somebody is giving me the runaround. It does sound suspicious to me, but it is better late than never. The people there said the orders would be sent off to Utah, and I should have some word within a week or ten days.*

From what they told me, I will then have to go to a STAR unit, whatever that is, and take more exams. There a board of professors selects the course and the school. And I might not even get Military Government. Most have been sent to an Engineering program. I sure hope that doesn't happen to me. I have been talking so much about Military Government. I'll let you know what happens, as soon as they tell me. In the meantime, I am still working, mostly in Col. Lawrence's office, and wishing I could have more exercise.

Still waiting, June 6, 1943: *I had a letter from my mother today. She said John was at the battle of Attu. I had rather suspected that, since the* Idaho *was known to be in the Aleutians. I had called their number in San Diego, but no one answered. He is now a lieutenant (JG), which corresponds with our first lieutenant. She also told me that Hilary Velten was in San Francisco, waiting to be shipped out. I'll try to meet him, if I can get a pass. Or haven't been shipped out. I'd like to see what effect army discipline has had on his ebullient personality.*

The next day: *I'm getting more and more to do in my job, but doing it in less and less time. The colonel gives me a new job, and then I find ways to make it shorter and easier. Last week he asked me to make all the assignments to the student officers for practice-teaching. The system had been a mess, with several people responsible for it. I reorganized it, and got out all of next week's assignments in a single afternoon. I do it, I suppose, because I like to see things running well. But since I should be leaving anyway, the changes won't affect my life. The main thing is that it gives me more time to work on my German. I'm trying to get out at least one lesson a week. And I'll be better prepared when I go to school.*

The Graduate, June 19, 1943: *Well, I am now a Bachelor of Arts, and have a diploma to show for my efforts. It seems strange not to have any work to worry about after the stresses of this past year. I suppose the difficulties are of my own making—for putting off the required courses for too long. So too much was crowded into the final semesters. I hate to say it, but I was working on a required paper right up to 9 p.m. the night before the graduation ceremonies. But I do have my degree, and as the years pass, I trust I will forget the agonies and remember the many fine teachers I have worked with. And especially Mr. Bilto. He has been my salvation.*

Three days later in camp: *Two matters of earthshaking importance, Marianne. 1. This is the first anniversary of our engagement. 2. I shall be coming home on furlough, after all this waiting. And how is this possible? The furlough, I mean. And it takes a lot of explaining. Captain Farleman decided to find out, once and for all, what was holding up my transfer to the ASTP program. "We'll miss you," he said, "but you do have a right to go." So he cornered another captain in the Classification office and wouldn't leave until they told him what was what. It seems that someone at this school, probably the colonel, had said I was "irreplaceable." Isn't it ironic, dear, that all this time I've been improving the running of his office, I was just doing myself in? The more I made time for myself to study German, the less likely I was to need it. Capt. Farleman did tell me, though, that the colonel could not prevent my transfer. That was a matter to be decided by the Ninth Service Command.*

To say that I was pissed off is the understatement of the ages. I'm afraid I acted somewhat rashly. This morning I marched into the colonel's office and announced that I wanted a furlough. But you're on orders to leave, he said. No, I said, somebody here told them I was irreplaceable. He looked reluctant. When do you want to go? he asked me. Tomorrow, I said. After all, I had been waiting for almost three months, unnecessarily. It turned out that it would take a week to process all the papers, but I might be able to persuade the first sergeant to give me a weekend pass as well. That way, I could be home early in the week. I'll telegraph you when I leave, so you and my folks will know when to expect me.

Colonel Lawrence then asked me to stay and talk about the ASTP. By the way, honey, you asked me earlier what those letters stood for. It's the Army Specialized Training Program. It began, he said, because colleges and universities were having a hard time—so many of their students had been drafted. From the first, there had been a lot of opposition from the "brass hats." (Those were his words, not mine.) They were interested in fighting-men, not scholars. But General Marshall, the army Chief of Staff, was in favor of the idea, and his support "carried the day." And the generals, though reluctant, did see one big advantage. The program gave them a place to "park" the many officers and enlisted men that would be needed later. Until Europe was invaded, he said, and the larger islands in the Pacific taken over, a great number of soldiers were "extra baggage." And that's what's happening around here, he said, in our OCPS program.

We have been doing our best to give the officers and noncoms who come here good training. But in one way, we are simply "babysitters," he said. Once there are large battles, men would be killed or wounded. Replacements will be needed. More privates and noncoms, and more lieutenants. At that

128

point, he thought, the ASTP would simply disappear. "And the OCPS will be gone in two months anyway," he said. It will just molder away. "Like a bunch of dry leaves." And also the main camp, probably. Several high-ranking officers here, including the general, are being transferred to Camp Blanding in Florida, he said.

He was telling me things he shouldn't, he said. And before that had been making decisions that belonged only to me. And I really had been "irreplace-able" in the running of his office. He knew everyone thought he was an old fogey. And he knew too that he would never have a combat command. He'd been passed over too many times. The "powers-that-be" would find him an office job somewhere in this country.

As for me, he was sure I would be accepted into the program. He'll write a good letter for me. But there were things I should know. First, the Mili-tary Government section never really existed. It was only a figment of some planner's imagination. In any event, as far as my immediate future is con-cerned, I will be part of the Foreign Area and Language section. I would study German, presumably, and speak and read it fluently. But I should be prepared to be sent anywhere, even to the Pacific. If I end up in Germany as part of an army of occupation, well and good. My records are impressive, he said, and should follow me wherever I go. "Just wish me well, dear friend," he said, "I shall need good luck too." And he shook my hand. I hope he is right.

P.S. All this is for your eyes only, for obvious reasons. No one else should know about it. Not Ellen or Sarah. Not our families. And especially not my dad. He might do something rash. And spoil everything. The army wouldn't like it. Please, dear, be careful. I'll see you soon.

❧ 6 ❧

The ASTP

From Dearborn after the second furlough, July 11, 1943: *Here we are, honey, taking up our correspondence again. I hope you will forgive me for doubting, but before you came home this time, I wasn't sure about us. I was afraid our love was getting to be—it's hard to explain—sort of apathetic. Just a lot of words. And that hurt very much. I know now that I was wrong, but it isn't easy to stay in touch with someone solely through letters—for an entire year. They can never take the place of seeing you and being with you physically. And then there were our disagreements, on religion and other things. I had hoped they could be reconciled, because we loved each other. And maybe too it was the war, all the worries, and my working so hard for so long that was getting me down. Anyway, everything came out when I first saw you this time, and I thought I didn't know you. You seemed like someone else, a complete stranger to me.*

And then you took my hand, and suddenly everything was all right again. I was certain that you loved me. You are all of my life, dear, and always will be. Your coming home, at this time, has done wonders for both of us. And in a way your frustrations of the past two months were a godsend, because you did get your furlough at an important time in our lives. If you had come home much earlier, you'd have found me too busy with trying to graduate to be with you very much. I hope you are able to get some sleep on the train, and that your trip back will be a pleasant one. My love will be with you, as always.

Thank you for your suggestion that we compromise on the religious question by joining the Episcopal church. That would certainly solve a lot of problems, wouldn't it? I am going to an Episcopal service the first chance I have and will let you know how I like it. I realize that it is not easy for you to give up the church you love and has been part of all your life. Again, thank you, dear.

I think I told you there might be a job for me in the office where Ellen works. It's a real estate firm in the Buhl building. I'm going to see about it on Wednesday, and if the pay is good, and they'll hire me, I think I will take it. Strangely, after all my complaints about how hard I worked this past year, I find I really do need something to do, something definite every day. Also the fact that I need the money. I'm practically broke, and I hate being so dependent on my father for so many things.

Two days later: *Well, dear, I have a job, it seems. I'm writing this in the office of Reaume & Silloway, where I shall be working for the rest of the summer. Twenty minutes ago I walked in here for an interview, and I'm starting in the morning. They need people so badly, they practically haul you in and rope and tie you before you have a chance to say "no." Mr. Kinsella asked me how much money I expected, and I said: "Thirty dollars a week." To my surprise, he asked if I could start tomorrow. I had planned to take a longer vacation, but it is a good opportunity to earn the money I need. I have a desk next to Ellen, and will be doing some of her work, I would guess. P.S. I'll make this a short letter, because I have to be up at 6:30 in the morning. Bright and early, as they say. God bless you, honey, and bring you back again soon.*

From California, July 16, 1943: *I was rather glad to be back here, not that I wanted to leave you, dear, and to leave home, but because the train ride was over. It was a tedious trip and almost impossible to get much sleep. In one way I was lucky, though, to be in the only new coach on the train. The others were very dirty. I arrived in camp about 1:30 Thursday morning. I was due back at midnight, but that was close enough. What I didn't tell you when I was home—so as not to worry you—was that I had left here early, without a pass before my furlough. I kept wondering what they would say when I got back. But nothing happened, and I'm not in the guardhouse. Or even the doghouse, though I was AWOL for two and a half days. When the major found out I had left without his permission, all he said was: "Well, I guess I'm not supposed to know about it." I was taking a big chance, that I might lose my rank or the chance to go to a college, but I suppose that I was still pissed off about everything. And the extra three days at home were worth a lot to both of us.*

Yes, darling, before I came home I did have a feeling that something was happening to our relationship. Especially, with our disagreements about religion. You remember I said in one of my German letters that maybe we would have to break up? And one month I had only two letters from you. Instead of realizing that you were under terrific pressure to finish your work at Wayne, I thought maybe you were changing your mind. But then I was home, and I saw you, and I knew that for me everything was OK. And so it was. Thank you, dear, for overlooking all my shortcomings. Those eleven days I spent at home were the happiest of my life. I'm glad you are considering our compromising about religion. It would mean a little hardship for each of us, but neither would have to do all the sacrificing. Our parents might be unhappy with us, but in the end it is our concern.

The next day: *I went in to the main camp yesterday and put in my application for ASTP again. Now all I have to do is wait and be patient. I should be pretty good at waiting. But patience is another thing. And no matter what happens, I'll never be sorry that I came home on furlough instead of reapplying at once. I had a wonderful time, and we may have saved our relationship. I'm back at my old job in the colonel's office, and all signs are that the school won't last much longer. The supply of officers coming to the camp has practically ceased. There were no new classes last week or this week. And it's not really my concern these days. If I leave here it won't affect me in the least. And if I don't, well, we'll just see.*

The ASTP, July 20, 1943: *Well, honey, I went before the board again today. Or rather they came to me, which was nice. The officers rode out to the school in a command car, and I went outside the office for my interview. It lasted for only a few minutes, and then they told me I had been accepted. They asked about my college work and gave me a few sentences of German to translate. They were really very simple, and I read them right off, in*

German and in English. So now I just wait. Some more. I'll let you know what happens.

The same day in Detroit: *I'm at work now and awfully busy. But I'm typing this short note before I forget. I ran into Marion Sheppard while I was out to lunch just now, and she asked about you. She says Verne Gibson is in Australia. He is in communications and is a Pfc. now, but expects a commission. Lots of love, dear.*

Three days later: *I started to write you last night, but I couldn't stay awake, and then this morning I didn't get up in time, so I'm writing again from the office. I have a few minutes left of my lunch time. I decided to save money by bringing my lunch, but I couldn't resist eating it at my desk. And so I had to go out with Ellen for another lunch. I get so darn hungry these days, you had better think very seriously before asking me to marry you—study your budget, and be sure you can afford me, dear. Otherwise I might eat you out of house and home. And I might even have to get new clothes!*

The war news looks very good these days, doesn't it? If we keep occupying Axis territory at this rate, they will soon need people like you in the governments of conquered territory. The army ought to realize that, and send you to school soon.

The same day in California: *I have a hunch from what people are saying that I'll be going to school sometime in August. In a way, though, the wait might not be so good for me—financially. I was red-lined at payday last month, and then again this month, and when I leave here I will be payless the following month. Luckily, though, I still have some poker money in my little box, and it will last me for a while. But then the first of October, wherever I am, I'll be getting a big pay—almost $200. And I could send most of it home to build up our joint account.*

There won't be much to do for a while in the school here—and maybe permanently. We have only 17 officers and 21 enlisted men at present as students. So I'll probably have more time to myself, to study German and to prepare for whatever is coming. The average workweek for the noncom instructors will be about ten hours, I reckon. The rest of the time the fellows just loaf—unless the colonel finds something for them to do, which he keeps trying to do. Without much success, because they usually succeed in staying out of his reach. So most of the work falls on my shoulders. After our talk I'm glad to help him, if I can.

Marianne replied from Dearborn, July 25, 1943: *You surprised me very much, dear, with the news that you had left Camp Roberts without a pass. You were really taking a chance, weren't you. I'm certainly glad you didn't tell me while you were here, because I would have been worried the whole time. Anyway, nothing came of it, and we were lucky to have those extra days to ourselves. I can remember the time when you wouldn't dream of taking such chances. You have changed so much, mostly for the better, I hasten to say. You needn't worry about having depleted our bank account. Now that I am working, I can start contributing again. And in the fall I should have a real job and a good income. The account has been a splendid idea, hasn't it?*

More from California, July 29, 1943: *No news yet about the ASTP, but rumors are everywhere that Camp Roberts is going to be turned into a training center for combat divisions. I just hope I'll be gone by that time. By the way, did you see where Roosevelt said the government proposes to give some soldiers and sailors further education after the war? It sounds wonderful, doesn't it, dear?*

News from Dearborn, August 2, 1943: *The war situation is getting better and better. With Mussolini out of the way, the Allies can turn their attention now to Germany. That won't be so easy, though, and might take several months—or even a whole year. You asked me once how I felt about the bombing of German towns. I have to say I have no personal association, because I don't know who most of my relatives are or where they live. I'm sure my father worries about his sister in Remscheid, though he doesn't talk about it. But I dislike hearing about cities being bombed anywhere, because it's someone's hometown being devastated, and innocent people are killed. I know it's the only way to end the war, but I wish they'd hurry up and get it over with.*

Ellen and I have decided where we will go on our vacation. We went to a Travelers' Aid Service in the Penobscot Building and got a lot of folders on places in Northern Michigan. If we can still get reservations, I think we will go to a sort of lodge on Cedar Hedge Lake near Traverse City. It sounds very nice. We'd get our meals and be able to swim, fish, and ride, and go boating.

135

From the brochures, it seems a real bargain. If we like it, you and I might go there some day. With our children even!

AT LAST! August 6, 1943: *Well, the day we have been looking forward to for three months has finally arrived! Yesterday I got my orders to go to Stanford University in Palo Alto and take my screening exams for the ASTP. I leave here on Monday, and it is none too soon for me. I'll be taking more examinations to determine if I'm capable of handling the requirements of ASTP work. Whether it will be Military Government is not quite clear. Col. Lawrence told me it would be something else, such as Foreign Areas and Languages. So we'll see. I know there is a school at Michigan for that, but I am afraid to hope too hard. People say the army keeps upping the requirements, and I hope I'll still be able to qualify. Otherwise, I'll be sent right back to Camp Roberts. That would really break my heart, dear, after all my planning and studying for the program.*

From Palo Alto, August 15, 1943: *I hope, dear, that you will forgive me for not writing you for a whole week. I trust you weren't worried too much. I wanted to wait until I knew whether I had passed all my exams here, before I sent a letter. But I passed all of them OK and was accepted into the program. Unless something unforeseen happens, I should add. With my fingers crossed. I'd better tell you, though, what has been happening since I left the camp. I got here Monday evening and was assigned to Company C and Encina Hall. The hall is an old dormitory used for years by Stanford freshmen before the army took over. Six of us have a room that was intended for two or three civilian students. The beds have no springs—in fact, they are just canvas cots, the kind you use when you are camping out, and not very comfortable. But in the context of my being on the way to a college curriculum again, they seem heavenly to me.*

Tuesday I didn't do much of anything except wander around the campus—it's very beautiful, and Wednesday I took the psych. examination. (Educators are gung ho about psych. exams, though I find them ridiculous, for the most part. Especially the true and false.) In the afternoon, I took a language-aptitude test, the likes of which I had never seen before, and then a written exam in German—mostly translations. The aptitude exam consisted of an artificial language and sixty-two questions to be translated. A list of verbs was given at the outset. For example MORI was "to be." GONDI was "to succeed." Add the prefix FE to get past tense, LO to get future tense, and no prefix was the present tense. Replace the final I with OP and you have a noun. Add AN to get an adjective, and EL for an adverb. The test, they said, was to determine how adept we were at learning a foreign language. I did pretty well; in fact my interviewer told me my score was one of the highest he'd seen. Of course skills used in passing tests are different from the skills necessary to acquire fluency in a language. But at that moment I was certainly grateful that a good score would ensure my entry into the ASTP.

Thursday afternoon I took an oral German exam and passed, though I didn't do as well as I hoped. So far away from people speaking the language, I've got mighty rusty. Then on Friday—the thirteenth, as it happens—I got my final interview, and was passed with no difficulty. So, for me, it was a lucky day. Now, I have to wait some more, until they decide where to send me. I doubt if I'll stay here, because the fall term doesn't start until October 15. And the chances of being sent to the East seem slim. Nearly three-quarters of the men accepted here, and sent out, end up on the West Coast. At present there are about 200 men in that category. They are all taking refresher courses while they are marking time, and I assume I shall be doing the same.

New road blocks, August 16, 1943: *I said yesterday that I'd be going to school pretty soon unless something unforeseen happens. And it looks as though it might. All the men here at Stanford who are waiting for language assignments were called in this morning and told they would be reclassified. It seems that the army doesn't need as many linguists as it thought, so the requirements are being raised. There was a list of names on the board this evening of men to be re-interviewed tomorrow, but so far my name was not among them. I hope that means I am O.K. But maybe I could be interviewed later. I'll just have to wait and see. People who speak a foreign language "fairly well," who have over 130 on the army IQ test, and have completed at least one year of college will be accepted. And that seems to include me. So the only thing that worries me is whether the people who judged my fluency rated me high enough. "Fairly well" could be interpreted a lot of ways. So we'll see. I would sure hate to be sent back to Camp Roberts—to the program that is obviously dying. Meanwhile, we are not doing very much, except going to a couple of classes, have athletics (exercises), and paddle around in the swimming pool. And wait.*

Good news! August 18, 1943: *I told you in my last letter that the language men were going to be reclassified, and that most of them would be eliminated. Well, that is exactly what has happened. About 85% of them were interviewed and told they didn't meet the new requirements. I was not interviewed and have been told by the major in charge that I will not be reclassified. So I must have satisfied the people who made the decisions. Thank God! I feel so lucky. But at the same time I'm sorry for so many young soldiers whose hopes had been raised and then dashed so quickly and arbitrarily. They must feel jerked around like a yo-yo.*

A day later: *Today I started my "refresher course." It's really a joke, though. Each morning I sit in on one class—the geography of Germany. But the instructor doesn't seem to know much about the subject. It's nothing like the classes I had at Wayne. And after that class I am supposed to go to the library, but they never tell us what to do there. So I find a book and read until lunch, looking studious the whole time. Maybe P. G. Wodehouse. Or something in German. I think the program is just a device to keep us busy until we are sent out.*

Life on the campus, August 22, 1943: *I stayed here at Stanford this weekend and spent the day washing and ironing my dirty clothes, which had accumulated alarmingly while I was still at Camp Roberts. It was fun for a change, and I really did a good job, if I do say so myself. It's tiring work though, and I wouldn't like to do it very often. Come to think of it, it's what women do in every country in the world. Do you ever think that is unfair, dear? Of course, when we are married we will have the latest washing machine with a good wringer, which may help out a lot.*

And speaking of the fair sex, Stanford is supposed to be noted for its beautiful women. And from what I have seen in the short time I have been here, it is true. I imagine it is difficult for the girls, having all these soldiers around—more men than women, it seems. You remember how the soldiers whistled at you when we were bike-riding at Rouge Park? Well, it's the same way here. The men aren't used to seeing so many women yet. As they will be, when they get to another university. One thing I noticed, though, is that so many of the girls seem so young—compared to the women at Wayne. When I first met you, you were only 18, but I thought of you as a grown woman. And also the women who worked on the Collegian *with me.*

Maybe it's because you worked outside the university to support yourself and to earn your tuition. The women I see here come from well-to-do families and have never worked, I would think.

The other day I was talking with a girl who sat across from me in the library, and she said people say Stanford girls were snobbish. But she was not, she assured me. But I was struck by the differences between you and her. At Wayne you were confident and self-assured, and you talked to me with a grown-up vocabulary. She asked me if I would like to go to a show, but I told her I was engaged. So she started talking with another soldier.

I had to interrupt this letter for about a half an hour, dear, to make a check on one of the classes. It was a hell of a trick, but it was done on the captain's orders. I had to see how many absentees there were and to report back to him with the names. I found only two present from our company. If there had been two absent, I could have marked them here. But there was no way I could cover up for so many. I hate doing things like that, because I am the shit-heel in all of this. I suppose the captain has to earn his pay somehow, but most of the classes we have to attend have very little value to us in the long run. We'd be better off in the library, free to bone up on what we will be doing later. P.S. A group of language students left today for Indiana. That wouldn't be a bad place to go, would it, dear?

About a spy ring on the home front, August 25, 1943: *I just read the morning* Free Press, *Bob, and there was a headline about Mrs. (Countess, according to the paper) von Moltke, the wife of our good friend. You have probably heard the news about the spy ring in Detroit, and she is alleged to be in with them. It seems odd that it could be someone we know, but Professor von Moltke was always a funny old bird himself, wasn't he? There were rumors around Wayne when we were there that he was a Nazi sympathizer, because he had been awarded some kind of medal by Adolf Hitler. Anyway, I doubt very much if he will be teaching at Wayne next semester.*

Mr. Reaume, my boss, was all aflutter about the ring-leader, Miss Buchanan-Dineen, who is a tenant at River Terrace, one of our super-duper, exclusive apartments. Our clients are investigated thoroughly before we rent to them, and Mr. Reaume approved her himself. So I imagine it was quite a blow to him to find that an accused spy was living in his pet terraces. We have a file on her, and she evidently was quite a socialite.

A letter from the North Country, August 29, 1943: *Here we are, dear, sitting by the light of a kerosene lamp in our little cottage deep in the wild woods of Michigan. Every now and then you can hear wildcats screaming or owls hooting. And maybe hyenas, who knows? Friday was my last day of working for Mr. Reaume, and Ellen and I came up by train yesterday. Mr. William Noteware, who owns the resort, met us at the station in Interlochen. We've built a wood fire in the stove, and it's very cozy in here. We arrived just before the midday dinner and were famished, because we hadn't eaten on the train. I think Ellen and I finished off a whole chicken between us. It was delicious. Then we went rowing on the lake and came back for a short nap. But we slept so soundly, that neither of us heard the bell and would have missed supper completely, if they hadn't sent a messenger to wake us up. It too was delicious. And I think in the morning they will be giving us pancakes for breakfast. All this for $2.50 a day! I'm sure I'll put on a few pounds during the week we are here. Tomorrow, I think I will try my hand at fishing. If I can get someone to put the worm on the hook, that is. They're so wiggly.*

Many thanks, dear, for all the presents you sent me from Chinatown—the shell necklace, the lovely box, and the statuettes. We'll have quite a collection of them, won't we. I have an idea—why don't we become Buddhists, since we are so well equipped? That might solve all our problems. Do you think you could sit cross-legged and contemplate your bare tummy?

News from Palo Alto, August 30, 1943: *I don't know how long this letter will be, because I am writing it in the library, when I should be studying—from nine to eleven every morning. But studying what, nobody knows. As a consequence, I have been using the time today to read a book on Plato's philosophy. I find it quite interesting, almost like a conversation, and not at all as difficult as I thought it would be. I don't think I'd want to be a philosopher, though, because they think about things eternal and ephemeral, and not at all about bodily comforts and things like sex, etc. Especially, if it's true, as you said, that they don't get married. I'll have to check with Professor Hoekstra about that, the next time I'm home on furlough.*

I went up to San Francisco this past weekend and managed to spend $10 without having a very good time. It's almost like throwing money away. It does go pretty fast when you spend $2 or more for a meal. Of course, I could have eaten at a cafeteria for a lot less, so I shouldn't complain too much. The *trouble is the town is noted for its eating places, and I am always tempted. This time I ate at Bernstein's Fish Grotto, which is famous. The first time I went there I had an abalone steak, which you probably never heard of. It's a big shellfish, and the meat is about six inches across and two inches thick. It's so tough, though, that before it's cooked they pound it for a long while to break up the fibers. Then it's delicious.*

Two weeks ago I ordered a complete fish dinner: A crab cocktail to start with, and then a bowl of clam chowder, and, as pièce de résistance, fried oysters. And on Saturday night I had another abalone steak, and yesterday some clam broth and a swordfish steak, which was even better than the abalone. Maybe I should take back what I said about having a good time, if fine food is so pleasurable. And maybe sinful. They say, though, that fish is brain food, so I can rationalize by claiming that I'm storing up intelligence for when I start my studies. I have to go to a class shortly—on the history of World War I. It will be interesting to see if they treat it differently from Mr. Kemmer's Western Civ course. So far we haven't had any of Stanford's high-powered faculty, probably because the fall term hasn't started yet for the civilians.

Thanks, honey, for the clippings about Mrs. von Moltke. I had read in the SF newspaper about the wife of a Wayne U prof. who had been charged. They didn't give her name, but I was reasonably certain it would be she. And I'm not surprised at all, since I knew all along that he had Nazi leanings. It's too bad it had to be Wayne, but they should have known about it years ago and taken some steps then.

News from Marianne at Cedar Hedge Lake, August 1, 1943: *Ellen and I have been practically having hysterics this morning writing a play. Each Tuesday night they have a program in the dining room where everyone performs, and since neither of us sings or dances, we decided to give a melodrama. It's corny, I know, but we think it is funny. The villain (Ellen) and the hero (me) get chummy at the end when they find they both belong to the ten-percent club and leave the heroine in the lurch. Three high school kids in one of the cabins are helping us put it on. One is Armenian, and he is the heroine (Waterlily). He is going to wear flowers in his hair that we picked this morning. I hope the other people enjoy it and think it's as funny as we do. I don't know, though, how Mr. Noteware will react to it. He's an old biddy. He likes things just so, and he glares at people who are late for meals.*

On the other hand, people here say he lives with the housekeeper (Mrs. Countryman), while his wife is in an institution!

The next day: *The program last night was a lot of fun, and our play came out swell. Afterward everybody was telling us how much they enjoyed it. We painted a black moustache (villain, you know) on Ellen with lamp soot, and shaggy eyebrows on me. Alec, the heroine, was a dream with two water lilies in his hair and a dirndl skirt on. I must say the fellows were mighty agreeable to let us do that to them. I doubt if you would do it, would you, dear? Even Mr. Noteware gave us a vote of thanks for our efforts. There's a professor here from the University of Chicago, and he played a guitar and sang in Russian. And he and his wife did a Russian folk dance. They are a young couple, and very nice. Not much like your typical professor, though. P.S. We still haven't been fishing yet, probably because neither of us could bait a hook. But I think we'll go out one of these nights and use marshmallow cookies. That's what we feed the baby fish that come to our dock, and they seem to love them. But then I don't know what I would do if I actually got one on my hook—probably cut off the line and let him go.*

At last! ASTP. September 3, 1943: *Well, it looks as though I am going to school, after all this waiting. And you will never guess where it will be. The University of Utah in Salt Lake City! I haven't seen the order, and it's still in the rumor stage. But several fellows tell me they saw my name on the shipping list. So it seems more authentic than most latrine rumors. And I'll be leaving in two or three days. I kept saying I'd rather be sent closer to home. But when you think of it, I'm lucky to be going to school anywhere. There are hundreds of thousands of men overseas who would give their right arms to be in my place, and I should be ashamed for all the complaining I do. And the University of Utah is a thousand miles closer than the West Coast—at least two days travel time, both coming and going.*

And I know that once I am on that train I won't be reclassified. Or have to take more tests. And all indications are that when I get started to school, I will go straight through. Some of the men were put in 9L, that is, they are fluent enough to need only three months training. But I was put in 4L, which means I need nine months, or three quarters at Utah. The more I get, the closer to a degree I will be. It's certain from what everyone says, that I will get college credit for all of it.

About the play you and Ellen wrote, it does sound interesting. I wish I had been there to see it. I wasn't aware that there was a budding playwright in the family. But I do remember at Wayne that you were an especially good speech student, so I think the reading of your part in the play must have been something to cheer about. At least, I'd have cheered. Your question about whether I could have taken a role played by the boys is unanswerable. With my short haircut the only way I could have had flowers on my head would be to glue them to my ears! So I am off the hook, along with that fish you are going to catch with those marshmallows.

I'm rather sorry to leave here, in a way, because the university is very beautiful. Then, too, the life I've led here has been quite pleasant, all in all. Stanford would be a good place to go to school, I think. It has an excellent reputation, the campus is ideal. Palo Alto is a nice, quiet town, and San Francisco is only an hour away. I am glad and lucky to have had this opportunity to be here for a month. I got a lot of exercise, which put me in good shape. I've read quite a bit, about philosophy and, of course, German literature. And it will be easier, I think, to get back into the habit of intense and consistent studying.

Good news from Dearborn, September 7, 1943: *It seems, honey, that I have a job, after all. Mr. Lowrey called while I was away, and he has a speech-correction position for me in Dearborn. I haven't signed a contract yet, but I think I will accept it instead of waiting to be assigned in Detroit. I attended meetings today, and school starts tomorrow. I must have met a hundred teachers today, and I saw a lot that I had in grade school and high school. It seems odd to be teaching with them now. There are two other members in my department, and both are young and very nice. One is the supervisor, but she doesn't act like one, so I'll probably be able to teach just as I please. I have a lot of ideas to try out. It's different from Detroit, where they seem to have more supervisors than teachers. Dearborn schools are more pleasant to work in too, because they are newer and so well equipped. And then I won't have as much traveling to do. The one drawback is that my pay here won't be as high as the Detroit salary schedule—probably about $1,500–1,600 a year. But I'll be living at home for now, and I won't have many expenses. I'll be able to save quite a bit, I think.*

The first letter from Salt Lake City, September 8, 1943: *I suppose my folks told you I'll be studying Japanese? I called them this evening to give them the news. It seems the ASTP has no German program here—Japanese, Italian, and Spanish, but not the language I was qualified for and have been studying for several years. Somebody in the army must have shit for brains, as we say. They must have known about the lack of a German program. Well, there's nothing I can do about that now, but go along with them.*

After we got here and were "oriented," we had to list our preferences. I put Spanish first, and then Italian, and Japanese last. I thought that way, I might be sent to Europe, and wind up in Germany somehow. But when the interviewers looked at the high marks I made on the aptitude tests, they thought I could handle Japanese better than some of the other fellows. I suppose I should feel flattered, but I really am disappointed. I had been building my hopes so and thought I could do more for the army in Europe. Well, "c'est la vie," to express myself in yet another language. And "merde." I think that's the right word for it.

They did say, though, that at the end of the nine months I would be able to take an intensive course in German. So we'll see. And from the news lately, it looks as though it might not be very long before the Allies are in Germany. Radio reports today are that the Italian armies have surrendered. From our point of view the war news is just swell, isn't it? The sooner this is over, the sooner we'll be able to be married and to live together. What do you think, honey, of our being married while I am home on one of my furloughs? Say in December or March? We could plan for it definitely, because I already know the dates when I'll be home. Think it over and let me know about your ideas.

The same day in Dearborn: *I'm at Sarah's house, honey, and have just had an interruption. Your mother called to say they had heard from you. And she said you'd be studying Japanese, rather than German. I wonder if that means you might be going to Japan whenever we occupy it. I suppose so. It does concern me somewhat. The Japs seem to be such sneaky little weasels, and they would probably go on killing people, even after they were conquered. On the other hand, it should be interesting for you to study an Asian society and language, an area we don't know very much about. At Wayne I used to be amazed that an Irishman could speak German as well as you do. And now you will be mastering Japanese. It will be much more difficult for you, but I have every confidence you can do it.*

144

I've been assigned the schools I'll be teaching at. One is Fordson High. (Worse luck!) I haven't had secondary-school training, and also I'll be working with kids not much younger than I am. But who knows? Maybe I'll like it. And I will have a football team to root for! That should interest you. I'll also be at the Oakman School—I went from kindergarten to the 6th grade there. They still have the same principal, and he is very nice. Some of the teachers have that patting-on-the-head attitude, but I think I can handle that. Also the William Ford and Henry Ford Schools—you can tell whose town this is—and they are both good schools too. I know I will like my job a lot. I feel so lucky about that.

Two days later in Salt Lake City: *I've really had an easy week since I came here—even easier than at Stanford, if that is possible. We don't do anything in the morning, except try to duck fatigue details, which I have done successfully so far. After all, I was a world champion in that area when I was at Camp Roberts. And we get passes from one in the afternoon till ten-thirty. They have been waxing the floor here in the field house the last couple of days, and we were told that if we stayed around, we'd have to work at polishing it. So it behooved me to get the hell out—and stay away as long as I could.*

I asked about doing some writing for the student newspaper here, maybe about the ASTP fellows, but the colonel in charge of the unit has forbidden the army men to take part in student activities. I hope he will change his mind, because it seems to me like an asinine rule. Of course, the soldier-students wouldn't have time to engage in sports—such as football or basketball. But we should be able to do something on the campus besides go to classes and study. I think I'm going to like living here even better than in Palo Alto. The school isn't as ritzy as Stanford, but the campus is nicer, I think, because the trees are more like home. Not so many palm trees, and stuff like that. It's a small institution, about 3,500 in peacetime, they say. Now I hear that there will be about 500 men from the military—350 in the ASTP and another 150 in the Enlisted Reserve Corps, and probably a thousand women, more or less. I say "women" advisedly, because those I have seen so far seem like high school sophomores. As I noted at Stanford, college girls here really do seem younger than when I was at Wayne. But then I'm a lot older than I was then. Almost middle-aged, if we are counting birthdays.

Salt Lake City is a nice place, a lot like Detroit with its trees and build-ings, but cleaner. In fact, the streets and the outsides of buildings seem immac-ulate, as if they were washed every day. It appears to be about the size of Akron, Ohio, where I was born. The school is a fifteen-minute ride on the streetcar from downtown, and there are good shows and shops. Right back of the university is Fort Douglas, where there are PXs and a GI movie theater. Of course, the only time I'll be able to leave here will be on weekends. The most unpleasant feature of the place is that we have to sleep in double-deck bunks—all 500 of us. We don't have much room for anything in the field house, nor any privacy. If they could move Stanford's dorms here to Utah, it would be perfect.

Hurrah! September 12, 1943: *I just had some very good news, dear. When I went to find out which platoon I would be in, starting tomorrow, I found I would be studying Spanish instead, after all. That's really swell, isn't it? It means I will be sent to the European theater of operations, rather the Pacific islands and—ultimately—the mainland of Japan. There's no way of knowing why, but I'm guessing that they had enough men in the Japanese unit and decided it made sense to put me in Spanish first and then in German. Colonel Lawrence thought there was little that made sense in the ASTP, but maybe there are some officers in charge who make sensible decisions. Sensible, as far as my future is concerned.*

The next day: *My schedule for the next three months will be about as follows: I'll have a Spanish class for one hour a day in which we learn gram-mar and other essentials from a "senior instructor." Then I have a two-hour session, six days a week, with a group of ten men, in which a drillmaster teaches us to speak idiomatic Spanish, and we have informal discussions in that language. This is followed by a two-hour period, five days a week, in which our group studies and discusses together. Then for two hours, five days a week, we'll learn about the geography and history of Europe and especially Spain. The other language groups have similar schedules.*

Each evening just before I go to bed I go out in front of the field house and watch the lights of the city for a while. The university is on top of a hill, and the whole city is spread out before it like a shining tapestry. There is no blackout here, as there is on the coast, so it is all lit up. I have no words to tell you how beautiful it is. Even San Francisco didn't have vistas like this. To the right of the city is Kearns Field, a large replacement depot for the air corps. It's several miles away, but it's so big the lights make it look like another city. And there are a lot of searchlights and beacons for the planes. All in all, it's breathtaking.

Problems already with the ASTP, September 15, 1943: *I'd been wondering why Richard Marks was complaining to Sarah about his lot in the ASTP. But after just one day, I can see why. It's not that we are kept busy. I expected that. But the military part of the organization is always dreaming up more asinine things for us to do. We have a commanding officer—the colonel—who used to be head janitor at this university. Someone said that he lost his job because he couldn't take charge of the men under him. And now he is over the whole military shebang. Probably he got his commission in the ROTC or the reserves, and now the army doesn't know what else to do with him. For instance, we had to get up this morning at 5:30 for some strange reason. Nobody could figure it out. I guess the colonel just wanted to be ornery.*

He is very unpopular with the men, especially the Engineering section. When he spoke to us at our orientation, some of the men hissed him. It was very impolitic of them, but it does show what they think of him. They are younger than the ASTP fellows, by and large, and have had only thirteen weeks in the army before coming here. Our language group seems to be mostly noncoms.

So far, I've liked the direct approach to learning a language. Our book is called Poco a Poco, *and we start with simple and obvious words. "La rata es un animal." "El elefante es un animal grande." And so on. We are thinking in Spanish all the time. And if we need to look up a word, we will be using a Spanish-Spanish dictionary. One anomaly, though. We are studying Spain and Europe, but our pronunciation is Latin American, rather than Castilian. And another interesting thing—I find that my German phonetics class at Wayne helps me a lot in pronouncing Spanish words.*

The same day in Dearborn: *I'm relieved, honey, that you won't be going to Japan. The military government of occupied Europe would be no easy job, but to try to set up a new regime in Japan would be something terrible. They have built up such a distrust of us, it would be hard to convince them they have been defeated, I would think. P.S. Yes, dear, I will marry you whenever you think would be a good time. I can give you many reasons, and maybe list them one, two, and three. But the most important, for me, are your*

147

wonderful letters. They have kept us together, when we have been apart. And cheered me when I felt unhappy and out-of-sorts. And now we need to do some planning. You can call me when you have a chance, and reverse the charges. I am making so much money now, I don't know how to spend it all!

The Utah rat race, September 19, 1943: *Here it is, the beginning of my second week at Utah—the end of one week of a tough grind. Spanish won't be hard to learn, though. A lot easier than Japanese with the thousands of characters I would have to commit to memory. We have spent this first week just learning to pronounce the words. Speaking is everything, and writing the language isn't stressed. But if I can say it, I can read it—it's that simple. So books should be no problem. Some parts make me laugh, though. Often, when I am asked a question, I start to reply in German! It just pops out, automatically. I think I'll like Spanish a lot. P.S. Here is a money order for $30, dear. Would you put $25 in our account and use the rest for my mother's present? Her birthday is on the 27th. I don't know what she needs, but flowers might be appropriate. A dozen or so roses, maybe. Thanks, dear. I love you very much.*

The next day in Dearborn: *I hope you like the briefcase I sent you. It's just the thing, I thought, for carrying your papers and books from class to class. I can see you now, looking very professorial, with your horned-rim glasses.*

You asked on the phone about my job, dear. I like it very well. Student-teaching in the Detroit schools was certainly not like this. I've been lucky to get a good room in each of the schools, and the children are all so angelic it still amazes me. I haven't begun teaching at Fordson yet, because I've had to spend the first two weeks getting a program organized. They've never had an official speech-correction program in the high schools, so I have to test all the freshmen to find candidates and get lists of people from the deans of girls and of boys and the counselors. I was doubtful about teaching at Fordson, because of the discipline problem. I didn't think I could get it through respect for my age. But I probably won't have much trouble, because the classes will be small, and I will let them know from the beginning that I mean business.

I'm pleased with the way the kids in the other classes are reacting. I decided I'd better spend the first week or so selling the idea of a speech class to them. Telling them they are something special. I noticed in my practice teaching that some children have disliked it a lot. I suppose because they don't like being made conscious of a defect, and there is a stigma to being singled out from a group. But one little kid told me yesterday that the other children in his class were going to start stuttering so they could come work with me. It made me so pleased with myself, because once you have the kids believing everything you say is right, you can teach them anything. P.S. I'll send your mother the flowers in plenty of time. I think I can get her two dozen nice roses for that amount. And I'll put some extra money in and get her some stockings. It's not very imaginative, but women can always use more stockings.

A scholar's life, September 24, 1943: *I'm really stiff today, and so is everyone else in my platoon. The powers-that-be directed that we take tests in physical fitness yesterday, and one consisted of hopping up and down, first on one foot, and then on the other. The point was that we would hop as long as we could, before we toppled over. We've been having these tests for a couple of weeks now, and I've found I have more muscles than I ever dreamed of. All of them sore.*

Yesterday we had to run 300 yards against time. There were three men in each race. I thought that I would start easy, and then at the last I'd spurt ahead. That's what we did when we ran in the Wayne gym. But I didn't reckon with the competition. I was racing against Dennis Paterson, who was a trackman at Berkeley—in the 400-meter relay, I think. He started fast and kept on running faster. I stayed about ten yards behind him all the way, so I was going as fast as he was. He finished in 37.3 seconds, with the fastest time in the company. I was timed in a little more than 39 seconds, and at the finish line I collapsed. I thought I was going to puke. Dennis said he thought I was going to beat him, but I think he was just being nice. It turned out that I was the fourth fastest of the lot, which is pretty good for an old man of 25.

From what I learned when I covered the track team for the Collegian, *forcing everyone to such excesses can be dangerous. It must have been the work of the janitor-colonel, who is also a sadist. No one else could be so cruel and so stupid. Still, I did get some satisfaction in performing well, under a lot of stress.*

I went to a concert here this week and heard the Utah State Symphony with Sir Thomas Beecham conducting. They weren't bad at all. Not like the Detroit orchestra, but Beecham certainly put on a show. I've heard he's been in this country, because of the war. I thought I had got my money's worth and more. The military authorities have relaxed their restrictions, and they are letting us go to football games and concerts, etc. I'm glad, because it is quite a grind to go so long without some kind of relaxation.

The next day: *I'm glad this is the end of the week, because now we have a day to rest and catch up with things. We really don't get enough rest around here. If we could get to sleep right away, it wouldn't be so bad, but the ERC men (the engineers) who live in the gym with us make too much noise at night. Worse than that, they sling empty Coke bottles along the waxed floor and crash them against the walls, breaking them into a million pieces. They seem to think that's funny. And nobody does anything to stop them. If I ever got to be sergeant of the guard or charge-of-quarters for one night, I would pull those bastards out of their beds so fast it would make their heads swim. I would put them under arrest, if necessary. Barracks are for sleeping, not for tomfoolery. Dangerous tomfoolery. They wouldn't last one day in the real army. Maybe the whole ASTP company should get together and beat the shit out of them a few times. Or the army could ship them all to the infantry. Anyway, that is off my chest, and I can turn to other matters.*

Changes, September 26, 1943: *Now, as to what you said about being married soon. When I asked you that question, I didn't know you would be getting a teaching contract. As things are now, the only time I am free is from Saturday at six in the evening until Sunday at five. It's been possible to get passes that would allow us to stay out until 11:30, but so far no one has been allowed to live off the post. Some of the men have their wives here, and they seem to get along OK. That's what the husbands say. But who knows what the women say to each other when they are alone? How is it for the wife? Alone in a strange city for six nights of the week and five and a half days. I would love to have you here, but not at that price.*

What I would like, dear, is to be married soon, on one of my leaves—in Detroit or Dearborn, probably. And then for the time being you could be there at home. And if things improved for us, we might live together, here or somewhere else. In the summer, say. But right now, my situation is so iffy, that I can't guarantee anything. Except that I love you, and want to be with you as soon as possible. Would there be any problem there with your job if you were married? I would think not, since there are so many teachers with Mrs. attached to their names already. And in any event, the Dearborn schools are lucky to have you. What are your ideas about all this?

℘ 7 ℘

A Wedding in the Offing

Settling in, October 2, 1943: *It's a Saturday morning and the end of my third week of school. Well, almost the end. I have a class this afternoon, but after that I'm free. Utah is playing Fort Warren in football this afternoon, and I am going to go. Like you, I now have a home-town team to root for. I don't know how good Utah is as yet, but they're probably better than Wayne, in a different kind of league. Fort Warren is an army training camp in Wyoming for the Quartermaster Corps. I hear they are pretty good. We'll see.*

I trust you will be somewhat surprised to get a money order for $100. I only wish I could be there to see you opening this letter—then swooning and lying on the floor. But you don't have to worry, dear. I didn't rob a bank or anything like that. Such as take part in an all-night poker game. I don't think the ASTP fellows are card players. And we don't have the time, any-way. It was just that I got paid day before yesterday—finally. And I drew $134.22! As I told you, I hadn't been paid for a couple of months. I should be able to do quite well on $34 for the rest of this month. Put it in our account, and I'll try to send more each payday I'm here. It's a good idea, I think, for me to put money in the bank, and for you to buy war bonds. That way, we'll have a ready supply of money for our current needs, and the bonds for a long-term investment.

I must have reached a plateau in learning Spanish. You remember in the psych. course that the professor said learning goes along in steps—a great deal

151

of progress, and then a plateau. I have learned a lot in these first weeks, but now I don't seem to be improving much. Sometimes, it's frustrating. But if I am patient, I believe I'll know Spanish even better than German. I keep being pleased how much the high school Latin is helping me—and it has been all of ten years since I was in the Caesar's Gaul class. Also the courses in English and German grammar make it easier now for me to put sentences together in our conversation sessions. Some of the men here are handicapped by not knowing the fine points of English grammar even. I don't know how they got to college without being exposed to some of it, at least. Simple things like diagramming a sentence on the blackboard.

The next day: *I went to the football game yesterday and saw our team get beat by Fort Warren 60-0! I hate to think what will happen next week when we take on Colorado, because they beat Fort Warren 35-0. Fort Warren—and I think Colorado too—have a lot of army or navy personnel from around the country, big, tough, grown men. Whereas, the team here consists of a lot of kids, most still in their teens, without much experience.*

The next day in Dearborn: *I went out to your folks house yesterday with Ellen, and we had a good time playing rummy with your dad and Eileen and Allen. Also your dad entertained us with some of his card tricks. On Saturday, I stayed out at Ellen's house, and she and I went to an Episcopal service the next morning. I liked the service very well, honey. The best part, I think, was the choir. They had good voices, mostly women. I suppose the younger men were off somewhere in the army or the navy. The music was especially beautiful, the hymns. It was not the "high church," that you spoke of. I'll try other Episcopal churches in the area when I have a chance.*

The service was a good deal like that of the Lutherans, so it doesn't seem it would be difficult for me to change. If we both agree, we can accept it for our church. It would be an ideal solution, I think, with both of us compromising. Incidentally, Jane is Episcopalian, and she has been telling me a lot about it. So I would agree to be married in either an Episcopal church or the Martha-Mary chapel at Greenfield Village. I don't believe it would be necessary now to take a course of instructions, or whatever is required to become a member—before we are married. We would perhaps join later, when we have a place of our own. Don't you think so, dear?

You asked me what effect our getting married would have on my job. I don't believe having a Mrs. in front of my name would make any difference, one way or the other. But if I did go out to live with you before June, my contract would still be in effect, and I could be sued for quitting. The Board of Education doesn't make a practice of suing for breach of contract, friends say, but it wouldn't be a good idea to quit now, because I would never be forgiven. The people I work with here have been mighty nice, and it would be letting them down pretty hard. The speech-correction program would have to fold up in three primary and intermediate schools, and also at Fordson after just getting started there. And I wouldn't be granted a leave of absence, because I haven't taught the required three years first. Under the circumstances, it seems a good idea for me to stay here at least until June, and perhaps longer, depending on the circumstances—if you were going overseas, or something like that. As we keep saying, we'll see what happens. If you were still in this country, I could perhaps come out to be with you for the summer. In wartime, it's difficult to make plans very much in advance, isn't it, dear?

Extra-curricular activities in Utah, October 7, 1943: *Last night I went to a debate between Lewis Browne, a radio commentator, and the novelist Sinclair Lewis on the subject "The Machine Age vs. Civilization." It was very interesting, and I feel lucky to be part of this intellectual exchange of ideas. But I don't think either of them made as valid points as he might have. Sinclair Lewis—didn't you read one of his novels in your course?—held that the machine unbridled was a detriment to civilization, and I agreed with his position. But I think I could have made more valid points, as could most of the fellows in my company who were there. Anyway, as I said, it was interesting to listen to them.*

Last Monday evening our company was invited to various sororities after our classes in the evening. Each platoon went to a different house—ours to the Chi Omega's. There was dancing, singing, and refreshments, and the girls made us feel part of the university community. One of the girls grabbed my hand and pulled me out on the dancing floor. "You're the tallest man here," she said. And before I could tell her I didn't know how to dance, I was dancing! Maybe the next time I come home, you will give me some lessons. It wasn't as difficult as I had expected. Every other Monday, the fellows will go to a different house.

We are going to have a parade next Tuesday—Columbus Day. We have been practicing each evening at the retreat formation, and should be fairly good by that time. But only fairly good. One trouble is that most of the men here are from the Air Corps, the Signal Corps, and the Medical Corps, and they don't know very much about being a soldier. How to move and to act like a soldier, and how to keep their uniforms neat and clean—their buttons and belt-buckles shiny. How to keep in step with everybody else when they're marching. And they don't want anyone else to be a real soldier either. So, we'll see.

Two days later in Dearborn: *In your last letter, dear, you spoke of our being married in June and said we might not have a chance to be together because you could be sent out soon afterward. I had understood that you would have at least three more months after that to brush up on your German. Are you supposed to go to school for the whole year, or am I wrong in that assumption? Perhaps June might not be such a good time to get married after all.*

I went to a sorority meeting on Thursday, and Elva Spicer was there, and some of us went out to her home afterward. She and Larry are home on his leave from Texas, and they both looked so happily married and so much in love. I was a little envious. Gerry Rapin was at the meeting too, and she and Bud Rollins are still going together. He finished OCS and is down in Virginia just now. I can get his address if you want to get in touch with him.

A weekend in Salt Lake City, October 10, 1943: *This will be a short letter, honey, because I have to study this evening for a big test in Geography. This morning I went to the Mormon tabernacle and heard the famous choir sing. I think their broadcast is at 12 noon on WJR. Have you ever heard it? It's really a marvelous group—about 300 members. The broadcast used to be open to the general public, but now only servicemen are admitted. If you have a chance, be sure to listen to it.*

Then I had dinner downtown and went up to Fort Douglas to see a couple of movies. Nothing very interesting. But I had a hard time sitting still for so long—more than three hours. After being in the army for over two years, moving around a lot, sitting gives me more trouble than you would imagine. In a way, women are lucky—to be more padded in the right places, so they don't have the troubles men suffer from. Or am I all wet about that? You might have learned about it in your anatomy class.

I'll have to really study this evening and tomorrow morning, because I want to make a good score on the Area exam. The professor gave us a list of 72 questions and said he would take about six from those for the exam. So if I know all of them, I should get by OK. The instructor, Charles Dibble, doesn't seem to know very much for a Ph.D. And he mispronounces so many words in English, that I wonder how he got his degree in the first place. (He's an anthropologist, someone said, who studies the Aztecs.) Most of all, though, he is a pretty nice guy. He had some of the men in our class over to his house for dinner last night. He told us that as soon as we get a good command of Spanish, he would give our lectures in that language. I think it's too early yet, but maybe next term we'll be able to handle it.

A week later: *It seems as though I have been neglecting you lately, honey, but only because I'm so darn busy these days. It's an old story, isn't it, for both of us. And next week I'll be even busier. I'll be having exams in both Spanish and Area Studies. We are supposed to be graded every three weeks, and our progress—or lack of it—reported to the army. And they do check up on us. I'm not too much worried about it, though I am trying to maintain my straight-A record.*

About my June furlough, at times you seem to be wondering if we should be married or not. Sometime yes, sometimes no. Maybe I'll never go overseas, or maybe I'll go over for years. Who knows? But I hope, when June comes around, that you will marry me, whether I will be here after that or not. We have been waiting a long time, haven't we? There is always some risk in marriage, even in the safest and surest of times. If we are waiting for a time when we will be absolutely sure of living together for months and months, that time might be a long way off. How do you feel about that? Some people say: "Let's wait." Or "What if he doesn't come back?" Or "What if I have a baby?" But the soldier in the dirty foxhole thinks if something happens to him, he would like someone to pass on his family name and family history. I wish I could make things perfect for you, so you wouldn't have to worry a bit. But I can't do that. Are you willing to take risks? The future is so unpredictable.

Ambivalence: *I haven't written you as often as I'd like, Bob, and I'll try to do better. But I seem so busy all the time. Last night I stayed at Sarah's, typing reports on the membership in my classes that were due today. And Monday and Tuesday I went to bed after coming home from work, because I wasn't feeling well. I hoped I wouldn't miss any school, because I have only three days off during the semester, and I would like to take them while you are home. Right now, though, I feel just fine, thank you.*

I like teaching at Fordson a lot. At first, I was a bit worried, because of my lack of experience, as I told you. I knew what I wanted to do, but not how to do it. So I've been reading up on what materials to use, and the ways to use them. The best part is that the kids in my class are all nice and appreciative. There has been a lot of talk about the problems of teenagers these days. They seem to have a general "what the heck" attitude toward their studies. Probably because many of them will be going into the service in a short time, and Latin and literature seem pointless to them. I don't have that trouble, I think because my class is elective, and those with serious speech defects would likely be turned down for military service unless they can correct them.

I'm sorry I puzzled you, honey, but I didn't mean that I wouldn't marry you this June. I was just thinking that if you are sent overseas right after your third term, we might have no more than a couple of days together. But then again, it might be longer, as you say. And I didn't think our getting married was being "too risky." But I hope you'll understand that, for me, there are a few things we want to be sure of. I do love you, and I want us to be married. But somehow it has always seemed pointless to me for people to be married one day and separated the next. But I do promise to marry you in June—after your third term—and take the chance that we could be together for some time.

As for what you said about having babies when husbands are going away, I guess you know I don't agree with you. And it is not because of "risk," but I just don't think it is right for the child. I can understand how you feel about wanting to leave some part of you behind, if you should have to go. I too would be happy to have someone who is part of you. And there seem to be a lot of people having babies these days with that idea in mind. The last war ended, and people such as our parents went on living together.

156

I know that we have to face the possibility that those who are dearest to us might be killed. But there is no point in dwelling on that possibility when the chances are better that they won't be. When the men all come back, some husbands might be presented with half-grown sons and daughters they have never seen. They will have missed a good part of their childhood—the "formative years," as we say. I think it would be too bad for the child, as well as the father. And it is generally agreed that no matter how good the care a mother could give their child, its life is very one-sided without the father.

The same day in Salt Lake City: *I have time for just a short note tonight, dear. I'm going to a party of the Spanish class, and I'm leaving in a few minutes. You might wonder, after all my promises, why I am writing you so seldom. But the demands of the program seem to get stiffer and stiffer every day. I do want to report, though, that I had a Spanish exam today, and I think I got a good grade. Not a perfect score, but least a 95. And in the exam in Area Studies I was so worried about, I got a 97, the highest in the class. So I think I'll stop worrying about trying to keep up with the "young fellows." Do you think I am bragging too much, dear? It's just that I am feeling pretty good these days. Maybe, though, I shouldn't be so cocksure until I find out how I did today. I must say, the competition is fierce in the Spanish group. Some of the fellows are Italian, and Spanish comes easily to them. Like Sgt. Bonfigli, who is beginning to speak it like a native.*

The best student in our class is Robert Bowen from Minnesota. His army IQ is 153, the highest in all of the area programs, so far as I know. I think he wants to be a lawyer when he goes back home. He likes to talk, so maybe that should be his profession.[7]

Our instructor says that at the end of our nine months we should know more Spanish than she did after two years of study. And she also told us that at that time she had gone down to the National University in Mexico City and at the end of two weeks had no trouble understanding any of the professors. So you can see that my Spanish should be pretty fluent. I only hope, though, that my German will still be as good. After all, that should be more important during the war in Europe.

---

7. Subsequently Robert Bowen had a distinguished career as a judge in the Twin Cities.

Two days later: *Today is memorable, dear. A day when no one should be forced to stay indoors. I don't think I have ever seen a day more beautiful, anywhere. And especially pleasant when we have already had some snow and ice. But I have another exam later in the afternoon, so here I am in the library, getting ready to study. That is, after this short letter, telling you I love you.*

I meant to write you last night, but I went downtown to a show with Sgt. Paterson. I had told my mother about being broke, and wanting to see For Whom the Bell Tolls. *So she sent me a dollar bill and said I should see it as a present from her. I wasn't hinting, of course, but I did appreciate it. I doubt, though, if she knew what kind of movie she was sending me to—especially the part about the sleeping bag and the earth moving. I liked it a lot and kept thinking Ingrid Bergman reminded me of you. Have you seen it yet? If so, you might tell me how it compares with the book.*

The same day in Dearborn: *I got your letter today, telling me you had done well on your exams, and I am glad to hear about that. No, dear, I don't think you are bragging—just reporting to me the facts, as you see them. But from time to time I do like to tease you about how egotistical you are. In a good way, that is. For me, it means that you are not content with being mediocre in anything you do. I remember that in Dr. Basilius's class your score was usually the best of all the students. Though I did tie you some of the time, especially when there was something about the subjunctive. Remember, dear?*

When I read your letter in which you thought women (me?) should take more risks, I realized you were up to your old tricks again. You play on my sympathies by putting yourself in dirty foxholes, being shot at by the enemy, while the women of this country are sitting safely at home in their warm living rooms. I guess there are some people who take advantage of the war, who are more concerned with their living in comfort than in ending it in a hurry. But not the women I know. Most of them, I think, would be willing to go out and fight alongside those they love in order to get this mess over with. They are the ones who now wait and worry. In spite of the pain and sweat the fellows have to go through, I still think it is easier to be doing something about the war—and knowing they are helping to end it. As long as you are busy, you haven't time to be tormented by worries about those you love. Perhaps the mental anguish of inaction is the worst sort of punishment to take. Reading the papers every day to see if your loved ones are in combat. Worrying about someone knocking at your door with bad news. Wishing the darn thing would end, so we can get on with our lives. You can consider yourself properly rebuked, dear.

A note about the snow in Salt Lake City, October 30, 1943: *This weather is bad for colds, I think, but so far I have been pretty lucky. I bought some Mentholatum yesterday and use that a lot, on my chest and throat, and it seems to do some good. I smell to high heaven though! And I could send home for my scarf, if it gets any colder. The mile-long one that you knitted for me, when I was at Camp Roberts. Also I can start wearing my long-johns, though I won't put them on when you are around, because they look too silly. Like the cartoons about hillbillies.*

There are some nice events starting here in a week or so, first the homecoming football game with Colorado, and then the Ballet Russe and the Don Cossack Choir. You can see that my cultural life is not being neglected. In fact, I think I'm going to more things here than I ever did when I was at Wayne. And it's so convenient, because the concerts and things are practically next door to the building where my classes are. I can leave a class at 8:15 p.m. and make it to concerts that begin at 8:30. Last Sunday I skipped the evening study period to see For Whom the Bell Tolls, *but that is too risky to do very often. So far, I haven't been caught out when I should have been studying. But eventually I suppose I will be, and they'll give me a little fatigue work to do. But it's worth taking the chance to see a good show. And the percentages are all in my favor.*

The next day: *This letter won't be very long tonight, because I'm going to bed early. Last night I was out—with Sgt. Paterson—until three in the morning. He's the one—remember?—I raced against. I'll probably be telling you about him from time to time, because he is now my best friend here. His first name is Dennis, but most people call him Pat. He is a few weeks older than I am and was an instructor at Berkeley before he came into the air corps. We seem to have a lot in common. We usually go to concerts, movies, and sports events together. I think you would like him—in fact, all the women I know here do, for some reason. He isn't especially handsome, but I guess it's his personality they go for.*

159

I went downtown today and had a Chinese dinner and then saw The Watch on the Rhine. *It was pretty good, I thought. And more serious and thought-provoking than most of the movies I see. I much prefer it to the Betty Grable stuff most of the fellows like. When I came back to the field house, I intended to take a nap. But our area instructor, Professor Dibble, was here, and he invited me and another fellow to supper. Of course, we accepted and had a very good time, talking about lots of things, especially Mexico. He has a boy four years old who can speak both English and Spanish fluently. He made me ashamed of the very little Spanish I can muster up for conversations. A funny thing happened, though, on the way to their house. The boy told his father his mother had said if he didn't stop asking soldiers over, she was going to throw something at him! I suppose she has to worry about their using up their precious ration points.*

There's another funny story about Professor Dibble's lecturing. I think I told you he's not the most inspiring teacher in the world. Anyway, the class is at one o'clock, right after lunch. And as he drones on, there's a tendency on our part to drift off. Last week, Sgt. Bonfigli's pen suddenly flew across the room. Afterward, we all asked him what had happened, and he said he had the pen in his hand as he was propping up his chin. He fell asleep and dreamed he was playing basketball. And he flipped his hands to make a shot!

The people here at the university say the professor is doing important research in Mexico, translating Aztec documents. I wish he could talk to us about that, instead of a subject he doesn't know very much about. I think they asked him to because he speaks Spanish so well. And it's true we are supposed to be studying the European area and learning Spanish at the same time.[8]

A note from Marianne on that same day in Dearborn: *Ellen came over yesterday afternoon and stayed for dinner—chicken and biscuits and cherry pie with ice cream. (I baked the pies in the morning.) Uncle Bob said I now have his permission to marry you, since it was evident that I can bake pies. (Do you get tired, honey, of hearing me boast of my many culinary accomplishments?) Then Ellen and I went out to the show to see* For Whom

---

8. Thirty years later Dr. Dibble and his colleague Arthur J. Anderson published their twelve-volume translation of Bernardo de Sahagún's accounts as *The Florentine Codex: General History of the Things of New Spain.*

the Bell Tolls. *We both enjoyed it, and I thought the acting was especially good. (You think I am like the Bergman character, perhaps because she seems so naïve. At first, that is. It's funny, because Gary Cooper reminded me of you—in a good way, I should say. Maybe because he is tall and lanky.) I was disappointed, though, that they left out most of the good parts in the novel. But then it is a long book. The film has been here for several weeks now, so it must be very popular with the public.*

Then today at our school—during lunch—we were talking about the film. And one of the older teachers (I had her in the second grade) said in a very shocked voice: "Oh my dear, don't tell me you saw that trash! I wouldn't allow any dog of mine to see it." She thought it was obscene. Maybe it was, in some grown-up ways, but it was a very good picture and worth seeing more than once. I hope I never get to be a fussy old biddy like that. I don't know if she could even be called a "teacher," although she has been "teaching" for almost thirty years now. If I ever show signs of getting narrow-minded and stuffy, I give you permission to put me in my place.

Doings at the University of Utah, November 3, 1943: *They are calling some of the men up before the classification board this week, and I'm not on the list. I had thought all the men would be interviewed, and decisions made about them. It seems, though, that it's just the ones who are in danger of failing, most of them in Engineering. A lot of those younger fellows don't seem to be taking seriously what we do here. And they will probably end up as casualty replacements for overseas infantry units. Which is a dreary prospect, I would think.*

The woman we have for our Spanish drill class told us today she was a Phi Beta Kappa, and she was surprised when we said none of us were. Of course, Wayne doesn't have a unit on the campus, and most of the other fellows have had only one or two years of classes, so they wouldn't have been eligible anyway. And it's clear most of the fellows in our class are a lot smarter than the teacher. I don't know if I've ever known a more brilliant group of students. Especially, Robert Bowen, as I said. By the way, I did beat him on our last exam—by one point. But then he never studies before a test, counting on his memory, and I stayed up late, reading over the materials.

The girl I talked to at Stanford was a Phi Bet, and I have met a lot of girls here—at the sorority parties. And talked with them too. But none them

Spanish platoon ASTP at the University of Utah.

are as smart as you are. That is, they maybe get good grades, but they don't know many facts or how to use them. About the country, the world, and the war, I mean. And the same goes for the girls I knew on the Collegian. Like you, they just knew more, I think, and were less parochial.

Sunday in Salt Lake City, November 7, 1943: *I didn't get very much done this past week, or this weekend, either. I did see Colorado beat Utah again, this time 22-19, and Utah looked very good. I guess the players were inspired by the homecoming crowd. I thought it was the best game I have ever seen anywhere. The kids can certainly be proud of themselves. Mostly, I have been resting when I get a chance. It's hard to keep going so many hours a day, day after day. But then I suppose you had that feeling last year when you were trying to graduate on time. How are you coming in your classes now, honey? I hope you like them, but not so well that you won't want to quit after we are married. I think we are agreed that taking care of a growing family is not compatible with a full-time job for you. Is that right, dear?*

Thanksgiving news a week later from Dearborn: *I meant to write you on the weekend, but we had a rather hectic time of it. And I missed a lot of sleep. Jane's son Paul is home on leave from the Navy, and something always happens when he is around. Friday morning about three he woke us up to say my dad's car had been stolen. My dad had let him borrow it for his date, and Paul must have left the keys in it, though he didn't tell us that in so many words. None of us got much sleep the rest of the night, with police-*

men calling us up. And my dad had to go down to the station with Paul and talk with the police while it was still dark. As you might expect, he—my dad—was pretty upset about it, especially because he had riders to drive with him to work the next morning. They would all have to make other arrangements, and that meant a lot of telephoning. And people taking busses. My car hasn't been used since last winter, and right now it is at a garage being fixed up, so he couldn't use that one.

Well, we had Thanksgiving dinner yesterday, early because of Paul's being home. And I baked a chocolate cake, and helped Jane stuff and roast the turkey. Kay and Bill were here with Barbara Jean, and everything was going fine. And then my pop got a call from the police saying his car had been found. They had picked it up on some deserted road beyond Redford, and the tires and everything were intact. And the keys were still in the ignition! So it certainly was Thanksgiving Day for Paul, after all. And for my dad too. He has been looking mighty happy to have his car again.

You asked me how I like school now, honey. I like it very much. Better than any other kind of work I've ever done. I am not concerned about teaching at Fordson High any more, although I still like the little kids the best. They are all duly respectful and very appreciative. A few of them have asked if they could have extra help, so one day a week I have classes after school hours. You also asked whether I'll be sorry to give up teaching when I marry you, and I suppose I will be. But I know I couldn't both have a family and work, and I'd rather be married to you than anything else. So when the time comes when we can be living together, I'll be only too glad to give up whatever I am doing.

And about your furlough, do you want me to draw any money out of our account and send it to you? Let me know about it pretty soon, so I can get it to you on time.

A reply, November 20, 1943: *I went to the university theater last night and saw a production of* Peter Pan. *It wasn't the best acting I've ever seen, but I enjoyed it a lot, because it had a lot of fairies, etc. in it. Some of the fellows didn't like it, but that was because they were too old in spirit and can't remember their childhood. I always did like to read fairy tales, so I thought it was good. I think stories like the ones the Grimm brothers wrote tell us a lot about a people, their customs, their values, and even their history. That's what Dr. Basilius said, anyhow.*

Busy days in Utah, November 24, 1943: *This, and the next week, will be very busy for me, with the final exams coming up, and I should at least do a little studying. I say a little studying because in part it is difficult to know what to prepare for. The Area final won't be so bad, because it covers only Spain. At the beginning of the course we were told the first six weeks would cover the geography of Europe, and the last six weeks would be on Spain. But the instructor kept talking too much, I think, and falling behind, so he didn't get to Spain until last week.*

The exam in the Spanish language, they say, is very hard, because it is the same as the one given to civilian students at the end of each year. They don't expect us to finish it, but we will be expected to do better—much better, I think—than the first-quarter civilians. It is entirely in Spanish, with no translation. And part of it will be to answer questions read to us in Spanish to test our oral comprehension. For the written part, it's hard to know what to focus on—not the textbook, certainly. But I can read through the book to recall the vocabulary and review the verb forms and the grammar. Sometimes though I have trouble with the meaning of words. Because of the Spanish-Spanish dictionary, that is. For example, I was looking up sin embargo *and found out that meant* no obstante. *And I still don't know what either of them means. Our teacher told us today that she would be giving us the forms of the subjunctive and conditional tomorrow and the next day, because they will be on the exam. That's a big order for just two days. But she is hoping a little learning will be a useful thing, to turn an old saying around.*

Anticipating, November 26, 1943: *Thank you very much, dear, for the gorgeous white-and-yellow mums. I am very fortunate to have such a thoughtful husband-to-be. There are no two ways about it—you are a sweetheart. And did you know that we—you and I both—are indebted to your brother Allen? He rode on buses and streetcars almost out to Dearborn, before he found a florist who would deliver the bouquet on Thanksgiving Day! Your mother told me about it when I called her. Be sure to thank him when you come home. He looks and acts so grown-up these days, it is hard to realize he is your "little" brother. I suppose, though, that one day he'll be in the service too. But maybe the war will be over by then. I hope so, anyway.*

I thought about you yesterday and the first Thanksgiving we spent to-gether three years ago. And did I ever tell you that it was about then I first began to be seriously interested in you? You seemed so at ease with my folks, whom you didn't know at all. And with me, whom you scarcely knew, ex-cept for a few cokes at the Cass-Warren. But the best was when I asked you if you wanted sugar in your tea, you said: "No, just dip your little fingers in it and stir." I thought you were fresh, in a nice way. And when you had gone home, Jane said: "You'd better grab on to him." Which I did. After that, you never had a chance.

You'll be glad to know, dear, that I drove my car yesterday for the first time in almost a year. It's been thoroughly overhauled, and my pop says I ought to drive it regularly, otherwise it will deteriorate too rapidly in this climate. So I believe I'll be driving it to school when the weather isn't too bad. As you know, gasoline is rationed these days, but I believe teachers are exempt, somewhat. I'll have to look into that.

Postponement, November 28, 1943: *The Spanish tests have been moved back a day, because some of us are on guard duty tonight. I'm glad, because my stretch was from two to six in the morning, and I'd have very little sleep before the exam. I spent most of today on my bed, because of my cold, but I'm still tired. I hope I can rest up on my furlough, but I probably won't, if the past is any criterion. I've been looking in the* Free Press *to see what is going on while I am home, but I don't think I want to waste time going out to a show. I'd rather be with you and my folks. We can always think of things to do at the time. I hope you will be able to get at least three days off, because every moment home is precious. See you very soon, dear.*

A reply from Marianne, December 2, 1943: *I've told my supervisor I'll be off work on Tuesday, Wednesday, and Thursday, and she understands, because she is a happily married woman. And I'll see Mr. Lowrey tomorrow to let him know my plans. And maybe I'll have a chance to drive you in my car. I'm still a little bit leery, though, about driving at night. So we'll see.*

Furlough's end, December 12, 1943: *By now you will be nearly back to Salt Lake City and very tired. I hope you haven't decided the fatiguing trip isn't worth the pain and discomfort of sitting up in a rickety train car all those days. I'm so glad you came home, darling. We seem to belong together, and when you are here I wonder how I could ever get along when you are away. You are dearer to me than I can ever tell you.*

I wrapped most of our Christmas gifts, and they are ready to be sent off tonight. Yours will be mailed on Tuesday. I sure hope it gets there in time. P.S. I have made a New Year's resolution early to write you oftener. I know I have said that before, but this time I really mean it. I know how much my letters mean to you, as yours mean to me. I love you very much, dear. Thank you for coming so far to see me. God bless you.

Alarming news from Utah: *We heard a pretty disturbing rumor today. An article in the* Chicago Tribune *said the army was doing away with the ASTP, either outright or gradually. I sure hope it isn't so, because I'd like to finish my nine months here. Or at the least one more term, because I don't know enough Spanish as yet to be useful to anyone. Maybe we'll find out about it in a few days. I know Col. Lawrence was pessimistic about the program.*

My furlough wasn't very long, but I did have a very good time. I hope you did too. But I still worry about what you said about not being sure you loved me, and that you wanted to be certain before you would tell me. It hit me like a lightning bolt when you said that, because I have never once doubted that I loved you. Maybe I was taking you for granted. If I was, I'm sorry, dear. I don't want ever to take you or your love for granted. Or maybe it was just something I did—like telling you to go home if you wanted to, when we were walking down East Grand Boulevard. If that was it, I'm very sorry, and I apologize. I love you too much to want to hurt you in any way.

About that "little incident," it showed that our marriage will be one of give and take. You made me come to the streetcar line for you. I'd have crawled all the way on my hands and knees if you had asked me, because I love you so very much, dear. But it would have been better if you had met me half way. I guess I'm making a mountain out of a molehill. But let's promise that our marriage will always be on a 50/50 basis. And we should be careful of the little things that come up, that maybe irritate us. And not lash out, without thinking. Let's try to tell each other everything and talk about our disagreements, instead of sulking about them, as we might do. And we will keep trying, each day of our lives. Maybe I don't use fancy language, but when I say I love you, I mean it, from the bottom of my heart.

A short letter from Dearborn, December 14, 1943: *Jane told me something I thought was funny the other day, and I had better tell you about it to clear myself of any suspicions you may have. And I strongly suspect my family of trying to marry me off in a hurry. My stepmother is doing her best anyway for the noble cause of romance. She said she felt very ambitious the day we came home to my house, and after she finished cleaning your room in the morning she spotted my atomizer and squirted perfume all over the room and on your pillow, because she thought the fragrance might inspire you. As if you needed inspiration, dear. I admit I am tricky, but this idea had never occurred to me. You can see you don't stand a chance.*

Two days later: *I won't have very long to write this evening because I am supposed to go out to a shower in a little while, but I do want to answer your letter tonight, dear. It deserves a longer reply. I will write until I have to leave, and then perhaps I can finish when I come home. I'm glad you brought up that night when you were home again, because I'd like to explain about it as best I can, and then I hope we can forget it. I can't tell you how sorry I am that I hurt you, and I hope, because you love me, that you will forgive me. I thought at the time I was being honest, but I shouldn't have said what I did, because when we have so short a time together things seem so important and out of proportion to how they really are. Please don't worry about it any more and berate yourself, because if it was true then, it isn't now.*

I have been trying since then to explain to myself why I felt the way I did, and I really don't know, honey. I thought the little incident when we said "goodbye" on the boulevard might have had something to do with it, but not much. It was sort of silly, and we really weren't serious. I didn't intend to go home, you know. I guess my pride was pricked a little when you let me go. I can see now that it would have been better, honey, if I had come back to meet you halfway. But I guess I was so glad to know you weren't going to let me go home, it didn't occur to me. It certainly seemed a long walk back to Kercheval and the streetcar. I kept my ears cocked, expecting you to call me. And I walked slowly so you could stop me, and kept wanting to turn back.

As for that Wednesday night, I had thought that it might have been be-cause it was strange to have you near me again, after such a long time, honey. Anyhow, I suddenly felt during the evening that I didn't know if I loved you or really even knew you, that the flesh-and-blood person standing in front of me was different from the one in your letters. It was an awful feeling, and it scared me. It seemed a fine state of affairs to be in since I ex-pected to marry you soon. I wished that I didn't have to see you, but at the same time that you wouldn't know how I felt.

Does all this sound silly to you, honey? I thought I had better give you an account of what goes on in my mind. I know now that I love you with all my heart, more than ever, if that is possible. It's just that I was confused that one night. And thank you, dear, for being so kind and considerate. I don't know what I would ever do without you.

I had heard the rumor too about the ASTP folding up. There was talk here that the unit at Wayne will be dissolved. But the Collegian *ran an ar-ticle denying the rumor. I certainly hope you will be able to finish your three terms before they discontinue it—if they are going to.*

A reply, December 19, 1943: *Thank you, dear, for the two good letters I received from you last week. I feel the same way as you do—that we belong together. And I pray that it won't be too long before we are married. June isn't too awfully far away, is it? Jane was rather tricky, as you say, putting perfume in my bed. But I'm sorry to say I didn't even notice it. Maybe I was too tired from the long train trip. Or there is something wrong with my smelling apparatus. Anyway, I went right to sleep!*

Did I tell you I got my marks this week and had A's in both Spanish and Area. So that last-minute studying of the subjunctive and conditional really did pay off. And incidentally several men in our class got higher scores than any of the civilian honors students. So we really are learning a lot, after all. I went with Pat last night to hear Yehudi Menuhin play the violin. We both thought he was great. And I'm going this evening to choir practice at the Catholic cathedral, and then I'll be singing in the Christmas Midnight Mass. There is a chance I will have a solo in the Gloria, but that hasn't been decided as yet. With the war and all they are fairly short of baritones, though. So we'll see. So far my studies have been keeping me more busy than last term, if that is possible.

An item from Marianne on the home front, December 21, 1943: *I haven't been very busy at school lately. So many people have been home with the flu, and in some cases my entire class was absent. For a while there was talk of closing all the schools, but now the worst of the epidemic seems to be over. Now I have just two more days of school and then a whole week of vacation. What an easy life I lead, honey!*

More about a "little incident," December 22, 1943: *I don't know how long this letter will be, because there's no way of telling how long I can stay in this study room. I hate to go back to the field house, because it's always so noisy after the lights are out. With the coke bottles and all. But maybe with all the rumors they just don't care what happens. More important, I received your letter about our "little incident," and was very pleased with it. Thank you so much for being frank with me, dear. I can't say that I'll be able to forget it. I don't think we should. The memory of that frightening moment can help us avoid such unpleasantnesses in the future—by meeting each other half way.*

In a way it's not difficult to see how you would feel "strange" with me. We have known each other for three years, but have been together for only a few months. And being together in stacks of love letters is not the same as meeting each other every day, face to face. What reality is there in pieces of paper with ink markings on them?

Pat said when he went home three months ago he and Margaret felt strange together. She seemed to be looking at him, and he was wondering what she was thinking about. But then he went back to California a couple of weeks ago to get married, and now both of them feel that they have known each other all their lives. There can be no secrets between them, he said. He appears to be very happy, and she is going to come to Salt Lake City right after the first of the year. They have rented an apartment, and they will be able to see each other for a couple of hours each day. And they will have their weekends together, from Saturday afternoon up to Sunday evening. It may not sound very much, but they do seem to be happy about the arrangement. And in many ways I envy them. A lot of men have their wives here and do quite well. Maybe I was wrong when I said our getting married was not compatible with my going to school. Perhaps one reason you felt as you did that night was that you thought I always putting off our wedding day.

Well, I would like to talk to you, honey, about changing it—but not putting it off anymore. After I've finished here, I don't know what will happen to me. We've been aware of that for some time. And I might not get to finish, if there is anything in all the rumors. And even if I do finish, I might not be able to get a furlough. Or maybe I would go directly overseas. And we wouldn't be able to be married in June, after all. So rather than wait, I think we should be married in March, when I will have another furlough. We wouldn't have much time together. But perhaps you could take four days off, and we could have a honeymoon of sorts. Close by in Michigan, or across the river in Ontario. Then if I'm sent back to Camp Roberts, or to some other base in this country, you could come there in the summer, and we would have at least three months together, before you started teaching school again.

If you will marry me then, sweetheart, we had better start planning— building up our bank account, deciding where and by whom we would be married. Things like that. Of course, a lot of the planning and work would be on your shoulders. Let me know whether you think it is wiser to have the wedding then or to take our chances and wait until June. God bless you, dear, and keep you safe. I love you very much.

More from Salt Lake City, December 26, 1943: *Thank you very much, dear, for the thoughtful presents. The cookies were classics and all too soon eaten up by my various friends. The game box was wonderful also—just the right size to take with me, even if I am sent to Europe. You are a real genius to think of it. But best of all were the pajamas. And they were neatly folded—just perfect for being stored under my bed—as you said, in case of fire. I wanted to call you tonight to wish you "Happy Birthday," but I have only 75 cents to last me until Saturday. There are times I almost wish the fellows here played a little poker or blackjack so I could pick up some change.*

A reply from Marianne in Dearborn, December 27, 1943: *I had a very nice Christmas, dear, although it was another one with you away, unfortunately. It was the first Christmas in my life I've had all the money I wanted to spend, and I had a good time doing my holiday shopping. Like you, I'm flat broke now, but I was able to give everyone the presents I wanted to. And thank you very much for the beautiful negligee. And for the red roses on my birthday. Jane thanks you also. I decided to put them in a vase in the living room as part of the Christmas trimmings.*

It hardly seems possible I could be 22 years old now—your age when we first knew each other. I can't say I feel old, any more than you did then. I always thought you were young in spirit. I do think, though, that we both are old enough and mature enough to get married. When I received your letter yesterday, I was in a quandary for a while. But not for very long. March seemed so close, and I wanted to be sure we weren't making a mistake. I asked my folks, but they said it was up to me to make up my own mind. And so it is.

You were wrong, honey, when you thought I felt you were putting off our wedding day. But one respect in which we are alike is that we are pretty conservative—in the good sense of the word. Not rushing into things. Like something as important as getting married, especially in times such as these. There was a time, I think, when we both thought we should wait until after the war. But we have changed our minds about that since. I feel now that the war—though things are better—could last for some time. The world is not going to right itself any time soon, so we had better make the most of our chances for happiness, such as they are.

I'll have to start making plans soon, because March is not very far off, so be sure to tell me anything you'd like me to take care of. I'll be seeing your family later this week, so I will tell them our news—okey, dear? Maybe we will surprise them this time. I had been thinking of trying to reserve the Martha-Mary chapel in Greenfield Village. It's the church I told you about that doesn't belong to any particular faith, and people of all denominations have their weddings there. And it has the advantage of being close to my home. What do you think about that, dear? I'll have to look into it pretty soon, because I've heard reservations should be made long in advance. But because our wedding will be on a weekday, and in the late afternoon or evening, perhaps it won't be hard to get.

I know you don't want too large a wedding, honey, and I don't, either. Besides, the chapel is not big enough to hold very many people. Do you want to invite anyone outside our immediate families? And tell me what you would like to do afterward for a honeymoon? (Such a question!) I mean, would we prefer to stay in Detroit at a hotel for three or four days, or go someplace that's not too far away—such as Kingsville or Leamington in Ontario? It's too bad everything has to be crowded into one week, isn't it, dear?

We will really want to start saving our money, won't we? I would prefer not cashing any of our war bonds, if we can possibly help it. I will have only two paydays till then and will be making my money stretch out very thin for the two months. Maybe I shouldn't have spent so much on Christmas presents. But then I didn't know we'd be getting married so soon. Just let me know as soon as possible what the date most likely will be.

News from Salt Lake City, December 29, 1943: *I am writing this letter from the hospital, dear, but don't worry, I'm not sick. I could leave now, but they are keeping me here an extra day after my temperature goes back to normal. I went on sick call yesterday morning, because I thought I had a bad cold, and while I was there I asked the doctor about a large sore I had on my ankle. He asked me if I had a pain in my groin, and I said yes, wondering how he knew. It turned out I had septicemia, blood poisoning, and that was what was causing the high temperature—it was 101 degrees. He gave me something he called sulfanilamide that I had never heard of, and said it would do the trick. I feel a lot better already.*

In case you wonder what caused it, it's a long story. You remember when I was home I told you I was taking swimming lessons here, because when they were checking us out, I told them I couldn't really swim. So I've been going to the pool three times a week for an hour each day. But the past month or so, the water has been so cold—I don't think they try to heat it, even in the winter. And we swam with no suit on—I think you called it "skinny dipping." It got so uncomfortable I started sneaking out when the instructor wasn't there—which was most of the time. I would go up to the men's gym and play basketball, which was much more fun, anyway. And because we wear our GI boots—no one has gym shoes—some of the fellows get kicked sometimes. And that's what happened to me, evidently. A big fellow went up for the ball and came down on my ankle. I didn't tell the doctor that, of course, because it might have got me in trouble with the colonel, who wanted to make sure we all swam well. So what happens now, we'll just see.

But, as I said, I am really okay now, and by the time you receive this letter, I will be up and around. I just hope, though, that I can stay here long enough to miss guard duty this week. This is a wonderful opportunity to get some sleep, and I am taking advantage of it. Of course, I'll have a lot of work in my classes to catch up with, but it is worth it.

New Year's Day, 1944: *You really took the wind out of my sails, dear, when you accepted my proposal of marriage so quickly. I thought you might be hesitant. And now I am trapped, with no way to out of it. But do I love it! I feel like a new man, with responsibilities, now that I am about to take unto me a wife—as they say in the novels. Ever since I got your letter yesterday, I have been walking around with my head in the clouds. I only hope the next nine weeks pass as rapidly as the weeks of this past quarter. We have a lot of things to do before the wedding, but two months should be enough, don't you think?*

Concerning the wedding party, I suppose you will have Ellen as your maid of honor. I think you once said the two of you had promised to be maids of honor at each other's wedding. At a small wedding like ours I would think we wouldn't have any more than the one bridesmaid. And only the best man for me? And there I find myself in a quandary. I would like to ask my brother John or Hilary Velten, who is my best friend at home. But of course they are both away in the service. I could ask Francis Ryan, but he works at a defense job and might not be able to get away. My brother Allen is big enough to stand up with me, but would he be considered old enough? Oh well, I'll have two months to decide about that.

I'll be talking with Paterson to see if there are things we might have forgotten. And be sure to let me know what your ideas are. After all, the bride is the most important person in the ceremony, and you should have the most to say—and the last say—about everything. And one final reminder—we will be needing Wassermann tests, I think within the month of the wedding. I can have mine here and send the results on to you so you can get the license. More later. Good night, dear. I love you very much.

❧ 8 ❧

A Dream Realized

January 1, 1944, from Marianne in Dearborn: *I'm sorry I haven't written you for the past few days, but I've been busy as two bees telling people about our marriage-to-be and planning for it. I told your folks the news on Thursday when I went out to your house. Your mother seemed more surprised this time than when I told her of our engagement. But they all said it was about time that we made our decision. They thought we had waited long enough. I wanted to tell them also about what church we would be going to. But I decided it was a more delicate matter, and perhaps you would like to tell them yourself.*

I called Mr. Koch at the Greenfield Village who takes charge of weddings in the Martha-Mary Chapel and asked him if we could be married there on March 14, and he said he thought it could be arranged. I'll be going out to see him next week, so I'll know more about it then. I'm glad we can have the chapel, because I think it's a good solution to the religion question. Mr. Koch sang at Elva Spicer's wedding, and I thought he had a good voice. Do you want me to ask if he can sing at our wedding also? I can't think of anyone I'd rather have, unless it is you, dear heart. But perhaps this is one occasion when you won't be front and center!

From Salt Lake City, January 4, 1944: *I just wrote to my folks, honey, and told them we were going to be married. And I also told them we would be married by an Episcopal minister. So by the time you get this letter you*

175

will be able to talk to them about it and make any plans for our wedding that are necessary. I never knew it would be so difficult to plan for a wedding. It's a wonder people get married at all. At the same time I never knew it could be so much fun! Always in the past, when we talked of our marrying, it was at some vague time in the future. But now the date is definite—Tuesday, March 7. Not the 14th, as I first thought.

I'm sending this money order for $30 to add to our account. How much do we have now, dear? It's important that I know, so I can tell how to make plans for our honeymoon. I'll send at least as much next month, and possibly more. I'm sure we will have a great time, in the Detroit area or in Canada. Maybe you can make inquiries about the hotel—the availability of rooms and the cost.

Planning for a wedding, in Dearborn, January 5, 1944: *I have been feeling so elated since we agreed on your happy idea, I will never come down out of the clouds again, dear. I'm afraid my heart won't be in my work for these next two months of school, and especially as it gets to be March. We have now only sixty-one days before the great event—I just counted them, and we have so much to do until then. I made a list for you, honey, of the things I could think of to do, and you can tell me if you think of anything else. I could handle most of them, except for the ring, maybe. And I can take care of the license and the waiver of waiting time from a judge beforehand, and save you having to rush around on our wedding day. I know it's customary for the groom to take care of a lot of the things you mentioned on the phone. But in times like these, when every day counts, it's up to the bride to handle most of the details. Since you won't be home until the night before.*

I thought four or five o'clock in the afternoon would be a good time to be married. Our friends who have to work would be able to make it, and it would give us enough time beforehand for whatever we still have to do. For instance, we might have to rehearse the ceremony. Then we can have a reception at five or six, either at my home or at the Dearborn Inn, which isn't very far away. I'll find out about the Inn, and if it isn't more than I can afford, we can have it there. It would save a lot of work at home for Jane. She seems to tire easily these days. We could plan on about an hour for the reception, and then I would have to change my clothes and get ready to leave for our honeymoon—at about seven or eight. I figure it takes about an hour and a half to get to Kingsville, so we would be arriving there at nine or thereabouts. How will that be?

I have been to both Kingsville and Leamington for vacations, but it was at the lake, so I don't know very much about the towns or the hotels. If it's all right with you I'll find out about the hotels—if they are open that time of the year, and what their prices are. The only advantage in going to Kingsville, I think, is that it is somewhat closer and not so far to drive to at night. I think it would be nice to have your brother Allen for your best man, honey. He looks old enough, even if he is only seventeen, and I don't think there is any law about a best man's age. He says he is six-two, so with Ellen as my bridesmaid we'll be a tall, and fair, wedding party, won't we? I think I told you I would like to wear white at our wedding. You and I will be married only once, and I have always thought I would like to have the traditional wedding dress. It won't be very elaborate, no long train or anything like that, but I will be wearing white, and Ellen probably will be wearing pink. I'll tell Allen to wear a dark business suit and a tie, if that is all right with you.

I was talking to your mother on the phone this evening about the wedding. I told her the church we planned to get married in and what we had decided about our two religions. That we were going to compromise. None of our folks seem to have been surprised or upset about it. I suppose they have all been expecting something like this. Your mother told me it was a decision for us to make. She had belonged to the Church of Christ, she said, but had converted to Catholicism ten years ago. I think we are lucky to have families who feel that way, because most of the difficulties that result from people of different faith marrying are caused by their families' interfering.

A short note from Salt Lake City, January 6, 1944: *There was a message on our company bulletin board today for me to call Mrs. Sullivan, who is director of the Choir at the cathedral. I haven't gone back there since I sang at Midnight Mass on Christmas Eve. I'm wondering if she wants me for anything special. She may want me to come down and sing on Sundays. I'll let you know later about that. I've been planning to go to the Episcopal church in town, and I can't very well do both, can I?*

My sore ankle is about healed by now. That sulfanilamide sure did the trick in a hurry. I've been going over to the dispensary every so often to get new bandages, but it doesn't hurt anymore. In fact, the nurse didn't even put on any medicine—just a bandage to keep it clean. I got a box from my folks today with a lot of things in it, including my field jacket I had sent home earlier. But what made a hit most with the fellows here was a lot of green and red popcorn that my dad had made for Christmas. It has become a tradition in our family, as you know. I'll have to learn how to make it for our own kids, won't I?

Two days later: *You remember I told you I had a call from the director of the choir at the cathedral? Well, she wanted me to come to a dinner the choir was having Thursday evening. I went, though I had a lot of studying to do then also, and had a really good time. And a very good chicken dinner. The bishop and monsignor were there, and we sang group songs. They asked me to do a solo, so I sang "Just Awearyin' for You." The choir mistress played the piano. But best of all was having a really good meal for a change.*

And the night before that I had dinner with the basketball coach. I told him I had never seen anyone shoot one-handed before. At Wayne it was all two-handed, including the foul shots. He said it started at Stanford, and was much more accurate, he thought. Utah has a good team, he said, though the players are mostly kids in their teens. Plus a Japanese fellow, Walter Misaka, who had been sent East from California. And the center, Arnold Ferrin, he said, would almost certainly be an All-American. He's that good. So we'll see.

It will be fine if we can be married at the Greenfield chapel, honey. Let me know as soon as you have found a minister, and find out what I have to do. I wonder if the Mr. Koch you mentioned is the Raymond Koch who sings in Wayne's "Messiah" every year. If it is, he has a very good tenor voice. It would be nice if he could sing at our wedding. I don't suppose the ceremony will take more than ten or fifteen minutes, will it?

The next day in Dearborn: *The most important thing I can think of to tell you, dear, is that I have my wedding dress! I had thought I would spend the next month or two looking around for one I wanted, but Ellen and I went downtown on Saturday to scout around and I found it. It's so beautiful! I won't tell you anything about it, so you can be surprised when you see me coming down the aisle. On my father's arm, naturally.*

I felt so "bridey" in the shop, trying on dresses and admiring them in the mirror. And all the salesgirls stood around and oohed and aahed. And Ellen has hers too. It's pink satin with a sort of mauve skirt, and she looks beautiful in it. According to Mr. Koch, my father and Allen should be wearing dark business suits, but I already knew that. I think my dad is really impressed with the idea of having to walk up the aisle with me, and to "give me away," as they say. He has a high silk hat that he inherited from a relative. He has been saving it for years and has been threatening to wear it to our wedding. It's hard to know if he is kidding me or what. He's been trying it on, and I keep telling him a dark suit is all that is required. He always walks too fast, way out in front of Jane and me, so he might just leave me behind in the chapel!

I went out today to Greenfield Village to talk again with Mr. Koch, and he raised a problem with me. He said he was quite certain that one of us had to be a confirmed member of the church to be married by an Episcopal priest. I should have thought of that before, because I know it's true of the Lutherans. So we'll see. Mr. Koch suggested we could get a Methodist or Evangelical minister to marry us, and then join the Episcopal church later. Does that seem all right with you, dear? In the meantime, I'll be trying to see if that is the case.

More wedding plans, January 12, 1944: *From now till March had seemed such a short time to get ready for our wedding, but the way I have been busy working on it, we could almost get married this coming week. I will probably have my suitcase packed, all ready to leave, and then have nothing to do but sit around and twiddle my thumbs, waiting for you to come home, dear. On Monday I talked again with Mr. Koch and arranged to have the chapel on the seventh instead of the fourteenth, as we had originally thought. He is a jolly sort of man and very efficient. He seems to get a kick out of helping inexperienced and young people like us plan their weddings. He is going to sing for us and asked what songs we would like. I told him I would ask you about that. I like all the traditional ones, like "Because," "Oh Promise Me," "I Love You Truly," or Grieg's "I Love Thee." Be sure to let me know soon about what you want. He says he will be singing two or three, depending on how long they are.*

He also asked if we have any preferences for the music the organist will be playing before the wedding. She plays for thirty minutes while the guests are coming in. He said the chapel furnishes all the things such as candles and a white carpet for the aisle. And they have a bus service to take the guests from the gate to the church, because cars are not allowed on the grounds. We will be having a rehearsal about a week before the wedding, and I can give you details about that. And then you will have to be there early on March 7, in case there is additional information for you.

The ceremony would probably last about twenty minutes, he said, so we can have the reception at 5:30—at the Dearborn Inn, I think. It's right nearby and wouldn't take more than five or ten minutes for all of us to get there. I talked with people at the Inn, and they said the date and time are okey. And it would cost me about $85 for fifty guests. My father will take care of that, he said. I figure the whole thing would be over at about 6:30, and we can be on our way sometime between seven and eight. Is that early enough for you, dear?

The same day in Salt Lake City: *I've been going over your letters again, reading what you have planned for March 7. Thank you for taking on so much of the responsibility. If you could do as much as possible before I arrive, it would certainly give us more leeway on that Tuesday. It looks as though we'll have enough money for our wedding trip without you're putting in any to our account. Our balance should be $85 now, if I reckon correctly, and I'll be sending $30 more next month to make it $115. From what you say, that should be more than enough for my share of the expenses. I hadn't realized that your part would be so expensive, honey. Are you sure I'm worth all that?*

I've been studying especially hard lately, and I hope I can keep it up. We had an exam today in Spanish—over difficult material. I finished fifteen minutes before the men who have always gotten the best scores, and a half an hour before the rest of them. I wondered how I could do it. And I hope I didn't make too many foolish mistakes. So we'll see.

Two days later: *I haven't written to Allen yet to ask him to be my best man, but it seems that he already knows about it. I'm afraid that he really will be the "best man," at my wedding, what with his being voted the best-looking fellow in his class at Eastern High. But I guess you'll love me any-*

way, even if I am an old broken-down wreck from my studies here. Maybe one of these days I'll get a good night's sleep in the field house. I can see from your letters that your dad is really impressed with the prospect of "giving the bride away." "Giving away!" What a terrible idea! I must say, that if you belonged to me, I would want to keep you all for myself.

Three days later: *I think it's swell we are going to have good music at our wedding, honey. In a few days, after the midterm exams, I'll make out a list of things I'd like us to consider, such as Bach's "Jesu, Joy of Man's Desiring," Handel's "Largo," the Intermezzo in "Cavalleria rusticana," etc. I don't know which songs I'd like Mr. Koch to sing, but I'll let you know before the week is over. I thought, though, that we were going to have a small wedding, and now you are talking about fifty friends. I didn't know we had that many friends! And when you talk about ushers, that sounds like a big production too. I would think people could just find their own seats. But then, as you say, we are only getting married once, so we might as well do it right.*

Your plans do sound O.K. to me, honey. And five seems a good hour for the wedding, for the reasons you wrote me about. I do hope, though, that we can keep to the schedule, because we will want to get away as soon as possible. And I'll take care of the Wassermann's test three or four weeks before I'm scheduled to leave here. That way the papers will get to Detroit in plenty of time. And I'll ask Dad to take care of the ring for me. Of course, the jeweler will have to know the ring size and the type of your diamond ring, so he can give us one from the set. You remember when we were there so long ago he told us we could get a wedding ring to match it any time. And I will send them some money to pay for it.

And one important point. Pat and Margaret said to be sure to remember to have everything packed and in the car before we leave. They said that at their wedding they had forgotten their license and a bag, and they had to drive all the way back to retrieve them—much to their embarrassment!

More thoughts from Salt Lake City, January 22, 1944: *I'm sorry, dear, I haven't written you lately. As I told you, I had to study for exams, and then I was in a quartet that sang last night at a dance. We had to practice every free minute for the past week. I learned the two songs right away, but the others, especially the tenors, had trouble right up to the moment we*

181

came on the stage, and then—miraculously—everything was fine. Because of the hours of practice, I suppose. Anyway, I'm glad it's over, so I can start writing letters again.

About music for our wedding, how about this: Before the ceremony the organist would play the Bach and Handel pieces I mentioned in my letter, as well as the Mascagni "Intermezzo" and also Schubert's "Ave Maria," if that isn't too "Catholic" for them. (Though I am giving up my church, I would still like to be part of its music, if that is possible.) And for the ceremony, I'd like Mr. Koch to sing something different from the usual songs—maybe "The Lord's Prayer" by Albert Hay Mallot, and "Where 'ere You Walk," from Semele by Handel. You might ask him how he feels about those. He might think they were too "big" and could detract from the significance of the ceremony. So perhaps it would be best to go with traditional music like "Oh Promise Me," or "Because." Why don't you and he decide, honey?

More information on the wedding, January 24, 1944: *I hope you weren't surprised at the kind of wedding we are having, darling. It really won't be a very large wedding. We are having only two attendants, and that in anybody's book is a small wedding party. And fifty guests may sound to you like a lot, but compared to most weddings these days it really isn't. So don't be worried about it. I'll send you a list of the people we are inviting, and if you think of any others you can let me know. I haven't ordered the invitations yet, but I'll have to do it very soon. My folks and I made definite arrangements for the Dearborn Inn last week, and today I received a letter of acceptance for the Martha-Mary chapel, so those two are definite.*

Questions from Salt Lake City, January 25, 1944: *I was looking at the list of things you made out for me, dear, and it looks as though everything will go off on schedule. But I'll still be keeping my fingers crossed. I do have a question, though, about the flowers for the bride and the maid of honor. Paterson said he got Margaret orchids for their wedding, but since you are having a wedding dress, I don't think you'd want anything like that to pin to the dress. I would think you and Ellen would more likely want to carry the flowers. Let me know what you prefer. And is that the bouquet the bride traditionally throws out at some point so all the young ladies get a chance to make a grab for it and determine their future?*

182

And what arrangements have been made for a minister? It doesn't matter too much to me, just as long as he can make it legal. Also, have you found out as yet about the hotel in Chatham or whatever town we are going to? When I get my furlough, I'll have to specify that I'm going to a certain town in Canada, so I'll have no trouble getting across the border. The army has to make sure, I guess, that I am not going AWOL. I hope the hotel won't be too expensive, because I won't have very much money left, after I get the ring and the flowers and give the minister something.

Last Saturday I went down to the R.R. station and made a reservation on the Zephyr from Denver to Chicago and for the trip back. I think I'll be able to make it this time, because the Moffat tunnel is open now, and the train here leaves early enough. I don't plan to be back here until Monday morning. Nothing happened the last time, when I was late, and I think nothing will this time either.

All my tests are over now, but I intend to study even harder than I did the first quarter. I see where some members of Congress are trying to close out the ASTP, so I had better make the most of my time here at Utah. The way Congress acts, though, it may be some time before they shut off funds for the program, if they do. And besides, the army has already contracted with the schools for students to go up to June of this year, so I doubt if it will affect us. But maybe there won't be any new ones coming in, after we leave. I hope I get to finish my three terms though, because it wouldn't do me much good to know the language only fairly well. We'll see, anyway.

I have corporal of the guard tomorrow morning from four to six, so I suppose I'll be pretty tired after that. But I'm hoping I can do some studying while I'm on duty. I'm really turning into an eager beaver, and it sure pays dividends. You remember I told you when I took the Spanish final last quarter I was twelfth in the class with a score of 58-plus? That was a good score, good enough to get me an A. But I wasn't satisfied with my class standing, so I did a lot of extra work this quarter. Well, she gave us that test again last week, and it was a surprise because there was no warning, and she wanted to see if there was any marked improvement in just six weeks.

Anyway, this time I was sixth in the class with a score of 73.72, which was better than the highest civilian student got in the most advanced class. The best student in our class—Robert Bowen—jumped from 73 to 80 this time. Some-

one said that was higher than the teacher ever got when she was a student here. I am getting so I speak it pretty well, and I have little trouble reading it. For practice, I have been reading foreign newspapers at the library.

An omen, January 29, 1944: It's a good thing we are planning to be married in March, because the colonel told us we won't be getting furloughs in June. That we will be shipped out on a troop train to wherever we will be going after our course here is finished. I sure hope I can go to some camp in the States, so you can come and stay with me for the summer. According to the papers, the army wants two-thirds of their men overseas before the end of this year. There are said to be big plans in the offing for an invasion of Europe. So, we'll see. Maybe, when we finish, I'll be sent to Europe. As what, nobody around here seems to know. And no one talks about Military Government any more.

More from Marianne about wedding plans, February 6, 1944: I went to the county building yesterday to find out about our license and medical certificates, and am enclosing yours. It seems the thirty-day rule applies only to our medical examinations, and I was glad to get that straight. We have to apply for our license—I can get it—within thirty days of the time the certificates are issued, but there is no time limit on when the license must be used. The clerk said if we decided to wait until after the war, it would still be good. And he suggested that we get it as soon as possible in case you get an unexpected furlough, and we decide to be married then. So we may as well get the license all taken care of and off our minds.

I think I told you about writing to the William Pitts hotel in Chatham, honey, and don't be surprised if you receive a reply from them soon. I gave them your return address. The main reason is that I couldn't figure any way of not letting them know we'd be newlyweds, if I wrote, and it might be embarrassing for the people at the hotel to know we were on our honeymoon. We probably won't get away with it, but we can at least pretend we are an old married couple. You can reply, if you like the sound of the place and the rates.

I believe your dad is planning on buying the wedding ring for you, and I don't think he will have any trouble getting it. If I don't go with him, he can take my ring for size. Also, I've heard that servicemen do not have to pay the ten percent luxury tax on jewelry, so your dad should tell them you are in the army. I have our wedding invitations back, and I hope you like them as much as I do. I'll enclose one in this letter. I couldn't afford engravings, though, because they are so expensive, but these are really good looking. It's too early to send them out as yet, but I'll start addressing them now to be all ready.

I don't remember if I told you about having talked to Dean O'Farrell of St. Paul's Episcopal Cathedral. He said that an Episcopal clergyman will gladly marry us at the chapel, and he seemed to think our plans to join his church were a good idea. He suggested I get in touch with Hedley G. Stacey of the nearest church in Dearborn. He is the man whose services I've heard, and I could hardly bear the sound of his voice. I don't know that I would want to listen to it every Sunday for the rest of my life. But maybe he would soften his tone a little for weddings. I hope this answers any questions you might have.

Complaints at the University of Utah, February 6, 1944: *I was going to write you last night, but for some reason or other, I was in a foul mood and decided to wait until today. But I'm just as mad today, so I'll write anyway. I don't know what started it. Maybe fatigue because I am working too hard. And something you said in one of your letters rubbed me the wrong way. Nothing worth mentioning now, because I know you didn't mean it that way. But then today I got even madder than I've been in a long time when I read in the papers that the Congress had refused to let soldiers and sailors vote in the upcoming elections! What's the matter with those bastards?*

I don't think anyone realizes what a strain we're under here. The most sleep we ever get is seven hours—and usually it's a lot less. Even on weekends its difficult to catch up. In fact, it's virtually impossible to make up for lost sleep. I wake up every morning more tired than the night before. And the work here is grinding. They keep expecting more and more from us. And when I try to have some recreation, to go to a show or to a concert, I just have to work all the harder. Even on Sundays there is no let up.

I'll be riding two days in a day-coach, sitting up the whole way, so I'll be worn out when I get home. I want our days together to be as peaceful as possible. All I want is time to ourselves—and peace and quiet. So I hope I don't have to rush around all day on the seventh, wearing myself to a frazzle, worrying whether we will get away on time or not. Let's plan, honey, to have everything on schedule. When we say we will be married at five o'clock, let's have it five sharp, no matter who's there and who isn't. If the photographer could take our pictures after the wedding, that would be swell. But we won't have time to go anyplace to have formal pictures taken. And then promptly at 6:30 we leave the reception, no matter what anyone says. Because we have quite a way to go. And in the dark. Is that OK with you? I hope I don't seem like an ogre to you. But you know what I mean, I think.

You said I should get a driver's license, so I could drive your car after the wedding. But I can't, because I haven't driven enough, and I have no opportunity, anyway, with the tight work program they hold us to. On our honeymoon, after we get through the tunnel and outside Windsor, I could chance it and drive all the way to Chatham, if you wanted me to, honey. But I've never driven a car at night before, or in traffic anywhere, so where does that leave us? Aren't you a little bit worried about that?

Another thing that's made me pissed off is the fact the results of my Wassermann test have to be on Michigan forms. I'll be goddamned if I see any reason why Michigan's forms are better than Utah's. But if that is the law, you'd better send me the forms posthaste, if you haven't already. And I do mean right away, *because it might take me two whole weeks to get the forms completed here. It did Paterson, because he had to take three tests before he was through. And you'd better send them airmail, or even special delivery. Then I can be sure to mail them back in time for you to get the license. Please, honey.*

I've finally decided to not worry a bit about the preparations for our wedding, honey. Paterson said he had his best man take care of all the things he was supposed to do before he came home to California. Such as order flowers, etc. So I wrote Allen tonight and told him I would expect him to see you and get everything ready before I got home on Monday the sixth. Otherwise, what purpose is there for having a best man who just hands over a ring he has been keeping in his pocket? Because I was mad about everyone and everything, I was probably gruff in my letter, as though he had done something wrong, I suppose. When you see him, you might apologize for me.

An anguished reply from Marianne, February 9, 1944: *I got home from school today and read your "mad" letter. I have been worried about it and thought I'd better answer it right away so we can see eye-to-eye about things again. It's funny how disagreements with friends don't bother me in the least, but when you and I have even minor differences they hurt so much it amounts to almost a physical ache, dear. I don't know what I will ever do if we have a serious quarrel after we are married. I want you to know that I love you with all my heart, for all our lives and don't think we ever need to be at odds about anything.*

As for our wedding, if you disapprove of the way it sounds to you, I hope you will tell me how. This isn't my wedding alone, it's ours, and I certainly want you to like all of it and remember it as being beautiful. All these plans may seem complicated, but they aren't really, honey. It will be a simple ceremony, and we're not having many guests. Fifty isn't a large number in a church, although to you that may sound like a lot of people. Yet you can see how easy it was to think of twenty-five friends whom you'd really want to come. And a lot of the people I am asking are relatives of Jane, but they have been so nice to me and are practically like my own relatives, so I almost have to invite them. I have very few near-relatives in this country, so you aren't going to be adopting a lot of in-laws.

If you expect that the reception will be big, you will be disappointed. All we are having is coffee, some little sandwiches, ice cream, and a wedding cake. The Dearborn Inn is very close to the chapel—it will take less time than it would to come out to my house for refreshments, and people won't stay as long. There isn't going to be any big supper. The guests will have to go home for their evening meals, and you and I can have ours on the way to Canada. Or wait till we get there. We won't take time to go to a photographer's because it would take another hour, at least. So if there isn't someone at the village to take our pictures, we'll just forget about it, dear.

Of course, the ceremony will start at five sharp, and it will take only 15 to 30 minutes, so the reception should be over by 6:30. The man at the Inn told me they usually take about two hours, but this one should be over in less. And if it isn't, well, you and I will just leave anyway. My friends say everyone does that.

And if this still sounds bigger than what you wanted, tell me now so it can be changed. If you would rather be married by a justice-of-the-peace, we could arrange that, even now, because I certainly don't want you to take part in something you don't approve of. My friends and relatives—and yours too—would be disappointed, but we could tell them about the shortness of your furlough, and the dislocations of a soldier's life, and they would understand. As it stands now, dear, you won't have any "rushing around" to do on your wedding day. Things should be pretty much taken care of by then, if Allen will order the flowers and your folks get the ring for you. So you shouldn't worry about any of that.

It doesn't matter to me if you get your driving license before you come home, honey. I had thought that if they weren't hard to get in Utah, it might be a good idea, because there could be an occasion here when you would want to use it. I had read somewhere that in some of the Western states like Wyoming, anybody could get a license just by walking into the office and asking for one. And of course we might not even be driving to Canada that night. If the weather is bad or icy, we will probably want to take a bus or a train anyway.

I'm afraid I haven't been much help this evening in spite of all this writing—because I haven't told you much you didn't already know. Write soon, please, and tell me what to do next, because I will be in doubts until I hear from you. The most important thing is that soon you and I will be husband and wife, and the details of the ceremony are not that significant. And we know that we love each other very much, and that we will be united for the rest of our lives after March 7.

The same day in Salt Lake City: *I'm going over to the infirmary tomorrow to see about my Wassermann test now that I have the form to be filled out. It says that the test must be given by an army station hospital lab. I don't know whether this infirmary counts, but I'll find out from the doctor. Tomorrow is a good time for me to take off, because it's the day we have wrestling in Phys. Ed, and I'll be able to get out of it by going on sick call. I'm just not in the mood now to be grappling with a fellow human being on the gymnasium mat. And besides that, I'll be able to study for a couple of hours that I wouldn't ordinarily have. These days every extra hour helps out in getting ready for the exams. So thank you very much, dear, for sending me the form at this time. I should have the results from the lab in a week or so, and I'll be able to get the form back to you in plenty of time.*

I'll also let you know when I hear from the hotel in Chatham. If their prices seem too high, we can always stay in Detroit instead. I don't think we'll have to worry, though, about people knowing we are on our honeymoon, because it will be evident to everyone who looks at us. I shall be glowing with some inner light that will be apparent to all and sundry.

I don't know if I told you about the report I was required to give to our European history course? Anyway, it was on Hitler and Nazism, and I put in a lot of time to the research for it. I must say, I learned a lot I hadn't been aware of before. I talked for about an hour and a half, and if I do say it, as shouldn't, I was pretty good. The fellows seemed to like it. They said I should be a history professor. Sometime, I think that myself.

The next day: *Thank you very much for sending me the invitation to your wedding, ma'am. In as much as I expect to be in Detroit on March 7 anyway, I will be very glad to be present at the church and at the reception afterward. I'm sure this fellow you are marrying is a very lucky fellow!*

I think this weekend I'll have a chance to usher at the Utah basketball game. I signed up for two of them, and the fellow in charge told me he thought I could. I can make two dollars for doing practically nothing, and I get to see a couple of games. The way my funds are these days, that amount means a whole week of spending money to me. Boy, it sure is hell to be poor! I hope I can do better after this war is over.

Comments from Salt Lake City, February 13, 1944: *I received your answer to my "mad" letter, as you called it, and was very much surprised— surprised because I had forgotten all about it. Or put it out of my mind, maybe. I'm sorry if you thought I was angry at you, honey. On that day I was just mad at everything in general, and the action—or inaction—of the Congress was just the straw that broke the camel's back. I'm sorry too that you felt called upon to give me explanations, because you have never—and I mean, never—done anything or said anything that needed an explanation. Everything you do or say is just what is right. I know that you will be the most wonderful wife any man ever had!*

And I don't object to one single part of your wedding plans, so, please, go right ahead as you are doing. As I think back, I see the reason I seemed to be objecting was that subconsciously I felt I was being left out of it all. In ordinary times you and I could be together, to talk things over, and to make our plans together. I guess it just hurt my male ego to know how little I could do to prepare for my own wedding. In the army I'm used to taking charge of everything. But in a difficult situation you have proved yourself quite capable of handling all the details, so far as I can tell, without any real difficulties. Thank you, dear, very much.

Bad news about ASTP, February 18, 1944: *You will have read about the ASTP program's being closed down. We've had a lot of rumors about it, but I'm afraid now that this is the real thing. We saw it in the papers and heard it on the radio. All but about 35,000 of the students will be taken out before April 1 and put in the ground forces.*

I don't know yet how this will affect me. Maybe by the time you get this letter I'll know. Because of our plans, of course, I would like to find out soon. And when I do, I will get in touch with you immediately by giving you a call—collect, I'm afraid, about eleven or twelve p.m. Detroit time. So far we haven't had any announcement about it from the colonel. It could be that some of the students will stay. The paper said "medical students," but there aren't 35,000 of them in the entire country. So I'm not counting on it.

The thing that worries me the most, dear, is whether or not we will get our furloughs. I hate to think about being shipped out right after this quarter without the chance of coming home and marrying you. That's what I want to phone you about. Oh my darling, I pray to God that we'll be able to be married when we planned, because we have waited so long now. And we have been so happily planning it all. But then there's no point in speculating about it until we know for sure, is there, dear?

Marianne responded to the ASTP news, from home, February 20, 1944: *I heard the news about the ASTP being disbanded this morning, which I know may mean that our wedding will be off for a while. I imagine you are feeling very disappointed today about leaving school, as well as about our marriage being delayed. I think it would be about the biggest disappointment I have ever had in my life, but at the same time I know you and I are strong enough to take it. We have had disappointments before, haven't we, dear? But when I think about it, I wonder why I should be pessimistic, when I haven't heard from you what will happen. How much better to be optimistic, as long as I don't know.*

I decided to go downtown and apply for our license anyway, because if you do come home we will need it, and if you don't, we can always use it at a later date. For some reason or other, I haven't sent out the invitations, although most of them are written and sealed, waiting for me to go to the post office. Maybe I was afraid something like this would happen. I'll wait some more, until I hear definitely what's going to happen. I'll be sure to be home in the evenings this week in case you should want to call. At the same time, dear, I know I will dread to hear the telephone ringing.

Hopeful news in Utah, February 21, 1944: *I may call you before you get this letter, so it isn't news to you, but I do have more information. Though none of it, of course, is definite. The officers here all seem to think we will get our furloughs as planned. They haven't received any word to the contrary, so they are going right ahead on that assumption. And if they don't say definitely in the next couple of days, I'll go see the new colonel, tell him my story, and see what he can do about letting me go home. Everybody says he is a decent fellow. Not like the old one.*

Now about our leaving here. The colonel, who is head of the Ninth Service Command ASTP, told us that he expected that Area and Language students who had just one more term would be allowed to stay and complete it. And the announcement from Washington about the reduction of ASTP said that "certain" language students would be allowed to continue. Whether "certain" means certain countries or those of us with higher grades or those with one more term, I don't know. If it's the first, then Spanish students may not qualify, because their language is not important to the war effort, I believe. But, as I said, nothing is definite.

All of the fellows here have been very sympathetic toward me. They say it will be hard enough for them, if they don't get furloughs. But for me it's a lot worse, because we have been planning for so long for the wedding. I'm keeping up my prayers, and I hope so much that they will be answered. I don't usually talk much to people about my religious beliefs, and I can't say that I am a truly religious person. But I do believe firmly that there is a God somewhere who listens to our prayers. And every once in a while, when I wanted and needed something very badly, I would offer to say a "Hail Mary" every night for a certain length of time. Like two months. I never asked for anything unless I thought it was very important. Once when Dad hadn't come home after work, and no one knew where he was, for example. (As it turned out, he was down at the Barnum & Bailey circus in the

middle of the night, watching them put up the tents and the sideshows.)
Usually my prayers were answered. Maybe it wasn't as a result of my pray-
ing, but no one can prove otherwise. And it's strange, because I have never
considered myself a "good" Catholic for years and years. Mostly, I go to church
because I like to sing in the choir. I've never told anyone about it till now,
but I wanted you to know at this important moment. And I hope you won't
think I am being silly.

Two days later: *I still have no definite news for you, and things look*
the same as when I wrote you on Monday. I talked yesterday with an officer
here and an officer from the classification section about my problem. And I
asked them what the chances were of getting a furlough. They both said that
so far the chances of getting a furlough are better than those for not getting
one. They said they are going ahead here as though nothing had happened,
until they hear otherwise. They are even going to start to make a schedule for
the next quarter's classes—just in case. They said we could go ahead on the
assumption that I will get a furlough. But the captain did say that I should
hold off until Friday before I called you about sending out the invitations. I
will definitely call you on Friday—at about eleven or twelve o'clock your
time. I hope the news is good.

We are going to have our finals this week and next, but, as you might
expect, no one is very much interested in studying for them. The army is giv-
ing us a Spanish test this Friday, and then we will have the regular depart-
mental exam next week, along with the test in Professor Dibble's history
class. I don't much feel like it, but I'm going to study harder than usual. I
have to think ahead to when they transfer my work here to Wayne. And
maybe bring up my grade average there. That way I would be in a better
position if I decide to go on to graduate school.

The same day in Dearborn: *I went out to the Greenfield Village this*
evening to give Mr. Koch the news about our wedding. Like the officers
there, he thinks it would be a good idea to go ahead as we have planned until
I hear something definite from you. He said he would be glad to sing "The
Lord's Prayer" and "Where 'ere You Walk," and the organist will play the
other selections you named, honey. I told him how we would be short of time
and that we wouldn't want to go to a photographer for marriage pictures.

He said that there is a Village photographer who always takes two pictures of each wedding, and that we can buy copies, if we so desire. So, we'll see.

From the start, the Army Specialized Training Program was opposed by General Lesley J. McNair, commander of the army's ground forces. He needed manpower, he said, good soldiers with demonstrated leadership qualities, more than specialists and college men. And later he complained that too many of the "good" ASTP men, including the noncoms, who had come originally from infantry or artillery units, were being sent back to other parts of the Armed Forces. But as long as the combat areas were limited in scope, the program continued to exist as an acceptable nuisance. The situation changed drastically in the last months of 1943 with the invasion of Italy. Then the armed forces began to need trained infantrymen and artillerymen to replace the many casualties—the dead and the wounded. And in November President Roosevelt designated General Eisenhower as supreme commander of the Allied forces with the mission of planning and carrying out the invasion of France. There was a sudden demand for a greater number of enlisted men who had completed basic training.

The replacements might be taken from existing divisions and shipped overseas immediately, but that was no real solution to the problem, because they must, in turn, be replaced quickly. On February 10, 1944, General George Marshall informed the secretary of war that more than a hundred thousand men were needed at once. There were two choices, he said. Ten existing divisions could be decimated, or the ASTP program would have to be cut. He recommended the latter. Within days, units around the country were put on notice that the program had been terminated.

On Friday I called Marianne to say my furlough had been cancelled. And I asked her if she would come out to Salt Lake City so we could be married there. I could handle all of the details, I said. She said she would have to think it over, and after an hour or two she called back to tell me she was making the train reservations. She would be arriving in Salt Lake City Monday morning the sixth, she said. Although neither of us had written or talked about that possibility, I'm sure it must have been in the back of our minds all the time.

I had only a few days now to organize our wedding, but I had no doubt I could do it, because Marianne's letters provided me with a detailed blueprint. First, I had to see if the chapel at Fort Douglas was available on Tuesday afternoon, and the chaplain was agreeable to performing the ceremony. That detail was taken care of quickly. It turned out that he was a Lutheran minister, but our religious differences presented no problems, he said, nor that Marianne and I intended, at some point in the future, to join the Episcopal church. As to the time, he checked his calendar and said how about four o'clock on the seventh. Fine, I said, and checked that item off my list.

And while I was at the fort I talked with the military doctor about a Wassermann test for Marianne. Utah required that the tests of both husband and wife be taken within that state, he said. I told him I would bring her up as soon as she arrived on Monday. And he agreed to have the results Tuesday morning. Then I would be able to go to the county building and get the license. I had already asked Pat if he would "stand up" for me, and Margaret to be the maid of honor, and they had said of course. So that matter was taken care of. And the unit captain agreed to take the place of Marianne's father and "give the bride away." A friend in the Spanish platoon had played the organ in church for years, and he said he could handle the music part. And Bob Bowen's girlfriend, Mary Jo Pallanch, would be more than glad to sing for us. She was part of the Tabernacle choir, he said. He doubted if she knew the "Semele" aria, but he would ask her about the Albert Hay Mallot piece. Then I went to a florist shop and chose two nice bouquets. I'll pick them up Tuesday morning, I said. And now, with the Spanish platoon promising to attend en masse, everything was arranged, I thought. But not quite.

There was the large question of a few days' leave to allow Marianne and me to have a honeymoon of sorts. The first sergeant was sympathetic, but his hands were tied, he told me. There could be no furlough or leave of absence. But having said that, he handed me two pieces of paper. "Here are two three-day passes," he said. "Just don't tell anyone about it. And let me know where you are or will be at all times." He might have to get in touch with me, if the orders to ship out should come through. Mostly I would be at the Utah Hotel, I said.

The Patersons and I were at the station to meet the train, which arrived from Denver pretty much on time. Marianne stepped down from the club car, and we took her baggage from the porter. She looked worried and tired. She had sat up two days and nights. "We have to hurry," I said. And the Patersons took her baggage. "You'll be staying with us," they told her. And I explained to her the need for another test. I hadn't had the chance to tell her that before. But it shouldn't take too long, I assured her. At Fort Douglas, everything went smoothly, and the doctor—a captain—promised to have the results by the middle of the next morning. Don't worry, he said, it's fairly simple. He could see the strained looks on our faces. As we were leaving, a large number of men in uniform were coming through the door of the clinic. And I took Marianne to the Patersons' apartment. She looked around. "You have a nice place," she said. But she really would like a chance to rest, she told us. It was a pretty grueling trip. And to me, she said: "I'll see you tomorrow, dear."

That night I slept scarcely a wink. The young engineers, who were being shipped out with the rest of us, didn't give a shit about anything at that point, and the coke-bottle brigade were out in full force.

In the morning I came up to Fort Douglas early, just in case, but the captain said he hadn't been able to get around to Marianne's test as yet. They had had a whole bunch of ROTC men come in for some kind of test or other, and the technicians were swamped, he said. They couldn't get around to Marianne's for a day or two. He was sorry about that, he said. My heart dropped down somewhere close to my lower extremities. But we're supposed to get married at four today, I told him. And I don't have the license. He picked up a stack of papers and leafed through them. She had the test in Michigan already? Yes, I said. He pulled out one of the sheets. "Then, I'll just go ahead and sign it." He scribbled his name across the bottom and filled out some blank spaces. "Good luck, corporal," he said. He handed me the paper and patted me on the back. "Thank you, sir," I said, greatly relieved.

Our wedding day.

But the ordeal was far from over. At the county clerk's office they told me they couldn't give me the license without Marianne's being there to sign it also. The Utah regulations were different from those of Michigan's, they said, maybe because of the Mormon traditions. I took a taxi to the Patersons' apartment. It was now after two o'clock. At the apartment I found the two ladies trying on their dresses. Margaret was pulling at something on Marianne's gown. "You've got to come with me, dear," I said. I explained why. "Like this?" she protested. She indicated the wedding dress. "We'll come back here before we go to the chapel," I said. The taxi had been waiting outside with the meter running. Within half an hour we had the license and were back on the street, hailing another taxi.

We arrived at the fort a good fifteen minutes early, the four of us looking as though we hadn't a care in the world. The chapel was nearly filled with my ASTP friends, and the organist was playing the Bach piece I had asked for. The company commander was there with his wife, and I was glad to see that Professor Dibble and Mrs. Dibble had been able to make it too. But where was the chaplain? No one knew.

Someone said he had gone somewhere to counsel a soldier who had had mental problems and was about to be sent off to a combat division. I kept looking at my watch, and I could see that everyone in the pews was fidgeting and looking at their watches, too.

At precisely four thirty the chaplain arrived, bringing with him many apologies. And the ceremony went off without a hitch, though Marianne said later she thought he had skipped some of the parts. The music was heavenly, and Mary Jo did sing "Where 'ere You Walk." It was a tenor aria, she told me, but she had thought she could handle it pretty well. Which she did, beautifully.

After the ceremony, my friends took their time about kissing the bride. And three or four got in some extra hugs, as well. It wasn't often, they told me, that they had been allowed to kiss such a beautiful woman. The few ladies present cried—as was customary in those days. And the chaplain acted calm and serene, as though marriages were an everyday matter to him, with no worries attached. I handed him an envelope with some money in it. He refused to accept it. It's all part of my job, he said.

The wedding was a resounding success, to be remembered and looked back on for many years to come.

ళ 9 ళ

Preparing for Combat

During the first months of 1944 the Allied nations began to reverse the fortunes of war. In January Soviet forces lifted the German siege of Leningrad, and in the Pacific theater American marines attacked and occupied the important Kwajalein atoll in the Marshall Islands. In Italy units of Mark Clark's Fifth Army made landings at Anzio to threaten the approaches to Rome. In February the Soviets pushed back the German armies and entered both Poland and Romania, while American naval and air forces destroyed the major Japanese base at Truk to allow more landings in the Admiralty Islands. Progress in Italy was slowed by the difficult terrain and the strong resistance of the Nazi soldiers, but by early June the Americans had occupied Rome. Beginning on June 6, with the largest military operation in history, hundreds of thousands of American, British, and Canadian soldiers were put ashore on the Normandy beaches. Nine days later American forces in the Pacific invaded Saipan in the Marianas Islands, and B-29 planes based in China dropped bombs on the home islands of Japan. And before the month ended, the American fleet in the Philippine Sea had decisively defeated the Japanese. Although ultimate victory was still far off, it was clear that the Axis powers would be defeated. The only question was how long would it take.

*　　*　　*

Leaving Salt Lake City, March 12, 1944: *I have a lump in my throat as I am writing tonight, because I miss you so very much. It has been only a little more than 24 hours since I last saw you and held you in my arms, but it seems like an eternity. I've said goodbye to you many times before, but none of those partings were like this one. It seems as though you must have taken part of me with you when you got on the train. I know that there is an empty feeling around my heart. But you've left something to make up for it, and I wouldn't part with that something for all the world—that is, the love of a wonderful wife. Thank you so much for coming out to marry me, my darling.*

And thank you for staying the extra day. I know you had missed a lot of your school as it was. Four days do seem such a short time to be together. But I must say you and I crowded them full of happiness, didn't we? We saw a lot of places here and did a lot of things. All in all, to me, it was the ideal honeymoon, though we never left Salt Lake City.

I'll probably be busy tomorrow getting ready to leave here. I have a box of books all ready to ship to you, and I think I'll send my suitcase with the clothes I won't be needing wherever I am going. Such as the pajamas. And the sweater you knitted for me so long ago, dear. Would you wash it, please, if you have the chance. It's the kind of thing that's hard for me to do at an army camp. Thank you very much. And I'll probably be asking you to send some things back, if I am staying any place for very long.

I meant to tell you I was sorry our goodbye was so brief at the station last night. It's a good thing I got off when I did, because the train had started moving. But perhaps it was better that way—there was no time for tears. I tried to see you through the window, so I could wave goodbye, but I couldn't. Downtown last night I met Pat and Margaret who were going to El Rancho Grande for a late dinner. They said they had seen the cartoon about the flea, and it was singing "Food around the corner," like you said. So you were right, wife darling, and I apologize most humbly. Let's hope that in the future none of our quarrels are any more serious than that!

On the train to Chicago, March 12, 1944: *It's very unsteady, and my handwriting isn't as clear as it should be, but I thought, darling, that you might like a letter from your wife who loves you very much. It may be the last one you'll get at the university, but I'll keep sending letters there with the hope that they will be forwarded to wherever you are going.*

I was thinking last night about the time long ago when you were going away for the first time, and we were on the bus riding home from Rouge Park. You were holding my hand, and you said it was going to be like leaving part of you behind. That's about how I feel right now, dear—as though I had left part of me in Salt Lake City. I guess it will always be that way now. Life will only be perfectly complete when you and I are together again. Especially so now that we are married, and the ties between us are closer and more tangible. You are now my "better half," dear, and I will love and cherish you for the rest of our lives. I pray to God that you will return to me as soon as possible—safe and sound. And thank you for the most wonderful five days of my life.

Moving on to Texas, March 14, 1944: *This isn't a happy day for me, honey, because I'm leaving tonight for Camp Bowie, Texas. But then I have a lot of company in my misery, because everyone else here is leaving too. And I've been in the army long enough to take these thing in my stride. I'd prefer to have stayed here, naturally, and finished the program. But if it can't be, why there's no use crying about it. I'll just have to make the most of it and do the best I can at whatever I am to do. And wherever I do it.*

When I saw all the soldiers and sailors in the same car with you, dear, I hated to leave you among those wolves. Maybe for two whole days! But then, I guess you are old enough and determined enough to take care of yourself in such a dangerous situation. More dangerous than a battlefield, maybe. Anyway, I'm glad you got back home safe and sound. (I got your telegram, by the way.) And thank you again for staying the extra day. Those were the most wonderful days of my life.

On the troop train, March 16, 1944: *We are now passing through the small town of Snyder, Texas, and in a few more hours we'll arrive at our destination. But before you get this letter, I hope I'll have wired you my new address. And I'll do that as soon as I am assigned to a unit. If you can't read my writing, blame it on the train, which seems pretty old and rickety to me. And my handwriting never was very legible, anyway. But I did want to tell you I love you, which you knew anyway.*

We've been riding in Texas all morning, and from what I've seen of the state so far, I don't care much for it. We go for miles and miles with no hills and no trees, and we haven't seen the sun since we left Utah. (By the way, the day after you left Salt Lake City we had thirteen and a half inches of snow—the most in Utah's history, the people said.) I expect that there will be a lot of raining at the new camp, but not much snow.

I didn't tell you when I wrote before that in a month or so we will probably be going on seven weeks of maneuvers in Louisiana. That's what the officers are saying, anyhow. I hate to think of going to that state with all its prejudices, but then maybe Texas will be just as bad. On the other hand, I'm curious to see what real maneuvers are like. We never had anything like that at Camp Roberts. And if I am going overseas, which is likely now, I should have some training like that. One thing is that there will be a lot of ASTP men in this camp, and maybe we can be placed where we can do the most good. And even if we are not all in the same unit, I will have a lot of friends there. Knowing all the men in this car has made the trip more pleasant. We have a lot of things to talk about. Good night, dear, and God bless you. I love you very much.

The next day: I just sent you a telegram which I hope you will get in the morning. The reason I sent it collect was not that I didn't have any money. In fact, on the train trip down here I played a lot of poker and won a few large pots. But we can't leave the area because we were quarantined for scarlet fever the minute we got here. And I'm afraid I won't be able to leave the camp before we go on maneuvers. So a furlough seems out of the question too. I'll probably be sending some money home to you when I get a chance.

Don't worry, honey, about my having an APO number. All of the divisions that have been activated have similar numbers. I won't be going overseas for some time. At least not until the maneuvers are over. And I'll know a lot more about that when I have been assigned to a permanent unit—to a division, probably. In the next few days we'll all be interviewed. From what people are saying, I would think I'll be assigned to the armored infantry— since I was in the infantry before. So, we'll see.

We're still in quarantine here, so I haven't left the area except to go to the PX. I wish I could get a chance to go to town before we leave here. As it is,

I haven't much use for all the poker money I have to carry around with me. So I might as well send it home. That is, if I could find someplace to get a money order.

We've been sleeping in tents since we got here, and it's really cold at night. I couldn't believe it. There are wool blankets, but that is not enough, and I have been wearing my clothes at night—and my long johns—and covering myself with my overcoat! This is sure a strange state. I wish you were here to keep me warm, dear, but then, I shouldn't ever inflict such misery on my good wife. Auf Wiedersehen, dear.

News from Dearborn, March 19, 1944: *Perhaps you have heard by now that your brother John is home from the Pacific and after his leave will be stationed in Dallas? He's training for the navy air corps, he says. So if you stay at Camp Bowie for a while, you might have a chance to see him and Betty. I looked at the map, and I see that Brownwood is not too far from Dallas. It was quite a surprise to your mother—and to everybody—when he called from SF and gave her the news.*

I haven't quite got used to being called Mrs. Quirk, and it surprises me a little—and pleases me very much—every time someone says my name. Everyone must know it by now, or maybe it's just that I am so conscious of it. My children walk in and out of the room saying "Good morning, Mrs. Quirk" and "Goodbye, Mrs. Quirk," and all the time I am beaming my joy back at them. It didn't take long to get my students trained, even the tiny ones—although I'm afraid you wouldn't recognize your name sometimes. I get Mrs. Quart, Mrs. Clerk, Mrs. Quick, Kirk, Quirt, Twerp, and Clark. And Kwoik and Kwalk from kids that can't pronounce their Rs. But I must admit that most of them had even more trouble with Gutzeit.

You asked me what kind of trip I had. I was lucky to have a seat all the way home, so I didn't have to sit on my baggage like some of the women—thanks to your taking me to the club car. And you were right about the wolves. I thought I had come across animals of that species before, but never any that were so aggressive and insistent as those on that train. But you need never worry about my being able to take care of myself in situations like that. I just held one of my bags on my lap and didn't pay any attention to them. And after a while most of them moved to other cars.

Getting ready for the maneuvers, March 22, 1944: *I wanted to write you last night, but I had to work on a detail and got back too late to do much besides washing up and going to bed. These days we usually go to bed at 9 p.m., because we are pretty tired after working all day. They are trying to toughen us up in three weeks for the maneuvers, which will come next month.*

The reason I had the detail last night was that the company commander didn't think my bed was made neatly enough, so he gave me a gig—the first one I've ever had in the army. I thought I had done a pretty good job. Maybe it was because I had just come from the ASTP, and he wanted to teach me a lesson. From now on I'll just have to work harder, I guess. I was supposed to go out with a group of privates and get some gravel, but we drove all over the countryside and never did find any. At least on public property. So, in a way, it was a break for me. It was the first time I'd been out of the camp since I came here. And I didn't have to shovel anything.

The quarantine was lifted today, but I was too tired to go anywhere tonight. So I just lay on my bunk and read some Free Presses *that came yesterday, and then shaved and washed up. Paterson came in from the PX and brought me a pint of ice cream, so I ate that. I'll write until about 9:30 and then go to bed. I've been sleeping better, now that we've got rid of the coke-bottle brigade. They've been scattered all through the division, I think. I had thought, dear wife, that I would be writing you often. But there always seems to be something we have to do in the evening, and, of course, we're busy all day.*

This afternoon I went through the gas chamber—and got a big whiff of chlorine, but it had no ill effects. Then we had a nine-mile march, and it was the toughest I had ever made. We did the nine miles in two hours. When you consider that the usual rate is two and a half miles an hour, you can see we were really traveling. I didn't get so tired, but my feet hurt me a lot, and they still do. The thirty-mile hikes we made at Camp Roberts never pained me like this one. I guess I must have really gotten soft in the last year or so.

More from Texas, March 26, 1944: *I got a pass yesterday afternoon and went into Brownwood. Around here it's called "Deadwood" by the soldiers. And at that it is dead, but also very interesting to me as a small western town. It makes me think of all the cowboy movies we went to every*

Saturday when we were kids. Tom Mix and Hoot Gibson. And Fred Thompson—we liked him the best. I got some lotion I had been needing for my face—it's getting burned by the sun here. I went with Pat and Otto, and we had a steak dinner and then went to a show. The steak was big—like everything in Texas—and tender, and it cost me only a dollar and a half.

When I got my pass the company clerk asked me if I was married, and I said "yes," so he made me out a pass until midnight. Otherwise, it would have been ten o'clock. I didn't tell him my wife wasn't here, but then he didn't ask me! Some of the men had to clean rifles today, so I went into town again, because I don't have one yet. I am writing this from the service club, which is a nice quiet place to be. And I think I'll have another steak dinner. After the war I plan to have a big steak every day, and maybe I can gain a little weight. I suppose I'll have to be rich to afford it, so perhaps I won't be a history professor after all.

Bob Bowen said the chaplain told them at services today that after maneuvers in Louisiana we would be sent to Fort Bragg in North Carolina. I had heard that before. I don't know how much truth there is in it, but it must be some kind of port of embarkation. Which would mean that we would be going to Europe. If so, I hope I'll be able to get a furlough before we go overseas. But we'll see when the time comes.

Oh yes, honey, I have been assigned to the 16th Armored Infantry Battalion. I guess it won't be too bad. At least we'll be riding around in trucks, while the regular infantry walks! What with my sore feet and all. Paterson got the artillery, although he is from the air corps originally. And a sergeant. I was classified as a squad leader, which calls for a staff sergeant's rating and $96 a month. But maybe I won't get it, because the outfit probably has its positions filled. It was the privates who were shipped out here as overseas replacements. So unless some of the noncoms are transferred, which is highly unlikely, I will be lucky if I remain a corporal. There's talk around here that all the ASTP people will eventually end up as privates in the ground forces, even the sergeants. I'd hate to take a cut in pay, but also one of the privileges of being a corporal is that I never have to do KP or walk guard. I'm sorry to see our bunch broken up like this. True, we will all be in the same division, but a division has between ten and fifteen thousand men, and it won't be like being in the same tight-knit platoon.

And still more news, March 31, 1944: *I have been assigned to C company permanently, but so far I don't know which platoon or what job I will have. As I expected, the company is full already, and all of the ratings are taken up. I'll see what happens in the next few days. The company commander interviewed me today, and he asked me about my former experience and what weapons I have fired. He was interested in my work in Information and Education and in tactics, and he seemed glad to have me here. But he said he couldn't guarantee anything about keeping my rank. He does seem like a pretty decent fellow. And fair.*

I think I'll be able to work on my German lessons here, so would you take the white index file that has all my lessons in it and send it back to me? Also the two German dictionaries and the book on Military German? I'd like to get that course out of the way before they ship us overseas. And would you look in the suitcase and see if my glasses are there? If so, would you send them to me? I'll need them for all of the reading I expect to be doing. I can't find them anywhere here, and that's the only place now I can think to look for them. I'm getting so absentminded these days. Maybe I should be a history professor after all! P.S. Did you see where Utah's basketball team won the national championship last night? Pretty good for a bunch of kids, eh?[9]

Yet more news from Texas, April 1, 1944: *They called in all the remaining privates and Pfcs in our company and told them they should get ready to go overseas by the 20th of this month. Any of them who hadn't had furloughs since November 1 get to go home for fifteen days. All in all, there were more than a hundred of them. I don't know where they will get men to take their places, because only thirty-five came in from ASTP. And since all the men leaving were privates, that still doesn't leave any rating for your husband.*

---

9. There were two tournaments in New York City, the National Invitational and the NCAA. Utah played Kentucky in the former, and was defeated in the first round, largely because of poor foul shooting. The *New York Times* reported that the "baby-faced" Utes seemed to suffer from stage fright. But the fates intervened to give Utah a second chance. The Arkansas team, scheduled to play in the regional NCAA, had a bus accident, and the Utes were asked to replace them. Utah defeated Iowa State, Dartmouth, and St. Johns—the favorite—to win the NCAA championship, and then beat Kentucky, the NIT winner, in a playoff. (Years later Arnold Ferrin was the university's athletic director.)

Sad news two days later from Dearborn: *I had some unhappy news this past week. You will never be able to meet my good friend Byron Tower who died overseas as a result of wounds on March 1. Shirley (Johnston) Sherman said she had seen his burial at sea on a newsreel yesterday. He had been in a photo unit and had taken shots of the landings of American troops in the South Pacific. The newsreel included shots of his being wounded too and then taken aboard a ship. I hope that I never see the newsreel, or that his folks won't either. It would just be too sad. His dad had died during the past year, and I know it will be quite a blow to his mother and his sister. They were always so close, when Byron was younger. It makes the war seem very near to home, when it takes someone you know well. And I know that will be happening more and more whenever we invade Western Europe and then Japan. I pray to God that the killing will end before it takes others who are so close and dear to me.*

Easter Sunday in Camp Bowie, April 9, 1944: *I've had some bad news too, dear. My mother wrote me that Dad was having some trouble with his heart and has had to take at least two or three weeks off from work. And maybe more. She told me it wasn't too serious, and I certainly hope so, because I worry so much when anyone at home is sick. Dad has always been so hale and hearty that it's hard to picture his being sick in bed. By the way, the fourteenth is his birthday, so you might get him something. When I go into town I'll try to find a good book he might enjoy. At our house my mother always baked special cakes for our birthdays. Mine is chocolate with a white icing. And Dad's, for reasons I've forgotten, is a white cake with a jelly topping. It's been like that for as long as I can remember.*

Paterson was telling me how he went to Fort Worth last weekend and got into a conversation with a woman in a restaurant. I think Margaret was out of town, though he didn't say so. The woman asked him to go with her to Dallas, but he said he couldn't. She invited him to come to her place in Fort Worth the next week (this one). And she would have a party for him, she said. He asked her if she had any friends so he could bring a friend— meaning me, of course. When he got back to camp his conscience bothered him, he said, so he tore up her address and threw it in the trash. I wonder, though, if he really thought I'd have gone with him? I hope not, because to me marriage means too much to jeopardize it, even innocently.

207

I still don't know any more about my job. I have been in charge of the ASTP men ever since I've been here, because of my work at Camp Roberts, and I've had a chance to show the higher-ups what I can do. So when they finally do decide to give us regular jobs, maybe my showing here will have some effect on where they put me. I'd sure like to get a staff sergeant's rating, especially because I'd get a $30 a month raise, plus a lot more responsibility.

Did I tell you that the maneuvers in Louisiana have been called off? They didn't make any sense when there has been so much upheaval in the division, with the privates leaving and all. Then we were supposed to go out on bivouac here for two weeks. But yesterday we heard even that has been called off. I hope so, because I might have a chance now to see John and Betty in Dallas.

From Marianne in Dearborn, April 10, 1944: *I mailed your books and notes to you Saturday morning, so I hope you get them soon. Your glasses aren't in the bag though. I looked all through it, in every nook and corner, so I hope you will find them there. I know how much you depend on them.*

When I saw your father yesterday he seemed to be looking well. And he laughed and joked like usual. But I guess he has been overtaxing his heart, so it will do him good just to rest it for a while. Your mother told me the doctor thinks it is because he had to throw all those tires around before he was a foreman. And then he had a job without much hard labor involved. But more stress, probably. I suppose it will be pretty hard for him to lie still in bed, when he isn't feeling sick, and I know your mom will miss not having him around. I know too what a financial drain it can be to have someone in the hospital, especially the breadwinner. Do you think she will need any help from you, honey?

I gave your mother the balance on our wedding ring, so we haven't any debts now, and I will deposit the rest tomorrow in our account. That makes the balance $78, enough for any emergency, such as your coming home, etc. If you have any to send home out of your next pay, maybe it would be a good idea to send it to your mother instead.

Troubles in Texas, April 12, 1944: *Our company commander put us in restriction today, so for a while we won't be able to get passes. Did I say he was fair? Maybe I should add strict to that. It seems he isn't pleased with the outfit or its attitude. And I can't say I blame him very much. This is really a snafu bunch of misfits. But then they haven't done much training together, and I doubt that restricting the men will make them snap out of it. What we need also is lieutenants and noncoms who set a good example for the men, who pay attention to details, and show they know what they are doing. As of now, most of what they tell us comes out of manuals that maybe they carry around in their hip pockets. Anyway, I hope the restriction doesn't last very long, because I want to go to Dallas this weekend.*

The next day: *We had a rough day today. We had to move up while artillery shells were shot over our heads. It wasn't too bad, although we got pretty close to where the shells were falling. They were about a hundred yards in front of us—about the length of a football field. A few of the men were closer and got hit by shrapnel. But we were all far enough away so no one was hurt badly. As you can imagine, it does give you some pause when you hear the shells whistling over your head. Right now the men in my barracks are having a discussion about politics and labor strikes. And it is getting to be a hot discussion, which keeps distracting me from my writing this letter. So I think I will close now with this page. I haven't had a good argument for a long time. It's interesting that we never seem to talk here about the war. As though we're putting it out of our minds.*

The same day in Dearborn: *I remembered that your dad's birthday was tomorrow, and I hope to go out to the hospital after school to see him. It's too bad he has to spend such an important day in bed, but at least he isn't feeling sick. Your mother said the other night that he is actually enjoying the rest he is getting. And especially having pretty nurses come whenever he rings the bell! I had thought too of giving him a book, and I will stop downtown tomorrow at Hudson's and get him something. Your mom said he will be on a strict diet for the next few weeks, because he is supposed to lose a few pounds. So I'll be sure not to send him anything to eat. Like chocolates.*

Three days later, April 16, 1944: *I drove out to your folks' house Friday night, and Allen and I went to the hospital after supper. Your dad was looking very well, better than I've seen him look for a long while. In fact, he seems so hale and hearty, he says everyone asks him what he is doing in the hospital. I got him a couple of books for his birthday—some crossword puzzles he could use to pass the time and* Under Cover.[10] *It turned out your mother had been to the hospital that afternoon, and she also gave him* Under Cover! *It would be funny if you sent him the same book. Three great minds with the same idea. I took back the one I had bought and exchanged it for Quentin Reynolds's new book,* The Curtain Rises.

Sarah and I got together last night and decided we would make something for you and for Richard Marks. He is now in Colorado, by the way. He finished the ASTP and is training for combat MP. We thought we would make upside-down pineapple cakes, because I had never made one, and you once said you liked them. They were fun to put together and looked beautiful when we put them in the oven. But after they had baked for a while, some juices ran down out of the pans, and the kitchen was so filled with billowing clouds of black smoke we could hardly see each other. I'm surprised one of the neighbors didn't call the fire department. And it was a good thing my folks were out for the evening. We had a hard time cleaning up before they got back.

I was afraid the cakes were ruined, but both of them did come out looking pretty good. So I sent yours on to you. Sarah is more of a perfectionist than I am, so she took hers home and said she would eat it. Or maybe she just threw it away. If yours tastes smoky and charred, you needn't eat it. But I thought you should know what had happened to it.

The next day: *While I was at Hudson's I picked up a book I had been wanting to read—*A Tree Grows in Brooklyn. *And as usually happens, I couldn't stop reading it until I was finished. I stayed up almost half the night. I thought it was a good book and believe you would like it too. It reminded me a great deal of some of Thomas Wolfe's works I've read. And then, interestingly, in Betty Smith's synopsis of her book on the cover, she said she was inspired to write it by one of Wolfe's novels. So I would guess her style is copied after his somewhat. Things like that keep happening, and I'm glad I had that course at Wayne in the novel—though at the time I had a lot of trouble, as you will remember, dear.*

---

10. By John Roy Carlson, a pseudonym for Arthur Derounian, an Armenian immigrant who spent several years as a self-styled undercover agent investigating and exposing alleged fascist organizations in the United States, "poised to stab at democracy" (including Detroit's Father Charles E. Coughlin).

I could hardly believe it, dear, but your mother called to say you had sent your dad Under Cover *too! That's really amazing, isn't it? The best thing, I think, is for me to keep it for our library, and you can get something else for him. Then you and I can read it sometime after you come home. If it's still timely by then. Is that okey, dear?*

Family news from Texas, April 18, 1944: *I went to Dallas over the weekend and finally got in touch with John and Betty. I had a very good time at their house, talking about old times. I couldn't locate them until Sunday morning, and I spent the night Saturday at a Jewish Center dorm. It cost me only 50 cents for a bed and breakfast—bagels and coffee mostly. (When I got back to the barracks I was talking to Bernard Koslow, who is Jewish, about it. He said he had been in Dallas the same night. Where did you stay? I asked him. He said at the YMCA!)*

My whole weekend cost me about ten dollars, which isn't bad. I went by car, and that was $3.50 each way. There's a big business in Texas of people driving private cars between cities. From what they say, they have no difficulty getting gasoline, though tires might be a problem. On the way back, we had a flat, and the man stopped to fix the tube, before we could get going again. It seemed to me like the jitney business in Akron during the Depression. It's certainly convenient, and quicker than the bus service. But to me it's one example of how things are run in this state during the war. For one thing, they don't seem to worry much about food rationing either. In restaurants they always have a lot of everything. Another thing that bothers me is the separate toilets in all the restaurants for colored people. Even colored soldiers, I've noticed. But then this is the South, so what else can you expect?

Saturday night I went to a Richard Crooks concert, and he was great, as usual. He sang some things from La Boheme *I had never heard before. Maybe someday we can have recordings of the entire opera, if there are any. I would think it would take a lot of single records. Incidentally, I found that I could get a free ticket and a dollar for ushering. And I even had a good seat. I am enclosing the check for one dollar for you to add to our account. Have you ever seen a check for a dollar? I hadn't till now. Maybe we should frame it and put it up on the wall, if we ever have a music room in our little house.*

Three days later: *It's a sultry Friday afternoon, and I'm not doing anything, so I'll write letters to you and to Dad. The reason I'm not doing*

211

anything, is that most of the remaining privates in the outfit shipped out this morning. It sure seems quiet around here. I can't tell you where they are going, of course, but you can guess that they will be overseas before long and maybe in combat. I noticed something that I didn't mention to anyone, but it had a lot to do with the way those that went were chosen. The company commander told the sergeants they could make the decision. In a way, that was a good idea, because the platoon sergeant and the squad leaders would know who were the most valuable to us. But one result, I think, was that almost all the Jews were put on the list. Even some who came here from the ASTP. Luckily, my friend Bernard Koslow wasn't.

I can't prove anything, and maybe it was just a coincidence. But it still troubles me. Most of the sergeants had their rank when the division moved here from California. And they weren't the most enlightened people in the world, to put it mildly. And I don't want to make difficulties for myself by asking questions. Maybe things like that will come out after the war, I don't know. Meanwhile, dear, please don't say anything to anyone, even your closest friend or our families. If I ever even hinted my suspicions to my dad, I'm sure he would raise a lot of trouble for a lot of people. And maybe for me too.

By the way, dear, I did get the box with the pineapple cake today. I ate a piece and gave some to my friends. You needn't have worried about how it tastes. It's very good. And my friends praised it to the high heavens. I'll have to admit that you have true culinary talents, in addition to your many other capabilities. Even your bad results end up tasting good!

Marianne commented from Dearborn, April 23, 1944: *By the way, honey, did you find your glasses? If you need new ones, maybe I'd better send you the money for some, because you don't want to go without them, do you? I'd probably have to send it from our account, because my pay will be spread out very thin to do me until May 15. They subtracted quite a bit for the time I was in Salt Lake City and on the train, and I only received a half pay this month. And after a bond deduction and I bought a tire and a tube, there isn't much of it left, unfortunately. But I've discovered another important advantage in being married to you, honey. My income tax deduction is less since I'm a married woman. These days it gets to be quite an item. You didn't know that the real reasons I married you were mercenary, did you?*

A bit of information from Camp Bowie, April 24, 1944: *I have some news about my stay here. It seems pretty definite that I can't be shipped out until four months after I left the ASTP, which would be not before July 14. It's too bad all those fellows who left last week weren't advised about that. I guess the reason for the restriction is that the generals who supported the program didn't want all of the fellows to be sent overseas as replacements without some kind of training.*

Anyway, I could be staying a lot longer, who knows? So maybe this summer you and I could drive down here together in your car. Is there any chance of that? I know that your father bought it for the tires, before he gave it to you. So would you have to get his permission or anything like that? If you were here for the whole summer, having a car would be mighty useful. Be sure to let me know when you are through teaching, honey, because then I can start looking for a place to stay in Brownwood. Since you will be paid in the summer, and we will have my salary and the government allotments, we should be able to handle it.

Marianne's reply from Dearborn, April 25, 1944: *Yesterday I got your letter of Friday, and I will answer it before I say goodnight. I had thought of taking the car down, too, honey, because it would be so handy to have in case I had to stay any distance away from you. But I am not sure it would be a good idea to take it such a long distance. It's not new, as you know, and it could be an awful nuisance if it started to give us trouble. I just bought a "new" tire, but it's a grade-3, recapped one, and I've heard they don't wear so well. I'll have to ask my dad about it, and maybe have all the tires checked at the garage to see if they will stand 3,000 miles of wear and tear. And then, although the car is mine to use, and is registered in my name, my dad did pay for it. I wouldn't feel that I could sell it, and I would feel responsible if something happened to it. So we can think it over and then decide the best way for the two of us to get to Texas—that is, if you do come home on furlough.*

From Camp Bowie, April 30, 1944: *So far, the married men have been able to go home practically every night, except when they have details, such as corporal of the guard or charge-of-quarters—and those don't come around very often. So I would think they will be no problem when you are here. Maybe we'll have some semblance of married life for a few weeks. As you said, we have been pretty lucky so far.*

I was talking to some German POWs [prisoners of war] *the other day in their language—just for practice. I guess we're not supposed to, but there were no guards around, and other fellows were talking to them also. They said they were captured in North Africa, and had belonged to Rommel's Afrikakorps. All newspaper and magazine accounts of German prisoners picture them as being "arrogant," etc. But these didn't seem any different from our own soldiers. And they talked a lot about their families. There are quite a few of them in a stockade here, and they work around the camp, hauling trash, digging ditches, planting grass, etc. It seems strange to see them working in denims, with no guard, while nearby in the stockade our own GI prisoners are being guarded by rifles. The POWs have a good deal here, and they know it. They get the same pay we do, eat the same food— and lots of it, and are out of the war for good. They could save a lot of money while they are here. I don't suppose US prisoners in Germany have quite as good a deal.*

More news from Dearborn, May 4, 1944: *I hope you will be able to get a furlough soon after June 4, as you say. But if you don't come home then, I will plan to leave right after the 16th—the last day of school—to come down to Texas. Is that okey, honey? I won't be driving, of course, because I would hate to try to find Brownwood alone. And I don't know of anyone who wants to go in that direction who could help me drive. So you can start looking for a place for us to live, if you like. I don't know if I told you what our finances will be like—more or less. I'll be getting paid each fifteenth of the month—$125 after deductions for income tax, insurance, etc. I'm having a bond taken from that, but I think I will discontinue it for the summer months, because we may need the money. With your earnings and the army marriage allotments it should make our income somewhere around $200 a month, which should be more than enough, I would think.*

Did I tell you, honey, about being offered a job as a policewoman in Detroit? I mean I received a letter from them asking me to come in and take some examinations. I think it has something to do with the summer job I had at the Methodist Village, because I would be working with juvenile delinquents. And I was always going down to some police station or other to take back a little boy who had run away. I declined, of course. You remember that I could hardly get through the summer in one piece. And I like my job in

Dearborn so much. But the salary did tempt me a little. It's $3,060 the first year of training, and $3,260 after that. A fortune!

Incidentally, I went to a party at Jean Larsen's a couple of nights ago—a hen party, for Betty, a sorority sister of mine who was married recently. She and Jake have one of these "modern" arrangements, and both still date other men and women, even after they have been married. To me that seems very strange as a basis for a strong marriage. You are the only one I want, dear, and ever will want.

A Quirk family get-together in Texas, May 5, 1944: *I finally got my three-day pass and went to Dallas to see John and Betty again. It rained on and off during my stay there, and John couldn't do any flying. But he did have classes each day. I had a good time, though we didn't do very much. There was a vacant room at their place, so I stayed there—$7.75 for the three days, which wasn't too bad. And better than a hotel. You can imagine that I felt very ritzy, what with my marble bath and all. For three days I was the lord of the manor. We talked a lot—about old times, of course, but especially about his experiences in the Marshall Islands. He said that the* Idaho *was protecting some troops when they were landing on a Jap-controlled island, and MacArthur wanted the* Idaho *to keep the enemy busy all night. The captain turned the job over to my brother. "You're always thinking you're smarter than everybody else," he said. And besides, the commanding officer wanted to get a good night's sleep.*

So John said he kept the ship's searchlights on the enemy encampment all night and sent in some shells from time to time. And the next day the American forces went ashore and took the island with very few casualties. For which the captain was later awarded a medal, John said. For heroism while sleeping, I suppose.

More training, May 9, 1944: *I'm late getting started tonight, so I'll write until about ten o'clock and then go to bed. It doesn't seem as though I get enough sleep these days. I guess it must be the hot, humid days—and nights. I hope it won't be too uncomfortable for you when you come next month. The reason I'm late writing is that we had an NCO meeting after supper. And it went on and on. I thought maybe the officers were going to tell us about what will happen, but then they probably don't know any more than we do. So tonight it was just the same old stuff—we've got to shape*

215

up. Officers always love to tell us things like that. It makes them think they are doing their jobs. But they never tell us how. Or show us. It's like one of my dad's favorite stories—about the mother who sent the little girl outside to see what her brother was doing and tell him to stop it. P.S. You'll be glad to know I've found my glasses, and in the most unlikely of places—in the pocket of one of my jackets! And here's a naughty story I heard today. One guy says to another: "Are you bothered by bad thoughts?" Says the other: "No, I enjoy them." That's enough for tonight. And there is nothing new on the furlough front.

From Dearborn, May 12, 1944: *It's a very warm night out, and the breeze comes through my window with the smells of summer. And a big, fat June bug just flew through also, which is a sure sign that summer is here. Just five more weeks, dear, and I will be with you again. I get nearly ecstatic each time I think of it, and my blood pressure jumps up about fifty degrees. I wonder if we will ever get used to the idea of being together and be sane and calm about it. About coming down in the car, honey, I have had more thoughts about it. I talked to my dad, and he thinks it would be a good idea to take it with us—if you are home on furlough, that is. He thinks it would hold up all right, and if we do have trouble, we could always sell it and go the rest of the way by train. And at the end of the summer, if I didn't have to drive back by myself, we could get a good price for it in Texas.*

Five days later: *When you do find an apartment tell me how we are set for dishes and pots and pans, for bedding, and for towels. Some or all may not be furnished. And for the time being you'd better not send your extra towels home. We might need them there. I have an alarm clock, but it is not reliable, so perhaps I can pick up one for us. It wouldn't do to have you be late when you go back to the camp in the mornings. And get restricted to quarters. Yesterday I received my contract to teach next year, with a raise of $260. I haven't signed it as yet, but I will soon, if you approve. By the way, your mother told me that John and Betty had given your dad his birthday present—another copy of* Under Cover. *I guess all of us are seeing to it that he reads that book—or else.*

About housing prospects in Texas, May 18, 1944: *Margaret Paterson says she has a lead that might prove good for them and for us. A man has a house that he rented to some people for fifteen years and is now vacant. He* *will rent it out, but he wants to repair it first. I don't know how long that would take, but Margaret says she has first call on it. The house would be rented by three or four couples, and they would have a bedroom apiece and a common kitchen and living room. She wasn't sure about the bathroom situation, but she's going to let me know. The rent would be $100 a month split three or four ways.*

I know it wouldn't be as nice as having our own apartment, but there would be some advantages, such as company for you during the day, and an electric refrigerator in the kitchen, instead of an icebox. And the men could all go to the camp at the same time in the morning. I'd rather have three couples, because it would give us a little more privacy, and $33.33 wouldn't be bad for the rent, would it?

More from Camp Bowie, May 21, 1944: *I won't send any of my towels home, if you say not to, honey. We could use them here, if you want, and save the new ones we got as wedding presents for later. These are pretty good towels, though. I think Cannons, and I have four or five too many. Besides, I have to start thinking about what to take with me if they decide to ship me overseas. And if I turned them in to the supply sergeant, they would just be torn up for rags, which makes no sense to me.*

About your job, dear, right now I feel that you should make your own decisions. By necessity, I can't contribute as much money to our partnership as you, so you should have the major say-so about it. And until after the war, everywhere I'll be is so iffy. You will have to do most of the planning for both of us. And even after the war I won't be able to contribute as much as you. I do mean to finish at Wayne, if it is at all possible. I would need about twenty hours, if my ASTP credits are transferred. I'll still have certain basic requirements to satisfy, but I figure I could do it in a year, easily. And if Wayne would count the ASTP grades, my honor point average would be 3.8, which would help me get into graduate school, I would think.

It seems clear now that the government will finance all veterans who want to go to a college or university, which seems to mean graduate work also. And they would pay them $75 a month, plus tuition and books.[11] I would want, of course, to apply for that. Providing you would be willing to

---

11. The GI Bill.

carry the burden of our money-making for another year or so, while I got my master's. Do you think that would be possible, dear?

I forgot to tell you, honey, that I'll be having a different job for the next three weeks. I was told to go down to the division ration warehouse yesterday morning, and I found I'd be working there. I have a detail of three privates, and we have to draw and issue rations for the entire division. So it is a really big responsibility, though of course most of it is manual labor. Sometimes we have to lift hundred-pound sacks of potatoes or flour. But I find I am enjoying hard labor for a change. It gives you a lot of satisfaction, that you can do it. And also the best part is that I get out of all company details, so I don't mind it in the least.

The next day: *There were a lot of prisoners working in the warehouse today, different ones, and I talked with some of them in German. I had some trouble, because I kept thinking of Spanish words, but after a while I spoke fairly fluently. I told them my wife came from Remscheid, and one man said he was from Solingen, which was close by. One spoke good English, and when he talked to me in German he used the Dufuss.[12] I wonder if he did it because he considered me his inferior? Or his equal? Maybe that's the way German soldiers talk with each other. I guess, though, that it's better not to get too familiar with them, when the army doesn't even want us to speak to them.*

Legal difficulties in Michigan, May 28, 1944: *It seems, dear, that there is a damper on our plans to drive the car to Texas. On Friday I went to the ration board to find out how we'd get enough gas for a trip like that. They said the only way was to have an affidavit stating that we are making a permanent change of address, and that I am unemployed at the present time. I asked your dad about it, because he's a notary public, and knows such things, and he doesn't think we could swear to that. We'd be liable, he said, to ninety days in jail for a felony, and have all our voting rights revoked for the rest of our lives. That seems pretty drastic to me, but he said it was the law.*

I admit that it's still a temptation, because by rationalizing a little the statements could be true. I am not "employed" in the summer, though I am

---

12. The familiar form of "you."

being paid. My dictionary says to be employed is to be "working for another person or a firm," which I'm not. And we are planning to be in Texas until the government changes our plans. I have known of other people who took trips under the same circumstances. But that, of course, doesn't make it right for us, does it? And do you think it would be worth the risk? In the end, it doesn't matter how we go down there. The important thing is that you and I will be together all the time. Even if you did get the furlough, we could both take the train down. We have enough money for that.

The same day in Camp Bowie: *I'm writing this letter from the orderly room, because I'm on CQ* [charge of quarters]—*only the second time I've had it since I came here. So the ration job doesn't get me out of extra duties, after all. But I hate to have a detail on Sunday, because it takes up my only free day. Still, it's not much work, and I can write letters.*

I just got back a little while ago from Brownwood, where I had dinner with Pat and Margaret. I had made the date before I knew I would have CQ, so my squad leader, Sgt. Peters, said he would stay here until I got back, which was very nice of him, wasn't it? They were both well, and I was glad to see them. I had been keeping in touch with Margaret by phone to see how her house-hunting was coming along. She said the apartment we had hoped to have June 10 wasn't going to be vacated, so that was out. They did find an apartment for themselves, and she said she'd keep on the lookout for another one nearby.

About my furlough, we got word Friday that the seven days leave I got in the ASTP didn't count as a furlough, so that means I am near the top of the priority list. When the first sergeant comes in tomorrow I'm going ask him for a leave as soon as my detail at the ration depot is over—which is June 9. So if I could leave here that weekend, I'd be home Monday morning. You'd still have another week to teach, but I could use those days to see my folks and friends. I would like to see Dr. Basilius, if that is possible, and talk with him about my work at Utah. And, of course, the nights would belong to you and me. I'm looking forward to a furlough in Detroit, so we can go dancing. All the best places should be going full blast then.

Travel plans, May 31, 1944: *I received your Sunday letter today, honey, and I thought I'd better answer it right away. I'm sorry to hear about the hitch in our plans to drive to Texas. I had so set my mind on it, that I hate to give up the idea without a struggle. I talked about what you told me with some of the married men here, and they said it was the same with them when they drove down here. They just said they were moving permanently, and it was as "permanent" as anything can be in the army these days. They said we should go ahead and get the gas, no matter what anybody said. In the army we are always looking for ways to get around regulations anyway. And as you said, we can rationalize it and come to the conclusion that we should get the gas.*

What I think we should do is first to see that the car is in good working order, especially the tires. And then when I come home, you and I can see the ration board and ask them what they have to say about it. As for being unemployed, well you are not employed until you sign next year's contract. Sure, I may be stretching things a bit, but the car would be of such value to us in Texas, that it would be worth our while to do that. We'll see what happens when I get home.

More travel plans from Marianne in Dearborn, June 1, 1944: *I still have my doubts about our taking the car. I have had several other people tell me lately that they drove to visit their husbands for a few months and then came back. But then I keep wondering about troubles with our car. I had a flat when I started out this morning—a nail went right through the tire, so now it's our spare and isn't in too good a condition. And I don't know if I can get another one. What would we do if that happened while we were driving to Texas? Have you ever changed a flat tire, dear?*

I understand that you will very likely go back to school when the war is over, honey, and I think it is the best time to finish up, because of your ASTP work and the experiences you have had since you joined the army. I've been reading about the new bill for servicemen the Congress is considering, and it sounds pretty good, doesn't it? Of course I won't mind working after you get back, dear. I like my job, and actually I'll be sorry to give it up. I imagine that there are a great deal of women in the same situation, who will be helping their husbands get an education.

I found an alarm clock, honey—finally. After trying all the department and hardware stores, I'd just about decided there weren't any in this entire area. But Jane heard a rumor yesterday at the beauty parlor about a place that had some, so I went down today, and he had a few left. It isn't very beautiful, but it's metal, and it runs and rings—I tried it out at the shop before I bought it. So I guess we are all set.

As far as I know, dear, I will be leaving here on Sunday the 18th. I'll wire you the time I expect to arrive in Brownwood, but it should be early in the morning on Tuesday. I was lucky to get reservations and a berth from Chicago to Fort Worth. The fare is $98, which seems like a lot of money— and more than I expected to pay—but now I'm sure to get there, and I'll have a place to sleep. So I'll be rested when I get there. And I would like to get started looking for a good place to stay in Brownwood. I hope that's all right with you. See you soon, dear.

CATASTROPHE IN CAMP BOWIE, June 16, 1944: *Right now, darling, I don't know where I stand about meeting you at the train or even what happens after you get here. Last night I had guard duty again, because my job at the ration depot was over, I guess. I was sitting in the guardhouse, trying to read my* Time *magazine, and the officer of the day—Captain Skoog—came in. It was two o'clock in the morning. He was so quiet, I didn't see him at first, and then I called everyone to attention. It's a regulation, when an officer comes in. I didn't think much about it then, but I did notice he had written something on a pad of paper he was carrying. He was probably prepared to find some fault or other.*

When I stopped by the company headquarters in the morning to see about a three-day pass to meet you in Fort Worth, the CQ said Captain Skoog had reported me for not leaping instantly to attention. Lack of respect for an officer, he said. And I was to be confined to the barracks area for two weeks as my punishment. The CQ said our company commander was away—he thought in Dallas. And he wouldn't be back for a day or two. I have no way of knowing what will happen, dear. I called Pat and Margaret, and they promised to meet you at the station in Brownwood. It's good to have friends like that. But right now your loving husband is up to his neck in the proverbial chicken shit.

❧ 10 ❧

Weeks of Uncertainty

From Camp Bowie, September 2, 1944: *It's hard to realize that you are gone from me, dear, and that once more we will have to rely on our letters and an occasional telephone call. And it seems strange to be spending my free time in camp, and in the barracks. I had become so accustomed to rushing "home" to Brownwood every time I was off duty, and being with you practically every night. For nearly three months. I know that each time we separate we say this is the most difficult, and the most painful. But it will be especially hard when there are thousands of miles between us, and we know that many months will pass before we are together again.*

You told me on Thursday morning when we said goodbye at the train station that you were sorry to be such a crybaby. And in public. But I'm not sorry, dear, because you were telling me how you felt, and I felt like shedding tears myself. And by a strange coincidence, at this very moment, the radio on my desk is playing "Oh Dry Those Tears."[13] Do you think the Fates are telling us something?

So I am not going to write you a sad letter, darling. We can't be together now or in the near future. But what we do have is far more important—a wonderful life to look forward to, for us and for our children. I've told you

---

13. By Teresa del Riego. This song was often recorded as a solo by a brass instrument, such as the trombone. And I sang it once in the thirties on our radio program.

often how much I appreciate you as a wife, and never more than now when we are apart again. I can brag to my friends about you and praise you, but I couldn't ever express in mere words my thanks to you for making my life so complete. You tell me that it irks you when I thank you for things that are self-evident, so I won't say any more about that. Just that it never ceases to amaze me that I am so lucky.

I'm still recuperating from the 25-mile hike we took on Thursday. In fact, I pretty much didn't make it, although no one else in my company knows about it. I was OK for the first 20 miles or so, though my feet were hurting me, but then I began to fall behind the rest of the fellows. Our captain had said he didn't care how long it took us, but he did want us to finish, one way or another. So I was limping along, and it was about four in the morning, and I was so far behind I couldn't see anyone in front of me. I had reached the outskirts of the camp, determined to keep going, when I saw a fellow I didn't know walking up and down. He was from a different company or battalion, because I had never seen him before.

He waved. "Have you seen a taxi?" He said he was going on furlough and had to get to Brownwood before six. I said I hadn't and kept trudging along. A few minutes later a taxi pulled up alongside me, and the fellow rolled down the window. "Would you like a ride?" he said. The temptation was too great, and I succumbed to his kind offer. Just drop me off before we get to the Company C barracks, I said. I didn't want anyone from our outfit to witness my shame. The next day the captain praised the entire company. Especially you, corporal. He was looking at me. "I thought you would never make it," he said. And my shame was doubled.[14]

Marianne made it back to Dearborn and wrote on the same day: *All in all, the ride home wasn't too bad. I slept most of the way to Fort Worth, where I had to change trains, and I got quite a bit of sleep most of the way to Kansas City. I guess I am getting used to traveling on trains and can even sleep while sitting up. For a time I was wishing I had spent the extra*

---

14. I owed the captain so much for helping me out in June. I had told him about Captain Skoog and his insistence that I be put in confinement. And that you would be here for the summer. He just smiled. He knew the captain even better than I did. "Don't worry, corporal," he said. "Tell me when she leaves, and you can serve your punishment then." Which was what I was doing. And most of it out in the field.

money for a Pullman bed—when I had to sit on my luggage from Kansas City to Chicago. But now that I am home, I'm glad I didn't. We can use the money for something else. If you would get another furlough, or something like that. I was about ten hours late getting into Detroit. I was supposed to have come in last night, but all the trains were late—which seems to be the rule these days. I did get a good night's sleep in my own bed, though, and now I feel almost human again.

Kay says Bill has been sent to Fort Belvoir in Virginia, so I guess they are going to draft a lot of married men with children. He was lucky to get the Engineers, because he is a draftsman and is eligible for OCS. He had been hoping for the navy like your brother Allen, but now that he is at Fort Belvoir he feels good about it. He likes his work already. And Jane is very much better than she was when you were here, so some medicine must be helping her a lot. She still needs help in the kitchen sometimes though. So she's glad I'm home again.

Two days later in Dearborn: *Kay and Barbara Jean came over to spend the day here yesterday. I got dinner and made some Parker House rolls to keep in practice. I must say they were pretty good, and everyone appreciated them. Especially my father. He ate several. He had gone fishing over the weekend, and caught several big ones. I don't know what kind they are, but maybe Jane can show me how to cook them. Seafood was your favorite meal out, wasn't it, when you went to San Francisco? I could see that Kay and Barbara Jean miss Bill a lot. Little BJ can't understand why her father can't be home like so many fathers. After they left I drove down to the train depot and picked up my trunk. I'm really glad, dear, that we didn't take our car to Texas. I don't know how I would have driven all the way back by myself. And I really do need it now to get to the different schools.*

I have to get up early tomorrow morning to go to a meeting for all the Dearborn teachers. School was supposed to start on Wednesday, but it has been postponed until the 18th because of the rash of poliomyelitis. A lot of kids seem to have it in this part of the country. Jane was in doubt about whether she should call me in Texas to tell me to stay there until then. But it's just as well she didn't. I'll probably have to help out at school with the rationing, and then I'll be needing to plan a curriculum for the next year—and doing something useful to earn my pay.

News from Camp Bowie, September 6, 1944: *They certainly are keeping us busy these days. And nights too. We left early Monday morning and didn't come in until after nine last night. After I had cleaned up my equipment and eaten supper, I was too tired to do anything but collapse on my bed. And it's started to rain again, so I suppose we'll have another sloppy, muddy problem. It was a lot easier in California. It might have been hot as blazes, but at least it was dry most of the year. Here it's hard to get any sleep in the field, when everything is so wet. I even tried to sleep standing up and leaning against a tree! I know it sounds silly, but I sure as hell hate to lie down in puddles of muddy water. One good thing is that my restriction is up tomorrow night. And it hasn't given me any troubles, because with all the problems we've been having, I couldn't have gone into town anyway. I surely hope I don't get another restriction. I've been watching carefully what I do when officers are around, to make sure I don't. Though some officers are more tolerant than others, obviously.*

Two days later: *We have been hearing rumors lately that we'll be moving out soon to a POE* [Port of Embarkation]. *Of course, after these many years you know all about the rumor situation. "Keep being skeptical" is my motto. But this information seems to be more than just hearsay. The dates are different, depending on who is saying it, but the rumors agree that we will be out of here in October or November. Which is why we are rushing through these problems, I guess. They have to get us ready for the final push in Europe or the Pacific. It looks as though the war in Western Europe is about over, with the Allies close to the German borders. And that means they would be sending us to MacArthur's army. I would hate to have to fight in both places, though, as many troops will have to do. And I sure hope the English and Russians will help us against the Japs. That would make things a lot easier.*

If we do find out we are leaving soon, I'll be sending more of my stuff home, especially most of the books, which are heavy. I would guess that we can't carry much when we get on the ship, with just the single duffel bag. Meanwhile, there will be more problems and maneuvers. General Wogan, the division commander, tells us our eight-hour days are a thing of the past. But I don't know what he means. We have been kept busy a lot more than that. Maybe he's trying to make us be tougher than we already are. But you can't do that with threats, I think. Example and encouragement work much better in the long run.

From Marianne on the home front, September 8, 1944: *I had our car fixed up, and we now have good brakes in it. The fellow at the garage put in new cables and linings, and a new distributor, and greased it, etc., so now it runs much better. And in the process I'm getting to know something about car engines. Not much, but something. Things can be dangerous, though. After having to put all my weight on the brake pedal to get the car to stop, I nearly went through the windshield the first few times I barely touched the pedal. The whole thing cost me about $28, which I thought was not too bad.*

Sunday in camp, September 10, 1944: *It's such a nice morning—no rain in sight—and I wish I had time to write you a long, long letter. But the army—in it's infinite wisdom—has decided otherwise. We're going out again after our noon meal for another problem. You'd think we have been so busy all the other days of the week, they'd let us have the Lord's Day to ourselves. But as they say in Gay Paree, c'est la guerre. I hear, though, that this is the last problem for a while, so maybe I will have a little time to read a book or one of the magazines that are fast piling up. Not to say, write letters to my dear wife. Which reminds me of something. If we are shipped out soon there won't be many more letters in which we can talk of our intimacies. I hate to think of a censor's reading about our private life. Especially some of the officers in our company I see every day. Had you thought about that, dear?*

The next day in Dearborn: *I've about decided to enroll in just one course at Wayne this semester, because I'll have an increased teaching load. I thought of taking "Psychological Implications of Brain Injuries in Children," I believe it is called. It's about the only class being offered that I haven't taken already. If I want to get my master's I should start doing something about it. And I should have more time now than I might later when you come home.*

The same day in Camp Bowie: *Well, it's looking more and more as though we'll be leaving the country before very long, honey. Today, in about an hour, we will go in for our physical exams to see whether we are fit for overseas duties. I don't know what that means—"fit for"—when they won't find anything they didn't already have in their records. Some fellows say two doctors look into your ears, and if they can't see each other, you pass! So, we'll see.*

We also had to sign a statement saying that if we went AWOL it would be treated like desertion. Which means they could shoot us, I suppose. They certainly are getting serious about this matter. I had thought they would just march us to the dock somewhere and lower the gangplanks. I keep hoping I could get a furlough first, but that seems to be wishful thinking now.

Health news from Camp Bowie, September 17, 1944: *It's late Sunday night, and I'll have just a short time to write before I have to shave and go to bed. I went over to the Patersons today and had dinner with them. Margaret cooked filet mignons, which were very good. It reminded me of the many times you cooked steaks for me when you were here, and for some reason I wasn't able to eat supper. Something about my stomach being upset, it always seemed. You looked worried, but you didn't say much about it. And the next day you had fixed Parker House rolls and something else that looked good, but I just lay on the couch and moaned. Not all the time, but enough that I decided to go in to the doctor after you left, so I could find out the reason.*

Yesterday they put a tube down into my stomach and took samples of what I had eaten. They kept the tube in there for an hour and a half, which was very uncomfortable, as you might expect. I have to go back on Thursday to find out the results. I'll let you know then what's what. Maybe I'm worrying subconsciously—about going overseas. I hope it isn't really serious, though.

We have to go out into the field next week for nearly a month. I don't much like it, but it does make sense that we have serious maneuvers before they ship us out. We haven't had any major operations since we came here. Another reason why it's a good thing you didn't stay here any longer. Some say we'll only be here a few days when the maneuvers are over. Others that we'll have another month. Sergeant Bundy, whom you met at the theater here, told all the fellows he would check our clothes for us to see if they are fit to be taken overseas. We were to have had it done at headquarters tomorrow, but now that job is out of the way. One more check before we take off, I suppose.

From Dearborn, September 22, 1944: *Happy birthday, darling, and many of them! I am propped up in bed in your pajamas—as usual, and I am listening to some good music on your radio. Something familiar, but I just can't think what it is. I seem to have your clothes and things all around to remind me of you. I hung your suits and jackets in my closet, because it seems so nice to see them whenever I open the door. But I suppose I should pack them away one of these days. No use having your clothes ruined by dust or from being eaten up by moths, just because I am such a sentimentalist.*

From what I read in the papers, and you tell me, dear, there isn't much doubt that you will be going overseas in the near future. I hate to think about it, and I try to find reasons for you to stay in this country a little longer. But for what it is worth, Jane's sister was reading my tea leaves the other evening, and she said you would be home one time before you left. And it looked as though I would be going down to visit you at Christmas time. I asked her when the war would end, but she said that was too big a question. I know you are a skeptic in these matters, but she has been right before. So we'll see.

Out in the field, September 25, 1944: *This will be a fairly short letter tonight, because I'll only be able to write till it gets dark—about eight o'clock, these days. Since it's almost 7:30 now, you can see there isn't much time. I just got through eating a cracker and cheese sandwich from the box you sent for my birthday. I'm especially glad to get food just now, because we'll be in the field for three weeks, and it helps to have a little extra. We bought some more stuff from Mom's in Brownwood before we came out, and we have it stowed away safely in the half-track.*

We didn't do much today. We laid out all of our equipment, so it could be inspected by men from the 4th Army to see if it is serviceable. Mine seemed to be. I napped awhile, read Time, *and played some touch football with the fellows. The life of Riley! It would be nice if every day were like this. But beginning tomorrow, I think, they will start making things hard for us.*

From Dearborn, September 28, 1944: *I'm sorry, dear, not to have written you for a few days. It seems every night I get home late, and then I just jump into bed. I suppose your maneuvers have started, and you'll be busy too, even busier than I am. I went over to your house Tuesday after school and brought your mother our birthday present—a pretty white slip and some handkerchiefs. She told me she had received the card you sent her, and she was pleased with the sentiments, which were just right, she said. Your father was busy rounding up people to register for the election. Mostly Democrats, he said. If he could help it! It's a very important election, he said. Your*

229

brother Allen got his notice to report for the physical by next Tuesday, so I guess his days as a civilian are numbered.

I went down to Wayne early this evening to study for my psychopathology course. I can tell it's not going to be a snap, but at least I'll do better than I did in the last two semesters. I'd just as soon forget all about that year. So far it seems very interesting. Two instructors I had at Wayne and the principal at the Lowry school in Dearborn are enrolled in the course also, so I have some grownups to talk to.

Two days later, on a Sunday: *I haven't heard from you for a week, so I suppose you have left camp. I hope you will be able to write letters while you are on maneuvers. But if I don't hear from you I will know why. I'll try to write you often so I can keep up your morale. We have had some beautiful fall days lately, and today was a perfect one. Ellen and I went biking in Rouge Park and then for a ride in the car after dinner. The leaves are beginning to turn color, and it was very pretty wherever we went.*

Did you find out anything about your stomach exam, honey? I hope there is nothing really wrong with you. When you are so far away, I worry a lot. Swallowing tubes and going without meals doesn't sound like much fun. I hope my cooking had nothing to do with upsetting your gastrointestinal system. Let me know when you find out.

A description of life on maneuvers, October 3, 1944: *Right now it's raining, and I'm sitting in the half-track, which is covered, so I won't get wet. Some of the men have pitched tents, but I think I'll sleep in the back of the track tonight. It'll be a lot drier, as well as warmer, though it's not as soft as the ground, of course. I guess I must be getting used to sleeping on hard surfaces, because it doesn't bother me anymore. Except when they are so wet and muddy, that is.*

We are supposed to shave every day, to keep up appearances, the officers say. But sometimes we're so busy we don't get the time. I use my helmet— without the liner, of course—to wash and shave in. I've washed my hair twice, and my feet once in the week. And my face and hands every day. With the same water, sometimes. My clothes are dirty, though I did put on a clean undershirt before we left. When I took it off, it looked like an old scrub rag. The last few nights we have had to sleep with all our clothes on, so I imag-

ine my feet are pretty perfumed by now. I wonder if you would sleep in the same room with me, like I am now.

Since Sunday we have been engaged in a problem in which we—the 16th Armored Infantry Battalion—are the Red, or enemy forces. All the rest of the division are attacking us. So they—obviously—have a lot more men and equipment than we have. Our platoon set up a roadblock, and caught a lot of the Blue forces, including a major from division staff. He had a small overlay map of their tactics with him, and he chewed it up and swallowed it, so we wouldn't get it!

At the crucial moment, when we thought we would be captured ourselves, a company of tank destroyers came to our aid and knocked out some enemy—our enemy, that is—vehicles. Our headquarters company got a lot of prisoners, including the commanding general—General Wogan—and his entire staff. I had never seen him before—up close, I mean. He was shorter than I expected, and looked like any other human being. All in all, we did pretty well for ourselves, we thought. Although the general was pissed off, I think. The last I saw of him he was chewing out some colonel. Our mission now is to protect a fortified position. Tomorrow and Thursday the rest of the division attacks our position. Tomorrow it will be just a "dry run," as we say, when both sides walk through the problem. And the next day will be the "real thing."

We pull out then to become the division reserve, while the division attacks, supported by bombers and fighter planes and additional artillery hitting the positions we are occupying now. Then the engineers move in to blow up and destroy obstacles with TNT and flame throwers. And finally the infantry come in to wipe up things. All in all, it should be a noisy and spectacular operation. I guess that after that problem, we'll rest up a bit, and then have a couple more operations before we go back to garrison.

I told you, I think, that we have a PX with us, with candy and pop and stuff. Yesterday I bought two cans of Spam, and I sliced it and cooked it for our squad on my shovel. The pickmatic we carry on our belts. I did wash it pretty well first, I should say. We had an open fire, and I also cooked some eggs. And they were excellent, if I do say so, who shouldn't—as my father put it. The fellows were leery at first, but then they all said "what the hell," and ate it, anyway. Sometimes I think I should decide to be a cook for a career.

Then I would always have good things to eat. Perhaps after the war, when we are home together, I can do the cooking for the family. While you are working and supporting me through graduate school, maybe? What do you think of that idea, dear?

The next day in Michigan, October 4, 1944: *I'm at Wayne, and we have about twenty minutes until class begins. I look around me, and everything reminds me of you. I guess the only reason I like the place now is the many memories. The main building is not in very good shape. It surely seems a long time since you met me at my locker by the Chemistry lab, and we would plan to study together for our seven o'clock class. Except that we never got around to studying, as I recall. Do you remember the time a mouse was nibbling on the cheese in the trap? And I made you take me someplace else, so I wouldn't see the poor thing getting caught?*

The place looks just the same as ever, and has that same stuffy, old-booky smell. The buildings are overcrowded—I always seem to be running into a lot of people. But I guess there won't be any changes until after the war. From your description, living out in the field doesn't seem so bad, although I wouldn't care much about sleeping on the ground when it's raining. Maybe you've had enough sleeping out to last you a lifetime. I'll be careful not to suggest any camping trips or picnic lunches when the war is over. I'll have to cut this short, honey. Dr. Strauss looks as if he would like to get started. So Auf Wiedersehen, dear. More later today or tomorrow.

And another day: *I'm home listening to the president's campaign speech on your radio and will try to write you at the same time, so you will have another letter from me this week. As he talks, I can tell that it's different from his first in that he hasn't said anything that is open to argument. He certainly is a better speaker than his opponent. You needn't worry about my being a Republican, dear. Mr. Roosevelt has my vote any time he decides to run. And I suppose it's a good thing for happiness and accord in our home, because I know it would almost be grounds for divorce if I were to vote for Mr. Dewey!*

Back in camp, October 6, 1944: *Our maneuvers are over now, and we have a little time off. The whole weekend, maybe. It was quite a problem, and it lasted from Sunday to Thursday. But the ending was sort of anticlimactic—for us, that is. We could hear it, but we were so far from the main action that we never saw it, much less got into it. I didn't mind so much, though, because I don't especially like advancing under artillery fire and bombs dropped from planes. I suppose we'll have to do it when we are "over there," wherever that is. But I don't think anyone would ever get used to it.*

General Ben Lear, Chief of Armed Forces, was here yesterday and today and inspected the division[15] *They had us working till midnight, cleaning up and repacking all of our equipment in the half-track for his inspection. But he didn't come near us. I knew he wouldn't, because the generals never do. They say they'll come, and then they don't. And all the officers are scared shit-less for nothing. He told the officers and NCOs of the division we'd be going overseas. But we knew that already, and he didn't say when or where. If he didn't know, who would? And I still wonder if we'll stay here long enough for me to get a furlough.*

The problem ended yesterday afternoon, but we were "tactical" until today noon, which meant we had to wear our helmets and carry our rifles even to eat our meals. But now we can do what we please. I went to the PX for a Clark bar, did a little reading, and am now writing this letter. For the first time in a long time, I can write a long one.

I thought you might like to know how we have been eating these days—out in the field, that is. Now, of course, we are back to the regular rations, except that we eat from mess kits. I thought I might get the GIs[16] *from dirty mess kits, but so far I have been lucky. It's hard to get them clean, dipping them in hot, soapy water, and then rinsing them in another large can that soon gets soapy also. The last two days of maneuvers we had canned food—C-rations, the kind you eat cold or prepare yourself in some way. They are pretty good, especially if they are heated. I'd imagine, though, that they'd get tiresome if you had to eat them every day and for so long.*

Some of the new fellows, who just came here from Camp Carson in Colorado, were put there on a two-months ration test to see how men could stand up under rugged conditions, eating the different rations. They said the ones who ate only K-rations nearly starved, and they finally were given five rations a day, instead of three.

---

15. He replaced General McNair who had been killed by an errant American bomb, while he was making an inspection tour of battle sites in Normandy.

16. Gastrointestinal problems.

This was the first time I had ever eaten K-rations, and they tasted pretty good, by and large. But they were skimpy, and you had to eat the same thing day after day. Each meal is in a cardboard container about the size of a Crackerjacks box. For breakfast there is a tin of ham and eggs, crackers, coffee, a fruit bar, cigarettes, chewing gum, and candy. In fact, in all the meals there are gum, cigarettes (4), and candy. In the supper box there is also some toilet paper. So the army evidently wants you to heed the calls of nature after you've stopped working for the day. Or fighting, I suppose, if you're on the battlefield. If you have to go after breakfast, it's tough shit, as they say.

Dinner isn't so good. It consists of a tin of cheese, with crackers, and lemonade. The fellows from Camp Carson said the people there said that cheese was "binding." So your innards didn't make the mistake of pooping at the wrong time, I guess. For supper it's a tin of pork, apple shavings, and carrots. That's what it looked like to me, anyhow. It isn't bad when you eat it heated. (I forgot to say that the fruit bar for breakfast makes good jam, if you heat it with a little water and put it on the crackers.)

The C-ration portions are a little bigger. They come in two tins, both slightly smaller than the evaporated-milk cans we use at home. One has biscuits, candy, and a drink—coffee, lemon, or cocoa. The other has stew, hash, or beans. I'm told that the new C-rations will have seven or eight varieties, but so far we haven't seen any. Those we have eaten taste pretty good if you heat them, but eaten cold they aren't too bad either.

You might wonder how we cooked our meals. Well, one time we put the cans next to the half-track motor and revved it up. They got pretty hot. But the best way is to take an empty C-ration can and half-fill it with gasoline from the half-track. (You siphon it out with a straw from the PX. But you sure as hell better suck on it VERY carefully. Otherwise you'll end up with a mouth full of gasoline!) Then you fill the can up with sand. You put the ring from a land mine over it, and you have a stove. It gives a good flame and heats very quickly. I made some good cocoa last night by heating water and using chocolate powder. I'll admit it isn't as good as the chow my wife cooked for me in Brownwood, but it tasted pretty good at the time.

The fellows just got back from supper, and they want me to play poker with them. I had skipped chow tonight, because I wanted to write this letter. They want to win back some of the money they lost to me over the weeks. It's true my luck has been changing lately. And yesterday I lost some, though not too much. I don't really enjoy the game, because I'd rather be reading a book or some magazine. But they do pester me a lot. And someone always carries a deck of cards in his pocket, just in case. P.S. Thanks for the letters you've been writing me lately. I tend to get depressed when I haven't heard from you for a while. And this was one of those times, for some reason or other.

A health report from Camp Bowie, October 9, 1944: *I'm writing this letter from the hospital, honey, and it won't be long, because I have to go back to the field very soon. A company truck will be picking me up out in front. I came in this morning to check up on my physical exams, and the doctor told me there was nothing organically wrong with my stomach. He said I should forget all about myself—just go to town and have a good time. "Paint the town red," he said. Then make sure I took a prophylactic! How's them apples for a diagnosis? Not welcome news for a soldier's wife. I was thinking, though, that the prof in my Abnormal Psych class would have referred to those ills as psychosomatic. What do you think about it? That's what you are studying right now.*

Yesterday was an easy day for all of us. I cleaned my weapons and equipment, etc. And I read through the current edition of Time. *In the p.m. I listened to the game between the Browns and the Cardinals, and then played some touch football with the fellows. I wasn't much interested in who won the World Series, though, now that the Tigers are out of it. Last night we had a fire, and drank some beer. We sang a lot of songs, some of them in harmony. I sang tenor this time, but I did have some trouble when I had to hit an f. It was fun, and a much better way of getting esprit de corps than the parade General Hogan was threatening to hold.*

A response about the health news from Dearborn, October 13, 1944: *I received your two letters from the hospital, honey, and I'm glad there is nothing organically wrong with you. But I don't think you could get sick because of worry. In all our married life I have never seen you really perturbed or worried about anything. Maybe you are a deep-down-inside worrier, but I doubt it. And I surely don't approve of that doctor's advice about "painting the town red," and then taking a prophylactic. He must be a member of the Freudian school, thinking that all ills are due to unsatisfied sexual desires. He reminds me of Dr. Hahn, former director of the*

235

Speech Clinic at Wayne, who had ideas just like that. He believed in free experience outside of marriage, and used to be very fatherly about it all, but I was always suspicious of the gleam in his eye when he talked with me. I used to be very careful not to be left in the building alone with him. And especially at night.

Sometimes the army makes sense. At least a small corner of it in Camp Bowie, Texas. On Friday the first sergeant looked me up and asked if I wanted to take a trip to Michigan. He told me there was an AWOL being held by the MPs in Detroit. Did I want to go there and pick him up? I had heard of NCOs who had taken such trips and gone back to their home towns. One of them was a squad leader in Company B of our battalion. He said the MP commanding officer had given him a three-day pass before he had to bring the prisoner back to Bowie. It was expected, he said.

Our first sergeant said I could leave on Saturday, if I wanted to. And he gave me a pair of handcuffs. "Do you know how to use them?" he asked me. Yes, I said. Actually, I had seen a cop use them in a crime movie, which is not quite the same thing. But I thought I could figure it out on the way home. And he handed me a .45 pistol. "You'll need this," he said. And the supply sergeant would issue me some ammunition.

We were scheduled to get back to the barracks late Friday afternoon. But I found a driver who was going in about noon, and I got him to give me a ride. I had already cleaned my rifle, and I knew there was an early train to Fort Worth, and with good connections I could be in Detroit by Saturday noon. The first sergeant had said I could leave on Saturday. But he didn't say I couldn't leave on Friday. So I didn't ask him. That way I would have an extra day at home—very important if we were to go overseas any time soon. I had learned through the years that there was an unwritten code that governed relations among all NCOs. It might be roughly translated as "You scratch my back, and I'll scratch yours." Or what the officers don't know about your business won't hurt them. As long as you don't go too far and tread on their toes.

From the train station in Detroit I called the number our first sergeant had given me and got the CQ. None of the officers were there, he said. They were gone for the weekend. Come in on Monday, he told me. Sometime in the morning. The officers wouldn't be in until ten or eleven. And he gave me directions to get there. I then called Marianne and told her I'd be taking a taxi. Never mind, she said, she would pick me up. Which she did.

On Monday both Marianne and I slept late. We had been out dancing and dining the night before. And there was a slight error in the way I had copied down the CQ's instructions, so it was after 11:30 when I arrived at the MP headquarters. I showed the captain my credentials and then asked him about the three-day pass. "Do you have your company commander's permission?" he asked. And suddenly I was impaled on the horns of an ethical and legal dilemma. I hadn't expected that. But I told myself that our captain, who had helped me so much with the Skoog problem, would certainly have said yes, if I had asked him. And the NCO in Company B had said a pass was always OKed. So I reached way down into and beneath my rubbery conscience and told the captain he did. And he didn't ask me for any papers, taking my word for it. And I knew that if there were questions later about it, all the blame would fall on my shoulders, anyway. If they demoted me, I was going to get demoted anyway when we went overseas, it seemed. So I took my chances.

The officer looked at some papers on his desk. This is Monday, the sixteenth, he said. And a good part of the day is past. We won't count Tuesday, so we'll say Wednesday, Thursday, and Friday for the pass. They weren't open on the next weekend either, so come back on Monday the twenty-third, he said. He looked at his watch. About this time, or after lunch if you prefer. There was no hurry, he said.

So the poor prisoner, who had gone AWOL and then turned himself in, would be confined in a cell, while my wife and I were having a good time. With this totally unexpected mini-furlough. And I even had time to go down to Wayne and talk with Harold Basilius about my education plans.

*   *   *

237

A letter from Dearborn, October 23, 1944: *It's hard to believe I left you only this morning at the MP headquarters. Today was like any other day at school, and it seems now that I must have dreamed the wonderful past week with you. In only seven days we did so many things, and went so many places. It's strange how everything seems so much more perfect when we are together. I liked especially our last evening at the Book–Cadillac, when we had a fine dinner and danced to our hearts content. The times I spend with you always seem too perfect to be real. If it weren't for the peanut shells in my car, and your clothes still hanging in my closet, I think I might doubt it really happened to us. Thank you for making it possible.*

I guess I'll be busier at school than ever before. Mrs. Thorne called today and asked me to take the Dearborn High and Salisbury schools in West Dearborn, in addition to my present load. One of the teachers had left, she said, and Mr. Lowery insists the rest of us are going to take over her schools. He was not going to replace her, he said. Or couldn't maybe. So it looks like I'll be busy spending most of my time driving back and forth and around the city and too little time teaching. I'll have a total of six schools to visit. And I mean just visit, it seems. But if Mr. Lowery wants to pay me for that, it will have to be all right with me.

I've been listening to the Bell Telephone Hour, *and Nelson Eddy just sang "The Kashmiri Love Song,"*[17] *which always makes me think of you, honey, and I started to cry all over again. Remember? "Pale hands I loved beside the Shalimar. Where are you now? Who lies beneath your spell?" Or something like that. You sang it, and I played the piano. Not well, but enthusiastically. That first time you kissed me on Christmas Eve. I'll never forget that moment, as long as I live. P.S. I hope your prisoner behaved all right, and that your trip back was without incident, as the newspapers say. Did you make him wear the handcuffs? I suppose you'll be glad to deliver him. Let me know what happened when you reported back to your company. I hope you didn't have any trouble there.*

The next day: *We just heard an announcement on the radio that the Jap fleet is engaging ours near the Philippines, so maybe this will be the decisive battle we've been waiting for so long. I hope so, and then we can get going*

17. By Amy Woodforde-Finden.

in the Pacific the way we are in Europe. If we get control of the sea, maybe the job of taking those islands back again will be simplified.

From Camp Bowie, October 26, 1944: *This will be a short letter, because I've got a lot of catching up to do, before I go to bed. The company is going on a 25-mile hike tonight, which I am not ready for. I hope I can stay here, because I'll be on CQ tomorrow. I wished I could have said more when we parted on Monday morning, but I just couldn't think of the right words at the time. It was like my tongue was tied in knots. I think all my good-byes are inadequate, but I guess we'd both be crying, if we said what was in our hearts.*

Not much has been said about my staying home for so long, so I guess I'm OK, in that respect. The company clerk—Corporal Hollis—told me I was lucky they were so busy around here, that they didn't notice it. They didn't miss me, I suppose. Or just looked the other way. All in all, you and I were pretty lucky, weren't we, to have seven whole days together? I'll tell you about my trip back, tomorrow, when I'm on CQ and have more time. By the way, when I came back I found that the entire company had been restricted for several days. It seems the fellows were out on the range, shooting at targets, and our platoon commander, Lt. Locke, was saying something on the loudspeakers, and someone said, into a microphone: "Fuck you, lieutenant." He demanded to know who had said it, but no one would tell. So he put everybody on restriction. A bad decision, I would think, but it shows a lot of togetherness in the company, to stick together like that. Not a bad quality, I would think. But it means I won't be seeing the Patersons for awhile.

The next day, October 27, 1944: *You'd think we were going overseas the way they are carrying on these days! And it seems we'll all have to work over the weekend, because there will be a big inspection on Monday. They have given us a list of things we can take with us, besides our clothes and equipment—a camera, a radio, five pounds of athletic equipment, an electric razor (though people tell me the current in Europe and the Far East is different from ours), etc. But we have to carry everything onto and off the ship, so that limits things, somewhat.*

After I left you on Monday, I went to the MP room at the police headquarters, and they took me out West Jefferson to Fort Wayne to pick up my prisoner. He had had some bad luck, they said, because he was AWOL only half a day. He had lost his bus ticket to Texas, and tried to find some way to get back on time. Remember, I said they take very seriously being AWOL in wartime? (I was doubly lucky, wasn't I? If the MPs had picked me up, I might have been shot!) Anyway, the prisoner was from New York, and he got as far as Detroit before he ran out of money, and had to turn himself in. Just think, honey, if he had stayed in New York, or hadn't lost his ticket, you and I would never have had those wonderful seven days together! But when you think of it, his plight does put a crimp on any celebration of those days, doesn't it?

Incidentally, he was wearing handcuffs the whole time, and I had my .45 on my belt. I felt sorry for him, but there wasn't much else I could do, after my instructions from the MPs. I did help him, though, to hide the handcuffs. And my pistol, too, as well as I could. And I was certainly glad to get back to camp with no difficulty. I hope they don't put him in prison, but then I'll never know, will I? My guess is that they will just confine him to quarters for a week or so. If we are going overseas, it doesn't make sense to leave a trained soldier behind.

A Friday morning in Dearborn, October 27, 1944: *There is no school today, because of teachers' conventions, so I am still in bed at this late hour— nine o'clock. I started to get up earlier, but I was so weak and woozy, I decided to rest some more. I got real sick at school yesterday afternoon and dismissed all my children and lay down in the teachers' lounge. And I went to bed as soon as I got home and slept until six, when I decided I felt well enough to go see* Othello. *But toward the end of the play, I began seeing stars and had to leave. So I missed seeing Paul Robeson stab himself in the tragic finale. The play was very good, though, as much as I saw of it. Robeson was wonderful, as usual, and José Ferrer, who played Iago, was so good, it's hard to say who stole the show. I know you would have liked it, honey.*

News from Camp Bowie about jobs, October 31, 1944: *I got a call last night about teaching a Spanish course for a couple of weeks. Frank Piano is the regular teacher, but he's on emergency furlough, and they want someone to fill in till he gets back. They called Dennis Paterson about it, but he told them I'd do a better job. I accepted, not because I thought I knew the language well enough to teach it, but because I wanted to get the teaching experience. For later on. The class consists mostly of phonograph records, anyhow, and I can play those as well as the next fellow. I'll let you know how it turns out. I find already that I am forgetting a lot of what I learned at Utah. Without having an opportunity to use the language. Perhaps we learned it too quickly and superficially.*

I find I have another job in the company, in addition to my regular chores as a corporal. I am now the Information and Education NCO. (That's another name for Orientation.) Remember I used to do that at Camp Roberts, before somebody said the lectures should be given by officers? Anyway, I'll have to contact the I&E man in the battalion and see what they have in mind.

Overseas plans, November 2, 1944: *We got word today about four o'clock that we were to stop all our packing. And I think they will have us unpack the stuff we've already packed. Somebody must have changed his mind somewhere. But not in our division, I would think. The armored forces need lots of space—with their tanks and all. And we'd be no use at all on the Pacific islands, even in the Philippines. And winning a big sea battle, which we seem to have done, is not the same as invading the Japs' homeland. That's a long way off, I would think. So maybe things in Europe aren't going as well as I had thought. I've been trying to keep up in the* Stars & Stripes, *and it looks as though the British are slowing down there, especially in The Netherlands and that area. So we'll see. I'll let you know if there are any further developments.*

I worked all day on my I&E job, trying to gather bulletins and books that were on the list they gave me, but seem to have disappeared. I haven't had much luck so far. None of the officers or NCOs at headquarters will admit to anything. So it remains a mystery. I like this kind of work, especially if I get to give any kind of lectures. And there's a big plus—when I'm working here at battalion headquarters I don't have to do other things. Such as take long hikes—maybe! I'm keeping my fingers crossed about that.

Politics at home, November 2, 1944: *I am writing this evening while listening to a political broadcast by the Democratic Party. It's getting closer and closer to the big decision—Roosevelt or Dewey. And the political rhetoric has become more and more heated. And every day I am more convinced that it would be a sad thing for this country if Dewey is elected. His whole tactic has become nothing less than a smear campaign against the president. He seems to have very little to say for himself. And, after all, what is there good to say?*

Ed, Jane's son-in-law, was here for dinner this evening, and he made me so mad. It was nothing but Dewey this and Dewey that. And just wait till the Republicans are in office. His chief objection to Roosevelt seems to be that his—Ed's, that is—salary is at a standstill. And he hasn't received the pay increases he is entitled to. It just rubbed me the wrong way, I guess. What with you getting ready to go overseas. I wanted to tell him off, but then I thought it would make Jane unhappy, so I didn't. People like Ed have been very little affected by the war. They eat well, and their businesses are flourishing, and still they complain. Don't get me wrong. Ed is a very nice person, and I agree with him on a lot of points. But not on this one. The Republicans are a disaster waiting to happen, I think.

The next day, November 3, 1944, at Camp Bowie: *We've had a long day, today, and a rough one, and I'm pretty tired, so I'm going to bed early this evening. We got up at four and had a firing problem with a company of tanks. To see how we could work together, I suppose. Team work, they called it. It was a good problem, but very tiring—trying to keep up with the tanks, for instance. But it does seem like a good idea to me. After we got back I had to clean my rifle, and then I decided to go to the show, to relax. (It was* And Now Tomorrow, *with Alan Ladd and Loretta Young.) It was not much, but at least it was worth the fifteen cents I paid to get in. And it was a good way to relax and not think seriously about much of anything.*

The next day, November 4, 1944: *I went to another class today—or rather, two classes. One was on Germany, by a T-5 who used to be a history professor at the U of Alabama. The other was on Democracy, by a lieutenant I don't know the name of. I didn't learn much from him either. In fact, I haven't heard much so far that I didn't already know. On the other hand, the talks might be useful for most of the fellows here, and I did get some useful tips about my own teaching techniques. What to do and what to avoid.*

A couple of fellows just came in from Mom's, and they brought me a quart of milk and a loaf of bread. I have a jar of peanut butter stashed away, and I'll have a feast before I go to bed. As you know, one of my favorite snacks is peanut butter sandwiches. I could eat them every day of my life and never get tired of them, I think.

Three weeks later, November 26, 1944: *It's a Sunday, and I don't have a detail for a change, but I didn't accomplish very much. I built a crys-*

tal set, which didn't take long, though I did have to rewind the coil. To make it smaller, so I could carry it in my duffel bag. But then I found the earphones didn't work. I had hoped to take it with me, if we go to Europe, because I'd always have a radio to listen to wherever I was. And I wouldn't need batteries or anything like that. I'll have to get another pair, I guess, the next time I go into town.

Camp Bowie, the next day: *This will be a short letter this evening, honey, because I went to a round-table discussion at the battalion headquarters and just got back. I didn't learn much about the proposed United Nations organization, but it was interesting to hear what some of the fellows had to say. Next week—if we're still here, that is—we'll be discussing the foreign relations of the United States. As you know, that is an especially interesting subject to me. By the way, honey, will you look through the books I sent home and find a white paperback book on National Socialism and send it to me? It was put out by the State Department and could be useful for me if we go to Europe any time soon. I figure I'll be able to take some of my own books, if I put them in with the I&E stuff the battalion will be taking.*

Views from Marianne at 6210 Payne, December 3, 1944: *The war news has been both good and bad lately, it seems to me. I hate to think of China losing it's war with Japan, and I hope that doesn't mean our men have to go to the mainland of Asia to retake the land the armies of Chiang Kai-shek have lost. The way he refuses to cooperate and carries on his private wars with the Chinese communists, I sometimes think he deserves to lose to Japan. And I get more than a little discouraged to look at what's happening to the little countries in Europe we've liberated. Maybe this is just the war for the extension of power around the world, after all, when our allies have a tug of war to see whether Britain or Russia controls Poland and Greece. And it looks as though the same is happening to Yugoslavia. Britain seems to be losing out all the time. But maybe I'm just being pessimistic on this cold and rainy afternoon. You're the I&E man in our family, dear. So maybe you can tell me if I have the wrong slant on things.*

Getting ready to go overseas, December 5, 1944: *I started taking the Expert Infantry tests today, and so far have passed them all. I had the physical part tonight—the part where the doctors put us through all kinds of contortions, and that was pretty rugged. I guess I must be getting old, but I was huffing and puffing before it was through. Or maybe I've been skipping too many exercises, because of my I&E work. But I did pass, and that's the main thing. Tomorrow will be the day- and then the night-compass course. I shouldn't have too much trouble there. I hope I can pass them all, though, because so many others have done it, and I'd feel funny if I couldn't. When I have spent so many years instructing others in those skills. And besides, if I pass, it means an extra five dollars a month in my pay.*

Pearl Harbor day, December 7, 1944: *I finished all the tests today, and now I'll be able to wear a medal on my chest with an image of a rifle. I'd have had a score of 100 on the Military Courtesy exam—it was multiple-choice—but the lieutenant in charge said nobody was perfect, and he marked me down to a 95! Which isn't too bad either. The field-firing, bayonet, and grenade courses took a lot out of me, and now the platoon is going out on a night problem. We won't be back before four in the morning, they say. So if I survive all this, you can tell people your husband is one tough son of a bitch. Or nicer words to that effect, dear.*

And we can use the extra money, because they're already breaking the NCOs in other units who are "over-strength." Which applies to me, of course. I can expect that our captain will be calling me in any day now to give me the bad news. He'll tell me it's "without prejudice," but what the hell satisfaction is that? I'll feel mighty funny when my sleeves have no stripes on them, and everyone addresses me as "Private Quirk." Not even a Pfc. I'll find my name from time to time on the KP list. And have to walk guard. After all these years of at least having some authority in this man's army, I'll be the lowest of the low.

❧ 11 ❧

The ETO

In the last months of 1944 German resistance toughened, as Allied armies threatened to invade the Homeland from the east and the west. At this point Adolf Hitler ordered one last, desperate tactic, totally unexpected by the Allied generals, a counterattack in Belgium to drive a wedge between the British and the Americans, and to recapture lost territory as far as the seacoast at Antwerp. Thus, on December 16, began the Battle of the Bulge.

Within days the Germans had retaken major road junctions such as St. Vith, and were battering the important American garrison in Bastogne. And when the German commander demanded that the Bastogne defenders surrender, General McAuliffe replied with the now-famous word of GI contempt: "Nuts!" But help was soon on the way—finally. Eisenhower directed the 101st Airborne to reinforce the garrison, while General Patton sent the tough and battle-tested 4th Armored Division to hit the flanks of the enemy penetration. And the clouds cleared away in time to give the Allied planes absolute control of the skies. Weeks of bloody fighting were ahead, with great numbers of casualties on both sides, all across Germany. As the new year began it was clear that Hitler and his Reich would be destroyed. It was just a matter of time. The 13th Armored Division, after all the waiting and wondering, played a role in those final battles.

Leaving Texas, January 5, 1945: *I'm sitting here in my barracks with the most forlorn feeling in the world—knowing that you are on your way home, and that I won't be seeing you again until the war is over. And that tomorrow I leave for who knows where? They have taken our bunks away, and our blankets, so there is a feeling of emptiness everywhere I look. Maybe we'll be going out in the night, but nobody tells us anything, so we just hang around. I thought you kept the door open a bit, when I left our room, as though you wanted me to come back for another embrace. And I started to turn around. But then I thought I'd better not even look back, lest we both break down in tears. And I was sure that each knew intuitively what the other would say and feel. My constant prayer, from now on, is that the day may soon come when there are no more goodbyes, and our home and family will be realities, instead of just hopes and dreams.*

The next day, January 6, 1945: *I'm writing this letter in the train on the way to wherever they are taking us. I don't think right now I am allowed to be more specific than that. We have to turn in our letters to the train commander for censoring, so you may not get it for a while. But I can say, I think, that you will remember the most recent rumors, and so far there is nothing to prove the contrary.*

None of us got much sleep last night, because we had to lie down on the bare floor, using our overcoats as a blanket. And we had to stay dressed, since none of us knew when we might be leaving. Well, during the night a major came through, inspecting the quarters. He looked around and told the sergeant who was with him to take down the number of our barracks, "because there was men and equipment scattered all over the fucking place!" I suppose he thought we should sleep leaning against the walls. Or hanging from the ceiling. What a farewell for a bunch of decent fellows going off to fight against their country's enemies.

I was checking in my pockets, and I realized that in my distress at our parting, I forgot to get some more money from you. I don't know what I'll need it for, but if we stay in one place long enough, I might call and ask you to wire me some. And in any event, I will be calling you when we reach our destination. The train has been stopped for some time—while they change engines, I think. So I'll take this chance to shave. When the train is rocking, there is always the risk that a fellow will cut himself and bleed to death. You must be almost as far as Chicago, if my calculations are correct, honey, and I hope you are having a comfortable ride. The seats on this car are about as soft as a pile of bricks, and my rear end is taking a lot of punishment. But they'll be making up the beds soon, so it should be pretty comfortable sleeping. Take care of yourself, darling. I love you very much.

Another January day: *It's early Sunday morning, and we're about to cross the Mississippi. At Vicksburg, it seems. I don't think much of the land we've passed through so far, but then I guess train tracks don't run through the best parts of the country. Louisiana looked like a big, swampy morass, with some sparse-looking pine or other coniferous trees. And a lot of Spanish moss hanging dismally from the boughs. Mostly, though, the trees were like gaunt fingers reaching, perhaps, for some sunshine. But then, this is January, and probably things will be different when the rice and cotton are growing.*

There are a lot of card games going on—in every car, I would imagine. But I don't feel much like playing. And besides, as I told you, I didn't bring much money with me. And I'll probably need that wherever we are going. The train just stopped at some kind of station, and I can see Red Cross ladies walking up and down, talking with fellows who have opened their windows. The ladies aren't allowed to come into the cars—because of the reputations for crudeness the GI has made for himself, I would imagine. So platters with cups of coffee—and donuts—are brought on the train by some fellows. I took a drink from one cup, but put it back on the platter. It tasted and felt like sweetened mud. I guess that in general people in the South don't know how to make good coffee. And I dream of myself, in the future, sitting across from you, drinking coffee brewed in a Silex coffee maker. With some good hot, buttered toast!

I didn't bring much literature to read on this trip unfortunately, and we're not allowed to get off the train to get any when we do stop. Bernard Koslow, who is sitting with me, is reading Madame Bovary *by Gustave Flaubert—which is supposed to be a classic. Maybe I'll read it after he does. He's a pretty fast reader. We bought some Sunday papers at the last stop. That is, the chaplain did. He was the only one, I guess, they trusted to get off. Anyway, he came through our car about 11 o'clock, and said a few prayers and read to us from the Bible, before he passed out two or three copies of the*

New Orleans Times. *Somehow it doesn't seem much like Sunday, with the fellows playing poker and saying "shit," and things like that, while the Good Book is being read to us!*

I said that Koslow was sitting with me. We have three men to each double-seat, so one of us gets the upper berth, and the other two the lower. Last night we flipped coins to see who got what, and I had to take the lower, with another fellow. Koslow got the upper to himself. Tonight the two of us who lost will flip again to see who gets the upper. And so on, until we get to our destination. I didn't sleep very well last night, because the other fellow was fat, and he turned over a lot. Plus, he talked in his sleep. If I get the upper, I can sleep diagonally and get to stretch out. So, we'll see.

I slept awhile, and then awoke to find we were in Mississippi. We're passing through a lot of shanty towns, and all the people we see are Negroes—who live in the shacks, I guess. And come to think of it, I haven't seen a single colored person on this train, except for the porters. No soldiers. They drive our supply trucks, but we don't let them on our troop trains. Is this the democracy we are fighting for? For the white folks of Mississippi and Alabama? And I wonder why Roosevelt doesn't do something about it.

Marianne's last visit to Texas, January 7, 1945: *Here I am, dear, writing you again while I'm sitting up in my comfortable, warm bed. And yet there is an empty feeling I always have when I am without you. I'm afraid I wasn't much help in making your leaving easier. When I left the door open, hoping you could come back for just another kiss or a few more words of assurance. But I think I know anyway what you would have told me then, because those are my feelings too. And sometime so much love is impossible to put into words. It has kept us together for three years of being apart, and will surely bring you back to me safely and soon. Thank you, dear for making my life with you so wonderful.*

I had quite a comfortable, though unexciting, trip home. I got an upper berth at Dallas on the 9:30 train and then also a berth at 11:00 when I got into Chicago last night. It made the trip seem much faster to sleep both nights, and also less tiresome. The train was crowded as usual, so I was lucky even to have a seat, I would say, from my past experiences. From Kansas City I rode in the same coach with Shirley Smith and John O'Greene, now Mr. and Mrs. O'Greene. They went to Wayne with us, remember? We talked a lot about our lives, and that made the time pass more quickly.

I got back to Detroit about nine this morning and went out to Kay's house first to get the car. It has certainly been snowing in the Detroit area since Christmas. It was deep when I left, but snowed every day since then. It took about an hour to dig the car out, and even little BJ did her part with her toy shovel! I really am proud of that car, because it started without any difficulty, after being left in the cold for more than two weeks. And especially it's being filled inside with snow. I'll never be tempted again to kick one of its tires, no matter what happens.

I talked to your mother on the phone this evening, and she said Allen's jaundice is a lot better. He was walking around outside today for the first time, she said. But it should keep him out of the service for quite a while, she thought. Or hoped, maybe. I'm sending this letter by airmail to your new APO address, honey. We got your card on Saturday. Do you think the censor will be reading my letters also? If so, I had better be careful what I write to you. I mean about national security, of course. And other things. In your first letter I thought you were trying to tell me where you were going when you said it was where you thought you would go. If you are in New Jersey, you can tell me your brother John is feeling better, and I will understand what you mean.

It certainly is cold in my bedroom right now, and the windows are frosted over. Maybe my dad didn't put enough coal in the furnace when he went to bed. Or maybe it's just colder than usual outside. I crawl under the blankets every now and then to get warmed up and just about fall asleep. I've been listening to the eleven o'clock news on your radio about MacArthur's invasion of Luzon. If we can beat the Japs in the Philippines soon, maybe the war in the Pacific won't be as long as we think. And you might never have to go there, after all. Will you be allowed to talk about things like that in your letters, when you are in Europe?

From Camp Kilmer, NJ, January 11, 1945: *This is the first letter I've written you since we came here, and the first letter I'm certain will be censored. You will notice that I have written just on one side of the sheet—according to instructions. So the censor can clip out anything I shouldn't have said. I assume it will be the same until the war is over. Both of us were hoping I might be here long enough to come home briefly—maybe on a three-day pass. But that seems out of the question now. A lot of the former occupants have written messages on the barracks walls—how long they were here before they were shipped out, etc. And the consensus isn't very hopeful. No one was here more than three or four days. There is a chance, though, that I can get to see New York. I'll know more about that later today or in the morning. As for the fifty dollars you sent me, I will probably use some of it, but I'll send the rest back to you. Where we are going, we won't be needing dollars, I would think.*

And the way the war is going in the Pacific, it may not be so long as we had thought. Of course, we were very optimistic last fall, and look what happened to the German front. A lot of trouble. I think some generals in Europe made some big mistakes. And both John and I had thought that perhaps MacArthur was not up to his job, either. But what's been happening in the Philippines recently makes me think he is doing a better job than we had any reason to expect. He has gone a long way in the Pacific, and with surprisingly few casualties. A great thing for the infantryman and marine, who always take the brunt of the enemy's attacks. MacArthur has done an excellent job there, I think. Sometimes, he talks too much. But after all, it is the results that count. So we'll see if events prove my optimism is not unwarranted.

The same January day at 6210 Payne: *It seemed good to talk to you again this evening, and I hope you will call me as often as possible and talk as long as you can. You sounded very close, better than last night, when there seemed to be some noises on the line. And for a little while, at least, we felt close to each other, almost as though we were in the same room. It's always such a disappointment to lay down the receiver, and to realize that you are really hundreds of miles away. You seemed so close.*

I was disappointed, of course, to know for certain that you will not be coming home now, even for a weekend. But neither of us really expected it, did we? All in all, we have been truly lucky to have had so much time together, when we might have been apart for so many months, or even years. Like a lot of married couples. And we have so much to look forward to in the years ahead. Our letters may change, because we are conscious that someone else is reading them, with his pen or scissors poised to deal with something "dangerous." But the best part of our letters will always be talk-

ing about our hopes for the future. For now, have a good time in New York, and don't worry about the money. It's there to be used. And again, call me as often as you can. I'll be staying home each evening, as long as you are in this country.

From Camp Kilmer, Saturday, January 13, 1945: *I hope to be leaving on a three-day pass in about an hour. If so, I will try to see the performance of Claude Debussy's "Pélleas et Méllisande" at the Metropolitan Opera. I'm not familiar with it, but I hear that it is perhaps the best of all operas. I'm eager to see why people would say that. According to the* New York Times, *the cast includes Lawrence Tibbett, Bidu Sayao, and the French tenor Martial Singher. I've heard Tibbett a lot on the radio, and like his voice, though lately he seems to be past his prime. He isn't singing as much as he used to. And although it may be incongruous, I want also to go to Madison Square Garden to take in a couple of basketball games. But you know my tastes, dear. And priorities.*

There are so many things to see, that I've read or heard about, for instance the NY Philharmonic or the NBC Symphony of Arturo Toscanini— maybe the greatest orchestra in the world. There is so much greatness here in this city, it will be impossible to comprehend it all in one short weekend. But I'll do my best. Whoops! The first sergeant has just told us we are free to go. And he says to behave ourselves. I wonder what he means by that, when everyone knows the typical GI is as pure as the driven snow. More later.

From the home front, January 15, 1945: *It's after eleven, and I suppose you won't be calling me this evening, honey. I've been sitting around, it seems for ages, waiting for the telephone to ring. I'm hoping you won't call me tomorrow evening between seven and nine. Ellen and I have decided to take a Spanish course at Fordson High, and the first class meets at that time. She is coming over for dinner, before we drive to the class. What if you should call then—for the last time? Would I ever forgive myself? You write me about the horns of a dilemma. I know precisely what you mean. I read today an article about the educational opportunities for women in the service— and after. We could get along nicely on $125 a month, going to school together. At Harvard, maybe. And I could get my master's degree. It almost tempts me to join the Waves or the Wacs. What do you think about that, dear?*

251

The same day at Camp Kilmer: *I'm back in camp after my memorable weekend in New York. I was certainly impressed with the big city, and will always think of it in terms of superlatives—the best of this, the greatest of that. But first, let me tell you about the opera. I got there without too much difficulty, after asking several people about directions. And as I was walking alongside the building, there was a man standing outside a closed door. Where is the main entrance? I asked him. Around the corner, he said, pointing. He looked at my uniform and handed me a pass-out ticket. That way, you won't have to pay anything, he said. He held the door open for me. But I would have to stand, he said. And so I did. For all five acts.*

I would have to know more about it before I could say it was the best. For one thing I had never seen it before and didn't know anything about the story. And because I don't know French, I couldn't understand many of the words. But I could sense an aura of mysticism about it, of magic maybe. Like the romantic stories we read in Dr. Basilius's class. And the production was magnificent. Every character had a fine voice. If you and I could have been seeing and hearing it together, holding hands, I might have comprehended some and appreciated it even more.[18]

The first sergeant just came by with some instructions, so I doubt if I will be able to call you tonight, dear—for many reasons. And this letter will be short. I hope you don't stay up late, worrying and waiting for the phone to ring. I'm sorry about that, but some times things are beyond a person's control. Incidentally, I had a letter from my brother John the other day, and he says he's feeling better now, and that he will be shipping out very soon. Wish him luck, will you? Good night, dear. I love you very much.

The next day in Dearborn, January 16, 1945: *Since you didn't call again this evening, sweetheart, I suppose you either have left the country or will be going before long. I'm sorry not to have the chance to hear your voice again, but we both knew you were going, and it would be one more sad and wrenching farewell. I was talking to Mrs. Thorne, my supervisor, this morning, and she told me the different APO numbers went to various zones in different parts of the world. She said the 200s were in Italy. I don't know*

---

18. The performance was broadcast on NBC, and a recording can be found through the simple manipulations of Google on any computer.

if that is true or not, but I would think you'd be as glad to go there as any other place. I've been reading that the Germans might be pulling out of that country completely. So maybe you will be stationed near the Mediterranean and can bask to your heart's content in the Italian sun and drink their wines until the war is over! While MacArthur is mopping up on the Japs. How about that, dear?

And the next day: *It's past midnight, and I've been waiting up on the offhand chance that you might call me. Someone is singing "In a Monastery Garden,"*[19] *which is one of my favorites. It always reminds me of the days when I was just getting to know you, and I used to listen to you sing it with the men's choir at Wayne. That seems like a hundred years ago now, but I still love to hear it, because of the memories. Sarah and I went to the Masonic Temple to hear Vladimir Horowitz play this evening. He certainly was wonderful, as good as any pianist I have ever heard. This is the night I go to Wayne, so we went together to my class and then to the concert. I didn't know whether to go, for fear you might call me, but I hated to disappoint Sarah, after saying I'd go. I enjoyed it a lot, though I kept worrying all the time that you were calling and wondering where I was.*

A Sunday letter from home, January 21, 1945: *I suppose you received news after you got back from New York that changed your plans somewhat. The chances are that you are aboard ship on the sea somewhere. And that was the reason you couldn't call me again. I hope it isn't too long before I hear from you to clear things up. The war news has been so good in the last few days, and perhaps it's not unreasonable to hope for a quick ending to the fighting in Europe. I wouldn't object at all if the Russians get to Berlin soon, before we do. How do you feel about that, dear? And then the army could station you in an occupation unit, in France or the Netherlands, say. And at the same time, the war will be ending in the Pacific, too, and everybody can come home. I think I'll submit my plans for you to the War Department for their serious consideration.*

Last night I had a funny dream about you, dear, and I woke up feeling so good about it. I dreamed you had come home, because you were medically discharged at the port of embarkation. And when I asked why you had

---

19. By Albert W. Kètelbey.

253

waited a week to tell me, you said you felt so ashamed about it and had gone with some other fellows on a bender. "Bender!" You even used that word in my dream. How ridiculous. I'll try to do better tonight.

A letter from the high seas, January 25, 1945: *So this is the Atlantic! Well, I don't like it. Or rather, it doesn't like me, which amounts to the same thing. I had once thought it would be pleasant to take a sea voyage when we are old and rich, but now I am dubious about that. I don't think my stomach was made for the undulating movements of the ship.*[20] *There are times when I wonder if the ship will survive. Great waves and swells toss the vessel without mercy, it seems. I will be sitting on the deck—clinging to whatever I can hold on to—and the top of the mast rolls down to the horizon on one side and then over to the other, describing an arc of 180 degrees! At the same time the ship pitches so much that the propeller is lifted out of the water, and the craft shudders like a giant whale in its death throes. And the navy cooks are feeding us greasy pork and beans! No wonder most of us are so sick. Or that I haven't written you for so many days. I think* mal de mer *must be about the worst ill of mankind.*

You might like to know about our life aboard ship—when we are able to get out of our bunks, that is. We usually get up about eight, because our company is the last to be fed, for some reason. We have breakfast in mess kits. At 10:30 we have inspection on deck—to see if anyone has died of seasickness during the night, I think. Or has fallen overboard. At noon there's just a snack, with a sandwich and coffee or soup. And then the main meal is at about 4:30, I think because at this latitude night comes early, and they want us below deck so they can turn out the lights, for security reasons. As I said before, they give us a lot of pork and beans, for some reason. I do like them,

---

20. I was aboard the 19,000-ton USS *General Grant*. It was part of a large convoy. The British dreadnought HMS *Nelson* was directly in front of us all the way to Europe, which gave us some feeling—wishful thinking, I am sure—of security. There were frequent booms from depth charges, though, which I couldn't mention in letters, and we all presumed German U-boats were operating in the area. It was Hitler's last hope for a victory at sea. From a Google Internet search I learned that the *Nelson* took part in the June 1944 D-Day operations, and struck two mines. It was then taken to the Philadelphia Naval Shipyard for repairs, and was being returned to duty—which accounted for its comforting presence in our convoy.

especially my mother's version, with ketchup, but a lot can be too much for a queasy stomach to tolerate. Which reminds me of my father's story from World War I, about the troops on a ship like ours crossing the Atlantic. "We must be almost there," said a soldier. "How do you know?" asked his friends. "Easy," he replied. "Everybody's hanging over the rail, and saying 'Europe, Europe, Europe!'"

The same day: *Right now there's a big crowd on my right—toward the bow, that is, looking at a sea bat. They have it in a bucket, and to see it you have to bend over and look in the bucket. Shining a flashlight, that is. As you might expect, the bat is really a lethal weapon, something like a cricket stick, and because you are stooping over, you get a wicked (wicket?) rap on your backside. Then everybody laughs. Except you.*

Luckily, I had heard about the ruse from John when I was in Dallas, and he had included it in his book. So they weren't going to catch me. But what's surprising, is that it worked all day yesterday, and there are still enough gullible men on board to give plenty of laughs. Every couple of minutes I hear a sharp crack, and I know someone has seen the sea bat and suffered the consequences. Barnum was right, there's one born every minute.

What's the ocean like today? Right now it is comparatively quiet. The waves are hardly as high as those on Lake Huron. There are no whitecaps, except for the path of the ship. The water is blue now—not aquamarine— but deep blue because it captures its color from the sky. It's like a mirror, with little color of its own. And when the ship throws up waves, they're of a greenish-blue like that of a swimming pool whose bottom is painted blue.

It's getting darker and more windy, so I'll have to go below before long. I hate to, because it is so uncomfortable in the hold. Our bunks (if you can call them that) are five high, without much vertical space between them and not long enough for a man 6' 2". If you are thinking of sardine cans, you are not far from the truth. And it's not like Chantilly after so many men have slept there in their clothes for so many days and nights. And because of the nightly blackouts, the sleeping quarters are always shut off from fresh air. But I suppose the time will come when that will seem like the acme of comfort. Everything is relative, I guess. At one time I thought Texas was a hell-hole. And I even complained at times about my ASTP lodging and the coke brigade! I didn't know heaven when I was there.

I just came down into the hold, and I'm writing this as I sit on a records box. The light is not so good here, but I can see what I am writing, which is all that's necessary. The sun disappeared over the horizon while I was writing, and it got cold suddenly. The sky and sea were quite beautiful for a minute or two, it seemed, and then it was dark. The reflected rays of the sun gave the water a pristine brilliance that is hard to duplicate in any picture, or even to describe accurately. And to tell the truth, I have seen more beautiful—and lengthy—sunsets back home. I think dust in the Michigan air adds to the brilliance of the sun's colors, and makes the landscape pink and purple. But out here on the ocean it was like molten gold for a moment or two, and then that was it. They're turning the lights out now, so I'll stop writing right here. Good night, dear, I love you very much.

The next day, January 16, 1945, from Marianne in Dearborn: *I worked at a nursery school for the first time this evening. It's fun, but it will be different from real teaching. They are all babies, and about all I can do is take care of them and entertain them. I don't get paid much, but it does add something to my monthly income. And I know the experience will help me later on when we have children of our own. I think I had better ask your dad soon to help me figure my income tax. If I have a lot to pay, I'll have to start saving up. Also, I had the car checked and will have to have it greased some day soon. It certainly has been a big item in my budget this month. Did I tell you I had to buy a tire? The old one was beyond repair, the man said. It's always something, isn't it, dear?*

Someplace in England, January 28, 1945: *It's about 9:30 p.m. our time, and we are anchored in one of England's many estuaries.*[21] *I won't say which, because I don't know if we are allowed to divulge it. I can't mail this letter, anyway—or any of the others I wrote on the ship—so by the time I can send letters, I might be able to tell you. We'll probably be going to France very soon, but I wanted you to get at least one letter written in Merrie Old England.*

Tonight was the first time we were allowed on deck after dark, and I was quite surprised that the heavens were the same as at home. I guess I had rather expected a new, strange world out there. And fortunately it was a

---

21. Southampton.

clear night. I looked up and discovered that Orion was still running across the sky, hunting whatever he hunts in our own constellations at home. And his sword was still at his belt. The moon is almost full—maybe you will see it later tonight—and orange like an October pumpkin. A harvest moon, we'd call it in Michigan. Every time I see the moon that full, it reminds me of our moonlight cruise in the paddle-wheeler down to Bob-Lo. And especially tonight, when the moon, shining on the water, turns the whole estuary into a pool of gold, so nearly real you'd think you could reach down into the water and dip out gold coins with your hands. Perhaps it's Spanish pieces of eight sunk during the rout of the Spanish Armada.

I could see Venus, the evening star, too, and it was large and as yellow as the moon. Remember the lines from Tannhäuser? "O du mein holder Abendstern, wohl grüss ich immer dich so gern." It is especially true tonight, because as I looked at it, I was poignantly aware that in that direction— several thousand miles to the west—you were. The evening star moving ever down and down, symbolizing my moving farther and farther away from you, my darling. But at the same time, we shouldn't forget that the star that vanishes beyond the horizon is also the morning star of tomorrow, epitomizing our bright new hopes for the future. The night may seem long, there may be false dawns, but remember, dear, that morning always comes. Morning always comes.

The next day: *Last night I went to a GI bull session for an hour, and the "Indian problem" was discussed. I'm not sure, though, if anything was solved in that short time. After that, we had a hymn sing, and I ran the gamut from tenor to bass, and thoroughly enjoyed myself. I like the Protestant hymns best, because they are easy to sing and to harmonize. And everyone is enthusiastic. The songs sung by the Catholic congregations are usually sappy, like "On This Day Oh Beautiful Mother." Nothing that stirs enthusiasm there. Or charges up your blood.*[22]

After the hymn sing, I got out my letter portfolio to write to you, but I stopped to talk to Glen Allen and another fellow from ASTP, Sam Brown.

---

22. Many years later when the first Catholic Mass in English was permitted in this country, in St. Louis, I believe, the congregation sang Luther's "A Mighty Fortress Is Our God."

We talked about the Henry Wallace deal and why Roosevelt replaced him with Truman, and then somehow got onto the race problem—in Michigan and elsewhere. You know Glenn's from Mississippi, and Sam's a New York Jew. It was the first intelligent and stimulating conversation I'd had in weeks, and we didn't break up until long after midnight. And me with no letter written. I hope you will excuse me this time, dear.

Though Glenn and Sam might have divergent views on matters, we were able to discuss the Negro problem rationally and dispassionately. Several times Glenn made innocent but pointed remarks about Jews, not knowing about Sam's background. But Brown seemed amused by it, I could see, because he kept glancing at me, and smiling. Glenn didn't say anything really bad, so maybe it was OK. Still, he did represent a southern viewpoint that I find objectionable and unhealthy in our republic. I keep wondering why the army should be segregated.

The little I have seen of England is much like the weather at home. There did seem to be quite a bit of snow all along the coast. I'm told that the winter in Western Europe has been the severest in a long while. I guess they run in eleven-year cycles, something to do with sunspots, no doubt. Like the ups and down of shortwave reception. Anyway, all the movies you see of the Western front show a lot of snow. I'd hoped to put off getting here until warmer weather sets in. As you know, dear, winter is not my favorite season of the year for doing anything. But I doubt if the generals will discuss the matter with me.

The same day, January 29, 1945, in Dearborn: *I'm sorry to say that this will be a very short letter tonight. It's after midnight, and I have to get up early in the morning. I came home a short time ago after spending the evening with your folks, and I stayed longer than I had intended. We talked so much after dinner, and your father kept telling his stories. Allen looks better and better each time I see him, but he is still not ready to go into the service. As always, your mother produced a delicious dinner with home-made bread. I will say no more about that, however. You might be reduced to eating K-rations these days, and there is no point in tantalizing you, dear.*

I suppose you are on some foreign shore by now. I hope it is England, because that's the only likely place I can think of away from combat. It seems strange to be writing you not knowing where you are. It's almost like throw-

ing the letter in the air and hoping the fair winds will carry it to you. But you have always got my letters, and I yours, so we will have to trust the army postal system to do its duty in that respect. And you will know that my love will be with you at all times.

The next evening in Dearborn: *It's just about midnight here and probably early tomorrow morning wherever you are. I hope that you are quartered in barracks or some kind of sturdy building, at least until the winter is over. We have heard so much about how cold it is in Europe. Be sure to let me know if I can send you anything, such as a sweater. I can't promise to knit one for you, because it might not be finished until the end of the year. And maybe you will be home by that time.*

Sarah and I went to a concert at the Masonic Temple this evening. The program wasn't as good as some of the others. It was a quartet—a baritone from the Metropolitan, a tenor, and two sopranos, singing selections from light opera. They sang Maytime, *parts of* The Merry Widow, *and Rudolf Friml's* Firefly *and* Rose-Marie. *The baritone, John Brownlee, was the best, I thought, and he reminded me of you, dear. The rest were just so-so. One of the sopranos was very attractive, though, and she sang "Vilia," which is one of your all-time favorites, I believe. And as you would say, "She had her points!" I could see them even from the fourth row of the balcony. You would have appreciated that, I know. And your GI friends would probably have whistled and stamped their feet.*

The last day of January, 1945, in Dearborn: *I have heard so much news and so many rumors on the radio this past week, I have all sorts of guesses about where you might be going, all of them probably false. Tonight they told us Eisenhower has about sixty divisions—half of them armored— in readiness for an offensive. I hope that has nothing to do with the 13th Armored, dear. And the latest reports are that Russians are sixty miles from Berlin. Perhaps by the time you receive this letter, Berlin will be captured. Things seem to be going that fast. And MacArthur seems to be doing all right in the Philippines, too. So we'll see.*

From the Seine Inferieure, in France, February 1, 1945: *I'm writing this letter on a farm about three km from "Somewhere in France." We have to go on a "little hike"—the lieutenant's description—in about a half an hour. To loosen our muscles, I suppose, after the long trip across the*

Atlantic Ocean. I'll write as much as I can, and then continue when we get back. We will be moving on, but right now no one seems to know when or where. I wrote several letters on the ship, which I obviously couldn't mail until now. I hope you will get them all OK. We had a mail call last night when we first got here, and lo and behold, I had two letters from you and one from my mother. Needless to say, I was overjoyed to hear from you so quickly. Because you had sent them airmail, I guess. It makes me feel I'm not so far from home.

We got to Europe a few days ago and came here shortly after. I can't tell you the name of the port,[23] or the towns around here—for security reasons. But I can tell you about this place. I'm in what we would call a barn, and we all sleep here. It's very crowded—the whole platoon, more crowded than we were on the ship. But it's infinitely more congenial, and none of the foul odors that plagued us down in the hold. We'll be here, I think, while we are being organized. There is a large chateau that belongs to the farmer, if you can call him that. Lord of the manor might be a better description. The house is where the officers live, and from the descriptions I've heard, it has pool tables, movie projectors, beds with soft mattresses, and many other conveniences.

When the Germans were here, they occupied this farm too. And I suppose many a Kraut has slept in our barn as well. 'Tis said that a German general slept in the CO's bed. I suppose one could be cynical, and say the people here "collaborated" with the Nazis. But then, they probably had no choice, with the French government collaborating, as well. Anyway, for me to sleep in a barn is no hardship. In fact, it is the fulfillment of a life's dream. When I was a kid, visiting my Uncle Frank Hall's farm in Ohio, I thought it would be wonderful to sleep in the hay, and in the daytime to jump in it. The smell of hay is almost intoxicating, I think.

It's cold here, of course, without any means of heating such a large building, but we have our sleeping bags, and we can pile the hay around us. And with a couple of blankets, and my overcoat on top of me, and my long-handled drawers on, I can sleep "as snug as a bug in a rug." I've found that the fetal position is the most comfortable and warmest. And I have visions of you

---

23. Le Havre.

joining me here. Except I don't think there is room in a GI sleeping bag for two people, no matter what María and Roberto said in For Whom the Bell Tolls. *Anyway, it would be pretty crowded for the kind of activity that Hemingway implies.*

The sun is shining now, and the weather seems to be improving. There was a lot of snow before, and we had a lot of difficulty getting here from the port of debarkation. In fact, we had to stop once to help dig out one of our trucks that had driven into a snow pile. Most of it is gone now, and the place is becoming a thing of beauty, as the poet says. If you and I could be here in the spring or the summer, with all the flowers, I think it would be the most beautiful spot on earth. It's so peaceful now, you'd never think there's a war going on only a few hundred miles from here. I'll draw you a little map to show where I am located—minus, of course, the place names—but showing the layout of the farm.[24]

There are several orchards—apple trees, I would assume, and fields for various crops. And before I forget, six families live here on the estate. All in all, a vast expanse, and quite impressive. I doubt if the owner does any work, except maybe to add up the profits. That's the life for me, I think, a "gentleman farmer," that people always tip their hats and say "sir" to!

Cpl. Helms and I went for a short walk yesterday to a village that is about a half-km from here—very small, perhaps no more that a hundred souls. It was interesting to us, because it is so different from what we're used to at home. I wanted to try out my French, meager as it is. Just what I picked up from the booklets they gave us on the ship. We stopped by one of the two cafés and ordered glasses of cider. It tasted good to me, and I thought also we could try some "hard" cider, that packed more punch. We also wanted some bread, so I looked in the book and said: "Je voudrais acheter du pain." There was no "boulangerie" in the village, the man said. So we talked him, with a lot of English and hand motions thrown in, into riding his bike to the larger village to get some. I paid them 16 cigarettes to get one kg of bread. I think I paid too much, but then the cigarettes cost me almost

---

24. This part of the page was cut out by the censor, interestingly the only such excision in the many letters I wrote in Europe. Perhaps I was more careful, or Lt. Locke more permissive.

nothing. The bread was dark, with a hard crust, and very good—far better than what they give us in the mess line.

It's funny the way we give away or trade our chewing gum and cigarettes. We're new to all this, having been here so few days. But there were soldiers here before, and the French have learned how to deal with us. The kids swarm all over us and holler "shween-gum" and "cigarettes pour papa." And because we have no francs as yet, we have to barter with the cigarettes—or sometimes with bars of soap, both of which seem to be scarce in France. Usually we pay a nickel a pack for cigarettes, so when I gave ten cigarettes tonight for a liter of cider, in one way I bought the cider for two and a half American cents. But the French pay a lot more for their own cigarettes—when they can get them. So both of us have gained in the exchange.

For example, the fellow who got the loaf of bread for us had to pay fifty francs for it, because it was obtained sub rosa—he didn't have ration coupons for it. Since a franc is worth five of our cents, he paid a dollar for it and got 32 cigarettes from us, worth a lot more to him. But to us, less than ten cents. Oh well, the more I think about it, the more tangled it gets.

I write more about France on the next day, February 2, 1945: *I'm finding in many ways how different the French are from Americans. It's to be expected, of course, because of our different cultures, but also because of recent events—notably, their defeat by Germany and the systematic looting of the country by the victors. The many shortages, for example. There are few autos on the roads, and I wonder where they get gas for those. But most walk—or ride bicycles, if they are lucky. To work or wherever, and for miles and miles, to other villages and towns. Something else: their attire. No one seems to have new clothing. And no hats like those we're used to at home, just berets or caps. And everyone seems to have red cheeks. I thought maybe it was the bitter cold, but now that it is warmer, they still have cheeks as red as the apples of this province. Not much need for rouge among the ladies here. I've about run out of paper, so unless I can find some in town soon, I will be in deep trouble. Having to write on one side of the sheet certainly has its disadvantages.*

Worries from Marianne on the home front, February 2, 1945: *Your mother called this evening to see if I had heard from you as yet, and, of course, I had to say no. There are so many things we can't know. Like how long it was before you sailed, how long it took you to get to wherever you are going. So, I suppose we shouldn't be impatient. I'll be very glad to have a letter to answer again. You must be tired of reading a monologue about my dull life. As for news about your family, Allen is working for the Post Office again as a mail carrier. He's pretty much over the jaundice, but the doctor won't give him an approval to join the armed forced for at least a month. So he will be with us for a while yet.*

I should bring you up to date about our money matters. We have a bank balance of $53.89, so our account has a start now, after being virtually depleted. I collected $2.25 at the nursery school Friday, which is what I am being paid for working there an hour and a half each week. Nine dollars a month may not seem much, but these days every bit helps. And my budget should be getting back to normal. I can deposit the money I get from the army and anything else I can save. Luckily there haven't been repairs on the car for a while, but maybe you should keep your fingers crossed about that item. God bless you, dear, and keep you safe for me and all of us here who love you, and pray for you.

News from France, February 5, 1945: *I'm sitting outside on a pile of oats writing this while the sun is shining on me. The French people are threshing the grain in the barn, mostly by hand. Imagine being dispossessed by a pile of grain! It's still somewhat cold, but in the sun it's not bad at all. I just hope it doesn't rain. In that case we might have to move temporarily to smaller buildings like the chicken coop or—God forbid—the outside toilet. You might be interested in hearing about that item of French sanitation— or lack of it. There are just holes in the concrete, and we crouch and hope our aim is good. And there is a stick to poke the stray stuff in.*

All of which reminds me of another of my dad's World War I stories— about the privy that had III printed all over the walls—in charcoal, it seemed. They finally figured out, he said, that it was because there was no toilet paper! It isn't that bad here, but in town the public urinals have chest-high walls, so they can talk with citizens as they pass by. "Bonjour, mesdam et messieurs," as they tip their caps. And I noticed a sign painted on the wall of the local church: "Defense a uriner." Each country has its customs, but I wonder if I could ever get used to—or not be embarrassed by— the Gallic bathroom procedures. We'll see.

And another interesting custom. Yesterday I was watching while a farmer was making cider in our barn. They have a horse walking in a circle to furnish power to crush the apples and then press them so the juice runs out into a dirty wooden trough and down into a vat. The workers didn't seem to mind when a little boy picked up a piece of paper from amid the manure on the floor, folded it into a boat, and floated it down the stream of apple juice! I think that in the future I should restrict my cider drinking to the hard version with the hope that the alcohol will deal with the germs. Or maybe there aren't human germs in horse manure.

I tried to get some writing paper in exchange for cigarettes, but the shop lady was adamant about that. She wanted real francs, which I don't have. So I will have to try some other way. And we've been told we can't buy bread anymore from the civilians. It's prohibited by the ETO [United States Army European Theater of Operations]. *About the only thing we can buy, then, is cider. And maybe eggs. I'm not sure about that. So I'll just have to take my chances and hope for the best. From time to time, I'll ask you to send me things, honey. I would especially like dried fruits, such as dates, figs, peaches, etc. Things that keep. You'll need a request each time, but then you can send several things, up to five pounds in a package—soup, canned meat, Nestle's chocolate. I'll probably think of more things later, such as books. Auf Wiedersehen, dear. I'll try to write again tomorrow.*

More news from the barn in France, Sunday, February 4, 1945: *I had hoped to go to Mass this a.m., but for some reason—not revealed to us— we were only allowed to go to the eight o'clock services, and it was after eight when I woke up. And it was about 9:45 when I ate breakfast. We're still making our own meals, and it usually takes us an hour to get it ready and cook it all. (Though the cooks seem to be bringing good meals to the officers in the chateau, I noticed. No C rations for them.) By the way, we're sleeping in the barn again. Which is fine for us, because it has been raining, and everything around the farm is muddy. Still, it's better than all the snow we had before, and we can get around better.*

This being all my writing paper, I'll have to use the lesson papers from the I&E class until I can get some more. It seems a waste of paper to always use just the one side. Perhaps I should use both sides, and if anything were to be cut out, it'd be just too bad. And the army should know that nothing we can say can help the enemy in any way. The newspapers and magazines tell everyone where we are anyway. And nothing is going to save the Germans now. Auf Wiedersehen, dear.

Two days later, February 6, 1945: *I just got back from a tour of three villages that surround us. We've moved to a new location, and once more we're quartered in a barn. This time, though, we have more room, and we're sleeping in clover hay, instead of straw. As you can see, I finally got some paper, and I can write longer letters again. The paper and envelopes cost me 15 francs, or thirty American cents.*

I went with Lamois, and we walked most of the afternoon. We stopped at cafés in three towns or villages and had cider in each. (I decided to forget about the paper boat and the manure or else to treat it as an aberration in that one isolated barn. I hope so, anyway.) In the first café the cider was five francs a bottle—about a dollar. In the second, we had applejack, which was pretty hard. But we enjoyed ourselves, sitting there and eating bread and reading a French newspaper. It's not too difficult—reading French, that is—because so many words about the war are similar in English, French, and Spanish. And you can guess a lot more words from the context. I haven't had any mail since the first day, but no one has had much. I guess it must come in batches, as planes arrive from the United States. I hope another batch arrives pretty soon. And tomorrow, if we aren't too busy, I'll be able to write you a long letter about life in the ETO.

The next day, February 7, 1945: *We've been out on our daily hike and are back now. I guess we are supposed to do some kind of maneuvers, but that seems impossible with all the farms and villages in the vicinity. So we walk instead. It didn't rain, for a change, and a stiff wind blew away most of the clouds, so we had sunshine, which made everybody happy. Incidentally, we saw an old German tank that had been knocked out months ago and was all rusted. It was the only item that made us think of the war. Sometimes I feel isolated, and cut off from the outside world. Especially when I don't hear from you for so long.*

It's pleasant to be walking along these country lanes—and more so when it is of our own volition. But even when the company is parading with some semblance of order. I find it interesting to promenade past the old farm houses, lived in for the many centuries the land here has been farmed. And to follow the winding lanes, lined with tall trees or hedgerows that lead into villages. Each farmer appears to have a goodly number of livestock, and as the company marches by, the cattle gallop over to the fence to see what we are and where we are going. They look well-fed, not what you might expect after five years of war. I guess the people who suffered most from the German occupation were the city dwellers. None of the people here seem emaciated.

Do you remember our trip on the bus from Cleveland to Akron last November, how the area was dotted with small farms and fenced fields? Well, this country is something like that—with an Old-World, bucolic atmosphere added. I'd like some day to show you the area in the spring and early summer. Can you imagine farm after farm of apple orchards in bloom? The two of us riding bicycles through the fragrant countryside. And staying at little inns on the way. Don't they call it hosteling? Remember the story we read about Mme. Curie and their bicycle trip in France?

Some school business from Marianne, February 8, 1945: *I haven't a letter from you to answer, dear, but I have hopes that it won't be much longer until I start hearing from you again. In the meantime, I have been kept busy at school. We are having our annual clinic next week to certify all our cases for state reimbursement, and it means records to get ready for each child. I am beginning to feel again the difference of doing a lot of someone else's work, in addition to my own. Unless Mr. Lowery decides to hire another teacher soon, I think I'll ask him for a raise in my salary, since he is saving that money.*

One of the mothers asked me today if I would give her son some private help at home, in the evenings, and I told her I would. He needs it very badly and is losing out in his other classes, because of his speech difficulties. The usual fee is about two dollars a lesson, so that is what I'll charge her. This is my first private case—not counting those at the university clinic, so it will be interesting. But I'll be on the spot, because parents will expect their child to improve or else, since it's costing them money.

From the village of Goupillières in the Seine Inferieure, February 8, 1945: *I received a letter from you today, for which praised be to the Almighty. It was the one in which you mentioned the concert of John Brownlee. I'm surely glad to hear from you, after so long. It had seemed an eternity. Some of your letters must not have come by airmail, because this one was not in sequence after the last one I got. I'm sending all of mine airmail, so they should get there fairly soon.*

Today I went to an I&E meeting at division headquarters and was gone most of the afternoon. We discussed current events, the French people around us, and the ETO policy of non-fraternization with German civilians, which you have probably read about in Time. *It was after supper time when we got back, so the cook fixed us three eggs and some ham apiece. They were from the officers' mess, he said. We never have anything like that. It sure was good to get a fresh egg again. Sunny-side up, they were beauties to behold. I had thought the only eggs we would get here in the ETO would be powdered. And maybe they still will be. In the enlisted men's mess lines. We also had creamery butter from Chicago, which on fresh-made white bread was quite a treat. For a little while, at least, we felt like kings.*

The next day: *At the battalion headquarters we broke open our I&E stuff that was sent with us from Camp Bowie. I had my German military dictionary in the box, along with the textbook for the course I took from the University of Wisconsin. Both of them should come in handy, one of these days. I read a few pages and was pleased that I could still understand quite well. With a little review, I should be fairly competent. Lt. Locke told me when we get to Germany, he wants me to translate for him. And the company commander too. It's interesting that a lot of the fellows here ask me to translate French for them. And some of the officers too. You'd think they would want to learn how to speak it themselves.*

It was the first time I had been in the town we hiked to today. It has a population of about 4 or 5 thousand, I would say, the largest in this area. There are modern shops, and the people actually dress somewhat like Americans—and there were good-looking women for a change. The farm women probably do a lot more hard labor than the townspeople. I'll probably come back one of these days, if we're still in the area. I'd like to check out the shops. I've been needing a pocket knife, especially when we do our own cooking—and for opening things, etc. And it will give me a chance to improve my French.

In one of our classes today a man dressed up like a German soldier so we could identify the uniform. Though because we have seen so many movies, I hardly think it was necessary. Anyway, one of the dogs that follow us around—hoping for something to eat—began to bark at him. In fact, he lunged at him and grabbed hold of his trouser leg! The captain who was conducting the class observed that the French dogs, at least, were not collaborators.

Sunday, February 11, 1945: *Our squad has fixed up a smaller building with a stove and an electric light, so I am writing there instead of in the barn. Sgt. Peters scrounged around and found a lot of the things we needed to make us comfortable. It could have been a chicken coop, but we've made it very homey, with hay piles for our beds, and the stove keeps us warm. Also it can be used for cooking. It burns wood, and we've collected some sticks and logs from round about here. When some general decided to put our platoon in the barn, nobody in the higher echelons considered that any of us needed to be at least a little comfortable. And warm at night. Except for the officers, that is. When we walk past the chateau, we can see through the windows that they are having drinks in front of what looks like a fireplace or an open stove. General Wogan was there a day or so ago. With a bunch of Red Cross ladies and some nurses. But with our little home away from home in the chicken coop, I shall not complain. Well, not too much. We are having a lot of good discussions these days.*

Honey, I've been getting your letters with large single sheets, and it occurs to me that you might rather use lighter paper, like onionskin. That way, you can include something of interest—for example, a clipping from the newspaper or a magazine. I would appreciate it very much. One of the fellows got a clipping of a Life *article about Bill Mauldin, the cartoonist. It was passed around, and we all read it eagerly. We do get the* Stars and Stripes, *but that's about all. You know what interests me, so send me something each time, will you? And be sure to send that article from the Sunday* Free Press *that summarizes the weekly news for servicemen. Some of my friends might be mentioned there.*

Another thing you could send me is my Baedeker's Southern Germany. *I trust the time will come when I find it useful as we move around. I don't think it includes the Rhineland, but it does have the rest of that part of the country. If you can send it airmail at not too great expense, do it, please. But send it posthaste, will you, honey?*

The next day, February 12, 1945: *I'll just write a short letter while I'm waiting for the first sergeant to get back from battalion headquarters. I was supposed to show a movie,* Doughgirls, *this afternoon to our platoon, but the lights kept flickering and going out, so we never did get to see it. The first sergeant is going to see if we can keep it longer and show it tonight. I hope we can, because the fellows were looking forward to it. According to the box it came in, it stars Ann Sheridan and Jack Carson. It's supposed to be good. At least, my mother said she has seen it and liked it. Something wholesome, no doubt. Just what the red-blooded soldier likes. P.S. The sergeant came back, and the answer is no. The schedule was tight, he said, and the officers wanted to see it in their chateau. Without us. The Red Cross ladies and the nurses were coming over, he said. So we were left to our own devices. I decided to play a game of hearts with the fellows, which I won, you will be interested in knowing. So I can go to bed happy. Good night, dear.*

❧ 12 ❧

Life on a French Farm

Gadding about in France, February 17, 1945: *I'm late getting started this evening, because I was writing to my mother, and then I was interrupted by the rest of the squad coming noisily into our little barn. They had gone out earlier on a night patrol to see if they could capture a chicken for our pot. Sgt. Peters had scouted around the area and identified the most likely place to look. As it turned out, the building was locked up, as tight as a drum, so they returned empty-handed. Unfortunately. I had been planning to try out our stove by stewing a big, fat hen. With dumplings, if I could get some flour and the rest from the cooks. Before they left, young Perry said that if anyone heard them, he would holler: "It's just us chickens in here." But Peters told him he would have to say it in French, which stumped the little fellow. They asked me how to say it, and I looked through both of my little books, but never did find such a phrase. You'd think that before they put us in barns the army would plan ahead and provide us with useful information like that.*

This afternoon four of us in my squad went to the large town the platoon had marched to last week. It seems there's a rule in the ETO now that no one can go anywhere by himself. I suppose it's for our own protection, though I've never worried about it before. The French around here seem to be peaceful folks. And friendly. So now if I want to go someplace I have to ask someone else or tag along, when another fellow is going. But I'm glad we did go today, because the town's off-limits now. I hear they've been charging too much for their drinks. *All we had today, though, was cider, and that never costs very much. I bought a jackknife and some writing paper, so my mission was a success. For the knife I had to pay all of 125 francs, which seemed a lot at the time. But I've concluded it's worth it, because it has six blades and gadgets, including an awl, a corkscrew, a screwdriver, and a can opener. I have the large knife your father made for me at Ford's, but it's unhandy for doing little things. It's shaped more for hand-to-hand fighting, if that ever should happen. I'll have to find some place to sharpen the blades, though, because they're pretty dull. Maybe I'll ask one of the farmers to help me.*

We stopped at a jewelry store, so I could pick up a leather watchstrap. Remember you and I bought one in Brownwood, but for some reason it got broken. This one cost 100 francs, which I thought pretty stiff, but you can't wear a wristwatch if the strap is broken, can you? The clerk was very pretty, we all thought, though a little plump, maybe. She held my hand while she was adjusting the strap, and Lamois said he had a notion to buy one, so she would hold his hand. But then he thought that would be a high price to pay for a moment of pleasure, when he didn't even need the strap.

We bought an apple pie at the boulangerie *and a loaf of bread, and took them to a café, where we drank cider, ate good food, and talked. The pie was different from ours and not sweet enough for our tastes. There's probably a shortage of sugar in this country during the war, but also the recipe could be different. You might know more about that. They charged us fifty francs for the pie, but we were supposed to have a coupon to buy it, so they upped the price. I guess it's rationed. The cider was good—and sweet— the best I've had for some time at a café. The girl that waited on us there spoke a little English, which helped us understand each other. But when she was trying to open the bottle, she said: "Jesus Christ!" And later, when she dropped something she said: "Shit!" So I guess she's learning her English from the wrong people.*

We walked all the way back—five miles, I think. (Going there, we got a ride part way in one of the Company C trucks.) And we stopped a couple of times to pick up some eggs. I traded a few old cigarettes for two eggs, and Head traded a bar of soap for four more. On the way we met some kids just getting out of school, and, as is their wont, they ran after us, yelling "chocolat" and "shween gum."

I talked a little French with the kids, telling them a few English words too. One was the prettiest little girl I've seen in a long time, anywhere— very blonde and blue-eyed. About twelve, I think. She reminded me some- what of you. When Cherwatuk gave them some gum, he gave her the whole stick, instead of breaking it in half, as we usually do.

About half-way back we had to heed nature's call—we had all drunk a lot of cider—so we just lined up alongside the road. Lamois said it was a good thing we were in France where such things were not taken amiss, when around the bend of the road came a lady. There wasn't much we could do but say "Bonjour" and keep on urinating. It's interesting that in the Anglican societies—England and the United States, anyway—these natural things are so hush-hush. We keep thinking of words that disguise what really goes on—WC, bathroom, toilette, and even the little boy's room. And over here we do it right in front of God and the whole world!

We got back to the farm a bit late for chow, but the cooks had a little food left, so we did eat something. Later on in the evening, I was still hungry, so I cooked a couple of eggs scrambled in butter in my mess kit. They tasted pretty good, as one thing I can cook well is an omelet. And it goes good with the French bread and the real butter I snitched from the kitchen. It certainly has been an interesting and pleasant day—for the four of us, I think. And we never even mentioned the war.

The next day: *This morning I went to Mass at 10:30 with some of the fellows in our platoon. The priest had us sit up in the choir seats, just in front of the altar. I felt very conspicuous, but never more so than when he began to refer to us in his sermon, and to welcome us as their liberators and the great fighters for their liberty. I felt myself getting redder by the minute. The Mass was sung in Latin by the congregation, which was a good idea, and I sang right along with them. They seem to pronounce some of the Latin words differently from us. Like* agnus dei. *It was led by an old fellow with a fierce mustache and a voice that might have been good several years ago. And as we filed out, many stopped us to shake our hands and to thank us for all we were doing for their country.*

This afternoon I went for a short walk with Head and Cherwatuk, and on the way back we stopped at a farm for some cider. The old fellow began to feel chummy, I guess, and he gave each of us a shot of Calvados. Wow!

That was like a bolt of lightning. And on an empty stomach. We were pretty dizzy as we staggered back to chow.

The next day, February 19, 1945: *No long letter tonight either, I'm afraid. We were kept busy most of the day with various classes—more about getting us ready to move out, I guess. Lecturing at us at this late date isn't going to do much good, though, except to give the officers something to do. Mostly I'm full of complaints today. But not about the food, this time. We're supposed to get a certain amount of supplies each week, but we go so long between the PX allotments that we never get what we're due to have. For instance, this week we got a single pad of stationery for each squad, when one man could use up that much in six or seven days. We've all had to start writing on both sides of the paper, with the hopes that not too much will be cut out. I've been trying to buy more paper in town, but it's expensive, and it's using up a lot of my francs. So maybe you could send me some paper in a package. In the meantime, if you don't get letters for a while, it's because I have run out. Of paper. Or money. Or both.*

The other night I was on guard, walking around the chateau for a couple of hours. And after I was through, I stopped in the large barn to talk with Lamois. It was about one o'clock in the morning by now, and he was still writing letters. Out of curiosity, I decided to see what it was like to milk a cow—both of us being city-fellers. We squeezed, and to our surprise milk came out! And the cows seemed to like the attention. They mooed to us anyway. We each got a canteen cup full and then decided to make ourselves some cocoa. (I've heard that in France it's not a good idea to drink raw milk.) I must say it really tasted great. And warmed the stomach, too. We'll have to try that again. And remember to save our Hershey bars. Good night, dear. Auf Wiedersehen.

The same day from 6210 Payne in Dearborn: *I'm sending a V-mail tonight, because I have time only for a short letter, and I'm told it's the quickest way to get to you.*[25] *The only letter I have had yet from France has been a V-mail. Sarah and I went to hear Lawrence Tibbett tonight, and we had*

---

25. V-Mail (Victory-Mail): A much more efficient and timesaving process in which our letters were written on special—and smaller—forms, censored, photographed, and flown to various parts of the world. A predecessor of today's e-mail.

dinner before at Cliff Bell's. The food was good, but not like when you and I were there and had those wonderful shrimp cocktails. I'll remember those for the rest of my life, I think. And especially because we were together. As for Lawrence T., he was polished and sang very well, though he didn't get much response, I thought. I believe because the program was so heavy. I kept wishing he would give us at least one or two songs that Nelson Eddy sings for us so well on the radio. Though, of course, Tibbett is better at the arias.

Tomorrow evening there's a dinner at the Lowrey school for all the teachers of Special Education, so I suppose I'll be pretty late getting home. Dr. Strauss, who taught the Psycho-pathology class at Wayne, will be the speaker. I'll try, at least, to write a short letter and to squeeze all my love into a small space—condensed, as it were. Good night, baby, till then.

The next evening, February 20, 1945: *So you are in France, honey. Let's hope you stay there for some time, and in the southern part of the country, away from all the fighting. I've been reading for some time about how relations between the French and the Americans are not what they used to be. And that it is evident in the changed attitudes of the people there toward the American soldiers. If that's so, De Gaulle had better mend his ways and not be so cocky, because we did hand his country back to him on a silver platter. And we don't owe him anything, as he seems to think. As for what you asked me, it was too dark when I got home to hunt in the attic for the book on Germany. But I'll look tomorrow and send it to you. Airmail. I'll also start sending you clippings from the* Free Press. *I should be able to get several in each letter. It's a good idea, and I'm glad you asked me.*

Our alma mater has been in the news quite a bit lately. The medical school came in for a lot of criticism, when it was threatened with being classed as a second-rate school, because fifteen of the best men had left recently. It resulted in Dr. Norris, head of the College of Medicine, being dismissed. Because he seems to have caused all the trouble, people said. Also a short time ago the Home Ec. building burned down. Goodnight, dear, I'll try tomorrow to answer your longer letter, when I can do it justice.

Tuesday, February 20, 1945, in Normandy I'm thinking about an end to war: *I saw an article in* Collier's *about a "complete" wardrobe for the returning serviceman. It says the basic essentials could be bought for about $150. So it seems that I'll be spending half of my mustering-out pay* *just getting outfitted. I do have some clothes left at home, but I know I will be needing a lot more. For one thing, I am heavier and taller, and my muscles are larger. And for another, I told Allen he could wear anything of mine that fitted him. So, after four years they could be worn out. After all these years of wearing a drab uniform, I might decide to break out in a riot of colors, and surprise even you, dear. So, we'll see. I've been in the army so long it's difficult to imagine what it will be like to be a civilian again.*

I still don't know where I'd like to go to school after Wayne, but I want to get as much information as I can about the different programs. Sometimes I think I'd like to be a teacher of Spanish or of history, though I wonder if I could be a good teacher. I wouldn't have the patience, I think. And I'd be too ornery. On the other hand, it might not be so bad in a college as in high school. I think I'd like the atmosphere of a university community. The give and take of discussions. It'd be almost like my going to school as a profession. Do you think you would like that kind of life, honey?

The next day: *I feel like a different man is writing you—a clean man! Today our company went in our half-tracks to a nearby town, where we all had a shower—wonder of wonders! The quartermaster corps has set up a tent, with lots of hot water. And each of us was allowed to wash himself for six minutes. It was brief, but the streams of water make your skin feel good for a long time. All the QM fellows were Negroes, and I was wondering if they were allowed to use the showers, too. Or maybe they would have to wait till we had left. It gives you something to think about, doesn't it?*

I'm writing this letter in a café while drinking cider. The proprietress is chattering away with some men at another table. Occasionally I hear a word I understand, but mostly they sound like a bunch of magpies having an argument about something or other. The men are playing dominoes, as is the custom in French bistros—or at least that's what the army guide book tells us. Jack Campey and I are the only soldiers here, so the atmosphere is congenial for writing letters. I just broke out a package of cigarettes I've been saving for such an occasion, and gave most of them away. The men in the café seem very pleased, by the looks on their faces, and the many thanks they bestowed on me. I feel like the lord of the manor passing out gifties at Christmas-tide. It's interesting, though, that I have no wish to smoke, even one cigarette. Maybe it's because they're worth so much for trading things. And coming back from the cafés, our clothes always smell of cigarette smoke, even our handkerchiefs. I'd hate to smell like that all the time.

I think I'd better close now and head back to our little barn. The proprietress is looking our way as though we shouldn't tarry too long. We have been here for most of the evening and the two of us bought only the one bottle of cider for five francs. A lot of pleasure for just ten American cents! And no one seems to mind. In fact, they seem to like us. Goodnight, dear. I love you very much.

The same day in Dearborn, February 21, 1945: *The only letter today was a V-mail notifying me of your present address, which I already knew. So I'll read over some earlier letters to make sure I've answered them. It won't be so bad now if the mail gets back and forth as it has recently. I reckon that you should be getting this letter shortly before our anniversary, and then I should hear from you about March 15. This is the night I usually go out to give Larry his lesson, but his mother called and said he has bronchitis. So I stayed in and spent most of the evening finishing the book* In Bed We Cry *by Ilka Chase. It's such a stupid book, I don't know why I wasted the time. She ought to stick to acting and let other people write books for us.*

I dug up your book on southern Germany and will try to get to the post office tomorrow, honey. I also took out some of your Spanish books. Maybe I'll be able to read them soon, when I get a little farther along in our course. I noticed that you have two Baedeker books, and since you asked for the one on southern Germany, I suppose you are somewhere in eastern France, close to Luxemburg. If you were sent to the northern sector you might have been marching through Cologne soon, and maybe Remscheid, the town where I was born. There aren't many relatives by the name of Gutzeit, I think. But there are quite a few on my mother's side—Klingelhofer. I seem to remember some Pauls and Wilhelms and Heinrichs. Not that you'd have much chance of meeting any of them if you're sent to Germany. But you never can tell.

If your division is made part of an army already in that area, I would think it would be the Third or the Seventh, from what I have been reading in the newspapers about the new offensive. I hope, though, that the 13th Armored Division could be kept in reserve till the end of the war and maybe used as part of an army of occupation. By the way, your folks and I have decided from all the hints you've dropped, that you are located somewhere near Nancy in eastern France.

More about food, February 24, 1945: *Usually you'd think of the main topic of army conversation as being sex or women. Or the lack of them. But of late, it seems—when we are not bickering about something inconsequential—the big topic is FOOD. We talk about delicious concoctions we ate at home, like hot homemade bread, oozing with creamery butter. Or strawberries and cream with shortcake. Or thick, juicy steaks with French fries. Or Southern fried chicken. Or hot milk-toast with lots of butter. Or navy beans with cornbread, hot out of the oven. All of us vow that after the war we will never go hungry for one day in our lives. I hope that our icebox and pantry will be kept well-stocked at all times, so I can have plenty to eat, and snacks, whenever I want them.*

And while I'm on the subject of food, I must say that one of the best things about being married to you is that you are such a good cook. I must confess that I had some doubts at first, because you always said you had done very little cooking, except for cakes and pies. And all new brides are notoriously bad cooks. In the folklore of marriage, anyway. But I can say I have been agreeably surprised. I can't remember a thing you've cooked that wasn't good, and most of it was very good. Excellent, I should say. I think the best meal I ever had in my life was the roast beef you prepared when John and Betty were visiting us in Brownwood. And what gravy! Ambrosia of the gods! I didn't brush my teeth for a week, so I could still savor the taste.

I mentioned the other day that I hoped you were continuing to buy books occasionally for our library. If you get a chance, would you pick up An Intelligent American's Guide to the Peace *by Sumner Welles? (He's the one who wrote our Good Neighbor Policy for FDR.) I've read that it is a particularly good book, and one we can use to guide us after the war. And if you see others you'd like to have, why buy them. But be sure to tell me about it, because I'm always interested in knowing what our library contains. And what shelf I can put them on.*

I haven't started to get my Time *as yet, though our platoon Sgt. just got his first* Collier's *since we've been overseas. He also had two issues forwarded from Texas, so now we have some reading material to work on. We get the* Stars and Stripes *delivered every day, and we are able to keep up on the news, especially about the war, of course. I've been reading from* The Loom of Language, *which one of the fellows brought with him, trying to improve my French. I think I'll copy a vocabulary from the book, and the four conjugations, to memorize them in my spare time.*

More on food and other things, February 26, 1945: *I got a copy of* Time *for January 22 yesterday, and it was very welcome. I read it from cover to cover. It had been forwarded from Texas, probably on a slow boat, which is why it took more than a month to get here. But I should be getting the Pony edition soon—directly. My subscription doesn't run out until June, but when you get the notice, I hope you will renew it. It's a very good source for background news, even though it might be a bit old by the time I get it. And I can use it in my I&E work.*

I went for a walk yesterday with a fellow from the second platoon named Ira Strauss. He's the one who lent me The Loom of Language. *He was in ASTP at Pasadena Jr. College. Well, we got down to the crossroads near here, and my friend Bernard Nee and his younger brother were waiting there just in case some of us should come along. They walked with us into town where we bought some writing paper, talking the whole way. And I got along a lot better in French than before. Bernard is 14 and seems to be a very smart kid. I gave him part of a pack of cigarettes for being such a good teacher. I was sorry, though, that I didn't have any food for him and his brother.*[26]

Jack Campey is giving all the men in our squad shampoos today. (I don't know if I told you Michael Cherwatuk is our barber.) So I'll close this letter and stand in the line. For some reason, I always did hate washing my own hair, maybe because it feels so good when someone else does it for me. I'm trying to think what I can do for the fellows like that, but maybe translating for them is enough.

March 1, 1945 in Dearborn: *I have been reading all the letters I received from you lately, and they are spread all over my bed. The letter you wrote when you docked in England is especially good, I thought. And*

---

26. After the war, Marianne and I sent the Nee family some CARE packages, and in 1962 we stopped by the area during a visit to France. We learned that Bernard was now the mayor of his village.

especially beautiful. I'm fortunate you describe things so well, almost like bringing them to life again. The ocean and sky from the ship, the symbolism of the evening star and our separation that will end when our lives are re-joined, as surely as the evening star rises again in the morning. That's the way I feel exactly. I know that someday all we have waited for will become real for us. And perhaps sooner than we think possible right now.

If you stay in France very much longer, you will know the language very well. And you'll be quite the polylinguist, to have a command of three for-eign languages. I loved your description of the children who beg for candy and cigarettes. It reminds me of the part in A Bell *for* Adono, *in which the mobs of children were organized into a sort of racket that dealt with* caramelle, *instead of with gum and chocolates. But somehow the French kids seemed more appealing to me, and I can tell from your letters that you feel that way too.*

Incidentally, dear, you'll be glad to hear that Henry Wallace was ap-proved by the Senate for Secretary of Commerce. I know you thought he should still be our vice-president, instead of Harry Truman. And after the passage of George's bill there probably isn't so much satisfaction for Wallace in getting the secretary job. I wish he might have control of the Reconstruction Finance Corporation, but at least he can still do a lot of good as secretary. And he's not lost too much politically, I would say.

The same day in the ETO: *Bernard Nee came over to our barn again to visit us late in the afternoon—they have no school on Thursday. And he brought his brother Robert. They stayed a while, and we talked, and then I went to supper. I wanted to tell them we weren't allowed to let French kids eat in the chow line. But they just stood by and watched with big eyes while the food was being passed out. Finally, I couldn't stand it any longer, so I gave them my bread and cheese and got a second helping of potatoes with some milk for them. They seemed starved to death—but now so was I, as well.*

I think before I go to bed tonight I'll go through the New York Times *book-review section. Ira Strauss subscribes to it, and he let me borrow it. Also I've been reading* Death *on the Nile, a mystery by Agatha Christie that's circulating in our platoon. I read it a long time ago, but in the mean-time I've forgotten who-dun-it. I'll still be surprised by the ending, I guess.*

Ira also lent me his copy of Thomas Wolfe's The Hills Beyond, *so I have a lot of reading to keep me busy. I've never read any of his publications, though my brother John says in his estimation Wolfe is tops. I remember your writing me about Wolfe a long time ago when you were reading* A Tree Grows in Brooklyn *for your class, I think. Perhaps I'll agree with John when I read the book. Or with you. Last night I saw another book I'd like to have for our library,* American Folklore *by Carl Sandberg. Maybe you can get a copy of it for us.*

The next day, March 2, 1945, from France: *I'm writing you this afternoon, instead of after supper, because we are having a night program. The platoon will be going on a compass course, which should take a couple of hours or so. The squad leaders were supposed to go out and mark the course. However, Sgt. Peters is working today at the motor pool, so they asked me to do it instead. There wasn't much to it, as I had done it often back at Camp Roberts. Jack Campey went along to help me. As the sun was shining, it was a very enjoyable walk.*

We designed it like a treasure hunt, which may or may not make it more interesting tonight for the men. It depends on the mood they're in, I guess. From what they're saying, I don't think they want very much to go out. And they may feel that a treasure hunt is teen-age stuff. And the truth is that they hate to do any training. Sometimes I feel the same way. I know I'll need it some day when we're in combat. And, as you know, all too often I've tried to get out of some part of my training. Some day we'll say: "If we'd only used that time to our advantage." But we tend to look the other way, and put all thoughts of the battlefield out of our minds. Until it's too late for some fellows, I'm afraid. I guess it's human nature.

A report from Marianne in Dearborn, March 3, 1945: *I went downtown today to buy some things to send you, and to have my gray suit fitted. I think I told you I'm having my slacks made into a skirt, so I'll have an extra suit. I was pleased to find cans of salmon and chicken and wieners at the store, but then I had to put them all back on the shelf, because Jane had given me the wrong ration book, and the stamps in it weren't good yet. I'll be sending you a few things, and then the canned meats another time. I'm finding I can't pack very many things in a five-pound box, so be sure to send me requests fairly frequently. Once a week, if possible.*

You told me about your budget, and what you intend to save, and I am sure we will be able to save $100 a month. And I'll try to do better once I get a full pay again. With your Michigan mustering-out pay we should have a good-sized account when you come home. Another source of savings is the retirement fund I have with the Dearborn schools. I can draw it out anytime I quit teaching. By this June it will be about $200. And something else, I am thinking of getting some kind of job this summer, because it would be dull doing nothing. That way, I could put all of my summer pay into savings.

You might as well start thinking about where you will be going to school when you come home. I can think of several universities where I'd like to take classes. As long as the gov't pays tuition anywhere, up to $500 a year, you could go to almost any school you chose. Even Harvard or Yale. There would be several advantages to going back to Wayne, though. For one, we'd be closer to home, and I would be able to keep my job. And I agree with you, Wayne does have a good faculty, whether you study languages or history and the social sciences.

I decided to take an incomplete in my psych. class, because I wanted to have more time to write the paper. As you know, I am making a study of aphasia. But because there are so few books on the subject, I will have to spend a lot of time at Wayne and at the speech clinic, if I hope to get enough information. Since the war started, the Univ. of Michigan has made some studies with veterans who have suffered brain injuries, and I could spend time up there as well. More about that later.

Military politics, March 3, 1945: *I took a walk this afternoon with Jack Campey, and we decided to go to a small town we'd been through before, but never stopped in. We went to the only café for some cider and talked about one of the fellows in our platoon who was giving everybody a hard time. That is, he brown-nosed the lieutenant and first sergeant until they got him promoted to sergeant—in another platoon, which was a great relief for all of us. Except that a good fellow had been busted to make room for him—allegedly for "inefficiency." Politics are politics in every institution, I guess.*

Today was a beautiful day for a walk. The sun shone, but it was a trifle chilly. These days we have to wear our overcoats when we go anywhere on pass. The generals want us to be more formal, I guess. We used to wear our field jackets in town, but the orders came down from on high, and we have to follow them. Even if they are stupid. The trouble with overcoats is that they are cumbersome for walking and a nuisance when it gets hot. I bet the general never took a hike wearing one. I admit though that they do keep you nice and warm on a chilly day. We had a little snow last night, but it melted as soon as it hit the ground. And the ice on the ponds has melted also. I hope that we can postpone our movement up to the front long enough for the weather to be good in Germany. I wonder about lying on the ground and shooting rifles when our hands are frozen. But then thousands of other fellows like us are doing it, and so can we, I guess.

The next day: *I'm writing this letter by the light of a burning C-ration can of gasoline. The electric lights went out last night, and they still aren't on—though they flickered and tried to come on a few times. I'll make this letter short, because the flickering must be hard on the eyes. I didn't get up until 7:40, and I barely got to breakfast on time. The eggs were gone, and there were no pancakes today, so all I had was a big helping of wheat cereal. Then I walked over to the church where Bernard was serving Mass, and back to his house with him and another kid named Roland. As in the other churches I went to, I noticed a conspicuous lack of young people. All those attending Mass were either old or very young. I know a lot of young men are prisoners, or in the army, maybe with De Gaulle. Or killed in the war. But when I take my walks, I do see young men and women on their way to work. But not inside the church, it seems. Perhaps they aren't as religious as their elders. And of course, the younger kids are made to go by their parents.*

There was a big excitement at four in the afternoon when a Red Cross clubmobile arrived, bringing us good—and hot—coffee, and two donuts each. There was a girl from Brooklyn and another from Illinois. The best part, I suppose, was that the fellows could engage them in conversation. All the men weren't here, so we had seconds, which I ate slowly to savor the taste. And they nicely helped fill the void between dinner and supper. Then, for supper we had chicken, which is usually good. But I must have had part of a tough old rooster, and, worst of all, the neck. I gnawed and gnawed on it without getting any meat. The last time we had chicken they gave me, as my father says, the part that went over the fence last. In all fairness, next time I should have something in between, like a breast or a drumstick.

283

The same day, March 4, 1945, from Marianne back home: *I've been listening to the news, and it still sounds good for us on all the fronts. I haven't been worried so far about your taking part in the new drive on the western front, because the First and Third Armies seem to be the only ones in action, and I think you are farther to the southeast. At least, I hope so. Our armies are already at Düsseldorf in the Rhineland, the city my mother was from.*[27] *And once American troops cross the Rhine at Cologne, I guess they'll be going through Remscheid. If ever you and I do get to visit my city, it probably won't look much like it did originally. We've heard that American and British planes have been dropping a lot of bombs in that area.*

The next day in France: *I'm writing this letter in the café I wrote you from a week ago. I came to town right after supper in a half-track with Jack Campey, James Head, Michael Cherwatuk, and Loyd Lamois. (Loyd is the one I brought to dinner in Brownwood, remember?) We all came in to spend the evening writing letters, playing dominoes or cards, and drinking cider. And I'm beginning to feel a little woozy now, because we've had a couple shots of Calvados. I wonder how coherent this letter will be, with me getting tighter by the minute. Having never been drunk, I have no idea how it must feel. You remember what I wrote you a long time ago at Camp Roberts about the fellow who was lying on the floor in his own vomit? And I swore it would never happen to me? So I plan to watch myself and maybe have just one more drink before we leave. I should say that we are not drinking it straight, but rather mixing it with a big glass of cider. But then the cider is somewhat hard too, so there is quite a bit of alcohol going somewhere. We'll see.*

I must say that the people here treat us well, and we get along with them better than I might have expected, from what I've read. The owners are nice to cook up things for us and to let us to use their café to write our letters and play games, and just talk among ourselves. And we listen to their radio (TSF). I spoke a little French with the owner, who gets his English from a phrase book, paging through it for translations. Sometimes the conversation becomes amusing. I tried to ask him if he were the fellow who lost

---

27. Marianne's mother was from the Hessenland (central Germany), near the city of Marburg.

his bicycle. (Actually, I think it had been stolen.) He looked at a page and asked me: "Do you wish to lend my bicycle?" Probably my French sounds just as quaint to him. But the point is that we were both trying to be friends. And succeeding, I think.

Good news from a French village, March 6, 1945: *Today I hit the jackpot at mail call, honey—three letters from you, one from Mother, one from Dad, and my new* Time *magazine. Yours were of the 21st, 23rd, and 24th of February. There are probably quite a few missing that will be coming by boat. We've found that V-mail is the most reliable. Koslow's folks have been sending him nothing but V-mails, and he gets a letter nearly every day. Of course, as you say, it isn't as personal as a letter written on regular paper and sent in an envelope, and you can't get very much on a page or include anything. But it's useful when time is pressing.*

Koslow also got two boxes from home today and Lamois one, so tonight we have—did have, I should say—a lot of candy. Hershey bars and things like that. I hope you will be able to send me packages once a week or so. I'll ask mostly for food, because that's what I can use most. I'll be watching, too, for the book on Germany. It sure would come in handy pretty soon. It's very old, but the cities should still be there—or at least there'll be places where the cities were.

Thanks, honey, for sending me the clippings from the Free Press. *And please keep sending them, especially the Sunday columns for servicemen. And also magazines like* Newsweek. *Because I'm getting* Time *now, I don't need to buy new copies of* Newsweek. *But if you have older issues that would be fine. Our platoon sergeant gets* Collier's, *which we all read avidly. Right now we are in the midst of a serial about a girl who hears that her lover is missing in action. She goes out with a "friend" because she can't face her family who wouldn't let her marry her lover before he went overseas. The "friend," a handsome second lieutenant, trying to comfort her, suddenly becomes a "darting, flaming arrow of passion" and overwhelms her with his officerly attentions. And he ships out the next day. Then she finds that she is* enciente.

Now we have to wait until the next week's issue arrives to learn how the plot develops. Is the lieutenant killed in action? Does her lover escape from a German prison camp to return and claim her as his bride? Baby and all? We're hoping the army doesn't send us to Germany until we find out. Such are the things we worry about these days. That and food, of course. Your and my folks' guess about where I am was certainly way off the mark. I'll probably be able to tell you precisely when we leave here. Our CO was saying the other day that almost anyone should be able to figure it out, just by the seemingly innocent things the men write home about—the weather, the type of country, the farms, the crops, the drinks, etc. of the local yokels. And I suppose it's true. I would think the Germans already know as much about us, and where we are going, as we do ourselves. And more, probably, because the army never tells us anything, and the enemy could have spies anywhere.

I got home OK last night, though when I came out of the café it was pitch dark—no moon, no nothing. It was the darkest place I've ever seen, I think. It was a good thing I had brought my flashlight. Otherwise, we might never have found our way back to the farm. Our total evening cost us 240 francs, which wasn't bad. We tried to give them an extra 60 francs, but they wouldn't take it. They said they were just glad we had come to their café and take the trouble to learn their language. I don't think any of us were "lit up," but we were filled with merriment as we found our way back. And when we entered our little barn we were laughing and whispering—sotto voce: "Don't wake up Koslow! Don't wake up Koslow!" Bernard likes to get his uninterrupted sleep.

The same day, March 6, 1945, news from Marianne in Dearborn: *I have just heard the news that Cologne is in our hands, and I'm glad, and very much surprised that it was so quick and easy. I know there's lots of fighting still to be done, but let's hope it won't be long until there is peace in Europe. I didn't write you last night, because I spent the night with Ellen. I went out to Larry's house, the boy I give lessons to, and she lives not far away. So I don't have to drive home at night. As usual, we talked and talked until it was after midnight, so I didn't get much sleep. And I'm still very sleepy this evening. I hadn't seen Larry for a couple of weeks, because of his bronchitis, so we had to start from the beginning. I have high hopes for him, because he is smart and works hard. And he's also a very cute little youngster. I'll be able to save at least the extra money I'm earning this month for our account. My pay has been short, because of the time I missed at Christmas.*

And also there are a lot of extra bills due since the new year, such as the car insurance and license plates, and long-distance telephone calls—money I owed Jane. Now I am back on my feet, though, and can start saving a lot more.

I called your brother Allen when I got back from school to wish him luck and to say goodbye. It's his last day at home before he joins the navy. I suppose your folks will find it very lonesome at 1418 Helen Ave. for a while. And I finally mailed your package, honey. Unfortunately, it doesn't contain very much, mainly because it weighed too much, and I had to bring it home from the post office and rewrap it. I'll try to do better next time. It's hard to judge the weight of anything without scales.

Best wishes from France on March 7, 1945: *First of all, let me say happy anniversary to you, honey. Perhaps by this time next year we can be together for the rest of our lives. You and I are always so hopeful and optimistic about the end of the war, aren't we? But with the Russians about to launch their all-out push to—or beyond—Berlin, and the Americans and British building up to take the Ruhr, the Germans can't hold on much longer. I realize that the going will be tough for us in the next few months. But when the Germans lose the Ruhr they can have no hope at all. They could lose Berlin and still keep going. Hitler and his gang could go to their castle in the Alps and still be in charge. But the Ruhr is their Pittsburgh, Detroit, Youngstown, and San Francisco all rolled into one. I don't speculate any more about when the war will end, because I have been wrong too many times. But all of us, at home and overseas, can pray and hope that the fighting ends as quickly as possible, and that all the soldiers and sailors can get home safely.*

Thanks for the pictures. They are wonderful. You told me a long time ago that I wouldn't have gone out with you if you had been homely. It's perhaps true, but only because the initial attraction toward a woman is the fact that she has physical beauty. And that is what made me notice you in the first place—in Dr. Colditz's class. But beauty can be skin deep, as they say. And to me you are the most beautiful person in the world because you personify all that's good in my life. But I have to admit that I'm glad you're so lovely, and that—for example—you have such good taste in choosing your clothes. I'm always proud to be seen with you, honey, and to introduce you

287

to everyone as my wife. Thank you very much, dear, for being you. I love you very much.

The next day in Dearborn: *Your mother called me to say your brother Allen is now a member of the United States Navy. He left this afternoon for the Great Lakes Training Station. So that's all the Quirks in the service now, two in the navy and two—counting Eileen's husband Bud—in the army. I think Bud's in the Philippines now, by the way. Your mother will be lonesome, with your dad working so many hours each day, so I'll have to try to keep in touch with her more consistently. For you, dear, I'll copy a few pages from Walter Benton's poetry and enclose them in the envelope. And maybe I can go through the entire book that way.*[28]

In France, March 8, 1945: *I haven't much time to write tonight, so I'll dash off a V-mail before I go to bed. I was on guard tonight from 7 to 9, and when I got off guard I scrambled a couple of goose eggs a lady had given me. They certainly were big, and they tasted different, but I have to say they will never take the place of hen eggs. Besides, the geese here, if they had the chance, would chase us all over the farm. Maybe we should turn them loose on the German soldiers and see how the Krauts like that. The war would be over in a day or two.*

Today, being Thursday, we went in our half-tracks for our weekly shower. I think I told you that each of us has just six minutes, and then we have to step out. Well, this time I happened to be in the shower at the same time as a colonel and a major, and I was rewarded with twelve whole minutes of luxury! It sure pays to be an officer in the ETO. Or in his vicinity. I've heard, though, that they take off their insignia when they get close to the battle zone, and try to act like plain old GI Joes. And even stand in the chow line. So the enemy won't aim especially at them, I guess. We'll see.

My French friends were here to see me again, this being their day off from school. And Jack Campey and I took a walk with them and stopped to see the lady with the peacocks. She asked us to come back tomorrow at 4 p.m. when her husband would be there. We had a heck of a time understanding each other, and it was a long time before I made out what she was saying. It was about that time that I realized how little I knew about the French lan-

---

28. *This Is My Beloved.*

guage. And I had thought I was doing so well. Or maybe it's that women's voices are softer, and they tend to mumble their words. I don't know. What does a speech correctionist think about that?

News on the next day, March 9, 1945: *I was on guard last night, and I walked three hours again today. Then I went for another walk with Campey this p.m. All in all, I'm all in. Today was a beautiful day, very sunny and moderately warm. We went back to the house of the lady we visited yesterday. Her husband was there, and he was a scraggly-looking guy with a scraggly moustache. We talked for some time, but I still had some trouble understanding him too. I had thought she had invited us to supper, but we didn't get much to eat. And we missed out on our evening chow here. But it was interesting what they gave us—preserved plums and peaches, some apples, walnuts, cider, and bread and coffee. The coffee was café na-tional—ersatz, probably, from the taste. We had a drink of something called kirsch, made from almonds. And mighty potent stuff, indeed. She was brewing onion soup, and it smelled wonderful, but she explained it was for their servant. Campey and I thought they must have had their main meal in the middle of the day. We came away hungry, but we both felt we had been treated as their honored guests.*

From Marianne on the home front, March 9, 1945: *We've been having such good news from the western front these days, and it was just announced over the radio that a new army—the 15th—was taking part. It didn't say where, though. I suppose your and Bud's [29] units might be part of it, though as far as I know you are still in France. The announcer said we had crossed the Rhine in strength, so with that barrier gone, the armies are expected to make a lot of headway now. With the Ruhr gone, as well as Berlin and the seaport of Stettin, it's hard to see how the Germans can hang on much longer.*

You wrote a while ago about your civilian wardrobe for when you get back, and what you'll be spending, and I believe $250 would be a more reasonable figure to plan on. I think you will be needing to replace almost everything. I doubt if you will be wanting to wear many of the things you left behind, even if they are in good shape. Four years is a long time. Clothes

---

29. The 20th Armored Division.

deteriorate, and styles change—even in men's clothing. I'd like to buy things for you occasionally, such as socks, shirts, pajamas. And even ties, if you don't mind, dear. It will make me feel as if I have a husband while you are gone. If it won't make you feel hen-picked, that is. Can you hear people whispering about you—"His wife buys all his clothes!" I promise to be very moderate about it. Especially with the ties. I had my eye on some at Hudson's.

The next day: *I liked the article in this month's* Reader's Digest *about the campaign on how to treat the returning soldier. It has been making me irritated for a long time to read all the advice from civilians to other civilians on how to "handle" him, what changes to expect, in him and in his behavior. I remember when you first went away, and when I saw you again after a year, I wondered what it would be like after such a long time. But we learned then that fundamentally we don't change that much, although we both had grown up a little, and any changes were for the better. It would be embarrassing, I think, for the fellows coming home, if the people they love treated them scientifically, as though they were a bug under the glass of a microscope—practicing the inane psychiatry on them that has been suggested. All of us, I think, will be so darned glad to see each other, we won't have time to worry about it. Love is a powerful and wonderful thing that neither the war nor anything to come can change—except to grow stronger.*

Unpleasant news from France, March 10, 1945: *Well, honey, at least I have something new to write you about. And not at all pleasant, I'm afraid. Today the company commander called me into his office to say he would have to reduce me to the grade of private. "Without prejudice," he said. He thanked me for being so helpful to the company with my I&E work and all. And he still hoped I could translate for him when we get to Germany. I'd been expecting it, of course, for some time, but I must say I'm sorry it had to come to this. For one thing, being a corporal kept me out of KP, as you know. And the extra $16 a month came in mighty handy. The CO said I'd make Pfc. on the first company order, but for the present I'm a plain old buckass private. For all I know, the only one in the division. I'll probably have to cancel my war bonds, which is too bad. We could have used the money when I got out of the army.*

In one of your letters you told me you would love me even if I were a private, so you are being put to the supreme test, Mrs. Quirk. I won't get used to being a private very soon, though. For lo these many years I have become accustomed to the aura of wearing the two stripes and of being addressed as "corporal." Now it's just: "Hey, you, do this and do that."

The next day: *Our French friends came over at dinnertime and stood around, but this time I didn't give them any of my food. I hated myself, and tried to look the other way. But I've been told we can get into trouble if we share with them. It just attracts other kids to hang around too, they say. Maybe I could try to get second helpings sometimes and put food for them in my pockets. After all, what can they do to a lowly private as a punishment? Rap his knuckles? Say "you naughty fellow?"*

Two days later, March 13, 1945, in Dearborn: *You spoke, dear, in one of your letters, of reading Thomas Wolfe's* The Hills Beyond. *I've never read that one, so I'll be interested in knowing what you think of it. The only novel of his I've read all the way through is* The Web and the Rock. *And I got about half way through* Of Time and the River. *I'm not so sure I would agree he is wonderful, especially, for example, when he is describing New York in* The Web, *etc. He seems never to know when to stop writing, and he goes on and on for 200 or 300 pages, when he might have been more effective being more succinct. And it's maddening trying to follow the thread of his stories, when he keeps interrupting the plot with a huge description of something that has somehow impressed him. At the end, when the story has become very complicated, and he has driven himself and his true love mad so that she leaves him, he winds everything up in a couple of pages by looking in a mirror. Deep stuff, maybe, but I wonder if it is great literature. What he needed most was a competent editor who was ruthless in cutting out huge chunks. I think you could give him a good working over. Let me know your impression when—or if—you finish it.*

On March 15 the 13th Armored Division received orders to move its units, first to the vicinity of Nancy in eastern France, and then across the border into the Palatinate to join General George Patton's Third Army. The pleasant days of sitting in a Norman café drinking cider with our friends were at an end. And the contents of our letters changed at once. I could write, but less frequently, and I had to be more careful about how much information I could impart.

At about midnight on the 17th of March our half-track pulled out on a tough journey that would take us north of Paris, first to Compiègne and Soissons, and then through Châlons-sur-Marne, Vitry-le-François, and Bar-le-Duc, to Nancy in eastern France, and ultimately to Germany's border with Austria. With many stops and various actions, some dangerous and some not, on the way. Late in the afternoon of March 19 we arrived at the small town of Moyenvic, still in France, where we stayed several days while the various companies of the division were melded into combat teams—tanks and armored infantry units working together, something we had never done before.

❧ 13 ❧

The Last Days

Moyenvic, France, March 22, 1945: *As I write this short letter, I can see all around me the rubble of war. The Germans were here once, but now they are miles away, across the border, leaving destruction and enmity behind them. And the nearest American troops—the First and Seventh Armies, according to* Stars and Stripes—*are somewhere in front of us. The population here is mixed. Most speak French, but very many are German, because Hitler's forces have been occupying Lorraine for a long time. There must still be a lot of hard feelings—on both sides—as a consequence. And I wonder how they will react to our being here. I doubt if we'll stay long enough to spend much time in cafés or in talking with farmers. Yesterday a boy of nine or ten was walking down the main street, smoking a cigarette. "Bonjour, garçon," I said. He took the cigarette out of his mouth. "Fuck you, you son of a bitch!" Not much like the French kids where we've been for the past month or so. But then some GI might have told him that was the American way of giving a friendly greeting.*

In your letter of February 20 that came today you mentioned that the French are pretty huffy about getting what they want in the post-war conferences, honey. A good many of the fellows here have the same opinion. They can't understand why the people don't always greet us with open arms. The soldiers say: "We're liberating them, aren't we? They should be grateful." And I can see their point, because none of us asked to come over here to risk our lives for people we don't know. And we want to make the road to victory as smooth and easy as possible for us, without too much loss of life.

But for a Frenchman who has been fighting a war since 1939, and has taken a lot from the Germans in the occupation, his fighting days are over. He wants to get back to tilling the soil or turning out goods in the factory. Yes, he likes Americans, even though the Yanks burn up his wood, eat his eggs while his children might go hungry, and even—God forbid—steal his chickens! And worst of all, it is said, they try their best to seduce the women by offering them bars of Sweetheart soap. They're glad and grateful that we have driven the Germans out, as the priest told us. But at the same time, they'd just as soon we don't stay here very long. And who can blame them? Certainly not I. All too few of our soldiers, I think, take the trouble to try to understand the "Frogs," as they call them. And they make no effort to understand their language or their culture.

The French certainly suffered under German rule, there can be no doubt about that. And there must have been a lot of looting by the Nazis. But there wasn't too much physical damage done in their country, because the major war for them was over within a month after the big May–June 1940 attack. When the Americans moved in during June of last year, they proceeded to ruin many of the towns and cities as they stormed their way across the country, killing or wounding a lot of the French people with our artillery and planes. Like the port we came through at the end of January. And the place we're in now, which consists mostly of a lot of trash. Maybe you'd call that "liberating" the French, and we say we have to do it because the most important thing in any war is to destroy the enemy. In this instance, to defeat the Germans and force them to surrender. And this is where they were. But we should understand and be tolerant when the French complain and want to take control of their own country once more. And without us.

I agree that General De Gaulle is making noises out of proportion to the cards he is holding in the international poker game. Acting as though he has a royal flush, instead of a pair of deuces. But France has a big stake in the pot, and the general is determined to get as much out of it as he can. So he irritates almost everybody and makes it easier for our soldiers to see the flaws in this country, instead of the beauties. But I want to look at the wonderful parts of France, the green hills and fields, the quaint towns and houses, and the hedgerows that take you to them. Especially the people, who are friendly, as a whole. And the kids, who ask us for chewing gum and chocolates and teach us something about their language. I wish each soldier could look into his heart and find a little bit of understanding and tolerance.

But somehow I doubt if they can. Maybe I'm a pessimist. I am apprehensive about the future when people refuse to understand each other and turn their backs. Perhaps the Dumbarton Oaks plans for a United Nations will pan out. I hope so, because I want this world you and I are going to inhabit after the war to be a good place to live in. I suppose we can just come home and look out for our own interests. Laissez faire all over the place. Survival of the fittest. I'm sure you and I will get along fine, because we have a lot going for us. But it would be nice if the whole world could get along too. Already German soldiers are talking about joining with us to fight the Russians.

I'm going to send you a couple of books I found while I was prowling about in the trash piles and destroyed houses. One of them is called Mutter erzähl mir von Adolph Hitler. *I haven't had a chance to read through it, but it should be interesting for a history class I might be taking when I get back to Wayne. The other is in French,* La Fontaine's Fables. *I think you must have read some of them in English translations. I got through a few here with the help of my little dictionary, but later I'll probably be able to zip through them, if I get more practice.*

The news that the Home Ec building burned down was of great interest to me, because the Collegian *office was upstairs. I spent many, many hours in those rooms, and they will always be a good part of my life. I certainly learned a lot about writing while I was doing it. Remember, you came a couple of times to meet me there? I hope no one was hurt. But then you would have told me about it, I suppose.*

I've been working on my crystal set, but so far I haven't been able to make it work. I scouted around the other day, asking about a shop where radio equipment might have been sold. And somebody directed me to a building that had belonged to some Germans. I found a lot of radio parts on shelves, and was able to wind a coil, but I still couldn't receive anything. From what someone else said, though, I realize that I need a lot more wire and something to wind it on—as big as a Mother's Oats box, maybe. Or even larger. I had been thinking of the stations back home, which transmit on the medium waves. And the Europeans are mostly on the long waves, they say. So I'll keep trying. And still hoping.

It's time to stop writing, dear. I've looked at the "black velvet sky," and decided to hit the hay. That sack is going to feel mighty good in just a few minutes. And I find that somehow I've written the longest letter since I came to France. There was just so much to talk about before we move on. I showed the pages to Lt. Locke, who will censor the letter, and he said he was not going to read it. He was too busy, he said. And besides I scribbled so, he could never make out what I was writing anyway. He said he'd have me sign an affidavit to the effect that it contained no military information that could help the enemy, and then he'll just seal the envelope. The lieutenant is a fellow who often skirts around the edges of army regulations. Sometimes he gives us trouble, but I think his spirit will be a good thing when we are in battle. Like General Patton, maybe. Auf Wiedersehen, darling. I'll try to write you again tomorrow.

The next day, March 23, 1945, brought a lot of mail: *Today was a red-letter day, honey. At mail call I received twelve letters from you and from my mother. It's almost worth waiting so long, for the pleasure of getting so many at the same time. I counted them over and over. Yours were written on the first, second, third, fourth, tenth, eleventh, twelfth, thirteenth, and fourteenth of February. So a lot of missing dates have been filled in. There was also an anniversary card from you, for which many thanks. And Mother said she had sent you the flowers for March 7, as I had asked her. I hope you liked them. I know red roses are your favorites.*

I don't think anyone has better described my feelings than Walter Benton in This Is My Beloved. *I'm glad you are sending me excerpts from it, and I hope you will send me something in each letter. Does it embarrass you, honey, knowing that other people might be reading your thoughts? The censors, I mean. But probably Lt. Locke doesn't read your letters either. I can find no evidence that they have been opened by the post office there or here. It's just my mail that the army is concerned about. And not one of the fellows here has had any trouble about that. Not even Ira Strauss, I think, who has strong feelings about some things and expresses them.*

I have to close now, honey, because I'm going on guard in a few minutes. I'll be thinking about you and hope I can write again tomorrow. But there are certain jobs around here the army has us do, so I might be busy. I think the CO wants me to do some translating for him. French or German, I'm not sure which. He needs to talk with some of the town officials, I think. Good night, dear.

Palm Sunday in France, March 25, 1945: *I thought I'd be writing you a long letter again today. But the mail has to be in by eleven this morning, so I'd better make it short.*[30] *I've already written to my mother, and I have to wash and shave before I go to church. There is a mass in English at 11, probably by the chaplain. And there is a French mass an hour earlier that I'd like to go to, so I can sing in Latin along with the congregation. But I probably won't have time to get ready for that. Last Sunday the chaplains came over from Germany, and had services in this area. It's interesting that there were about three times as many people at the Catholic services as at the Protestant. They probably thought that their attendance at mass would help them in the days ahead. A few extra "Hail Marys" never hurt. Works vs. faith, and all that. The old argument between the Papacy and Martin Luther. And you know what they say about atheists in foxholes.*

Rumors on the home front, March 27, 1945: *I have been listening to the late news, and the announcer said we could expect the end of organized resistance in Germany anytime within the next thirty days, according to Eisenhower's statement today. There were a lot of peace rumors floating around. The kids came to school very much excited by what they had heard. There would be "big news" sometime this afternoon, they said. So I listened to a radio in the teachers' lounge for awhile, but heard nothing I didn't already know. When it comes to rumors, civilians are as bad as soldiers, I guess. Or worse. I realize there will still be fighting now, but you and I can be thankful the news has been so good. We have had a lot of good breaks lately.*

Somewhere in Germany, March 28, 1945: *As you can see, honey, I am now in the land of your birth—the land of my enemy now. It seems strange to be here, because everyone is an enemy, from small children to old ladies*

---

30. When we were moving out, the mail had to be turned in early. But of course I could not say that in a letter.

and men. I'm glad your folks decided to come to the United States so long ago. I can't see myself treating you as my enemy. But what about your relatives, your cousins and aunts and uncles? I wonder if any of them are in the German army. It's a real problem, isn't it? In a way, it'll be hard to know how to treat an enemy. We're not supposed to "fraternize" with them, and that means, evidently, no conversation, no visiting homes, churches, restaurants, no nothing. We're not supposed to treat them cruelly, of course, though many soldiers don't understand that. They generalize and say we ought to "murder the bastards." With all the news about concentration camps coming out now, it's easy to hate all the German people.

I found a book yesterday that I'd like to keep and show sometime to the people at Wayne. It's called Der Giftpilz *(Toadstool). It's a long series of calumnies on the Jews, telling children how to distinguish them from the "good and decent people" of Germany. On one page the teacher is pointing his ruler at the blackboard and saying: "Die Nase steht wie ein Sechser."*[31] *I doubt if books like this will be needed after the war. But it should be kept somewhere so people will know firsthand what the Nazis were like. And even ordinary people. Already we're meeting foreign workers who say they were enslaved by the Germans and want to go home now.*

And while I'm on the subject of sending, I still haven't received any packages since I came to France, except for an eight-ounce packet of dried fruit from my mother. If the truth were told, I think somebody is dumping them into the Atlantic Ocean. And I could be using the Baedeker you sent me so long ago. Where we're going it would be a big help for all of us, I think.

The next day: *I think I'll write a letter while I'm guarding our half-track, because I might not have a chance to write tonight. I feel silly watching over the vehicle, when the enemy is so far away. But realistically I know that some bastard from another GI outfit might decide they need it more than we do. So here I am, at three o'clock in the morning, sitting in the front seat with my Garand leaning against my knee. They're keeping us pretty busy these days, so I don't have much chance to write. I've been doing a lot of translating, and I still make mistakes, I'm sure, but each day I am getting better. I talked with a priest this morning who showed me where*

---

31. "The nose is like the number six."

the German soldiers had buried land mines. So our vehicles could go around them. And he assured me that there were very few Nazis in this area. Like so much baloney! I bet we can go from here to Berlin and get the same story. But it is difficult. How do you tell if a man's a Nazi anyway? That's one of the things we're trying to find out right now. Searching their houses for things. Interrogating the town officials. And I'm sure it will be a problem for the occupation authorities when the war is over.

Somewhere in Germany, March 31, 1945: *They've been keeping us so busy these days that we hardly have time to sleep or to keep ourselves clean, much less write letters. Our squad is lucky today, though, because we got to sleep later this morning and have some time to ourselves. I think the CO gives us more to do, because we have a couple of good sergeants, and I can handle lots of things that the NCOs are usually used for. The rest of the company had to get up at five, but I slept until 8:30, because I had been on guard from eleven to three in the morning and was really tired. I fixed myself some ham and eggs from our 10-in-1 rations when I got up and felt a lot better.*

We're not allowed, of course, to say precisely where we are, but I think it's safe to reveal that the area stinks—literally. The last part of France I was in was bad enough, with the manure piles in the front yard. But here they have the manure piles, and their houses are attached to the barns. We had to go into some houses for purposes I can't write about, and even their bedrooms smelled of the animals. Ira Strauss pointed out that because of the horses and cows the houses are warmer in the winter. It saves fuel. But at what price? There are some things, though, we didn't see in France—like running water inside the house and electricity. Right now the current is off, because there was some fighting here not too long ago. But the bürgermeister *assures me they are working to restore the service. Incidentally, I'm the one who tells the officials here what to do. And when. Of course, I am just repeating what one of our officers has said. But it does give this lowly private a sense of power when I utter the words in German to the priests and* bürgermeisters. *And they can be very obsequious, even to me! But then they were obsequious to Adolf Hitler, and he was just a corporal in World War I.*

What really astounds me, though, is the amount of furniture and cloth-ing they have stashed away in closets and attics, and most of it apparently never used. Sometimes rooms full. Eight to ten beds in a house with a couple of bedrooms. Are they the haul from years of looting in the rest of Europe? But then they wouldn't be so new. Ira thought maybe they were the result of the many bombings and the destructions of towns and cities. Collecting someone else's house things. Or from furniture shops. I guess I'll never know. But it is strange. And I'm still suspicious.

In the Palatinate, April 1, 1945: *It's Easter Sunday, and I'm standing guard over some public buildings. I'm very dirty, and I didn't get a chance to go to church. In any event, in my disreputable condition, no one would want me in their church. Except maybe God who, they say, is all-forgiving. I think tomorrow they will take us somewhere to have showers,* Gott sei Dank. *On the other hand, some of the fellows think we'll be moving out again real soon. So we'll see. I had hoped to write earlier, but my writing portfolio and bag with the pen and ink didn't catch up with me until a short time ago. I had thought I might get letters, but all that came in last night's mail was the latest* Time. *This copy was for March 26. I still haven't received any packages from you, and only the fruit from my mother I told you about. Maybe the army intends to feed all the refugees from the boxes that are being piled up somewhere. All of my Toll House and Nabisco cookies.*

Today is payday, but alas not for me. I was redlined again when I was made a private. Nobody can tell me when I'll be paid. I do have a bunch of francs I got by trading cigarettes, but of course we can't spend them here. So I might have to start playing poker again. The other fellows were paid in occupation marks, but then with nonfraternization they can't buy anything. It's interesting, though, that the exchange rate is ten cents to a mark. Before the war it was a quarter. I don't know what that means. It could make everything cheaper for us, I suppose, when the fighting has stopped. There's talk that we will also get a ration of liquor, or of wine of some sort. Up to now the only ones to get liquor—from the army, that is—have been the officers. Some of the fellows did 'liberate' some stuff in a liquor shop, but I'm not supposed to talk about that.

I almost forgot to tell you we finally got some Stars and Stripes *yesterday and again today and found out how the war has been progressing. The way Patton has been racing along, I think the fighting here is about over. It seems the Third Army is on its way to Berlin. Wouldn't it be wonderful, dear, if the Russians launched a big drive too and linked up with the Americans?*

News from Marianne at 6210 Payne, Dearborn, April 4, 1945: *I fin- ished up my ironing this evening, and I am in bed as usual, and it's 10 p.m. I'll try to answer the four letters I received from you today. You are right that there is nothing like a lot of mail for boosting one's morale. A letter from you makes the day worthwhile, but four all at once, and I feel like skipping on clouds! I mailed you a package this afternoon with some chocolates, popcorn, fruit, and magazines, and I hope I hear soon that you've received some pack- ages. I've been sending you one each week for more than a month, so you'll be getting them regularly once you receive one, I suppose. Jane dug up some baby's scales, which solves the weight problem—they all weigh five pounds on the nose now, and I never have to repack them. Next week I'll send you some toilet articles that you requested.*

I wasn't criticizing the French people, honey, when I said De Gaulle was in no position to be choosy for turning down Roosevelt's invitation to a conference. Although I agree that most of us are inclined to be intolerant and look down on others because their ways are different than our own. I was peeved at De Gaulle's lack of cooperation. But the same thing is true of Stalin and of Churchill. Each one seems to be looking out for himself and thinking what he can get out of the situation, instead of giving a little for the sake of future world security. I suppose nations, like individuals, will always put first their own interests. But it's hard to see how a lasting organization for world peace can come out of an attitude like that. Unless we can have an in- ternational government strong enough to make an offender behave, even a great power. I'm sure that whatever happens you and I will get along, as you say. But I would like for us and our children to be able to live in a world where peace is assured.

From the Palatinate, April 4, 1945: *Come to think of it, dear, isn't the second Sunday of May, Mother's Day? Be sure to get something for both our mothers. I'd like to send them a present from Germany, though I doubt if I'll be able to find anything suitable. We still can't mail packages, so the few things that I want to send I'll have to hang on to for a while longer. Any- way, it's hard to acquire things, because we are not allowed to buy them from civilians, and looting is—of course—verboten. (Incidentally, there were ru- mors that some escaped Russian prisoners were looting in a town not too far from here. But when I checked it out, I found it wasn't true. In fact, I couldn't find any Russians at all.) About all I could send home would be military equipment that we found or took from soldiers, such as helmets or weapons. I don't suppose you'd want an almost brand-new German helmet, dear? It even has a bullet hole through it! To put on our mantel some day as a memento?*

Two days later: *I'll write this afternoon on the pieces of stationery you sent me, honey. I don't think I'll need any more for quite a while. I found a lot of onionskin paper and some ink in a bombed-out building that had until recently been the* bürgermeister's *offices. I tried a little bit of the ink, and so far it seems to work OK in the Parker 51. What I do need, though, is envelopes and several 6¢ stamps you could put in your letters. I have several German stamps, but they're no good now. Anyhow, I decided to save them for my collection. And by a curious coincidence, all of them have Adolph Hitler's picture on them. Not a popular image right now.*

I told you we can't mail any packages home right now, so the books I meant to send you I put in my duffel bag. It stays back of us, somewhere in France, I think. It also has some of my clothes in it, and some things I don't want to lose track of. I found a good copy of Mein Kampf *in Merzig. It seems to be a present to a recently married couple and doesn't look used at all. Probably people buy them for show purposes and to impress the officials, and not for reading. Maybe some day when things aren't so hectic, I can put the books in a box and ship them all home.*

As I said, the towns of Germany seem to be more modern than those we've come through in France. And they have real toilets. Though they're shaped somewhat differently from those back home—with a flat place where bowel movements can lie intact and be examined, maybe, before they are flushed. And poked at, to see if they are gesund, *I imagine. Dr. Basilius used to talk a lot about the German mania for things being* gesund.

The people here are much more like Americans in appearance, which surprised me. I had always pictured them like in the movies, the men stern-faced, and the women fat and blonde. But there aren't many men at home now, only the old ones. The girls are beautiful, more so than in France, and they take good care of their hair and are well groomed. But very few in this part of the country are blonde, with that Nordic appearance I had expected. I was surprised that some of them, at least, have silk stockings. The fellows keep talking about what they would be doing, if it weren't for the nonfrat-ernization policy. But as far as I can tell, they've obeyed the rules, despite the temptations. At least in our outfit.

I was talking with a Belgian soldier today, and he said the German women were all putains, *who could be had for a bar of chocolate. But I haven't heard it from any American source. The people don't seem too hard off. Perhaps food is a problem now, from what I've observed in the houses we've taken over for a night or two. On the surface they don't seem too un-friendly. Not that they wave at us as we go through their towns, like the French people. But they do try to be obliging—or I should say, obsequious. A little girl said to me today, ungrammatically, albeit succinctly: "Mir nichts Hitler haben!" I wouldn't want to trust them very far, though. Not yet.*

Questions from Marianne on the home front, April 6, 1945: *I re-ceived your letter saying you are now "somewhere in Germany." I'd been ex-pecting news like that, because of the hints you've been dropping lately, but I had been hoping it wouldn't come quite so soon. I assume you haven't moved very far into Deutschland, because the latest letter I have from France is March 26, and this one was dated the 28th. I still don't know where you are. The newspapers haven't mentioned the 13th Armored yet. The Allied armies are speeding along so fast they are more than half way across Ger-many by now, so I think you must be somewhere in the rear.*

We were pretty stupid to be so far off on where you were in France. I guess I was looking for subtle hints and overlooked the obvious. The apple trees and the cider. But then I didn't know much about the geography of the country. I'm sorry you didn't get any of my boxes before leaving France. And now it will probably be even longer before they catch up with you. The war news does sound good every day, doesn't it? We are going faster in the Pacific than I ever thought we could—and also in Germany. The latest news now is that the end of hostilities in Europe will be declared when the Russian and American armies are joined. And that could be before you get this letter at the speed they're advancing.

Yes, dear, it does embarrass me somewhat to put the words from This Is My Beloved *down on paper, knowing they might be read by someone who is censoring my mail. It isn't a book we'll want to leave lying around for our children to see, is it? At least until they are grown up enough to know what life is all about. But I'm glad you gave me the book for Christmas, and I'll continue to put a selection in each letter I send you. P.S. I'm glad you are a Pfc. now, dear. Does that make any difference in what you have to do?*

During the last week of March 1945 General Eisenhower made a significant decision to change Allied strategy in Europe. Instead of driving on to Berlin, as the British general Bernard Montgomery had planned, the main thrust would be farther south, in the direction of Leipzig. In any event, the Russians were only thirty miles from the German capital, and were preparing to invest it. The British protested, but to no avail. To precipitate a race between allies, so Montgomery could reap the greater glory, was imprudent, and would only serve to irritate Stalin. The American planners believed they would be needing the assistance of the Russians in the final campaigns against Japan.

Meanwhile, the American Third and Seventh Armies had been assigned the task of clearing out the Saar-Palatinate and eliminating the last German position west of the Rhine. Once across the Rhine, George Patton's Third Army would head north in the direction of Kassel, led by the battle-hardened 4th Armored Division. Montgomery had conceived a huge assemblage of forces somewhat like the D-Day attack, with lots of artillery and air support, to be the first commander to cross the Rhine. Instead, infantrymen of the American 9th Armored Division approaching Remagen stumbled on an intact bridge and were across the river before the Germans could destroy it. Two weeks later Third Army units of the 4th Armored Division crossed silently at night and were on their way to Kassel. The next day Montgomery had his whoop-de-do engagement, but by then it was an anticlimax. The headlines belonged to George Patton. And the 13th Armored Division remained in the Saargebiet to protect the tunnels and bridges of an important rail line bringing supplies and replacements from France to the Third Army.

As we moved forward our orders were to be on the lookout for Nazis. But also for any evidences of Nazism and to destroy them—placards, signs, pamphlets, and especially books, anything with a swastika on it. Or a picture of Der Führer. To impress the citizens of the town, and to show them we meant business, we were to bring everything to the public square and burn it. As the pile got bigger and bigger, I could see that the men had no idea what was dangerous and what was not. Very few of them, of course, could read German. And swastikas were everywhere. I knew it was ridiculous, but when generals tell you what to do, you do it. And don't ask questions. Aloud, anyway.

For me it was an opportunity to find interesting and useful things to send home. Children's fairytales in the local dialect. A *Grosse Duden* and a German dictionary published in the 1890s, both in pretty good shape. Ten books in all. I couldn't carry them with me, but I thought I might be able to put them in my duffel bag to be sent home later. If it caught up with me again, that is. What a shame, I thought, as a sergeant poured gasoline on the heap, and the collection went up in flames. I had had so little time to search through the pile. The people of the town who walked by tried not to look in that direction.

On a farm near the city of Kirn one of the men in our platoon found a motorcycle without wheels hidden in a haystack. Lt. Locke told me to ask the man where they were. The farmer shook his head. He had kept them from the Nazis for years, he said, and he sure wasn't going to tell us. He would be needing the motorcycle, he said, now that there was no longer any fighting in the area. Tell him we'll be leaving soon, and that we'll bring it back, said the lieutenant. So I brought the village priest as a witness and assured the farmer in my best classroom German: "Ich geb' Ihnen mein Ehrenwort dass wir Ihr Fahrrad zürichbringen werden."[32] For a couple of days Lt. Locke zipped around on the motorcycle, having a great time, and as we loaded up for what lay ahead of us, he was still riding it. "Are you going to give it back, sir?" I asked him. He looked at me as though I were out of my mind. "Hell no," he said. So much for a soldier's word of honor. We were getting ready to join the Third Army again and to do battle with the enemy. I will say, though, that for years we had been told of the atrocities the

---

32. "I give you my word of honor that we shall bring your motorcycle back."

German people inflicted on other peoples and were reluctant to do good things for them.

On April 6 our division was ordered to proceed to the vicinity of Alsfeld in the Hessenland south of Kassel. We were to relieve the 4th Armored Division and spearhead the drive of Patton's army in the direction of Leipzig and Chemnitz. We would be—it seemed—the first Americans to meet the Russians face to face. We asked Cherwatuk, who was Ukrainian, what to say, and he told us something like "yuk-sheh maish." ("How are you," he said.) There would be a lot of picture taking, and perhaps our photos would be in the newspapers. Sergeant Bundy reminded us that there might be some serious fighting on the way, but we tried not to think about that eventuality. It was a formidable task, but that was what we had been trained to do, for so many months and even years, most of us.

We pulled out shortly after midnight, and at 6:35 of the following morning our half-track eased its way onto a pontoon bridge and crossed the Rhine at Sankt Goar. By now there was no resistance. We drove all day on the Autobahn, through Limburg and Giessen and talked about the 4th Armored. "Tough," said someone. They had turned things around at Bastogne in the Battle of the Bulge. The Germans called them "Roosevelt's Bastards."

But then, for whatever reason, our orders were changed. We wouldn't replace the 4th Armored after all. In retrospect I would think that the generals, George Patton himself perhaps, preferred not to rely on untried troops to lead his army in the race to beat out Montgomery. Let the fellows of the 4th Armored reap the rewards of final victory. An official history of the last days of the European war indicates that we were to turn about and to join the First Army of General Courtney H. Hodges, now fighting in the Ruhr area. We would give an "armored component," to the XVIII Airborne Corps, headed by General Matthew B. Ridgway. The next day—April 8—we loaded up our half-tracks, and the following morning we headed south and east through Marburg again and then Siegen to an assembly point near the Sieg River. The going was slowed by heavy traffic in both directions and damaged bridges that had been sabotaged by retreating Germans. The generals must not have counted on that when they drew their targets on large pieces of paper and added a lot of arrows.

Our "baptism of fire." That's what the historian called it. On April 10 we were to pass through troops of the 97th Infantry Division and drive rapidly on the flat terrain close to the Rhine to get behind the Germans who were opposing the 8th, 78th, and 86th Infantry Divisions. A "lightning advance," somebody said. General Hodges thought in terms of a quick "mop-up" to release most units for the drive to the East. It didn't work that way. The men and equipment of the 13th Armored were "worn out" by the two road marches, to the Kassel area and back, with no time between for rest or for servicing their vehicles. And Ridgway was equally insistent. He refused to approve a halt in the Siegberg area before the attack so we could regroup and coordinate our tactics. And inadvertently he slowed our attack by directing the men of the 13th to "destroy" the enemy.

General Wogan, who had never led troops into battle before, took that exhortation to be a command. "Destroy," to him, signified staying in one place until the enemy was totally eliminated—which ran counter to traditional armored tactics that involved driving ahead and leaving the "mopping-up" chores to the infantry. Moreover, rains that turned some of the back roads into muddy sloughs hampered the attack. Units lost contact with one another, and some were lost. One of our three combat commands never showed up until it was too late.

On April 12 Ridgway told Wogan what he really intended, and the following morning this information was passed on to the officers of our 16th Armored Infantry Battalion. Late that evening we reached a position opposite Cologne where we should have been a day earlier, only to find that units of the 8th Infantry Division had already occupied that area—without help from the armored forces. At that point the Reserve Command of the 13th Armored Division that included our battalion was attached to the 8th Infantry. The rest of the division proceeded north along the Rhine. On April 15 General Hogan, who had been investigating a roadblock that was holding up the advance, was shot and seriously wounded by a sniper. He was replaced by General John Millikin, who shortly before had been removed as commander of the III Corps of the First Army, because his superiors thought he was doing a poor job.[33]

Against sporadic resistance our battalion proceeded northeast from Bergisch-Gladbach through Hückeswagen and Gevelsburg, then west again, rejoining the rest of the division north of Düsseldorf on April 17 and connecting with the Ninth Army. It was now only a matter of dealing with the thousands of German soldiers who were surrendering. The next day the united division received orders to move to the vicinity of Freudenberg with the mission of supporting the military government in that area. Then the 13th Armored would rejoin George Patton's Third Army, which was on its way to Bavaria.

Personal memories: Someplace, I don't remember where, we were held up by machine-gun fire. We couldn't tell where it was coming from. But I do recall feeling this is silly, someone could get killed. Why were we moving up? It's interesting that I was not afraid. Rather, I felt as though I were part of an invisible chain of compulsion, some people ahead of us and some behind, all moving forward. We had no choice. Each time anyone crossed the road there was a burst of fire, and bullets kicked up shards of concrete. Now it was my turn, and as I ran my belt got twisted, and the bayonet in its holder slipped between my legs, tripping me up. It was almost laughable, and certainly ridiculous. Nothing like the real soldiers you saw in Hollywood movies.

Down in the ditch on the other side, where I had tumbled, I saw an American tank coming right at me, buttoned up so the fellows inside couldn't see me. I jumped up on the road again, with another burst of enemy fire, only to see the tank right behind me. It was tilted, as the rear end was still in the ditch. Suddenly its 76-mm gun fired right beside me, or over my head. What a noise! My ears rang. And all the while our platoon sergeant, Edward Levandoski, was banging the side of the tank with the butt of his rifle, and hollering at them to be more

---

33. Charles B. MacDonald, *The Last Offensive* (Washington, DC: Office of the Chief of Military History, United States Army, 1973), 362–68.

careful. When it was over, we all laughed. We never did find out, though, where the MG fire was coming from. But the platoon shot up a lot of houses in the town, trying to stop it.

One night they put us infantrymen on the outside of the tanks to guard them from ambushes. We had always thought the tanks were there to guard us. I remember the feeling of panic, in the dark, trying to hide behind the gun turret, as we barreled down a side road to someplace we weren't told about. And later, in Bavaria, I was on guard often—by myself—in the middle of a woods. I dreaded every strange noise. I think it was the dark that was so fearsome, not the situation. In the light you can see everything that happens and do something about it. At night any noise might be an unseen enemy.

Renewing communications with home, April 18, 1945: *I'm sorry, honey, not to have written you for so many days, but circumstances beyond my control have made it impossible. I probably won't be able to write too often still, but I'll try to write as frequently as I can. Our mail situation has not been so good either. I had four letters from Mother and Eileen yesterday and today, but I haven't had any from you for more than two weeks. Oh well, I suppose in a short while I'll get another big batch of mail. And maybe some packages too. None of those have arrived as yet.*

I had hoped to get the book you sent me, but now I doubt if I'll need it— in the near future, anyway. Perhaps some time later it'll come in handy. I won't make this a very long letter because the things we are permitted to say are very limited. I think they'll let us say we are giving the Germans hell, so I'll say it now. Loud and clear. Things haven't been awfully bad, though, and I've been fairly safe so far. Don't worry about me too much, but keep saying a prayer now and then. It helps, I've found.

I feel pretty clean now, having washed and shaved yesterday for the first time in a week or so. I had a couple of pictures taken of our squad, and I must say we looked pretty rugged. Like the movies about men in Alaska during the Gold Rush. We had the picture taken just before we cleaned up. Whenever we stop long enough I'll have the roll developed by the PX and send you the positives. I have just one more roll, so if you can

The Company C squad in Germany.

*find some somewhere, I would appreciate it. I know .35 mm films are hard
to get everywhere.*

*I've been picking up a few souvenirs lately, besides the books I mentioned
before. I have a couple of Luger pistols .38 caliber I took from two officers
who were surrendering to me. Also a small .25 caliber French pistol I found
in a house we were looking through. I carry a couple of the pistols and let
Campey carry the third. I'd give it to him, but I promised to save one for my
brother John. And another for Allen, if he wants it. I'll have to ask Mother
about that. He's still pretty young, though after all he is in the navy where
everybody grows up quickly.*

The next day, April 19, 1945: *We had mail call a short while ago, and
there were a couple of letters from you, one from Eileen, three copies of* Time,
*and a five-pound package from my mother, the first since we came overseas.
It was mailed March 9. My sister has been writing me pretty regularly these
days, which pleases me very much. She said Mother's asthma has been bothering her, but perhaps when the weather gets warmer there it won't be so*

bad. Mail is going out in less than an hour, so I'll make this letter short. I'd like to write to Eileen also, to thank her.

I feel pretty good these days about the war, and even being away from home and all. I got a good night's rest and slept until 9:30 a.m.—in a real bed, wonder of wonders. And I took advantage of this little break in our activities to have a bath and do my laundry. The day is very sunny, and I can hang out my things to dry. The people in this house don't have a real bathtub, so I used their laundry tub full of hot soapy water. I must say I seldom have had a better bath. It made me think of my uncle Frank Hall in West Virginia, who worked in the coal mines and took his baths in the kitchen. He always seemed so happy to us kids, except when he whomped my cousin Franklin, because he didn't keep the cows out of the potato patch.

From what I've seen of Germany so far, I don't see why they fool around trying to rule the rest of the world. The next time anyone tells me the Krauts need Lebensraum, I'll tell him bullshit! Most of their countryside is in forest—half of Germany maybe. The country is the most beautiful I've ever been in, I think. The women are really super women, *their houses are modern and well-built. What the hell do they want? We finally got some newspapers today with details about Roosevelt's death. I hope Truman is man enough to step into his shoes. Perhaps only days from now we will see the end of the war here. I hope though that the German civilians don't give us trouble. There are signs everywhere announcing "Wir capitulieren nie." So we'll see. P. S. Here's a paper dropped from Allied airplanes to help the Krauts decide to surrender.*

A stopover, April 20, 1945: *This morning I had to go to battalion headquarters for an I&E lecture on what will happen to Germany when the war is over. It was interesting, but I think the officer emphasized the wrong points. Then this afternoon I had to give my own lecture to the fellows in C Company. They asked questions, and there was a lot of give and take. I'm thinking more and more that teaching history might be a lot of fun.*

We're staying at a house here on the outskirts of a town, and the farmer has a small garden. He's living someplace else, but he comes back every day to tend his garden. I had always thought the Germans were modern, but maybe with the war and all, they can't get fertilizers. Anyway, he opens up his cesspool and gets human excrement to put on the garden. Does it stink around here then! Worse even than a manure pile. And I would think it's not a sanitary way to grow things. Campey says though that the germs are the farmer's family's germs, and we'll be gone from here in a day or so. So we don't have to worry about it. Still, I would as sure as shit hate to live my life out in the middle of a latrine.

In your letters you are always hoping that I'll be staying out of combat— in a nice, quiet rear area, or someplace doing occupational duties. I have to admit that I've been pretty lucky for nearly four years. But eventually they caught up with me, and since I left France I've had to do that for which I have been training since June of 1941. Maybe you have guessed by now that we were in the Ruhr for a while? It was in all the papers, I think. No combat is easy—it's people shooting at each other. But this time it was far from the hell many of our troops have taken, with so many casualties. Did you read in Time *about how the enemy surrendered in droves? Well, it's true. You might have thought they would fight hard for cities like Remscheid or Düsseldorf, etc. that we went through. But once they were cut off, they gave up, mostly. They did "capitulate," after all.*

Mostly, that is. It isn't so bad when they just walk up to you and surrender. Those are the "pretty good" Germans. (To the GIs a "good" German is still a dead German.) But what pisses me off now, and all the rest of us, are the bastards that shoot at you until you overrun their position, or they run out of ammunition, and then come out, hands high, shouting "Kamerad!" It's hard to take prisoners like that. I know there are supposed to be international laws, but where were they when the Germans were attacking Leningrad? They know the Americans are soft-hearted, in the main. But sometimes it seems we shouldn't be. To see the fellow next to you get shot one minute, and the next minute they are hollering "Kamerad!"

Did you read in Time *about the liberated prisoners and slave laborers wandering all over Europe? We captured one town where there was a large prison for the French who had to work in the Ruhr industries. As we moved down the street in our half-tracks they all came out of their barbed-wire homes and cheered us as we passed. It gave me a lump in my throat to think of all these people being free to go home after five long years in servitude. We tossed them packages of cigarettes, and they cheered all the more. I wonder what all the German civilians thought about what they had done before the end of the war. "Nicht Nazi!" they all said, and it was all right what they had done. It was always somebody else who had committed the atrocities.*

I told you about Cherwatuk, the fellow in our squad who is Ukrainian. Well, he has talked with Russian and Polish refugees. They tell the same story as the French and the Dutch. They have had to work 13 to 14 hours a day, seven days a week, for four or five years, for which they got two meager meals per day and 30 marks a month (about seven dollars, I figure). Germans doing the same work get 300 to 400 marks. The refugees tell of being beaten if their work didn't suit the Superman. The Superman who now says "Kamerad," and bows and scrapes in a most obsequious manner. One Squarehead who spoke English, with a British accent, told me: "You've won the last round, and we've lost. Just bad luck!" As though it was a game of cricket! "Bad luck," he said.

And now that the war is over, we'll forget what they did to the Jews, the Poles, the Russians. Forget Lidice. These people are just like us, they say. Like Mr. and Mrs. Schultz back home in Detroit. Our next door neighbors. They're just like the Americans. In a pig's eye, they are. They're butchers. I wish the folks back home could see this country we're in now—the work-slaves, wandering around, hoping to get home somehow. The women wear kerchiefs, most of them have no stockings. Some go barefooted. The men are not healthy looking; they haven't had enough to eat for so long. Some stay here at their work, because they don't know what else to do. And going home to communism might be just as bad. Even the French—three million, it's estimated—can't get home because there are no trains or trucks to get them there.

Because I speak their language after a fashion, the French are sent to me when they are looking for information. They tell me their troubles, how hungry they are, and how glad they are to see us. But what can I do? A lowly Pfc. All we have now is our boxes of K-rations, and often don't get enough of those—when we're moving up so fast. In one place I found a couple of un-opened German mail-packages. Both had cookies in them, and I gave them to a Ukrainian who was talking with Cherwatuk. You should have seen how some Russians fought to take them away. And there was a warehouse full of goods where some Russians were cleaning it out—who can blame them? But some of the townspeople came and chased them out. Cherwatuk

313

and I put an end to that. We threatened the Germans with our rifles and let the refugees back in. Looters, my ass. Liberators is more like it.

In another place there was a Dutchman, all lit up, for the first time in years, probably. He talked and talked—in Dutch—and waved his arms about. A speech full of sound and fury—signifying nothing to us. I told him we couldn't understand, to tell us in German. But he paid no attention. He raised two fingers in the universal V for victory and shouted "Wilhelmina gut!" He held out his arms as though he was embracing his fat vrow *and the three kids he hadn't seen in years. He was happy in his tipsy bravado, and he wanted us to know it. He was free. He could go home.*

And another Hollander in a different town—he talked to me at length in German. I gave him some cheese and a few crackers, more than I could spare. I went without my so-called dinner that day. And I let him take several swigs from the bottle of Cherry Herring we had confiscated from some German prisoners. He said it was the first spirits he had tasted in years. And as we pulled out, he waved and shouted after us: "Amerika prima! Amerika prima!" He was free!

At 11:00 a.m. on April 24, 1945, in Neunkirchen General Patton talked to the officers and higher noncoms of the 13th Armored Division and welcomed them back to his Third Army. Because of my I&E and translating work I was allowed to attend. The general minced no words. He told us that he wanted every German to remember that George Patton had been there. We were not to just go into a town or a village. Shoot up the place first, and then go in, he said. It's safer, and fewer American soldiers would be killed. And the best aiming point for your artillery was the church steeple. The next day the division moved to a forward assembly area, preparing to cross the Danube River.

In the Third Army again, April 26, 1945: *I'm writing this letter at the company Command Post where I am the "runner" for tonight. The weather is good now, and the sun is shining. But for a while this afternoon it was raining pretty hard, and it didn't look so good for sleeping on the ground, which we have to do from time to time. As the dog says, it's "ruff" in the ETO! Actually for the last two nights we slept in a house. I had a reasonably soft bed to myself, with a feather comforter. It's the first time I've ever used a feather bed. It's very warm and really comfortable, though that may be by comparison with a sleeping bag.*

The way we operate this billeting situation is this. When we are going to stay in a town or village overnight, or for several days, the CO looks over the houses and picks out enough for the entire company—one squad in each house usually. Then I do the negotiating. Actually that's the wrong word. I tell the owners "heraus!" Which they do posthaste. So we have our little home away from home for a while. We have a place out of the rain to cook our meals, wash up, and above all to sleep. After being on the move I had a couple of good nights' sleep. Sometimes there aren't enough beds for the entire squads, and we have to throw dice to see who will sleep on the floor in his sleeping bag.

We got the Stars and Stripes *a while ago, and in a way the news was disappointing. I had hoped that by now the Russians and Americans would have been linked up. But I guess not so far. Patton's army is said to be only 35 miles from Austria, so it should be pretty soon. I don't see how the fighting keeps on. And why. The Germans know they can't win, but they keep on shooting at us. And they shell their own towns, destroying buildings and killing their own people. They should realize that they'll have to rebuild all this wreckage some day. They must be insane. There is so much beautiful here that is still being destroyed. On the other hand, maybe it's better this way. Then the German people will think twice before they set out on another war. P.S. The box situation is still not very good, but you might try again to send some cookies, candy, etc. Kozlow's family sends him these large Hershey bars every so often. Some with nuts in them. Could you get any of those, honey? They might be scarce at home, though.*

During the last week of April we crossed the Isar River east of Munich. The Germans had blown up bridges everywhere, sometimes just ahead of us as they retreated. We could see them on the other side of the river, taking off in their vehicles. While we looked for some way to cross over to a town—called Mamming—we flushed out two German soldiers in ill-fitting uniforms. Both seemed to be about sixteen. By then most of the army recruits were boys or old men. They came out of the bushes with their hands up. "Kameraden!" they said, obviously scared. Lieutenant Locke shouted: "Kill the sons of bitches!" We had heard everywhere that the Germans—especially the SS troops—had been shooting their prisoners. But I wasn't going to kill boys, though it might constitute failure to obey an officer's orders. Besides, they hadn't fired at us. So the lieutenant just said "Shit!" And he told us to take their rifles and bang them against some rocks and then throw the weapons in the river. I told the boys to go past us and find someone else to surrender to. They thanked me profusely and called me "Herr" several times.

Because of the melting snow in the mountains the water level of the Isar was high and the current both cold and swift. We might have waded across, holding on to parts of the bridge that were sticking up out of the water, but no one wanted to get his clothes wet. And if you fell off you would be swept downstream. So the entire platoon elected to crawl over, slowly and carefully, on our hands and knees. Up and down, slantwise, up and down the girders, for perhaps a hundred yards, completely in the open and vulnerable. A single sniper on the other side might have picked us off, one by one. There were none. Others weren't so lucky. In Mamming we found that a sergeant had been shot. Through the chest, it appeared. By now it was dark.

Lt. Locke communicated by walkie-talkie with the other side, and the people over there said they would send a medic on a raft. It might take a while, they said. The medics were busy elsewhere. I told the lieutenant I could meet the raft because I was still awake. I was standing guard for two hours and had just been relieved. And most of the fellows were sleeping. We woke up Peters and Campey, and Lt. Locke told them what we had to do. Down at the bridge we found a Russian DP, escaping from the Nazis and trying to get home, and he and I carried on a halting conversation in German. When I said I was from Detroit, he smiled from ear to ear. "Detroit!" he said. "Henry Ford!" Rolling his Rs. He told me he had read Jack London, Theodore Dreiser, and Mark Twain. He had been a teacher before the war, he said.

316

Suddenly all hell broke loose up in the town—tracer ammunition in the night sky and explosions. Like a Fourth of July celebration in the States. We shivered and wondered what was happening. When the medic arrived it was long after midnight, and Peters sent me with him to find out, while he and Campey tied up the raft and brought the stretcher. By now the shooting had stopped. There was a full moon, and the road seemed as light as day. Halfway up we saw some ghostly figures ahead of us. At least a dozen, it appeared. Were they the enemy? I couldn't distinguish their uniforms. I was carrying one of my Lugers, and I thought of throwing it away. We had heard that if the enemy caught you with any of their weapons, they would stick it up your rear end and pull the trigger. But I had given my rifle to the medic, and all I had to protect myself was the German pistol. And maybe they weren't the enemy. I called out: "Kozmac?" That was the name of a platoon sergeant. "Yes," was the reply.

Relieved, we continued up the hill. Just then something black and hard rolled toward us, making metallic noises, and the medic and I dived into a convenient ditch beside the road. Whoom! It was a hand grenade. And whoever had thrown it scurried up the hill. Were they Germans? How could we tell? The medic and I waited, alone in the night with our fears. When Sgt. Peters arrived we let him go up first, to find out what had happened. We found no one.

I knocked on the door of the house where the wounded man was. Silence. I knocked again and hollered: "Kozmac, you son of a bitch, open the goddamn door!" It opened a crack, and two eyes peered out at us. Then they let us in and told us about the shooting. Four of us carried the sergeant down to the river. His face looked very gray, like old putty. And I was surprised how heavy he seemed. He died a few days later in the field hospital. And I never did learn if it was a German or American grenade. The official reports later said there had been three attacks by SS troops. And that our fellows had acquitted themselves well. The men, who had seen some of them, thought they were from the Home Guard. They looked like boys, they said. But if the general wanted to assume we were heroes, so much the better for us. It gave us something to write home about.

View from Hitler's house, Obersalzberg.

The next day we were pulled back across the river to be replaced by part of the 80th Infantry Division. They were all wearing red neckerchiefs, and their clothes looked as though they had never been dirty. We whooped and hollered and used words such as "fairy," but we were glad to see them. After this extremely minor engagement we felt like seasoned veterans. As we waited on a hillside for our vehicles, a German artillery unit somewhere zeroed in on our position. We could hear the captain shouting into his walkie-talkie: "Somebody help us! They're shooting the shit out of us over here!" He must have received some slight wound in the brief bombardment, because later he was awarded a Purple Heart, and a silver medal for high bravery. I never noticed any bravery on his part at the time, but then—as I've said frequently—officers did tend to get more awards than the enlisted men.

The 13th Armored Division was the first American unit to cross into Austria, and our company's mission was to lead an attack on the German town of Burghausen on the border. By now enemy resistance

A French comment.

was practically nonexistent, but there was no point in taking chances, said the lieutenant. "Go loaded for bear," was the way he put it. So each man carried several hand grenades and a belt full of ammunition, in addition to his rifle and the pickmatic. But the bridges over the Inn River at Marktl were down, so we commandeered an antiquated ferryboat, and left our vehicles behind. And we took no food with us. We were already weighted down by weapons. Burghausen was about ten miles away, and none of us had walked that far in a long time. All of us were tired and anxious when we reached our destination. We had never been required to occupy a town as large as Burghausen. But there was no resistance. The Germans had had enough.

We took over a large apartment building so we could sleep. The officers reserved several rooms on the top floor for themselves. A *Bierstube* was on the first floor, and I think some of the fellows helped themselves to some *Brot* and *Würsten*. I also found some jars of preserved fruit in the basement, and that helped a little bit. Among the

Allied bombers have destroyed Hitler's headquarters in the mountain.

enemy personnel were some young women. They told me they were telephone operators, but the lieutenant decided they were prisoners of war also, because they wore uniforms. He took them up to the officers' rooms. During the night I was awakened and told to come upstairs. The women were crying. "Tell them nothing's going to happen to them," said the lieutenant.

"I can't say what's going to happen to them," I protested. "I don't know what will happen to them." I refused to take any responsibility. And I didn't want to know.

News from Marianne on the home front, April 28, 1945: *For a short while this evening we thought the war in Europe was ended. Ellen and I had been planning to go to a movie, but we changed our minds and came home about 8:00 p.m. My folks were very excited, and the radio announcer was proclaiming that this was V-E Day. It certainly sounded like authen-*

tic news. But then Mr. Truman said it was only a rumor, started by some-one in San Francisco. The rumors of peace in Europe certainly are coming thick and fast. But I can't believe that it will be very long before the Germans surrender.

At last I had two letters from you, honey, one dated Easter Sunday, the other April 18. Evidently you were not able to write anything on the days be-tween. You certainly aren't allowed to say much, are you? I don't know how you can fill so many pages, when you're not saying anything! But I am glad and relieved to hear from you, dear. I worry a lot when I don't get letters.

The next day: *Well, honey, now we know where you are—with Pat-ton's Third Army, and from all the news reports lately you have been very busy. Your mother called this evening and said your dad had run across a mention of the 13th Armored in the Sunday* Free Press. *I must have missed it somehow. I'll check and send you a clipping so you can see your division has finally made the news. Now I can trace where you have been for the past few weeks. It looks as though you are so far across southern Germany that you might be joining up with the Russians. In Austria maybe. I'll feel much better about you, knowing the war in Europe is over.*

Somewhere in Germany, Thursday, May 3, 1945: *I have a five- or six-day beard, and I'm dirty all over. Today I saw myself in a mirror acci-dentally, and the shock made me vow not to look into another mirror until I get a chance to shave and clean up a bit. I'm writing this letter in the local Polizeiamt, and when I want anything—water to drink or some coal for the fire—I just send the police chief out for it! And he calls me "sir." So life isn't too bad for this lowly Pfc. right now. I think I'll revel in it while I can. And I don't have to stand KP. (I should have said that the cooks and the kitchens have caught up with us, finally.)*

The news today has really been wonderful, hasn't it, honey? Berlin has fallen to the Russians, Italy has turned over a million prisoners to the Allies, Hitler is dead, and the war is about over, Gott sei Dank. *It's been a happy day for all of us.*

The next day: *As we marched into town we found a large prisoner-labor camp. There were hundreds of French, Poles, Serbs, etc., and they cheered us as we took it over and pushed the guards around a little. The pris-oners were locked up inside barbed-wire enclosures, and they told us some of them had been here for as many as five years. You can imagine their joy at finally being liberated! Lt. Locke, who was now the acting company commander, told me to give one the keys and tell him to wait five minutes to give us a chance to get out of the way. And the prisoners could do whatever they wanted with the guards, he said. But they pushed and shoved and broke out and ran after us, yelling, kissing us on the cheeks, and shaking our hands. What a happy, delirious mob! I can tell you it made us feel pretty good.*

By now, German soldiers were coming into town to surrender by the dozens, and I put them in a Bierstube *and told them to stay there. There must have been several hundred of them. The next morning a Greek came to the* Rathaus *where Lt. Locke and I had an office, and told us there were some American POWs a few kms away, so the lieutenant and I, with several other fellows, went out in two jeeps and a German truck to get them. They had been working on farms and were really glad to see us. It gave me a lump in my throat that made it hard at first to talk with them. They looked in pretty good shape, actually. They said they got more food (such as it was) on the farms than at the Stalag where they were kept. The farmers were pretty decent people, they said. The Americans had just received some Red Cross parcels, so they shared them with us. Imagine prisoners feeding their liberators! They told us one of the guards, who had lost a leg in the war, had mistreated them, and they wanted to shoot him. The lieutenant gave them some rifles, and I heard some shots, so I assume they did.*

Last night I helped Lt. Locke make arrangements for keeping the German prisoners elsewhere, and we put them in a church. I counted about 1,100. By morning the total had reached 2,600—taken by our company and B Company, and we had to use another church as well. Across the river in Austria a Stalag with American prisoners was taken over. A bunch of them are swarming about town just being happy. I think, though, that they emptied all the Bierstuben *of their contents! Several of them stayed at our lodging and listened to the radio with us. Of course, the news made them all the happier.*

Good news on May 8, 1945: *Today is V-E Day, finally and officially. No more 88s to sweat out, no more machine guns. The war here is over. We were in some dangerous situations for a while in the Ruhr, and at first we messed up somewhat. But we learned a lot, and now I think we are a pretty good outfit.*

❧ 14 ❧

Winding Things Up

From Germany, May 9, 1945: *The war in Europe must really be over—officially and in every other possible way. We'll be standing reveille in the mornings, and this afternoon we're having both rifle and person inspections. By the major, no less. And yesterday an MP stopped our jeep to see if we had a trip ticket. I wouldn't be surprised if we had to start polishing our shoes again!*

I'm going to battalion headquarters tomorrow to see if they know anything about the educational programs the army is supposed to set up after V-E Day. I've heard rumors that some men will get to go to universities in France and England. I'd sure like to be part of that. To go to England, if I can, to Oxford or Cambridge. And if I had a chance to go to the Sorbonne in Paris, I certainly wouldn't turn it down. I know I'd have trouble with the language at first, but if I could study something like history, I think I could pick it up pretty fast. I'll let you know what I find out.

The next day: *This afternoon I went to an I&E meeting and learned that some fellows will be going to civilian universities. But the percentages are pretty small. And they'll probably take fellows who already have undergraduate degrees. But I'll buck for all I'm worth, to be selected, and see what happens. I did hear too that some divisions here have already been selected to go to the CBI* [China-Burma-India Theater of Operations], *the outfits that have had the least battle experience here. That doesn't look so good for my chances. In the meantime, I'll keep busy perfecting my command of both German and French. There will be a school program in the division, and if we're here long enough, I'll be able to teach a Spanish or English course, I think. In addition to the school, we'll have an athletic program and a military-training schedule. That will keep us busy as long as we are in the ETO.*

I'm making this letter short because the squad wants me to play a game of volleyball with them. And they need another tall man up front. I haven't played for a long, long time, in fact since we were in Normandy, and I'm not in very good shape. Being in a battle situation doesn't do much to build up a fellow's muscles. More tomorrow, dear. I love you very much.

The next day, May 11, 1945: *You said in a recent letter that you wondered if I'd be able to get out of the army before the war was over. We heard a broadcast last night on the army radio station about the details of the point system for discharges, and I doubt if I can make it before the fighting ends in the Pacific. A man gets one point for each month of service. That gives me— at the end of June—48 points. Then there is an additional point for every month overseas. At the end of June I'll have five more points. Children count 12 points apiece up to a maximum of three kids. On that score you and I draw a blank. At that, though, even one child wouldn't have made a big enough difference for us. As for battle honors, all I have now is the one star—which is the equivalent of five points. There are rumors that we might get a second star for middle Europe, the fighting in Bavaria, so we'll see. Right now— or at the end of June, rather—I would have, at the most, 58 points. And a man needs 85 to qualify for a discharge. So you can see that I am quite a way away from it.*

About my Spanish, I haven't had an opportunity to use the language since I came to the ETO. There's a fellow from Mexico in the platoon named Cantú, but he prefers to speak English. Anyway, the other day I was on outpost guard with José. Our duty was to check the identification documents of German men who passed through an intersection. Enemy soldiers are required to carry a Wehrpass. *Everywhere they were surrendering in droves. But some just changed their clothes and tried to go home. The pass would distinguish military men from civilians. You might think my job was dangerous, but as it turned out, I had no trouble. At least with the identifications.*

Germans seem to obey regulations, even when there is no official government. And I never worried.

But something else more interesting happened at that intersection. There was a Panzersperre—*tank trap—to stop or at least slow down the American tanks. It consisted of about eight large logs on either side of the road sunk upright into the ground—a couple of meters deep. There were a lot of other logs that fitted across the road into the vertical logs. Luckily, they were never used, because there was no fighting in this area. But the people of the village asked me if they could have the logs for firewood. I said it wasn't my wood, and they could take all of it if they wanted to. Pretty soon the whole population was out sawing and digging away.*

But back to Cantú, who has very dark skin. A girl asked me if he was a "Neger." It seems that the Germans are scared to death of the Negroes in our army. She wanted to know if he was böse [bad], *as her soldier friends had told her. I think the reason is that the Germans fought against French colonials, from places like Senegal or the Congo, and the Africans were fierce warriors, I'm told. I told her he wasn't* böse. *By any means.*

The girl is very pretty, about 20—and from Hamburg, I learned later. She had left during the bombings there. She was wearing a thin dress, insecurely buttoned up the front, with just panties and a brassiere underneath. She was sawing wood with an old man I assumed was her grandfather, and with each motion, we could all witness the openings and closings of her dress and the exposure of flesh. And I have to admit that she was stacked like the proverbial brick shithouse. At one point the two were having a lot of trouble with a log that might still have been green. So always the helpful fellow, I offered a suggestion. "Fräulein," I said, "haben Sie eine grosse hache?" For some reason, the French word for axe had come into my mind. She reddened and laughed. "Meinen Sie eine Axt?" she asked. I assured her that was the case. She must have thought I was inquiring about the state of her derriere. That's what I get for being, as you said, a polyglot of sorts. When I told Kozlow later about my mistake, he suggested that it might have been a perfectly understandable Freudian slip on my part. Because of all those priapic logs, he said.

While I'm writing this there's a USO show going on, with girls and comedians from the States, and I'd like to be seeing it. But they wouldn't let me in the door without a necktie. I told them mine was in my duffel bag, still back in France, and they said that was just "tough shit." The general gave orders, they told me. To say I'm pissed off is a gross understatement. Just wait till Patton wants me to do something for him! So here I am, alone in Frau Rommel's living room, listening to music on her radio. Radio Prague, I think. Loud and clear.

Sunday, May 13, 1945: *In one of your recent letters you mentioned that you had baked a rhubarb pie. I don't remember having eaten one, but I think it would be good. While we were still in France, in the small town of Bourdonnay, I picked some rhubarb and cooked it in a C-ration can over our little stove. I used some water and sugar and simmered it a long time until the sugar caramelized slightly. It made a wonderful sauce, and everyone liked it on the crackers that come in our C-rations. (It was from Bourdonnay, by the way, that I sent you the box with the several books. Did you ever get it? You didn't say in any of your letters.)*

I saw the other day in Stars and Stripes *that Switzerland was buying up German marks at 300 to the dollar. So they must really have inflation here in the civilian economy. I wonder if it will get as bad as in 1922–23, when your family came to America. I should think our military government wouldn't allow that. It caused so much trouble then. Some of the men tried to send home money of that ancient vintage, but the censor bounced them right back. It was lucky the officer didn't know where they got them. They might be in real trouble. It seems the lady of the house where we are staying, Frau Rommel, was away someplace, and the fellows were rummaging through her bedroom. She had a large chest of drawers filled with those bills. Thousands of them, they said. I tried to explain to them the history of that money, but they didn't seem interested, so I gave up.*

News from Marianne on the home front, May 13, 1945: *This morning Ellen and I went to the early services at the Lutheran church near my house. This was proclaimed a national day of thanksgiving for the peace in Europe. We have good reason for being grateful that at least half of the war is over, and I pray it won't be long before they cease firing everywhere, and I have you home with me again, dear. By the way, I read today that St. Mary's on Jefferson Ave. is celebrating its one-hundredth anniversary. You went to that church and sang there, didn't you? The "Seven Last Words of*

Christ" at Easter time, as I remember. I suppose that whatever church we decide on, you will want to be part of the choir.

From Germany, May 14, 1945: *After dinner we are supposed to go hear our commanding general talk. No one has said what he will talk about, but maybe it's the point system. Around here that is the one big topic of conversation. We have a new division commander now, General Millikin. General Wogan was hit by some lead in the Ruhr, and he's recuperating somewhere, no doubt. Nobody is unhappy about the situation. Old-timers here say that for some reason Walter Winchell had it in for Wogan. He used to write columns about "Wogan's playboys," vacationing in sunny California. And about the former cavalry officers who lounged around wearing their riding uniforms, their boots, and spurs. Before the division moved to Texas, that is. I don't know if he has written anything about us recently. I do know that the division changed a lot after so many privates—and maybe officers, too—were shipped out as replacements.*

Two days later: *Wonder of wonders! We had mail call just a few minutes ago, and I didn't get a letter from you, but I did have two packages and my* Time *magazine. So it was a pretty good mail call, after all. Thanks very much, honey, for the packages, especially the things to eat. The regular meals here are good now. We have no complaints about that. But it helps to have that extra bit from the PX, or as in France, a half-dozen eggs in the evening. One funny thing at Frau Rommel's—there are some ducks, and the fellows keep following them around to see where they hide their eggs. It's a kind of game for them now. Duck eggs aren't as good as the hen variety, but in a pinch they are better than nothing.*

It's late in the afternoon now, and I have to take care of the washing I did this morning. I can't say I like very much washing clothes by hand with a bar of Ivory, but I guess it's necessary sometimes. It's hard to get laundry soap here, which is why I have done so little washing, I guess. And I have been wearing some of my things a long time dirty. Like the underwear. I hope you sent some in one of your packages. I'm down to the last pair of shorts, and no one knows when, or if, we'll be getting any. I found a German undershirt that was about my size, but it had a swastika on it, and I was reluctant to have the fellows see me wearing it. They might forget the war is over and use me as a target.

And thanks for the clippings. I'm glad to see that the 13th is in the news these days. I heard on the BBC last night that the chief-of-staff of the Hungarian army was captured in Tann, which is just three km from this village. Actually, he just walked in and surrendered to the charge of quarters. There are a hell of a lot of Hungarians around here, and they are getting to be quite a problem. They were out of the war before the Germans, so they weren't our enemies when we arrived here. At the same time, they are not on our side, because up to a few days before that, they were fighting against us. We didn't take any of them prisoners, because we wouldn't know what to do with them. Herding together all the German soldiers is bad enough. And nobody here speaks Hungarian. So they wander around and salute us all over the place. They should just go home and leave us be, but they're afraid of the Russians, they say. I'm glad it's not my problem. I have enough trouble these days, trying to keep my single pair of underwear from falling apart.

More from the Bavarian region of Germany, May 17, 1945: *I'm sorry I didn't write to you yesterday as I planned, honey, but in a way it's your fault. For sending me that Ellery Queen mystery, that is, because once I started I couldn't put it down till I was finished—at 12:30 this morning. In one of your letters you asked if you could buy me some ties and socks for my birthday. If you love me, and I trust that you do, you will never buy ties or socks. Well, hardly ever. They may be perfectly good choices. On the other hand, it's been my experience that women seldom are good pickers of either. Menfolks have learned to their sorrow through the years that at Christmas time or on Fathers' Day the ladies are going to let all sorts of fanciful patterns run amok through their good intentions. The artist's palette pales by comparison. So please, dear, wait till I come home, and you and I can walk through the men's department at Kerns, and I can point at this and that. After all, I did work for over a year at the tie counter, as you must remember.*

From Germany, May 19, 1945: *I waited to write until after mail call, hoping to get some letters—but no luck today. Except for a box of Sanders candy from my folks. That was very welcome, of course, but I think I'd rather have letters these days. Anyway, in a squad of ten ravenous men even a large box doesn't last very long. Especially Sanders candy. And shortly all you have left is a white box and a lot of pieces of crinkled brown paper to dispose of. I think the mail clerk must have alerted Sgt. Peters that the box was coming.*

Though how he knew what was in the package I don't know. Unless he tore open a corner of the paper to see. He was hanging around the barracks when I opened the box, so, of course, I had to offer him some. And then all the others.

We played some softball this morning, the first time since I was at Utah, I think. We just got up a scrub game with one of the other squads. Your husband made three hits in four times at bat, not bad for a decrepit old man, eh? I'll be glad when my duffel bag catches up with me, because I have a pair of shorts in it. I've heard that we are going to be issued German shorts for recreation. The army bought out an entire factory, I think. But from what I've seen, the German variety are baggy and too long. They have funny ideas about what athletic shorts should look like. I think they are more for hiking in the mountains, than for active sports. So, we'll see.

I had to give part of an orientation lecture this morning—extemporaneously. When Pfc. Wood didn't show up from battalion headquarters, and everybody had been assembled in the school auditorium. I talked about the German people for the umpteenth time. Then this afternoon we had a short-arm inspection—everyone wearing raincoats and nothing underneath, while the doctors did their business of looking for evidences of venereal diseases. Quite a show for the villagers, I must say. We must have made a spectacle they'll no doubt talk about long after we have left here. And tell their kids about it.

The next day: *We have a division newspaper called the* Black Cat, *and in today's issue they told about our exploits since leaving the Ruhr. I'll try to send you a copy so you can see how we did. I think the reporters were able to use some of the division papers, and it gave me some ideas. Since I'm not too busy here, maybe I could write something for them. About some of the fellows in our company. Those like Sgt. Peters who got medals, for example. P.S. Almost all restrictions on what we can say in our letters are off now. Even where we are located.*

From Marianne at 6210 Payne Avenue, May 21, 1945: *No letters from you today, dear, but then we learned that mail might be delayed by the movement of troops, prisoners, refugees, etc. around Europe. Maybe that's why the mail from you is so irregular. I'll be anxious to get a letter from you dated after V-E Day. And maybe if censorship is lifted you will be able to tell us where you are and what you are doing. The papers say the 13th Armored Division has been with the Third Army, so I assume you are somewhere in Bavaria. But then you might have moved. And also you might have information about what is next for you. I'll be hoping that you won't have go to the Pacific. Some of the fellows have been having furloughs on the way there. I would love to see you, but I would much rather have you stay in Europe in the army of occupation, if that is possible. So you can use your German. I hate to think about you landing on some godforsaken island—your father called it the "atoll of creation." Ha! Ha!*

From the village of Schildthurn, Germany, May 22, 1945: *This will be a short letter tonight, honey, because it's late, and I just got back from a show. I saw* Here Come the Waves, *with Bing Crosby and Betty Hutton. I enjoyed it a lot. It wasn't the best Bing Crosby picture I've ever seen. But it was a joy to have a look at feminine pulchritude again. Most of the Bavarian women aren't so hot on looks, I must say. And I've been surprised at how many of them work out in the fields—barefooted too. Some with teams of oxen. But as Sgt. Bundy says: "They seem to get prettier every day!"*

Frau Rommel is not here now, though she still has a room upstairs. Her home was in Munich, but because of the Allied bombing there she moved to this village some time ago. I don't know when or where nonfraternization stops, but I've talked with her a lot about her life in Germany. She told me her husband was a cousin of the Field Marshal. She is well educated—at least she speaks English, French, and Italian fluently. And she has read many of the books you and I used in Dr. Basilius's class. But I was surprised by her lack of knowledge of German history since 1930. She seems to know less about it than I do. She didn't know who was chancellor before Hitler (von Schleicher). She didn't know who had been killed in the Blood Purge of June 30, 1934 (Roehm, von Schleicher, etc.). And she didn't know that Heinrich Brüning, the former chancellor, was teaching at Harvard now. Or maybe she just closed her eyes and ears to everything unpleasant that was happening in her country. Because she could do nothing about it.

She was moved (by army orders) to another village, Babbing, about two km from here. There was an ugly incident when one of the fellows went into her bedroom, and she thought he was trying to rape her. Which he probably was. She hollered and woke us all up. But because he was a sergeant, nothing happened to him. None of the privates wanted to say anything about it and get themselves in trouble. While she was here, she kept our kitchen clean, washed dishes, etc. So now we have to do the chores. And as I said, I did like to talk with her. We are scheduled to go to a lake for a few days, I think in Austria. And the fellows say we might be visiting Berchtesgaden on the way. So I'll let you know what happens.

The next day, May 23, 1945, in Dearborn: *Oh happy day! Mail from you, honey. There were three letters, dated April 6th, May 3rd, and May 6th. Also the* Black Cat *newspaper with the whole story about what you have been doing. I haven't worried about you exactly, but I was beginning to get a little impatient. The story explained a few things I had been wondering about—your visiting the city of my relatives and being in the Third Army. We had heard that Remscheid was about 85% destroyed. So maybe, from what you wrote, it wasn't so bad, after all. And your letters about the prisoners you took were very interesting. I read them over the phone to your mother, and I know your father will want to read the article in the paper. Perhaps it's just as well we didn't hear all this before the war was over in Europe, because we would have worried that much more.*

I haven't mailed you the box yet, but maybe I should just pack up your old things and ship them off to you. They'd be better than nothing. But maybe you wouldn't get them before the end of summer anyway. I would think the army should have enough underclothing for the soldiers who are fighting for their country!

From Dearborn, May 30, 1945: *You'll be glad to hear that I finally have some undershirts and shorts for you, dear. They aren't 36, the size you gave me. But they were the only ones I could find, and I looked all over Dearborn and in downtown Detroit. At Kerns I told the salesman you used to work there, which helped, I think. He said he remembered you, and he assured me they would fit someone of your build. Never having bought underwear for a man before, I know nothing about sizes. While the salesman wasn't looking I measured them against myself, just to make sure, and I think they will be okey. Your old trick from San Francisco days. Anyway, they are better than none at all. Right? And they do look stretchy. I'll send them to you tomorrow, with the hope that they arrive before the summer is over.*

You asked me if I'd like any souvenirs, like a soldier's helmet. Thank you very much, but I don't think so. Uncle Bob, Jane's brother, carried home some empty shell cases after the last war—all the way from France. He keeps saying he is going to make flower vases of them. But for 25 years they have been collecting dust in the attic, she says. Which reminds me, dear. Lets build a house with no attic, so we'll never have to face that problem. My folks too have so many things in the attic that they will never use.

The next day in Germany: *Last evening I went to another village with a German friend of mine named Fritz to visit some Hungarians. They had been professors at the university in Budapest, he said. Fritz was a major in the air corps who was severely wounded early in the war and retired from the service. The MPs had taken him into custody, but he must have had a good record, because they turned him loose. He and his wife seem like cultured people, whom you'd expect to see in a city such as Munich or Cologne, not a small village like this. But maybe they came here for the same reason Frau Rommel did. He didn't talk much about his past, except to say he had been a student at Heidelberg. He was interested that you and I had taken that course with Dr. Basilius, and we talked about* Tonio Kröger *and* Die Brücke.

Mostly I wanted more practice in speaking German—that's the main reason I agreed to go with him. And, I suppose, curiosity too. I wanted to know what the Hungarians were like. And their universities. But they kept talking about the Russians, whom they both hate and fear. The Americans, they said, must join the Germans in protecting Europe from the "barbarians." But I didn't want to deal with that question, so I kept trying to change the subject. I must say that my command of the German language was taking a beating. And finally I told them that the Russians and Americans were allies—it was a fait accompli. *Period. And I left and walked home by myself. In a way, though, the Hungarians were right. Once the communists have control of a country, I doubt they'll let it loose.*

And the next day, June 1, 1945: *I just got through playing six games of volleyball, and for some reason my hand is shaking. We were playing against the anti-tank platoon who are about the best in the battalion, I think. And maybe the whole division. One of their players was an all-state basketball player in Minnesota. I usually have to play against him, because he's so tall—I think I told you we don't rotate positions. It was a real battle, with lots of bodily contact. They usually whomp us, but today we held our own, and won half of the games. We thought it was a moral victory, anyway. It's getting to be a ritual. The anti-tank fellows come and stand under our win-*

dows at Frau Rommel's house. They holler their challenge: "The third pla-toon runs rabbits, eats shit, and barks at the moon!" We denied that we ran rabbits or barked at the moon, and the warfare would begin.

Two days later, June 3, 1945: *Today was a very lazy on-again-off-again day, and now the sun is shining. I'm sitting in Frau Rommel's kitchen listening to good swing music from the army radio station in Munich. About the only thing useful I did was to read a P. G. Wodehouse book,* Hot Water. *It was pretty good, though not one of his best. I think people underrate him sometimes. He writes so many books. But if you look at his prose, you have to admit his use of the English language is tops. Or should I say "British English?" The book belongs to Frau Rommel, and it was printed in Germany—in English, of course.*

By the way, I was talking with her the other day, and she told me her fa-ther had been ambassador to France at the time of World War I. And her brother was ambassador to Ethiopia and then Chile. But he left Chile in 1943, she said, I suppose when that government broke relations with Germany. Oth-erwise, Chile couldn't join the new Organization of American States, I read in Time. *She didn't say what he is doing now. I was curious too about her hus-band, but I thought it better not to ask her—whether he was still living or not. And also if he was in any way involved in the plot to kill Adolf Hitler. And the Field Marshal committed suicide. That would be a very interesting story.*

The next day, after volleyball: *A great victory! This evening, after supper, we played volleyball and beat the anti-tank platoon two out of three games. And both of my shins are bloody again. Some of our men won a lot of money betting on us. With good odds. I guess we just didn't want to let them down. And now I am going to lie in my bed and listen to the Munich GI station, which has all the best radio programs from back home. And with no ads. Can you believe it? We're really living it up these days!*

From Schildthurn, June 16, 1945: *Today's* Stars and Stripes *has a story saying the 13th will be going to the CBI by way of the United States. So now, honey, it's official, and we can stop wishing and start planning for it. You haven't submitted a treasurer's report recently, but I would think we'd have enough to have a really good time, bother the expense. I know you're concerned not to use it up "foolishly," as you say. But if, for example, you could meet me in Chicago, and if we stayed at the Stevens for only a couple of days, I don't think it would break us.*

The next day, from Marianne in Dearborn: *Today is Fathers' Day and I decided to take your dad to a baseball game. But the Tigers were playing out of town for a couple of days, so I sent him a card and enclosed a note saying I would like to escort him to Briggs Stadium on Tuesday. That is, if he is free. Ellen said she would like to go some time, so she will be joining us. She and I had planned to go biking out at Rouge Park today, but it was raining—as usual. So we just stayed inside and talked and didn't get much done. If this kind of weather keeps up we might as well plant a rice crop, because there doesn't seem to be much hope for our victory garden this year. We've had some vegetables, but the only thing that's really flourishing is weeds, weeds, and more weeds. I wish they could invent something to just get rid of them without so much work. Some kind of spray.*

A relative of mine—Uncle Albert—came over this afternoon and stayed awhile. He is my father's cousin. But they're not very close, and I've seen him only a few times in my life. He's old, about 64 or 65, and has never married. He was born in what is now Lithuania and is of Russian extraction, as are my father's parents, I suppose. So you'll be interested to know that our children will have some Russian blood in their veins.

The next day, June 18, 1945, in Schildthurn: *I had to give a talk this morning on "Fascism." I dwelt on the causes of Fascism in Germany and Italy, and then showed how it could happen in the United States. It was a lot better than my earlier talks, I think, perhaps because I was more prepared and familiar with the topic. I feel very strongly about the home-grown variety that might crop up after the war if we're not careful. People like Father Coughlin in Royal Oak.*

A letter from home brings lots of news from Marianne, June 19, 1945: *I took Sarah out to a show this evening. She's leaving Friday for Denver where she will be going to school this summer, and I wanted to meet her and say farewell. She has resigned her job and says she's not coming back for a while. I hope, though, that it's not permanent. She has been an important part of my life. We saw two very good pictures at the United Artists. One was* The Enchanted Cottage *with Dorothy McGuire and Robert Young. She is supposed to be ugly, which is hard to believe. But it was wonderful still—all about the magical powers of love. I hope some day I can see it again, with you, dear. I know you will like it as much as I did. I didn't ex-*

pect much from the second film, Pan Americana. *But it turned out to be pretty good. I liked the music, and especially the Spanish dancers. They did a snake dance that was very realistic.*

Also Jane and I had a very busy day. Because tomorrow is my father's birthday, we shopped for a present for him. And we drove out to a little poultry farm on Outer Drive to see what we could find to fill our kettle tomorrow. We were very lucky to get a couple of chickens. They are scarce these days, the meat situation being what it is. I have been doing most of the shopping of late. I find it amusing—and sometimes frustrating. Shopping, that is. Soap, meat, and potatoes are high on the list of things you talk about in whispers in the grocery shop.

Yesterday, for instance, I could see there was no laundry soap on the store shelf, but I thought it wouldn't hurt to ask Ray about it. He said: "No, we haven't had any for a long time. What kind do you use?" I told him. That was all that was said, but on our way out, a sack was dropped quietly into my shopping bag. And sure enough, I found some Rinso when I got out to the car. It must be hard these days to be a grocer and still keep your friends.

My dad had a nice birthday. I gave him a tie and a shirt, and he didn't complain about it. Like some people I know. Also I baked his favorite cake— white with coconut icing. Barbara Jean sang "Happy Birthday," which pleased him very much. Kay told me that Bill has gone overseas now, which surprised her. But the papers say that all men now in this country will be going to the Pacific. They didn't leave here until after ten, and I took them home, because my dad hasn't much gas till his next coupon. Jane went along so I wouldn't be alone driving back. And she doesn't get out very much. I've been pretty lucky about the gas situation. Because I'm not teaching, I don't have an allotment for the summer. But I have some C-gas left, and if you come home soon we'll be able to drive. I believe you will get an allotment of gasoline for 30 days, and I'll save what coupons I have in case we want to take a little trip.

News from Schildthurn, June 20, 1945: *Now it can be told—we're coming back to the States before very long! Of course, it's been in the newspapers and on the radio for some time now. But for us it's been a military secret. We will be going first to Camp Atlanta, a new redeployment center near Reims and Vitry-le-François. According to* Stars and Stripes, *we should be there from ten to fifteen days. And then we'll be sent directly to a port, I would imagine. The voyage shouldn't take as long as the trip over, because we won't be in a convoy this time. It'd be nice to sail on a big vessel like the "Queen Mary"—a five-day trip. I wouldn't be seasick for so long! We'll probably be in the States for a few months (very few) of training. Mostly for amphibious landings, I would imagine.*

The next day: *They tell us we will move to France in boxcars—you know, those 40 & 8s of World War I fame. Forty* hommes *or eight* chevaux. *We've seen them in lots of movies. But those boxcars are so small, I don't think they can fit forty American men in them. Maybe we'll have to sleep standing up! But the main thing is that I will be coming home.*

Our battalion commander said that while we are in France, he will try to see that every man who has not been to Paris gets the opportunity to go there. I'd like to very much. There are so many things to see. But I've heard it costs an arm and a leg to see the town, and I have no desire to spend money I could use better at home. The fellows who have been to Paris say it's not safe to be on the streets after dark. The women grab you as you come out of the hotels or restaurants, and practically rape you on the spot. A lot of the fellows I know here won't fight too hard, I imagine, to resist the young ladies' blandishments.

From Dearborn, June 24, 1945: *Only a short note this evening, because I'm very sleepy. I just got back from Wayne where I was writing the final exam in my Psych. class. It wasn't as bad as I expected, or maybe I knew more than I thought I did. The test certainly was comprehensive, though. We started at seven, and only two people left before nine. I didn't finish until 9:30, and I had writer's cramp long before that. If I passed, it wasn't because I had studied much for it. In fact, I took only ten minutes in the hall to look over my notes. I doubt if I'll get an A this time. Or if I deserve one. And I still have to write a paper, before I can get a grade for the course. The professor gave me a four-week extension to turn it in. I don't think I'll be taking courses at Wayne next semester. My teaching job is enough, I think, for a change.*

Two days later at Camp Atlanta (BQ): *I don't know what to write you tonight, honey. I have so many letters from you—nine of them—that it's hard to decide where to start. Besides, I am tired after riding so far in that boxcar and then the French train. As it turned out they put only 25 of us in the boxcar, so it wasn't that crowded. But it was difficult to stretch or to move about. And, of course, there were no toilets. From time to time the train stopped at a station to let the men heed the call of nature. But in one station—somewhere in Germany—there were hundreds of Russian DPs [displaced persons] going back home, who also had stopped. It seemed to us that they were all crowded into the men's room. Both males and females. We could see the urinals, but couldn't get close to them.*

And then the whistle on our train blew, and the bell clanged imperiously, and we had to get back on without accomplishing our mission. Some of the fellows peed on the tracks before they got on, but most of us couldn't bring ourselves to do such a barbaric thing. It was one thing to do it in France at the side of a country road, and quite another right in the middle of a large German city. We just hoped we could hold it until the next stop. And if not, someone could slide the door open a little bit and hope there wasn't too much wind.

We should be back home about the middle of July. From a port on the East Coast I'll go either to Indiantown, Penna. or to Fort Sheridan in Chicago. If the former, I'd like to stop in Akron to visit with my folks. And you can come down, with my father and mother, if possible, for a family get-together. I'll call you from the port station, probably Camp Kilmer. Also you'd better have some money available, in case I arrive home on a weekend, and the bank is closed. Most of all, I want to be with you every minute possible. We know now that the furlough will be a full 30 days! And the army pays for the train fare, coming and going.

You asked in one letter how the men could talk to Germans when there was a nonfraternization policy. Maybe it hasn't been in the papers at home, but it seems those policies are not being carried out. Stars and Stripes *says that 99% of the cases are not being reported. The generals were unrealistic when they laid down those rules. Right or wrong, the policy will have to change, I think. As long as the soldier has his needs, and the Frau or Fräulein is willing to satisfy them, they're going to get together. Every outfit I know about has the same problems—if it really is a problem. An army report says the women are "frustrated" by being away from men for so long. And because of war casualties, there are now in Germany a lot more women than men. Anyway, most of us will have left Germany before too long, so if it is a problem, it will be only for the military-government people to deal with.*

337

Camp Atlanta, July 2, 1945: *We were supposed to leave tomorrow to go to a port, but they've told us we can stay here until Saturday, or even later. I'm glad, because now I can go to Paris. They've started to go in groups of six from each platoon this morning. We're supposed to leave at 0600 in trucks and get to Paris in about three hours. Then we'll have all day to look around, and start back at 2130. As you can see, it doesn't give us much time. But at least I'll be able to tell our grandchildren that I "saw" the great city. The fellows that are going with me want me to stay close, so they can accost the ladies of the night— that is, those who ply their trade in the afternoon. I told them they should take the Metro to the Pigalle, and they'd have no trouble at all. But after much persuasion, and offers of some Hershey bars, I agreed to take them to the Metro station and see that they took the right train. I told them, though, that after that they were on their own! Then I'd go visit the famous churches and take pictures of the Champs Elysées, Arc de Triomphe, Eiffel Tower, etc.*

Memories: It was late in the evening as we entered Le Havre. The city was alive, bursting with noises. There were lights in buildings everywhere and tricolors over doorways. Cars were honking their horns. People leaned out of windows, waving at us. A grateful population, I thought, was thanking us for driving the Germans out of their country. I waved back, as did the others in our truck. Then a young woman threw a bucket of water. Almost as though she was aiming at me. I was drenched. Some gratitude! And the noises increased. Church bells were ringing. And for some reason I looked at my watch. It was after midnight and now the 14th of July. Bastille Day—the first since the liberation from Nazi rule. That's what they were celebrating. Not the GIs. But I wondered about the bucket of water. Was she saying: "I'm glad you are leaving?" Or was it just a harmless prank? I'll never know.

The voyage back—the southern route—was much more pleasant than the January crossing through cold and troubled waters. And I can recall only one incident. For the first time in my army career I volunteered for an unpleasant job. It all began when we were ordered to turn in the weapons in our possession. They would be tagged and put in Cosmoline to protect them from the salt air, we were told. We could understand that.

But then came the shocker. No one could take back more than two pistols. And I had three, two of them promised to my brothers. We all knew the reason. Many of the officers had been so far back of the fighting that they had no trophies to show to their loved ones, and they wanted one weapon, at least. But I had four years of army experience behind me, and I knew how to get around regulations. On the last day before we docked they said they needed someone to wipe off the Cosmoline. I raised my hand. I worked all day, skipping my noon meal, and as I got to the little French .25 caliber, I cleaned it and stuck it into my pocket. And no one was the wiser. With that important job done, I claimed the two Lugers with my name on them. All was right and fair in this world. We were going home. For a month, that is. Then off to the war again.

On August 6 and 9 atom bombs were dropped on Hiroshima and Nagasaki that destroyed those two cities and most of the populations. At noon, Tokyo time, August 15, 1945, the Japanese emperor announced the conclusion of hostilities between his country and the Allies. The war had been ended without an invasion of the main island. We could really go home now—by way of Camp Cooke in California. It was just a question of how long we would have to wait. And that depended on how many points we had.

In September the people of California showed their appreciation for our contributions to the war efforts. The mayor of Los Angeles proclaimed a "Thirteenth Armored Division Week." Governor Earl Warren awarded the Black Cats a Certificate of Merit on behalf of the people of the state. "California's Own," he said. Then the movie stars played host to the division with an all-star show in the Hollywood Bowl that featured Orson Welles, Eddie Cantor, Bob Hope, Frances Langford, Kay Kyser, Edward G. Robinson, Dinah Shore, and Lionel Barrymore, as well as a host of lesser luminaries. All of this for us soldiers. We had returned in triumph to a state that years earlier had given birth to our division. And if they exaggerated our accomplishments, what did it matter? The war was over, and it was a happy time for all of us.

Robert E. Quirk, a corporal once again.

❧ 15 ❧

The Final Days

Chicago, August 28, 1945: *I'm writing you from the USO at the Union Station while waiting for the train to Camp Grant. We were due here at nine, but were 40 minutes late for some reason, so I'll have to take the 11:30 p.m. train. I'm OK—or I should say, not too late. Since the war is over, I don't think anyone will get upset by just a few hours. I've talked here with several of our men from the 13th AD, and none of them seem worried.*

I see by the Chicago newspapers that men with 60 points won't have to go to the Pacific, for which many thanks to God and to the newly found wisdom of the US army! I hope to get out by the first of the year, but so far that seems unlikely. At least I should be able to start classes in the summer session. I'm sorry I didn't have more time at the station in Detroit to tell you goodbye, but we seemed so rushed in those last precious minutes together. And in any event, you know what I wanted to say, don't you, dear? That I love you, and that I will be thinking of you each minute until we are together again.

The same day in Dearborn: *Well, dear, here we are again—you're back in the army, and I'm writing you once more. We are lucky to have had such a perfect month together. And though I will be missing you very much, we know now that our separation will be short, and that our future looks bright. Don't worry about the car—or about me. I didn't have any more trouble. The tire was fixed, and I got home in plenty of time to have supper with my folks. Jane says she knows that both you and Bud will be home quicker than*

341

*you think. And she is rarely wrong when she has feelings like that. I tried
calling up your family several times, but they must have gone somewhere,
maybe to a late show. So I'll try again in the morning.*

The next day, August 29, 1945, and Marianne sends news: *It was
nice, dear, to hear your voice again and to learn that you will not be going
overseas. With your 67 points it shouldn't be long before you are back with
me. And spending some time in California shouldn't be too bad. Before long
you will be in civilian clothes and enrolled in Economics 201. And maybe a
course or two with Dr. Basilius. Do you think it's too early for me to start
apartment hunting? And where do you think I should be looking? While you
were home you said it might be nice to be near Wayne. On the other hand, I
need to be fairly close to my work, so I can go from school to school. I would
like also to be close to Jane, in case she has any sort of trouble. And I think
places might be less expensive in Dearborn. At least, I can look in the newspapers and get some ideas about the cost of an apartment, before we have to
make a decision.*

*Today I helped Jane wash clothes and then cleaned house. And tomor-
row I'll do the shopping for her. On Friday I have an appointment with the
doctor for a checkup before I start school again. I'll let you know what I find
out—whether to expect an addition to the family. Or maybe it's too early for
that. Right now I'm tired, so I'll close with this one page. I think it's better
anyway, to write short letters every day.*

The same day at Camp Grant: *Being here again makes me think of
those days more than four years ago, when I got on my first troop train. So
much has happened, hasn't it, much of it to the good? And I think that later,
when I am home, I can look back and say I'm glad I was in the army. I complained often, as you well know, but for a lowly Pfc. I think I have accom-
plished a lot. And I'll be a far better student with my many experiences.
Thank you for loving me, dear, and thank you for all the letters that have
kept us together for these many years.*

The next day, August 30, 1945, in Dearborn: *If it wasn't too hot
while you were home, the weather is certainly making up for its unusual
pleasantness. I've been going through the house in shorts, with my hair
pinned up, and carrying a glass of lemonade, trying to find a cool place to*

write. As of now I'm out on the back porch, where there is a breeze of sorts. But it's still as hot as all get-out. So if you see blotches on the paper, you will know that it is honest sweat. But then, I suppose it will be even hotter where you are going, so I should just shut up about it and get to writing. This morning I received the letter you wrote me from the Union Station in Chicago. That was good news about the sixty points, wasn't it. So now I can stop worrying about your going to the Pacific like Bill Rollo.

The next day: *Another hot day, dear, and Jane and I have been sitting in the living room just melting away. I spent most of the day ironing, I took her to the hairdressers, and then I went to the doctor this afternoon. There is nothing wrong with me, he said, and I'm not even going to have a baby. Darn it! He gave me a prescription for some vitamin tablets and told me to eat lots of butter, cream, and other fats and get lots of sleep to build up my resistance. So we'll see.*

More from Dearborn, September 1, 1945: *I just got home a little while ago, and I sat in the parlor and talked with Jane—mostly about our plans and hopes for our future. By the way, thanks again for fixing her radio set. It's so hard these days to get anyone to come to the house for things like that. We heard the broadcast of the Japanese official surrender. That makes it more definite, doesn't it? But I've read that some of their soldiers have kept on fighting on some of the islands. The announcer said they will pay attention to the emperor now. So we'll see.*

Camp Cooke, September 3, 1945: *I'm sitting here at a desk in the Service Club, trying like mad to write with this damned SOB of a pen I "borrowed" from Allen. No wonder he didn't take it with him. It's called Inkmaster, and you have to mix the ink yourself. He sure paid a lot of money for it. I'll be going to the PX this afternoon to see if I can get me a Parker 51. It would cost me even more money, but I'll know it's worth every penny. I came here because I'm staying away from the barracks as much as I can—so the first sergeant can't find some chore for me to do. Like KP, most of all. The main problem is that as fellows with the most points leave to go home, there are fewer and fewer here to do the dirty work.*

People say that before the war ended the army had planned to have us stay here for six-months training in amphibious warfare, as I thought. Then they would take us across the Pacific in LSTs [landing ship tanks] *(sixty days) and land us on the coast of Japan. On D-Day plus four. They expected casualties in the tens or hundreds of thousands for all our forces. So we can thank the atom bombs for saving a great number of American lives. We talked about that on the train coming out here—whether the bombs should have been dropped. The consensus was that we were sorry so many "innocent" civilians lost their lives. But were the American soldiers "guilty" of something? Were our lives less valuable or less worth saving? You take a young man of from 18 to 30-some years old, and put him in a uniform, and then it's OK to shoot him.*

And were the atom bombs that were dropped on the Japanese cities so much worse than the firebombing of Tokyo? Or Hamburg and Dresden? After all, the Japs started the war by bombing Pearl Harbor. And the Germans shelled the towns and cities of England. So I'll just be glad I'm coming home earlier than I expected and leave the explanations to the policy-makers and the theologians. And to the historians of the future.

Later the same day: *As you can see, honey, I have acquired a new pen—which cost me the sum of one dollar. I don't know how long it will last, but at least it writes better than the blasted Inkmaster Allen paid $20 for. And the fellow at the PX said they might be having a shipment of Parker 51s any day now. So I'll keep checking there every day or so. And it won't be long, anyway, before I'm home and won't be writing you any more letters. I doubt if they'll be giving us any military training here, so I'm planning to spend a lot of time in the base library, getting ready to go back to Wayne. I checked it out this afternoon, and it seems to be very good. I figure if I read up on enough economics here, I won't have to take Econ 101.*

When the library closes, I think I'll go see a Shirley Temple show, "Kiss and Tell." Everyone says it is good. It's funny, when she was little I hated her films, especially when she danced and had ribbons in her hair. And the way she talked. But now that she is a teenager, she is much more simpática.

The next day, September 4, 1945, from Marianne in Dearborn: *The news gets better all the time now. It was announced officially today that the point score for going overseas has been dropped to 45. And it would seem that pretty soon the fellows in the high sixties will be let out. I hope so, anyway. Jane says that Bud is not so lucky. He has only 41 points because he was drafted fairly late, and he is 33, which means his age won't send him home. He does think though that the 20th AD will not be going to the Pacific after all. It doesn't make sense, he says, to send so many fellows and their equipment—tanks and things—all that way, when there is no war.*

This was opening day at school, and as usual nothing much happened. So far as I know, there are now just three members of our department, Doris Cuthbert, Ann Thorne, and me—instead of the five, as we had expected. I don't know if there isn't money enough or if they just couldn't find anyone. They haven't given me my assignments as yet, so I'm not going to worry about it. But I don't see how it can be done. Some of the kiddies will have to be shortchanged. Or else I'll be awfully busy when you come home. So we'll see.

The next day from Dearborn: *After reading what your division's assignment might have been, I certainly thank God that the war has ended. I must say that you and I have been very lucky throughout these four years. And although you have been gone a long time, and we have been apart, you haven't been in danger for more than a few weeks. Do you have any idea, dear, what you will be doing at Camp Cooke now. A lot of I&E work, I would suppose.*

From California, September 5, 1945: *I'm trying out the Inkmaster pen again, so don't be surprised if I suddenly leave off and switch to the dollar pen again. If I didn't have to return the Inkmaster to Allen some day, I would have thrown it out the window a long time ago. But in a way, I hate to give up on a project, and I keep thinking I can figure out how to mix the ink. More water or less water, different temperatures, etc. It's a challenge for me.*

I wish I could be getting out now so I could start back at Wayne in the fall term. It makes a lot of sense, because I'll be doing nothing important here. But I've been reading that there are various problems, with important people and institutions pushing this way and that. Some in Washington think that "dumping" too many servicemen on the job market too soon would lead to a lot of unemployment and misery. And the transportation people say they can't handle the millions coming home on busses and trains. I guess I can understand that. But I still want to leave here as soon as possible. Let them pack us all on a train like a bunch of sardines. I certainly wouldn't mind sitting on my baggage.

I did go to the show last night and saw Kiss and Tell. *I must say it was one of the best I've seen in a long while. It was very funny, and at the same time risqué. The fellows did a lot of clapping and hollering. I kept thinking the Hays office must have been asleep at the switch, letting so much slip through. Maybe little kids shouldn't see it, but even a teenager wouldn't be corrupted by it. As I said, Shirley plays the part of a 15-year-old, who is supposed to be pregnant. We tend to get films here before they come to Detroit, so maybe you and I will be able to see it together when I come home. To laugh a lot, but also to think about serious questions.*

From the Service Club, September 6, 1945: *Just a short letter tonight, honey, so I can go to the PX and pick up a few things and then to bed. I worked pretty hard this afternoon for a change, and I'm tired. Besides, we have to arise at 6:15 for reveille, if you please! And next week we will be going out on the range to fire our rifles. Maybe to see if they work. I had thought for a while that the war was over. I suppose the general thinks we might get into mischief if we have too much free time on our hands. Which is probably the case with some of the fellows. They're starting to play a lot of poker again, even in the daytime. On government time.*

I decided to get a three-day pass this weekend to go to LA. It's not my favorite place to go, by any means, but SF is too far. And besides I don't have much money to spend. I won't get paid, of course, until the end of the month. I'll be able to sleep at the USO, and I can go to shows—I missed a lot of movies while I was in the ETO. And there is usually a lot of traffic on the highway, so I should be able to hitchhike both ways. The main thing is to get away from camp duties for a few days. From what people are saying, I doubt if there will be a 13th AD very much longer. Now that they don't need divisions any more, it will be broken up and the low-point men sent to the Pacific somewhere to goof off for a while.

From Dearborn, September 9, 1945: *Kay and Barbara Jean were here to help us eat a large turkey my dad had brought home. The biggest I've ever seen. He says he bought it, but Jane thinks he won it in a raffle at the Catholic church. She says he spends more money that way than if he went to the supermarket. But then he does have a lot of fun playing the games. Because she couldn't handle the turkey, I did most of the preparation, the stuff-*

ing and all—though she gave me directions as we went along. With the lights on in the dining room, it was just like Thanksgiving around here.

Which makes me think, dear, wouldn't it be wonderful if you could be here for the real holidays. It will always be so special for the two of us because that's when we began to think we might be in love. I did, anyway. You said nothing about it then—only that I should put my little fingers in the teacup instead of sugar? Remember, honey? And if not Thanksgiving, almost certainly by Christmas. Wouldn't it be wonderful if you could go shopping for gifts with me?

Kay told me that Bill has been assigned to a mapping unit in the Philippines. He says he wouldn't recommend it as a place to live. At least for very long. It rains day and night, and the mosquitoes are big, plentiful, and voracious. The fellows have to keep taking pills, he said, because of malaria. Thank God, dear, you won't be sent out to all that misery. Not to mention being shot at by the Japanese. Lately I've been thinking of taking summer courses at Wayne and getting serious about a master's degree. What do you think about that?

And another day: *I've been listening to the 11 p.m. news, and everyone in Congress is getting excited about demobilization. That's all right with me, because that's what I am most interested in too. I've been thinking it might be nice to go house-hunting together. But on the other hand, I'd like to be able to move in soon after you come home. I was talking to Doris Cuthbert about her apartment—she's paying $65 for three furnished rooms in Dearborn. Most of the furnished apartments I've heard about are much more than we expected to pay—with my salary and what you would be getting with the GI Bill. What if we rented a small unfurnished place, and then bought a bedroom suite and some pieces of living room furniture with our savings? What more would we need? I think kitchens usually come equipped with a stove and a refrigerator. Jane says she can give us pots and pans and some dishes to get started. I suppose we can know better, though, when we see what there is for rent.*

I know now what my teaching schedule will be, and I don't like it one bit. I'll be taking four schools in the West section, and the Maples and Woodward jr. highs in the East, so I guess I'll be kept very busy. I don't like giving up schools and the kiddies I'm familiar with, but I'm the one who goes to West Dearborn, because Doris doesn't drive. Which means my getting up earlier in the morning and driving long distances in all sorts of weather. I guess speech correctionists are hard to find right now. They say at Wayne that most of the university graduates are being taken by hospitals, especially because of the increases in cases due to war injuries.

More from Marianne in Dearborn, September 13, 1945: *My new schedule at school isn't going to be so bad, after all my worrying and complaining. I like the west-end schools I have been assigned to, and the principals are nice, cooperative people. And I have several cases that are interesting. Two of the schools are way out in the country. It's a pretty drive, out and back, though there might be problems when it snows, because of the narrow roads. One of the schools in southeast Dearborn is newly built to take care of the transient population that moved here during the war. There are only five rooms and the clinic—no principal. The teachers are girls just out of college. And very nice, all of them.*

The same day in California: *There has been a big change in my life here, honey, and I am very excited about it. I told you earlier that I had written an article for the division newspaper, about fellows in our platoon. Well, someone in battalion headquarters must have seen it and liked it, because the major called me in and asked if I would be interested in writing a history of the battalion. It seems they will be putting together a book about the 13th AD, with pictures and text of our operations in the ETO. Of course, I said yes, so I went this morning to the major's office to work through the records. I said I might not be here very long, but that my work in journalism classes and on the* Collegian *had prepared me to write things quickly. He told me he was pretty sure I wouldn't be leaving before the end of October. So far it's been interesting to read battalion materials that have a different perspective from my own. Oh yes, they also asked me to be the battalion reporter for the* Black Cat. *So I should be pretty busy, all in all.*

The next day, September 14, 1945: *I wish I could have been there to help you eat the turkey. And perhaps I'll be home by Christmas to help you prepare our own bird. I would think though that we might start out with a chicken or a duck that we could roast in the electric oven my parents gave us. I think I'd even rather have a duck, anyway. For me it has more character than a turkey any day. How does that sound to you, dear? I might even cook it myself, if you don't mind, that is.*

I've been thinking of one problem, though, with your working five days a week. You tell me that you are looking forward to preparing meals for the two of us. But would you have enough time? So what would you say if I was self-sacrificing, if I did some of the cooking? Getting things ready for you when you came home. And even experimenting with some dishes I read about somewhere. In France or in Germany. Or making up the recipes. It sounds like a lot of fun to me.

Also, I think it wouldn't be fair to have you working all day and then doing all the housework. I would be willing to take over some of the chores. I know I'll be busy with my classes, but much of my school work can be done at home—writing term papers, etc. I have had a lot of experience, cleaning the barracks and all.

In Dearborn, September 15, 1945: *I went shopping this morning and got some woolens to make two skirts with. I met Marion Sheppard downtown, and she said to be sure to tell you hello. Verne Gibson is in Japan, and she said that Hortense Groves had married somebody whose last name is Young. She didn't know his first name, but you might remember him, she thought. I also deposited $50 in our bank account, so we have exactly $700. It should be about $800 when you are discharged. I'm glad we didn't have to spend as much as we thought while you were home, though I might be sorry I didn't buy that formal we talked about or get to go to Chicago. We can always go there some day when we are settled down.*

The same day at Camp Cooke: *This will be a short letter again, honey. I have guard duty this weekend, and I'd like to get a good night's sleep tonight. As good as possible, that is, with all the noise that goes on around here. The end of the war has brought about an understandable lack of discipline, but still there should be more common sense. It's almost as bad as the old coke-bottle brigade. I'll sure be glad when I am home in my own room—"our room," I should say, and I can sleep at night.*

We were up and about early this morning, as usual, and I went to the battalion headquarters to check on their records. Then I walked down to the 45th Tank Battalion to see their after-action reports, because C Company was attached to them most of the time in the Ruhr, and I want to make sure

I present a well-rounded account of that battle. I also went to the division headquarters to see the editor of the division newspaper and let him know I'm going to be the 16th AB reporter. I also took my war pictures to battalion, and several fellows there asked if they could have copies of them. I told them the negatives were at home, but I guess if they want to use them for our history book, I should send for them. Could you pick out those that I took in Europe, and send them to me, honey? And be sure to wrap them well in Kleenex so they don't get damaged in the mail. Thanks very much.

The next day at Camp Cooke: *Is there anything you'd like me to buy while I am still here? I've been looking around, and there are some Cannon towels and wash cloths at the PX that are a lot cheaper than any place outside the army. Before I get my discharge I plan to buy up a lot of things, like razor blades. They don't cost so much any place, but as we start off our life together, even small savings are important, I think. As usual, there is a lot of noise around here. There is a poker game going on, and everyone has to react when he wins—with some shouting. Also the losers, as well. They've been tempting me to join them, but I said I was too tired. They said how about tomorrow, and I said maybe. But I feel that my good luck might be over. And thinking of all the expenses we'll have when I come home, I don't want to take any more chances. The stakes are just too high these days, with fellows throwing ten dollar bills on the table. I wonder where they get the money.*

September 19, 1945, from Marianne in Dearborn: *Concerning our financial situation, I'd better tell you what my salary is and what we can count on. During the summer I was getting $155 dollars each month, after all deductions. But it seems that the summer pay is always a little higher than the year-round pay, for whatever reason. My pay check for September was $138, so that is what I'll be getting each month until next summer. Every summer I assume I'm getting up in the world, and then BANG—in September I am right back with the proletariat. (My actual salary, according to my contract, is $242.50. Then the deductions jump in, income tax, retirement fund, summer pay, and the war bonds.) In the fall, I think we will cut out the bonds, and I will be getting a small travel allowance to help pay for my transportation. It doesn't sound like much, does it, honey? But with* the $85 Uncle Sam will be paying you, I think we'll be doing quite well. I'm not worried, anyhow.

You can have anything you like for Christmas dinner. With the help of my handy cookbook, I should be able to roast a duck with no difficulty. We can invite your folks over to celebrate with us, or my folks—or even both. Then we might have to roast two ducks, I suppose. It should be quite a festive occasion. It's very good of you, dear, to be self-sacrificing and offer to cook. I have no doubt you could do it. And I will let you in the kitchen now and then. But that's my territory, and I'll do the cooking, if you please, at least for the first five years. Anyway, I know you will be busy trying to catch up with your work at school.

And I would think that taking care of an apartment would not be too much work, especially since no one will be there during the day. My job is better than most, because I have Saturdays free, and most days I get out early. I'll probably wash and clean on Saturdays. Right now my school hours are from 8:30 to 4:15. It's going to be changed soon to 8:00 to 3:45—but that's fine with me. I drive out to the west-end three days a week, and it takes me about 20 to 25 minutes, and ten minutes to the Woodward school on the other two days. I think we should be able to have supper about six. I usually eat my lunch at school, except for the days I help Jane with the wash or take her to the hairdresser. All in all, we'll be able to get along very well, I think.

I have been wondering about Jane, though, and I suppose you have been too. She couldn't manage without help, and I really hate to leave her. I know my dad would like to have Kay and Barbara come to stay with them. So perhaps they will, at least until Bill comes back from the Pacific. Kay doesn't have a job and would be more help to Jane than I can be. And Barbara will be going to school before very long. It would be nice for her if she could get a start at least in the Dearborn system, which I think is better than the Detroit schools. They get so much support from the Ford family.

The same day in California: *I've been thinking more about our housing situation, and I think it is probably better if we got an apartment in Dearborn, as you say. If we found something fairly close to Warren or Schaefer Rd. I could easily take the streetcar or the bus and ride to Wayne. And if we could get an unfurnished apartment for—say—$42, it wouldn't be so* *bad. That is, if the kitchen things were furnished. I have some things at home I can bring—a chair and the desk I always considered mine, but that's about all. I don't suppose any of the stuff at your house belongs to you, does it? You might let me know how things are progressing as we get closer to the time of my discharge.*

So you saw Marion Sheppard the other day. We always had a fine time on the Collegian, *she and I and Verne Gibson on the sports section. I don't suppose she is still there. Or any of the people from that time. Unless some of the serviceman are coming back. It will be almost as if it is a new generation, with different experiences from ours, maybe even different values. It should be interesting. What do you think of my plans for the future—graduate school, the teaching profession, or the diplomatic corps? Or working for the* Free Press? *Maybe I shouldn't rush into anything until we've had a chance to talk over all the possibilities.*

The next day, September 20, 1945: *Even better news, honey. From the paper today, men with only 60 points will be eligible for discharge on the first of November. So it looks as though I might be home before Thanksgiving, after all. Oh happy day! I'll write more about the prospects tomorrow, because I'm tired and it's late. I just got back from seeing a movie,* The Isle of the Dead, *with Boris Karloff. Very scary, and one of the best I've seen for a long while. But before I forget, will you send me a money order for fifty dollars as soon as you get this letter? The PX is having a sale on good watches, and if I don't hurry they might be sold out.*

More from Camp Cooke, September 21, 1945: *I'm down at the Service Club this afternoon, so I'll write you now, instead of waiting until tonight. I should be working at the battalion, but I have been waiting for some information from a couple of companies that are dawdling about sending me things. I'm not worried about getting this history project done, because I've been told it should be limited to 1,500 words, and for me that is no problem. Besides, if I finish it too quickly, I'll have to go back to the company, and there's the chance—the certainty, really—that I'll be put on details again like KP or walking guard.*

I've been looking here through all the men's magazines to see the latest in men's clothes. Not zoot suits, of course! It seems I should be able to get a good suit, fairly conservative, for a little more than $50. Then some black shoes *will cost me about $10. My brown shoes are still okay. With a good shine they look almost new. I'm not sure about a top coat, whether I can still wear the one I left at my folks' home. I have put on a few pounds, as you know. If so, I still think that with a couple of ties, a sweater or two, a few shirts—a dollar and a half for each—and socks, it shouldn't be much more than $150. And shopping at Kerns with my discount will be a big help.*

Tonight there is going to be a bull session or maybe a round table about the soldiers and labor. It's a subject I have a great interest in, and I should be there to insert my two cents' worth into the discussion. One of the speakers is a friend of mine from Utah, Fred Hackett. I'm eager to know what he will say, and what his political leanings might be. It could be a controversial subject.

My birthday, September 22, 1945: *Well, here I am 27 years old, and I don't feel any older than I did yesterday. Of course, there is no cake or candles, and no one out here knows what a momentous day it is for civilization. Some day they will be sorry they missed it. I'm down at the Service Club again, this time to talk with a captain from division about something or other having to do with the book I'm working on. Actually, I came here to "hide out" again, because the battalion is having an inspection I want to avoid. Otherwise, I would have to be working on my clothes, shining my shoes, and all those things that are now completely unimportant in the history of mankind.*

The bull session, "The Veterans' Stake in Labor," was interesting, but I didn't learn anything. I did talk for two minutes about a statement by one speaker that the labor unions were full of racketeers. When I asked him to name them, he said "Browne, Bioff, and Scalese," which is about all anybody can name.[34] I said I could name three crooks in industry, but that didn't mean all businessmen were racketeers. When I got back to the barracks I had a discussion with some of the fellows in our platoon, and I gathered that most soldiers believe that an unskilled laborer shouldn't be paid a decent, living wage. There's a lot of bitterness here about the various strikes around the country. It makes me wonder about how much—or little—many Americans value the lives of people around them.

Later the same day: *I'm about ready to go to bed, but I want to write you this short letter. Not that I will sleep much. The fellows are playing poker*

---

34. George E. Browne, Willie Bioff, and Gino Scalese.

again, and I expect we will have mayhem in the barracks. But I wanted to thank you for the birthday present that arrived today, right on time. Especially the tie, though of course I'll not be wearing it for a while—until I get home probably. And I take back all I said before about women's choice of men's clothing. Again thanks.

I got a German grammar book from the library here, and I'm going to try to refresh my memory. Already I am getting a little rusty. When I get back to Wayne I know there will be some required courses, but I would like to take a German grammar and composition course. I inquired today about working full time on the division paper. I think that would be more helpful to me than the I&E work I have been doing. I know there is a chance the division will be breaking up. But before it does, I'd like to be attached to some unit in the meantime.

The same day in Dearborn: *This will be a short letter, because Kay and Barbara Jean were here, and I drove them home a short time ago. Coming back it was storming and raining so hard it was difficult to see where to drive. In fact it was scary at times. And knowing our headlights, you can believe that they weren't much help. My dad has been saying I should take care of such things, but I keep putting it off, because I hate to spend the money. One of these days, though, I'm going to treat our old car to all the things it needs—headlights and adapters, tail wiring and light, right windshield wiper adjusted, seat covers, ignition lock repaired, floor covering, and new tires. If I do it now I might have to go into our saving account, but my dad says he worries every time I take the car out. He has offered to pay for it, but I'd rather not be dependent on him for anything.*

The next day, September 23, 1945, at Camp Cooke: *I've just been taking it easy all day, resting and reading some German literature. And now I will answer your letter of last Wednesday. As far as I can tell now I am almost certain to be home by Thanksgiving.* Gott sei Dank! *Nearly all the men with more than 80 points have already been discharged—except for a few whose records have been lost. All of them seem to be from the ASTP. And I can imagine a lot of pissing and moaning about somebody's inefficiency or carelessness. I sure hope I'm not one of them. If everything goes OK, though, I should be leaving shortly after November 1. The discharges are being handled now by battalions instead of the division, so things should be going more quickly.*

I was wondering too how Jane would make out when you leave her and your dad. I could see when I was home that she doesn't get around very well. I don't know much about Parkinsonism, but I think I read somewhere that there is no cure for it. Your dad doesn't seem to realize how bad off she is. I would think he could help her somewhat around the house. Or at least get someone to do the cleaning. I hope Kay and Barbara do come over, at least until Bill comes home. But what then? I remember your telling me about how devastated your dad was when your own mother was ailing and then died of cancer. And now, maybe, he has to go through that agony again, with Jane. I hope when I'm home we will be able to help them. But your job keeps you busy, and I'll have so much to do at Wayne to catch up with all I have missed while I've been in the army. Somehow, though, we should be able to figure something out. I hope so, anyway.

Camp Cooke, September 25, 1945: *I can't write much now because there is going to be another GI Forum tonight at the Service Club. This time on race prejudices, especially Senator Bilbo's "Dear Dago" letter. You probably read about it. It should be interesting, because a lot of the fellows here are from the South. Even from the senator's home state. And they share his prejudices, I think. So I don't want to miss it.*[35]

The same day in Dearborn: *I'm sorry I haven't been able to send you the money order for your watch, honey, but I'll do it for sure tomorrow. I haven't been in East Dearborn during banking hours lately. You asked if you should be picking up anything there at the PX. It seems a good idea to get a watch that will last you a long time—and maybe things like percale sheets, if the PX would have some. Also a wool blanket. Your G.I. blankets are okey, but only temporary. I prefer white, if you could find one. Also I could use a few linen dish towels. But maybe you wouldn't have room for that in your duffel bag, with all your books.*

More from Marianne about cars, September 26, 1945: *I thought I could write you a long letter tonight, but once again I have been thwarted. I was going out after dinner to get your mother something for her birthday,*

---

35. Senator Theodore Bilbo of Mississippi wrote to a young woman of Italian descent who had criticized his policies, addressing the letter "Dear Dago." He also addressed a Jewish protester in New York as "You Kikes."

and the starter button wouldn't work. The motor made no noise at all, and nothing happened. My dad gave me a push to a nearby gasoline station, but they didn't have anyone who could work on it. So I had to take it to an all-night garage where they have repair parts. The man wasn't sure whether it needed a new starter, and I left it there so the boss could work on it tomorrow. I'll have to take a bus to the Oxford school in the morning, and probably hike to the Edison school, because there's no bus service out there.

Damn! Damn! Damn! Excuse my English, dear. If it isn't one thing, it's another! Every month something comes along, without fail, to put a hole in my budget. I've decided making budgets is just a waste of time, because I never spend my money for things I think I'll be spending it for. Maybe, though, when you come home we can do some more realistic planning together.

The same day in California: *The bull session last night wasn't as interesting as I thought it would be. The same people come to meetings, with the same ideas and opinions, and no one seems to want to engage in a discussion. They are thinking more about going home, or baseball scores, or their girl friends, than talking about important issues. And I must confess that I was glad to go back to the barracks early and try to get a good night's rest.*

About those GI boots I left at home for you to send to me, I think I'll just leave them there. They aren't much use to the army, and would be thrown out anyway. Besides I can use them when we go hiking or if there is a lot of snow. I can wear my civilian shoes home, and nobody will care. Or notice, probably. The army says I can keep one suit of Ods [olive drabs], one of suntans, an overcoat, and all my socks and underwear. If I want them. No one said anything about my field jacket, so I'll just bring it home also. It will be very useful to wear in the fall.

Now I'm going to read a mystery story, because the fellows are having another poker game, and I couldn't sleep anyway. How can they play, day and night? But maybe they're tired of the things we read about these days. Like all the problems in the world. And the strikes. How wonderful it will be when I am at home, and quiet is the order of the day. Or the night, I should say.

The next day, September 27, 1945: *You don't need to worry, honey, about my discharge being held up by the history project. Nothing would stop* *me from leaving when they tell me I can go. Actually, though, I finished it today, and it just has to be retyped in the battalion office. I'm glad it's done, because I was tired of stretching it out. Don't tell anybody, dear, but I don't think it's very good. I didn't have enough time to do a real job of researching the records and talking to people. I think they just wanted to get something the fellows could have at home as a remembrance. Incidentally, when you get a card, send them $5, and they'll send you the book. It won't be worth that much, but we can always have it to show to our children some day. And I did have a few of my photos in it.*

From Dearborn, September 29, 1945: *At last, honey, I'm getting around to answering all the letters I've been getting from you lately. I hope you haven't been worried or anything. I don't know what happens to the time, but the days surely go by in a hurry when I have so much to do at school. I do know that in a month you will be home, and that's all that counts. I went to a show yesterday with your sister and then to dinner. We ate at Marco's and sat at the table where you and I sat the night this summer we got our drinks mixed up. Remember? We gave the waiter our orders, like people who knew what they were doing. Then we got up and danced. When we came back to the table, the drinks were there. One was pink and the other one was light green, but we didn't know which was which. And we were too embarrassed to ask the waiter. We just drank them and said nothing, and no one was the wiser. Least of all us, dear.*

Our car is acting up again, so I took it to the garage this week. They replaced the cables connected to the starter and cleaned out the starter, which was corroded—all of which cost me about nine dollars, not as much as I expected. All in all, it has cost me about fifteen dollars this week, aside from the gas and oil. So I guess we should plan on it's being an item in our budget. And about the gasoline strike in Detroit, if it doesn't end very soon, the car won't be much use to me anyway, because it's running very low. I don't think I could get enough gas from the Board of Education to go back and forth. And if the busses stop, maybe they will have to close the schools.

The next day: *It's after midnight, and I am just now going to bed. It seems I was waylaid by a mystery story I started this evening,* Calamity Town *by Ellery Queen. You're right, his books are hard to put down. Each page I would think I could put a marker in it and finish it tomorrow. And then I told myself maybe one or two more. Ellen was here this afternoon and we cut and sewed the skirts we both are making. She had a date this evening with Jim Tencza, who is home from the army, and after dinner he came over to pick her up.*[36] *I played a few games of pinochle with Uncle Bob, Ruby, and Jim, and I won. I did have good cards, but my dad kept looking over my shoulder and saying: "No, not that one. The other one." I'm afraid I'll never be much of a card player.*

More from home, October 1, 1945: *I didn't go out to Larry's tonight because of the gas situation. I did get some today from the Bd. of Education. I was running low and was going to the Administration building anyway. So after talking with Mr. Lowery about my schedule, I checked with Mr. Mitchell, the business mgr., and he said I could have a couple of gallons. It's not much, and I don't know what any of us will do, if the strike doesn't end pretty soon.*

The same day in California: *Well, it looks as though I'll be working on the battalion history for a while yet. I turned it in to division headquarters this morning, and then they said it was not what they wanted. They should have told me when I first started what it was, and I wouldn't have wasted the time. Actually, it's what I had wanted all along. So back to the old tread-mill. They want it by the middle of October, but as I said 1,500 words is not very much for me. Two or maybe three days of writing. But there are other things I need to be doing at the same time. I had promised the division news-paper an article about some fellows in our company, and I am supposed to be covering a football game for the sports page. Also, for I&E I am making a checklist of things for dischargees to do when they get home. There are a lot of things they might not think of. I have been reading a lot of articles in magazines about that. Then I plan to have it mimeographed and pass it out to the fellows when they leave.*

I'm making plans too about my own coming home, of course. Once the process starts, I should be on my way in three days. I haven't decided yet about the route, but I do know I'll be traveling by day coach. That way I can save at least $100, and that ain't hay, as the farmer says. This time I won't

---

36. Jim Tencza took part in the Guadalcanal operation and was wounded twice. Subsequently he and Ellen were married.

mind sitting up the whole way. In any event, I should get to Detroit on or about the tenth of November. So if you can find us an apartment by then, it will be all ready when I get home.

The next day, October 2, 1945, from Marianne in Dearborn: *There are so many reasons I am looking forward to your getting home in a hurry. And one is the weather, which has been so beautiful these days, an especially pretty autumn. There was an early frost, and it's been turning all the leaves. It will be nice to take walks and go together to football games. And now that the strike is over, there will be plenty of gas for rides in the country to see the foliage. Like you, dear, I certainly hope we can find a place to live quickly. Jane and I have been checking the newspapers every day, but so far all the listings have been in "undesirable" areas, if you know what I mean. Maybe I should start putting ads in the paper myself. Jane thinks that might help.*

I deposited the two checks for this month, so our account now stands at $630. There was a notice included that you would be paid for the entire month you are discharged, no matter how small a part of it you have spent in the army. Even a single day! Every little bit helps, doesn't it, dear?

October 3, 1945 in California: *I thought for a while today I might be discharged as a corporal, but that fell through. The major called me in this morning and asked me if I wanted to work in battalion headquarters as a corporal, taking care of all the records. I said I'd do it because of the rating. It would be for only a short time, of course, but he wanted me to straighten out some things, the way I did at Camp Roberts for Col. Lawrence. And I'd get only a little more money. But it was the good feeling I'd have, the recognition of all I've done since I was in the army.*

But then they told me they couldn't promote me because I had too many points. It seems that a lot of units had been giving fellows last-minute pro-motions—for no ostensible reason. So the army put an end to it. I said I wouldn't do it. It was just too much work for a private's pay. It makes me mad, though, that all the punk kids around me, with fewer points, are being made corporal or even sergeant. And they can tell me what to do.

October 3, 1945 in Dearborn: *Jane hasn't been feeling at all well the past few days. The new medicine has been making her ill, and has affected her kidneys. She's stopped taking it for now, and will be going back to the other in a few days, I think. After she has talked to the doctor, that is. So*

I've been doing most of the housekeeping this week. My dad has asked us to stay. But I don't think it's right, as we start a new life together, that we live here, or at your folks' place either. I'd rather try to live close by, so I can get over from time to time to help with the housekeeping. Once or twice a week, say. But I wish I could come up with a more satisfactory solution, so I wouldn't feel that I'm deserting my stepmother, who needs me. It's hard for older people, isn't it, dear, with your mother's asthma and your dad's heart problems?

From Camp Cooke, October 11, 1945: *Big news, dear! I'll be working at division headquarters until I am discharged. This morning the CQ woke me and said an officer wanted to see me. Fairly quickly, he said. For some reason I had overslept. They'd give me some breakfast, he said, and there was a jeep waiting outside my barracks. It seems the colonel in charge of the history project liked what I had written, and he wants me to write the division history that would be in all the books. He said he knew I would be rushed, but they would give me all the help I needed. And most important, he said I would be discharged as a corporal. The general would see to that!*

So here I am, hard at work, with my own desk and typewriter, and a pile of histories of the other battalions I've read through. They're not very good, in my estimation, but I won't have time to rewrite them all, obviously. The main thing is to get busy on the division history, which will be much longer than the individual battalions. After I finish that I can touch up the others. And with the four photos they've already chosen, most of the book will be mine. I feel like the times I was in the bürgermeister's office telling German officials what to do. I'm writing about the lives of ten thousand men. What a sense of power!

The next day: *I'm sitting here on my bunk after a "tough day at the office." I was looking through division records and trying to put together a good story. From what the colonel said, they want a "feel-good" version of events. For example, in my first version of the battalion history I had written about how the POWs at Burghausen had given us some food. They took that out. I guess the colonel thought it reflected discredit on him and the other officers. And at Mamming they wanted me to include attacks by SS troops, when I was sure it was the Home Guards, the boys and old men. So, I'll give them what they want. It will make it easier to write, because I won't have to be so careful about all the details. Not so good for a potential historian, though.*

I'm finding that there has been very little sense of direction in the whole operation. I guess that is why the colonel took it over. And in a sense dumped it in my lap. It makes me mad, though, that during all the time I spent in the 13th AD I wasn't good enough, or talented enough, they thought, to get out of the infantry. While other guys, just fresh out of high school maybe, had safe jobs as Press or some other cushy position. And now I have to rush to finish off what they couldn't do. But what the hell! The war is over, and I guess I should be flattered that they picked this lowly Pfc., out of all the thousands in the division to do the job. It might be helpful for my record when I go to graduate school back home. Or look for a job later.

I think before I go to bed I'll pack my two duffel bags, so I'll be all set to go. I will put in two blankets that I had been hanging onto for some time. I'm sure the army doesn't need them, and they will come in handy when we are furnishing our apartment. You might not like the color, but we could always cover them with a bedspread. Some of the fellows are saying they might try to bring home their carbines. I doubt, though, that they will get away with it. A rifle wouldn't fit very easily in a duffel bag, no matter how it is camouflaged.

From Dearborn, October 16, 1945: *We almost had a house yesterday. I was driving up Schaefer Road to the Lowery school, and I noticed the Boles real estate office that I hadn't seen before. They had an ad in the paper saying they have a housing service for veterans. So on a hunch I stopped to give them our name, and he told me about an address near Michigan Avenue. It was close by, so I stopped there after school. It was a cute little brick house with white shutters and a picket fence. There was a fireplace and a console piano. I thought immediately of you, dear. There was a catch, though, as big as a mountain. The owner, who is handicapped, wanted to retain the right to keep one room for himself. I'm sure you wouldn't want to share a house with any stranger, any more than I would. We might rather live with my folks. It surely was a beautiful house, though. So I'll keep on looking.*

From Camp Cooke, October 18, 1945: *I turned in the division history today. Now five copies go to senior officers, including General Millikin, for their approval. And overnight I have been thinking there could be a better ending. More upbeat. I'll be taking care of that tomorrow or the next day. Unfortunately, my name will not be on the cover, and there's to be no indication of who wrote the book. I think sometimes I should go with a megaphone to wherever it is sold and holler: "Bob Quirk wrote this book!" Of course, you can say I will get satisfaction out of knowing I did a good job. But what is satisfaction compared with a little recognition?*

I picked up some Rinso tonight at the PX, as you asked me to. I find I can buy only one in a day. But I can go back each day I'm here and get another. For your information, honey, it costs 22 cents for a large package, which would seem to me a bargain. Anyway, I'll send them home in my duffel bags, which are filling up alarmingly with all the books. You will be interested to know that I'm still working on the history book, but in a different way. It seems that the other battalion histories have needed more attention than I expected. That should take a couple of days, at the most. And I've set myself an absolute deadline of the end of this week. Period!

And now for the latest news, honey. The 69s will be discharged this Saturday, and I figure I will be out a week from then, on November 3. And that means I should be home on the sixth. To be certain, I'll call you the night before I start my processing, and you will know then that six days later I will be in Detroit. It hardly seems possible, does it? After being apart for so very long.

The last letter from Camp Cooke, October 24, 1945: *This will be just a short letter tonight, dear, to tell you I love you very much. How many times have I written that in all the years we have been apart? It's been the story of my life in the army, I guess. I decided to get lots of sleep tonight, because I'm certain to be out late tomorrow night. The fellows are having a party to use up the company fund that would otherwise have disappeared into some deep hole in the army's finances. It's better that we use it up, the first sergeant told us. We deserve it, he said. It includes a steak dinner, drinks, and dancing. I don't think I'll be going for the last named, but how could I pass up the opportunity to have a $2.50 porterhouse steak—at government expense! It's going to be at a restaurant in Santa Barbara, so we're sure to be back here pretty late.*

I had two letters from you today, for which much thanks, honey. I suppose, though, that there is no point in your writing again, because by the time the letter got here I'd be gone. It isn't sure yet whether we will be going to Camp Beale or to Fort MacArthur in Los Angeles for processing. In any event it will be soon. It makes some difference in how I'll get home, that's all. Which trains I'll take. But I do know I will be going through Chicago. If I can, I'll call you from there. And when I arrive in Detroit, will you be waiting for me at the station? Even on a school day? I have visions of you, dear one, standing there, looking this way and that, with maybe a spotlight shining on your hair. Waving at me. The warrior has returned!

The last letter from home, October 27, 1945: *Your letter came today telling me not to write you anymore, dear. But I am going to take a chance and write again because I have so much to tell you. And in the confusion of your homecoming I might forget. I'll take it to the post office and have them put a special delivery stamp on it. First, though, I'd better tell you about our new home. We have an apartment, furnished with refrigerator, stove, etc., etc., and light, heat, and gas. I rented it yesterday. It's in Dearborn, and the address is 6900 Bingham Ave. The rent is $43.50, due each 26th of the month. When I got your letter telling me you might be coming home earlier than you thought I decided it was time to get busy and look around seriously.*

The Dearborn paper comes out once a week, so during my lunch hour I drove to their publishing office and picked up a copy, before they were distributed. And then I drove directly to the house. I got there just ahead of six other people, and the poor woman was flustered trying to decide whom to rent to. But I told her I was there first, and I was the most insistent. She wasn't sure about renting to us, because she had advertised for an elderly couple, and she didn't want any drinking or "wild parties," she said. But I told her we were quiet, sober, etc., and when I said you were writing the division history and sang in the church choir, I think that convinced her. I paid a month's rent in cash, plus $15 to insure against breakage or other damage to her property, she said.

We have four rooms on the second floor of an income bungalow. It has coal heat, and when I was there it seemed plenty warm, you will be glad to hear. The woman and her husband live downstairs. I didn't meet him, but she said he was from French Canada. It's nothing very beautiful or luxurious—the furniture is their old cast-off things, with a heavy, old-fashioned *"mission furniture" look. There are no curtains. I've already priced them, and I've found I can make them for about $20. And when we get it cleaned up and shined, and have brought a few things of our own, I think it will be nice. And convenient. You'll be glad to know that transportation to Wayne and to town is good. We're close to both Warren and Schaefer Road.*

I'm going to take some money from our account to pay for the curtains. After paying the rent, my purse is about empty. I think I won't deposit the allotment check on the first, because we'll be needing to pick up a lot of things when you get home. To this "new home," I should say. Meanwhile, I'll be busy, making things shipshape for the homecoming "warrior." I'll be waiting at the depot, if you can call me about what time your train arrives. And if I seem to be glowing, it is because I know that you won't ever have to leave me again.

Maybe, some times, I'll miss writing letters. I don't know. But now the thought of saying goodnight and telling you in person how much I love you seems so much better. You thank me for writing to you. When it comes to passing out bouquets, they go to you, honey. In all these years we have been apart you have written me so many beautiful letters. And lately almost every day. It seems a shame sometimes that no one will ever read them but me.

Postscript

In early November 1945, back once more at Wayne University (present-day Wayne State University), I enrolled in two special classes, put together for the veterans, as well as two more German classes that were already close to the midterm exam week. In addition, the university awarded me a semester's credits for having served in the Armed Forces. And I received full credit for the work I had done at the University of Utah. As a consequence, I was able to graduate with my BA in June 1946. During the summer of that year I edited the *Collegian* and took upper-level courses in history. The university's returnees formed a veterans association and elected me their chairman. As a consequence, the federal Office of Price Administration appointed me to the local rent board. By then, my career aims had been determined. I would be a college professor. But where? The History Department needed someone immediately to teach the freshman surveys, and the chairman, Raymond Miller, asked if I could handle three sections. I said of course, though at first it was a matter of keeping a half step ahead of the students. I recall in one lecture that I mistook England's Henry I for Henry II. But the class was always glad to help me, and we got along very well. And if I ran out of things to say, I could always reminisce about my experience in Patton's Third Army. In the meantime I applied for admission to the graduate school at Harvard University and was accepted.

Because of the shortage of student housing in the Harvard area, Marianne and I lived in Waltham—fortunately near the train station. I commuted daily to North Cambridge. The landlady was reluctant at first. Were we Irish? she asked. My husband is, Marianne said. We don't like Irish people here, was the reply. Marianne assured her I was only half-Irish, which seemed to be sufficient. During the two years we spent in Massachusetts, Marianne taught first- and second-graders in Winchester.

I had come to Harvard intending to study German history with Sidney Fay, only to learn that the distinguished professor was no longer teaching. A quick decision was required, and I asked if I could switch to Latin America and work with Clarence Haring instead. At the time I had no more experience in the area than the lectures of Charles Dibble at Utah. And the brief ASTP language experience had left me with a shaky conception of what the conditional tense and subjunctive mood were all about. But the people in the history office were agreeable, and a totally unexpected career was launched in the fall of 1947.

The university allowed me to transfer the graduate credits I had earned at Wayne, and I completed Harvard's course requirements in two years. I passed the oral exam with the welcome help of fairly easy questions from my committee. The professors were more interested in what I knew than in what I didn't know. It was a policy I adopted for my own use as a professor. And during the summer of 1949 Marianne and I drove our new Ford to Mexico City. Her careful guarding of our income had allowed us to pay cash! And I began work on my dissertation—the conflict between the Mexican Revolution and the Catholic Church from 1910 to 1929. To get more experience I accepted an offer by Mexico City College to teach a course in Latin American history. And the president of the college introduced me to priests and laymen who had document collections I could use in my research. The pay was minimal—$45 a month. But Harvard had given me a generous fellowship, and with the added income from the GI Bill we were able to lead a comfortable life in the Mexican capital.

We had been told by other graduate students that entering Mexico with a tourist pass was far easier than securing a student visa. But that meant leaving the country after six months, driving to the border, and then applying for another pass. We decided, however, to drive back to Detroit first. My father was ailing, and it gave us an opportunity to see him. He seemed quite recovered, and was happy to talk with me about my dissertation and to make several helpful suggestions. I paid a call also at the Wayne campus to meet friends there. By sheer happenstance, I ran into Richard Burks at the History Department. Indiana University was looking for someone in the Latin American area, he told me. Why don't you stop on your way back and talk with them?

Marianne and I looked in my dad's atlas. Bloomington wasn't too far out of the way. So why not? We never told anyone at Indiana we were coming. We pulled into Bloomington about 4:30 on a cold and snowy February afternoon. And *mirabile dictu!* we found John Barnhart, the chairman, still in his office. We talked for less than an hour. He was impressed by my teaching in Mexico and at Wayne. And that in the army I had written the division history. As we left, and shook hands at the door, he suggested that I write him about my life and record in the profession. Which I did, as soon as we were back in Mexico City. In May Professor Barnhart sent me a telegram. The job was mine, he said, if I could complete the dissertation by September—when the fall semester began. The salary would be $3,200, two hundred dollars less a year than Marianne had been making when she left Dearborn. But it was a job, at a fine institution, and I quickly accepted the offer, though I had not begun to write yet.

As with the history of the 13th Armored Division, I began composing at a furious pace, sometimes five or even ten pages in one day. Then there was the rewriting, and the cross-checking. Marianne typed away, mostly in the evenings and on weekends. She was taking art classes at the college, and spent her days painting and sculpting. One afternoon some film people came by the college and asked her if she would like to take part in a movie being made in Acapulco. With the famous actor Tin-Tan. They were looking for a blonde American, they said. She told them she couldn't. She was too busy typing her husband's dissertation, she said. Clarence Haring was in Brazil at the time, so I worked with a Mexican professor whose command of English was only so-so. Professor Haring never saw the dissertation until it arrived at Harvard already bound. I met with the committee in early 1951. About halfway through the examination Crane Brinton said: "We'll assume Mr. Quirk has passed, so let's stop and have some sherry." Everyone agreed. My Harvard PhD was assured.

The book was published twenty-two years later, after much more research in public records and private papers. It received the annual award of the Catholic Historical Association. I had by that time published three other books on the Revolution and on American relations with Mexico. Marianne was a therapist in Indiana's Speech and Hearing clinic and later, because of her skills in three languages, she interviewed young students for the overseas travel programs. At the same time she was also a docent in the university museum. In 1958 we adopted Anne Elisabeth. At the time we were planning to build a house, and I thought I should check on the tenure situation. Professor Barnhart, in his office, wrinkled his brow. "Well," he said, "if you weren't coming back next year, we'd have told you in December. And it's already March. So I guess you have tenure." Five years later we adopted Thomas Michael.

In the 1960s I directed the Latin American Studies program and edited the *Hispanic American Historical Review*. In the next decade I taught at Hamburg University for a year and lectured at several East German institutions, and then edited the *American Historical Review*. I retired in May 1983, and wrote a biography of Fidel Castro. It took me twelve years and was used by Hallmark to make a TV film for Showtime. And then I found those boxes in our attic.

Editor's Note

The reader will be rightly disturbed to learn that after I completed this book, I made a sudden decision to shred all the original letters on which it was based. At the time, we were renovating my study, and on the first day the builder pointed to the largest pile in the room and said, "Get this trash out of the way, and we'll save you some money." Obviously, that was not the reason for my destroying the letters, but it gave me the incentive to do so.

One might wonder why the letters were not sent to a library or other suitable archive. In my own research, I have encountered such collections, but these were usually the letters of famous individuals—former presidents, such as Woodrow Wilson (Washington, D.C.) and Venustiano Carranza (Mexico City). All I can say is that it never occurred to me that my own letters perhaps belonged in such a collection. Moreover, throughout my work on this book, I was troubled by the fact that should the original letters somehow be made public beyond the excerpts used in this book, other people—most of them strangers—would be reading the very personal exchanges between two real-life lovers. Many of them are just plain embarrassing to an old fogey. For the destruction of the letters, I accept all responsibility.